Aspects of
ALICE

Still she haunts me, phantomwise,
Alice moving under skies
Never seen by waking eyes. —LEWIS CARROLL

Aspects of
ALICE

*Lewis Carroll's Dreamchild
as seen through the
Critics' Looking-Glasses*

1865–1971

EDITED BY *Robert Phillips*

ILLUSTRATIONS BY
Sir John Tenniel
AND
Lewis Carroll

THE VANGUARD PRESS INC. NEW YORK

Library of Congress Catalogue Card Number: 70-178822
SBN 8149-0700-8
Designer: Ernst Reichl
Manufactured in the United States of America

"Today's 'Wonder-World' Needs Alice" by W. H. Auden, copyright 1962 by The New York Times Company.
"The Thinking of the Body" from *Language as Symbolic Action* by Kenneth Burke, copyright 1966 by the University of California Press.
Material from *How Does a Poem Mean?*, copyright 1959 by John Ciardi.
"Lewis Carroll—the First Acidhead" by Thomas Fensch, from *Story: The Yearbook of Discovery* edited by Whit and Hallie Burnett, copyright 1969 by Scholastic Magazines, Inc.
"*Alice in Wonderland* Psycho-analyzed" by A. M. E. Goldschmidt, from *New Oxford Outlook* (1933), copyright 1933 by Basil Blackwell.
"Alice" by Robert Graves, copyright 1961 by Robert Graves.
"Alice" from *Lewis Carroll* by Roger Lancelyn Green, copyright 1960 by The Bodley Head, Ltd.
"The Character of Dodgson As Revealed in the Writings of Carroll," from *Swift and Carroll* by Phyllis Greenacre, copyright 1955 by International Universities Press, Inc.
"On Lewis Carroll's *Alice* and Wordsworth's 'Ode' on Immortality" from *The Shield of Achilles* by Horace Gregory, copyright 1971 by Horace Gregory.
"About the Symbolization of *Alice's Adventures in Wonderland*" by Martin Grotjahn, from *American Imago* (1947), copyright 1947 by George B. Wilbur.
"Alice Meets the Don" by John Hinz, copyright 1953 by Duke University Press.
"The Philosopher's *Alice in Wonderland*" by Roger W. Holmes, from *The Antioch Review* (1959), copyright 1959 by *The Antioch Review*.
"Did Mark Twain Write *Alice's Adventures in Wonderland?*" by George Lanning, from *Carrousel for Bibliophiles* edited by William Targ, copyright 1947 by Duschnes Crawford, Inc., New York.
"*Alice in Wonderland* in Perspective" by Elsie Leach, copyright 1964 by *The Victorian Newsletter*.
"Escape Through the Looking-Glass" from *Victoria Through the Looking-Glass: The Life of Lewis Carroll* by Florence Becker Lennon, copyright 1945, 1947, 1962, and 1971 by Florence Becker Lennon.
"Wonderland Revisited" by Harry Levin, from *Kenyon Review* (1965), copyright 1965 by Kenyon College.
"A Note on Humpty Dumpty" from *I For One* by J. B. Priestley, copyright 1921 by The Bodley Head, Ltd.
"Alice's Journey to the End of Night" by Donald Rackin, copyright 1966 by the Modern Language Association of America.
"Further Insights" from *Magic and Schizophrenia* by Géza Róheim, copyright 1955 by International Universities Press, Inc.
"Psychoanalytic Remarks on *Alice in Wonderland*" by Paul Schilder, copyright 1938 by the Smith Ely Jelliffe Trust.
"White Rabbit" by Grace Slick, copyright 1966 by Copperpenny Music Publishing Company, Inc. and Irving Music, Inc. (BMI).
"Lewis Carroll and T. S. Eliot as Nonsense Poets" by Elizabeth Sewell, from *T. S. Eliot* edited by Neville Braybrooke, copyright 1958 by Neville Braybrooke.
"Lewis Carroll's Adventures in Wonderland" by John Skinner, from *American Imago* (1947), copyright 1947 by George B. Wilbur.
"Logic and Language in *Through the Looking-Glass*" by Patricia Spacks, from *ETC* (1961), copyright 1961 by the International Society for General Semantics.
"Last Days of Alice" from *Poems* by Allen Tate, copyright 1931, 1932, 1937, 1948 by Charles Scribner's Sons; renewal copyright 1959, 1960 by Allen Tate.
"Through the Looking-Glass" from *The White Knight* by Alexander L. Taylor, copyright 1952 by Alexander L. Taylor.
"C. L. Dodgson: The Poet Logician" from *The Shores of Light* by Edmund Wilson, copyright 1952 by Edmund Wilson.
"Lewis Carroll" from *The Moment and Other Essays* by Virginia Woolf, copyright 1948 by Harcourt Brace Jovanovich, Inc.

THIS BOOK IS FOR

MASTER GRAHAM VAN BUREN PHILLIPS

who can still look forward to his first fall

down the Rabbit-Hole.

Contents

III.   Comparisons with Other Writers

IV.   Philosophical and Others

V.   Church and Chess

VI.   Language, and Parody, and Satire

VII.   Freudian Interpretations

VIII.   Jungian and Mythic

IX.   Psychedelic

Illustrations

All illustrations on part titles are by Sir John Tenniel.

ACKNOWLEDGMENTS   IN PREPARING this volume I have incurred various debts, which are a pleasure to acknowledge. The living contributors, or their publishers or representatives, have been most gracious. John Lehmann of London, Derek Hudson of Surrey, Mrs. Anne Clark of the Lewis Carroll Society, and Robert Gorham Davis of Columbia University made helpful suggestions. Robert Emmet Long, formerly of Queens College; Howard L. Applegate of Syracuse University; Jerome Mazzaro of State University of New York at Buffalo; Hedy Shulman of New York; and Philip Lyman of the Gotham Book Mart helped locate several elusive essays. Bernice Woll of the Vanguard Press helped in ways too varied to enumerate. She has been the ideal Editor.

While my bibliography is selective and considerably updated, I—like most recent Carroll students—am indebted to Florence Becker Lennon for the checklist appended to her *Life of Lewis Carroll.*

And my wife, Judith, has helped beyond the possibilities of acknowledgment. As others have remarked, she *is* Alice.

For their kind permissions to reprint material in this book, I should like to thank the following persons, magazines, publishers, foundations, and universities:

"Today's 'Wonder-World' Needs Alice" by W. H. Auden, reprinted by permission of the author and his representatives, Curtis Brown, Ltd. Copyright 1962 by The New York Times Company.

"The Thinking of the Body," an excerpt from *Language as Symbolic Action* by Kenneth Burke (1966), reprinted by permission of the Regents of the University of California.

Material from *How Does a Poem Mean?* by John Ciardi, reprinted by permission of the author and Houghton Mifflin Company.

Extract from *Lewis Carroll* by Walter de la Mare, published by Faber and Faber Ltd., reprinted by permission of the Literary Trustees of Walter de la Mare and the Society of Authors as their representative.

"Alice in Wonderland: the Child as Swain" from *Some Versions of Pastoral* by

William Empson. All rights reserved, reprinted by permission of William Empson, Chatto & Windus Ltd., and New Directions Publishing Corporation.

"Lewis Carroll—the First Acidhead" by Thomas Fensch, reprinted by permission from *Story: The Yearbook of Discovery,* edited by Whit and Hallie Burnett, copyright 1969 by Scholastic Magazines, Inc.

"*Alice in Wonderland* Psychoanalyzed" by A. M. E. Goldschmidt, reprinted with the kind permission of Sir Basil Blackwell and Basil Blackwell & Mott Ltd., Oxford.

"Alice" by Robert Graves, reprinted by permission of Collins-Knowlton-Wing, Inc. Copyright 1961 by Robert Graves.

To The Bodley Head for the extract from their monograph, *Lewis Carroll* by Roger Lancelyn Green (copyright 1960).

From "The Character of Dodgson As Revealed in the Writings of Carroll," reprinted from *Swift and Carroll* by Phyllis Greenacre, M.D., by permission of International Universities Press, Inc. and of Dr. Greenacre. Copyright 1955 by International Universities Press, Inc.

"On Lewis Carroll's *Alice* and Wordsworth's 'Ode' on Immortality" from *The Shield of Achilles* (1944) by Horace Gregory, reprinted with the kind permission of the author; also Grove Press and Greenwood Press. (Copyright 1971, Horace Gregory.)

"About the Symbolization of *Alice's Adventures in Wonderland*" by Martin Grotjahn, and a selection taken from "Lewis Carroll's Adventures in Wonderland" by John Skinner, both originally published in *The American Imago* (1947), reprinted by permission of George B. Wilbur.

"Alice Meets the Don" by John Hinz, reprinted by permission of the author and Duke University Press. Copyright 1953, Duke University Press, Durham, North Carolina.

"The Philosopher's *Alice in Wonderland*" by Roger W. Holmes, from *The Antioch Review* (1959), reprinted with permission of the editors and the author.

"Did Mark Twain Write *Alice's Adventures in Wonderland?*" by George Lanning, reprinted by permission of William Targ and the author.

"*Alice in Wonderland* in Perspective" by Elsie Leach, reprinted by permission of William E. Buckler and *The Victorian Newsletter,* copyright 1964.

"Escape Through the Looking-Glass" from *Victoria Through the Looking-Glass: The Life of Lewis Carroll* by Florence Becker Lennon (copyright 1945; 1947; 1962; 1971). Reprinted by permission of the author.

"Lewis Carroll and the Oxford Movement" by Shane Leslie, reprinted by permission of Lady Leslie, Literary Executor for the estate of Sir Shane Leslie.

"Wonderland Revisited" by Harry Levin, from *Kenyon Review* (1965), reprinted by permission of the author.

"A Note on Humpty Dumpty" from *I For One* by J. B. Priestley (copyright 1921), is reprinted by permission of the publisher, The Bodley Head.

"Alice's Journey to the End of Night" by Donald Rackin, reprinted by permission of the Modern Language Association of America, from *PMLA*, 81 (copyright 1966, Modern Language Association of America), and by permission of Mr. Rackin.

"Further Insights" from *Magic and Schizophrenia* by Géza Róheim, reprinted with permission of International Universities Press, Inc. Copyright 1955 by International Universities Press, Inc.

"Psychoanalytic Remarks on *Alice in Wonderland*" by Paul Schilder, from *The Journal of Nervous and Mental Disease* (1938), reprinted by permission of Carel Goldschmidt, Trustee, the Smith Ely Jelliffe Trust.

"Lewis Carroll and T. S. Eliot as Nonsense Poets" by Elizabeth Sewell, reprinted by permission of the author; Neville Braybrooke; Books for Libraries Inc. (1969); and Garnstone Press Ltd. (1970).

"White Rabbit" by Grace Slick, copyright 1966 by Copper Music Publishing Company, Inc. and Irving Music, Inc. (BMI), reprinted by permission of Irving Music, Inc.

"Logic and Language in *Through the Looking-Glass*" by Patricia Spacks, reprinted from *ETC.* (Vol. XVIII, No. 1), by permission of the International Society for General Semantics.

"Last Days of Alice" is reprinted by permission of Charles Scribner's Sons from *Poems* by Allen Tate. Copyright 1931, 1932, 1937, 1948, Charles Scribner's Sons; renewal copyright 1959, 1960, Allen Tate.

"Through the Looking-Glass" from *The White Knight* by Alexander L. Taylor, reprinted by permission of Alexander L. Taylor. Copyright 1952 by Alexander L. Taylor.

"C. L. Dodgson: The Poet Logician" (1952 version) by Edmund Wilson, reprinted by permission of the author.

"Lewis Carroll" from *The Moment and Other Essays* by Virginia Woolf, copyright 1948 by Harcourt Brace Jovanovich, Inc., and reprinted with their permission.

"Introduction" by Alexander Woollcott, reprinted under the title "Lewis Carroll's Gay Tapestry," from The Modern Library edition of *Alice in Wonderland, Through the Looking-Glass*, and *The Hunting of the Snark*, published by Random House, Inc.

Thanks are also offered to the Princeton University Library, the New York Public Library, the Houghton Library of Harvard University, the Butler Library of Columbia University, the British Museum, and the Limited Editions' Club for their cooperation in supplying the photographs and illustrations.

Foreword

SHE HAS SURVIVED the Victorian Age, several wars and depressions, the Age of Anxiety, and when last seen was thriving in the Post-Christian Era. Lewis Carroll's Alice may prove to be the hardiest perennial of them all. Certainly she is one of the most popular heroines of world literature. So popular that for Christmas, 1871, her author had to publish a sequel to her 1865 adventures. *Aspects of Alice* is a *Festschrift* for Alice—a critical celebration published one hundred years after *Through the Looking-Glass*. Some reference books postdate *Looking-Glass* a year; several of the essays that follow refer to 1872 as the date of publication. However, the book was in fact published in time for Christmas, 1871.

Lewis Carroll's two *Alice* books, *Alice's Adventures in Wonderland* and *Through the Looking-Glass,* are part of the background of every educated Englishman and American. They are also books that are read the world over. By 1965, Alice's adventures had been translated into forty-seven languages, including Latin, making it one of the world's most-translated books. And better than merely being read, the *Alice* books are remembered. Their degree of memorability can be judged by the number of people who make allusion to them daily—not only invoking characters such as the Cheshire Cat or the Mad Hatter, but whole phrases of dialogue and entire poems as well. After Shakespeare, it has been said, Carroll is perhaps the world's most quoted author. Moreover, the world of his imagination is often borrowed from to lend a proper dreamlike quality to certain aspects of our modern life: witness books with titles such as *Alice in Hueyland* and *Malice in Blunderland.*

Besides being translated, Alice has been animated and annotated, musicalized and televised. In printed versions she has been illustrated numerous times: the New York Public Library alone holds editions illustrated by fifteen different artists, including Peter Newell, Arthur Rackham, Charles Robinson, Thomas Maybank, Harry Furniss, Fritz Kredel, and, of course, Carroll himself. In 1970, Salvador Dali attempted to wed his surrealistic vision to Carroll's nonsensical one. Yet all attempts fail to match the truly inspired efforts of Sir John Tenniel, who prepared the illustrations for the original trade edition (a number of which are reprinted here, to lend instant Alice-ambience to our pages).

Carroll himself prepared two private editions of the first *Alice* book, originally called *Alice's Adventures under Ground*. His first, which may have had no illustrations at all, was probably destroyed by the author after he had made a much more careful and elaborate copy to present to Alice Liddell, his Muse, on November 26, 1864. This second version did indeed contain illustrations, thirty-seven in number, drawn by Carroll. Luckily, today there are several facsimile editions extant with Carroll's own drawings. They lack the polish and grace of Tenniel's, but in some ways help underscore the author's intentions more graphically than those of the professional illustrator.

Tenniel's illustrations were, then, for the third version of *Alice's Adventures*. (There ultimately was a fourth in Carroll's lifetime, a *Nursery Alice* rewritten for young children and incorporating twenty of the Tenniel illustrations enlarged and in color). It is Tenniel's illustrations one always recalls, and perhaps more so than with any other book, the illustrations for the two *Alices* are considered an integral part of the work itself. As Austin Dobson versified in his "Proem" to a 1907 edition of *Alice's Adventures:*

> Enchanting Alice! Black-and-white
> Has made your charm perennial;
> And nought save "Chaos and Old Night"
> Can part you now from Tenniel. . . .

Yet, just as the merit of *Alice's Adventures in Wonderland* was questioned at first, so too were Tenniel's illustrations. One reviewer thought them "grim and uncouth"!

It was perhaps this inexorable association with Tenniel that accounts for the relative failure of Walt Disney's animated version on the motion-picture screen (1951). Live film and stage versions have fared rather better. In Carroll's lifetime there was an *Alice* operetta, a dramatization of both books by Savile Clarke that was produced initially during the 1886–87 season at the Prince of Wales Theatre, with Phoebe Carlo as Alice. Carroll attended on several occasions. In 1888 a second mounting, with Isa Bowman as Alice, played at the Royal Globe Theatre.

Since then there have been more one-, two-, and three-act versions than you can shake a hookah at. In our own time these include a rather adult version by Jonathan Miller of England; an Afro-American soul musical for the New York stage in 1969 (retitled *But Never Jam Today*, with Carroll's characters and lines serving as a vehicle for commentary on racial inequality); a stage musical, *Alice*, directed by Christopher Hewitt and produced by David Black; another musical produced by Leonard Rosenman; and a highly imaginative and energetic *Alice in Wonderland* staged by the Manhattan Project, directed by André Gregory, that won awards during the 1970-71 season and is now on a world tour. One should perhaps mention as well Edward Albee's drama, *Tiny Alice* (1964), since so many critics were able to discover in it a debt in source and symbol to Carroll's works.

Writings about the two *Alices* are, of course, far more numerous. There is even a magazine devoted entirely to pieces about Carroll, or essays that would be of interest to Carroll enthusiasts. Called *Jabberwocky*, it is issued in London by The Lewis Carroll Society. A superficial survey of Carroll criticism reveals that in the two *Alice* books there is surely a little "something for everybody." Most recently Alice has come to be seen as the mother of all psychedelic divertissements, a reading based upon the books' underground settings, "groovy" characters, magic and antiestablishment commentary. (See, for instance, *Alice in Acidland* by Thomas Fensch.) As such, Alice has even influenced Rock. Grace Slick has made Alice the subject of an acid rock anthem, misquoting the Dormouse, presumably as an encouragement to American youths to "turn on."

Which goes to prove, one supposes, that Alice is what you make of her. It should be said quickly that no one has known exactly *what* to make of her, including Carroll himself, who always stressed the nonsense aspects of his literary works.

Certainly not all the critics knew what to make of her at the time of publication. One anonymous reviewer (in 1865) found Carroll's attempt to manufacture a dream unconvincing, and concluded "we fancy that any real child might be more puzzled than enchanted by this stiff, over-wrought story." Another, writing in 1887, found "nothing extraordinarily original" about either *Alice* book, and all but accused Carroll of plagiarizing from Tom Hood, a charge Carroll quietly denied in 1890, pointing out that the Hood book, *From Nowhere to the North Pole*, was published in 1874, after both *Alice* books were in print.

While not pleasing to all the critics, the *Alice* books were certainly well known and widely enjoyed during Carroll's lifetime. After his death in 1898, interest in his work waned somewhat, but the 1914-18 war sent many readers back to Carroll's unreal world. There they found the solace and pleasure that so many have discovered since. When the manuscript of the first *Alice* book was sold in 1928, it fetched more than any other manuscript ever sold in England up to that time.

The "glory, jest and riddle" of English literature is one epithet that reveals the rich and quixotic nature of both the *Alice* books. Written originally for children, they have transcended that audience. Like all true classics, they are multileveled and continue to entertain one with subsequent readings. Yet after a time the educated mind requires more than mere entertainment. After a time the reader insists upon asking, "What does it mean?"

Many critics have tried to "explain" or "explicate" *Alice*, but how do you explain nonsense? As Derek Hudson has observed, you might just as well attempt to dissect a soap bubble. Yet every year new and different explanations are offered, many of which make amazing good sense. (Kenneth Burke's 1963 essay, in which he interprets the acts and symbols largely as excremental images, is remarkably convincing—at the time of reading. So too is Shane Leslie's piece alleging Carroll's books are reflections on contemporary ecclesiastical history.) Carroll himself, while maintaining that all his books "meant" nothing, was quick to add in a speech echoing his own Humpty Dumpty:

> *Still, you know, words mean more than we mean to express when we use them; so a whole book ought to mean a great deal more than the writer means. So whatever good meanings are in the book, I'm glad to accept as the meaning of the book.*

Carroll's phrase, "good meanings," is a salient one; he might not take such a charitable view toward criticism were he to encounter some of the interpretations given his writing in the last four decades. Most especially, the numerous psychoanalytical readings, with their emphasis on bodily functions, would probably disturb if not destroy him. What would Carroll say to Florence Becker Lennon's assertion that his verse indicates an unresolved Oedipal conflict with a strong attachment to mother? Or Martin Grotjahn's belief that Alice represents the "symbolic equation for the phallus" and her adventures "a trip back into the mother's womb"? Or Géza Róheim's theory that Alice's story is clearly one of oral trauma, with her manipulations of time, food, words, and reality being highly schizophrenic? Or A.M.E. Goldschmidt's suggestion that the whole course of the story can be explained "by the desire for complete virility, conflicting with the desire for abnormal satisfaction"?

Perhaps Carroll would have torn the books into his characteristic shreds had he foreseen such commentary. For him the essential was that he enchant thousands of children with his dreamchild. In his Preface, penned on Christmas Day, 1871, addressed "To All Child Readers of *Alice's Adventures in Wonderland*," he confessed:

The thought of the many English firesides where happy faces have smiled her a welcome, and of the many English children to whom she has brought an hour of (I trust) innocent amusement, is one of the brightest and pleasantest thoughts of my life.

"Innocent amusement" is another key phrase for Carroll. Doubtless he would have been equally disturbed at readings that accuse him of contriving elaborate theological and political allegories. He would agree with his twentieth-century defender, Lord David Cecil, who saw the books' unique quality as their total lack of allusion or implication. Lord Cecil railed in 1932:

Of course there are people who find such allusions in them, who say that the caterpillar is a satire on Oxford logic and the Duchess a skit on Cambridge paradox. But they belong to the same tribe of pedantic lunatics who think that Macbeth is a topical hit at Essex and Cleopatra a satirical picture of Mary Queen of Scots.

The truth must lie somewhere between the extremes of the "pedantic lunatics" and Lord Cecil's own conclusion that "the central, splendid truth about the *Alice* books is that one needs no outside information of any kind to see their point; they are as absolute, self-sufficing, supreme creations of pure humor as the Parthenon is an absolute, self-sufficing, supreme expression of pure form. . . ." Martin Gardner's *The Annotated Alice* (1960), with its 198 annotations—some, quite lengthy—clarifying the jokes, games, puzzles, tricks, parodies, private and contemporary references that riddle the text, dramatizes Lord Cecil's simplistic claims. As Gardner explains, ". . . no joke is funny unless you see the point of it, and sometimes a point has to be explained."

Whereas *The Annotated Alice* is a copious representation of one man's researches and conclusions, *Aspects of Alice* attempts to gather the most interesting, if not always the most illuminating, interpretations by many men. Some are thoroughly outrageous; others are in themselves finely wrought works of literature about a work of literature. A glance at the Contents page reveals that some of our finest critics have brought their sensibilities to bear on *Alice,* usually with happy results. In any event, the reader should note that what has been attempted here is a serious symposium. It has been a pleasurable bonus for the editor to discover essays about Alice, written in earnest, approaching the wit found in Mr. Frederick C. Crews's *The Pooh Perplex* (1963), that compendium of parodies on criticism which *might have been* written about Milne's *Christopher Robin* books.

My title, *Aspects of Alice,* intentionally echoes that of E. M. Forster's informal and witty 1927 guide to the novel, which ultimately is a discussion of experience and of life as well. I have attempted to draw from the full range of Carroll commentary, though certain of the mathematical and scientific investigations seem too specialized for an omnibus directed to the general reader. Those who are interested in these interpretations will find the proper citations given in the checklist that concludes the volume. William Empson's plaint, voiced in 1935 ("It must seem a curious thing that there has been so little serious criticism of the *Alices,* and that so many critics, with so militant and eager an air of good taste, have explained that they would not think of attempting it. . . .") could not be voiced today. Indeed, beginning with the centenary of Carroll's birth in 1932, Carroll criticism has multiplied in Malthusian manner. It would take several volumes the size of this one to begin to gather it all. The present book is purely a personal selection. Choices were made for readability as well as for scholarship. Not all are essays. A few poems are included as well, since some writers have best approached Alice in that form. When Robert Graves proclaims her to be "That prime heroine of our nation," we are encountering the critical mind at work, albeit within a poem. Alice, one finds, has been the Muse of many poets. Had I not used W. H. Auden's essay, for instance, I would have been tempted

to include his fine sonnet, "The Door" (from *The Quest*), with its ultimate image of "enormous Alice" peering through the tiny door at Wonderland that lay beyond. The door, "simply by being tiny, made her
cry." In the essays I have resisted the urge to edit what may seem to
be needless repetitions of certain facts or opinions. From repetition itself
comes a pattern that may be useful for evaluation. Spelling and punctua-
tion have been standardized, abbreviated titles of the two Carroll books
have not been. The title *Alice in Wonderland* seems to be with us, even
though it is not Carroll's. Footnotes are those appended by the authors
to their individual essays on original publication unless otherwise indicated by the notation [Ed.].

The varieties of methodologies and conclusions set forth here tell us
in themselves a great deal about the *Alice* books. That they can be compared to Wordsworth and Henry James as well as to Eliot and to
Cervantes is extraordinary. That few critics quote from precisely the
same passages in support of their critical claims also attests to the books'
richness. Within the essays collected here Alice is called a heroine and a
supremely destructive force; a critic and a myth; a conventional children's-book character and a protagonist within decadent adult literature!
That one critic can find so many meanings in any one book is truly rare:
Yet Horace Gregory, one of this country's most impeccable critics, has
explored the first of the *Alices* on four different levels in his excellent
"Foreword" to the Signet Classics edition (not reprinted here in defer-
ence to another essay by Mr. Gregory). Gregory sees the *Alices* as alert
and critical psychological novels (with the adventures related as though
coming from inside the dream); as parodies on children's literature; as
satires on then-current theories of education; and as political satire. It is
equally remarkable that the books prompt such a wealth of different
responses from so many and varied academic and professional disciplines.
Indeed, Alice's critics remind one of Carroll's description of the pur-
suers of the Snark:

> *They sought it with thimbles, they sought it with care;*
> *They pursued it with forks and hope;*
> *They threatened its life with a rail-way share;*
> *They charmed it with smiles and soap.*

Alice's life has more than once been threatened; yet undeniably she lives
on.

It also seems undeniable that Carroll is one of the few writers who produced one masterpiece as a sequel to another. (Think for instance, of the failure in tone and inspiration of Faulkner's *The Town* and most of *The Mansion* in the Snopes trilogy, as compared to the comic original, *The Hamlet.*) Yet it is safe to say that of the two *Alices, Alice's Adventures in Wonderland* has enjoyed the greater popularity among the general reading public and literary critics alike. In July, 1899, the *Pall Mall Gazette* conducted a poll to determine favorite children's books, and *Alice's Adventures* won overwhelmingly. *Through the Looking-Glass* was among the top twenty, but much farther down the list. (A similar poll was conducted in July, 1898, by the *Academy,* and *Through the Looking-Glass* was not in the top ten.) Most critics agree with Stuart Dodgson Collingwood, who proclaimed in 1899 that nothing else Carroll wrote had the originality or freshness of the first *Alice* book. Not many individuals agree with Henry Kingsley, brother of Charles and author of *Ravenshoe.* Kingsley wrote Carroll in 1871 on the sequel:

> . . . I can say with a clear head and conscience that your new book is the finest thing we have had since *Martin Chuzzlewit* . . . I can only say, in comparing the new *Alice* with the old, "This is more excellent song than the other."

As Carroll's first biographer tells the story, the most ingenious comparison of the two books was the answer of a little girl when Lewis Carroll had asked if she knew them: "Oh yes, I've read both of them, and I think,"—this, more slowly and thoughtfully—"I think *Through the Looking-Glass* is more stupid than *Alice's Adventures.* Don't you think so?"

To prevent the *Adventures* Alice from dominating her *Looking-Glass* counterpart too completely, I have selected the study of the sequel whenever a critic has written a piece on both, as in the selections from Mrs. Lennon's and Mr. Taylor's books.

Attempts at creating a balance of another sort prompted the editor to commission a pair of essays especially for this volume. The first is Professor Jan B. Gordon's remarkable study of the child in Victorian literature (as well as of Victorian children). The second is Judith Bloomingdale's Jungian interpretation, with special emphasis upon the *anima* concept. Ever since the Dean of Rochester playfully alluded to a possible mythic structure for "Jabberwocky" in a letter to Carroll in 1871 (suggesting the Tumtum tree as the modern Yggdrasill!), the mythic possibilities have remained unexplored. While legions of Freudians have been beating poor Alice with their big sticks, the Jungians have bided their time.

(Jung himself discussed *Alice* in print only once, and that in his last essay completed before his death, "Approaching the Unconscious," in which he noted Alice's dream of growing infinitely small or infinitely large to be "a typical infantile motif.") The essays by Donald Rackin and by Miss Bloomingdale seriously take up the cudgel of the jesting Dean.

For all their ingenuity, none of these critics shall have claim to the final word on *Alice*. As Louis Untermeyer has said, the books comprise "the most inexhaustible fairy tale ever composed." Carroll's own Tweedledee would caution us: "If it was so, it might be, and if it were so, it would be; but as it isn't, it ain't." *Alice* remains delightfully enigmatic to the end. If this anthology entertains as much as it informs, its intentions will be fulfilled. Above all, the editor hopes the essays will send the reader back to the Carroll books with something like new wonderment as well as new understanding.

ROBERT PHILLIPS

Düsseldorf-Benrath, Germany
July 4, 1971

I
Personal
and
Biographical

Today's
"Wonder-World" Needs
ALICE
by W. H. Auden
(1962)

IN THE EVENING of Friday, July 4, 1862, the Reverend Charles Lutwidge Dodgson, lecturer and tutor in mathematics at Christ Church, Oxford, wrote in his diary:

Atkinson brought over to my rooms some friends of his, a Mrs. and Miss Peters, of whom I took photographs, and who afterward looked over my album and stayed to lunch. They then went off to the Museum and Duckworth and I made an expedition up the river to Godstow with the three Liddells: we had tea on the bank there, and did not reach Christ Church again till quarter past 8, when we took them on to my rooms to see my collection of micro-photographs, and restored them to the Deanery just before 9.

"The three Liddells" were the daughters of the Dean of Christ Church, one of the authors of the famous Liddell & Scott Greek lexicon. Their names were Lorina Charlotte,[1] Alice, and Edith—nicknamed Matilda. Alice was ten years old.

This was by no means their first expedition together. For some years they had been seeing a lot of one another. In the winter, they would go to Dodgson's rooms and sit on the sofa beside him while he told them stories, which he illustrated by pencil or ink drawings as he went along. Four or five times in the summer term he would take them out on the river, bringing with him a large basket of cakes and a kettle. On such occasions, Dodgson exchanged his clerical suit for white flannel trousers and his black top hat for a hard white straw hat. He always carried himself upright "as if he had swallowed a poker."

Outwardly there was nothing to distinguish the Godstow expedition from any other. And nobody today would remember that it ever took place but for what seems almost a pure accident. He had told the children many stories before, to which they had listened with delight, and they begged him to tell them another. This time, perhaps, he was in better storytelling form than usual, for his friend Mr. Duckworth was evidently impressed:

I rowed *stroke* and he rowed *bow* . . . the story was actually composed and spoken *over my shoulder* for the benefit of Alice Liddell, who was acting as "cox" of our gig. I remember turning round and saying "Dodgson, is this an extempore romance of yours?" And he replied: "Yes, I'm inventing as we go along."

Anyway, this time Alice did what she had never done before—she asked him to write the story down. At first he said he would think about it, but she continued to pester him until, eventually, he gave his promise to do so. In his diary for November 13, he notes: "Began writing the fairy-tale for Alice—I hope to finish it by Christmas."

In fact, the text was finished on February 10, 1863. Tenniel's illustrations were not completed until September, 1864, and *Alice in Wonderland* was published by Macmillan in 1865 (which is also, incidentally, the year of the first performance of another masterpiece, Wagner's *Tristan und Isolde*).

These events are memorable because they reveal a kind of human being who is, I believe, extremely rare—a man of genius who, in regard to his genius, is without egoism. In other respects, Dodgson was neither selfless nor without vanity. As a member of Senior Common Room, he was a difficult colleague, forever complaining about some minor negligence or inconvenience. He held strong and conservative views upon almost every question affecting the College or the University, and the savagery of his polemical pamphlets, like "The New Belfry of Christ Church" or "Twelve Months in a Curatorship," cannot have endeared him to his opponents.

He was proud of his photography, and justly so, for he was one of the best portrait photographers of the century. He had great hopes for his theory of Symbolic Logic, which is, I understand, more highly regarded today than it was at the time. As his diaries show, he also thought well of his little inventions—and he was always inventing something: a *memoria technica* for the logarithms of all primes under 100; a game of arithmetical croquet; a rule for finding the day of the week for any date of the month; a substitute for glue; a system of proportional representation; a method of controlling the carriage traffic at Covent Garden; an apparatus for making notes in the dark; an improved steering gear for a tricycle; and he always sought publication for his light verse. But when it came to the one thing which he did superbly well, where he was without any rival—namely, telling stories to children—the thought of himself, of publication and immortal fame, never seems to have entered his head.

The two *Alice* books were no freak achievements. There are passages in letters to children where the writing is just as good. For example:

It's so frightfully hot here that I've been almost too weak to hold a pen, and even if I had been able, there was no ink—it had all evaporated into a cloud of black steam, and in that state it has been floating about the room, inking the walls and ceiling till they're hardly fit to be seen: to-day, it is cooler, and a little has come back into the ink bottle in the form of black snow.

He went on telling impromptu stories to children all his life, which were never written down and, for all we know, may have surpassed the ones that were.

Though no human character can be explained away in terms of his upbringing or environment, it is legitimate to look for influencing factors.

In Dodgson's case, one such factor may have been his position as the oldest boy—the son of a clergyman—in a large family: he had seven sisters and three brothers. By the time he was eleven he had made himself the family entertainer. He constructed a train, built out of a wheelbarrow, a barrel, and a small truck, which conveyed passengers from one station in the rectory garden to another, and in the rules he drew up for this game, the Lewis Carroll imagination is already evident:

All passengers when upset are requested to lie still until picked up —as it is requisite that at least three trains should go over them, to entitle them to the attention of the doctor and assistants.

When a passenger has no money and still wants to go by train, he must stop at whatever station he happens to be at, and earn money— making tea for the stationmaster (who drinks it at all hours of the day and night) and grinding sand for the company (what use they make of it they are not bound to explain).

Two years later, he became the editor and chief contributor for a succession of family magazines, the last of which, *The Rectory Umbrella,* was still appearing after he had become an Oxford don and first printed the opening quatrain of "Jabberwocky."

Thus, at the beginning of his career as a writer, he was writing directly for an audience with which he was intimate and in which he had no literary rival. The average writer, at least today, has a very different experience. When he begins writing, he has no audience except himself; his first audience is likely to be one of rival, as yet unpublished, authors, and his only chance of acquiring an audience of his own is to get published, in little magazines or popular ones; and this audience consists of readers whom he does not know personally.

It seems clear that what, as an imaginative creator, Dodgson valued most was the immediate and intimate response of his audience, and its undivided attention (hence, perhaps, his passion for the theater). His writings for adults, no less than his children's stories, are for the "family" —Oxford to him was another and larger rectory. Even in the only company with whom he felt so completely at home that his stammer disappeared, the company of little girls, he preferred to see them singly. As he wrote to one mother:

Would you kindly tell me if I may reckon your girls as invitable to tea, or dinner, singly. I know of cases where they are invitable in sets only (like the circulating-library novels), and such friendships I don't

*think worth going on with. I don't think anyone knows what girl-nature
is, who has only seen them in the presence of their mothers or sisters.*

Many guesses, plausible and implausible, have been made as to the
historical origins of the characters and events in the *Alice* books, but one
may be sure that many allusions which were apparent to the Liddell
children are now irrecoverable. When he told a story, it was always for
a particular child. One of them, not Alice, records:

One thing that made his stories particularly charming to a child was
that he often took his cue from her remarks—a question would set him
off on quite a new trail of ideas, so that one felt one had somehow helped
to make the story, and it seemed a personal possession.

Very few writers, I believe, however much they desire fame for their
books, enjoy being a public figure who is recognized on the street by
strangers, but Dodgson hated publicity more than most. He refused to
allow any picture of himself to appear—"Nothing would be more unpleasant for me than to have my face known to strangers"—and he gave
orders that any letters addressed to L. Carroll, Christ Church, Oxford,
were to be returned to the sender with the endorsement "not known."

But thanks to Alice Liddell's importunity, and luckily for us, the
intimate narrator became a world-famous author. As usually happens
with a masterpiece, the initial critical reception of *Alice in Wonderland*
was mixed. The *Illustrated London News* and the *Pall Mall Gazette* liked
it; the *Spectator*, though generally approving, condemned the Mad Hatter's tea-party; the *Athenaeum* thought it a "stiff, overwrought story," and
the *Illustrated Times*, while conceding that the author possessed a fertile
imagination, declared that Alice's adventures "are too extravagantly
absurd to produce more diversion than disappointment and irritation."

When, seven years later, *Through the Looking-Glass* appeared, the
critics knew, from the enormous public success of its predecessor, that it
must be good—though I can think of no more unlikely literary comparison than that of Henry Kingsley, who wrote: "This is the finest thing
we have had since *Martin Chuzzlewit*."
And the book's fame has continued to grow.

I have always thought one might learn much about the cultural
history of a country by going through the speeches made by its public
men over a certain period, in legislatures, in law courts, and at official

banquets, and making a list of the books quoted from without attribution. So far as Great Britain is concerned, I strongly suspect that, for the past fifty years, the two *Alice* books and *The Hunting of the Snark* have headed it.

How do American readers react? Though nearly all the Americans I know personally loved Lewis Carroll as children, they may not be representative of American taste in general. Certainly, in every American book read by children—from *Huckleberry Finn* to the *Oz* books—which I have come across, nothing could b⸱· more remote from their worlds than the world of Alice.

The American child-hero—are there any American child-heroines?— is a Noble Savage, an anarchist, and, even when he reflects, predominantly concerned with movement and action. He may do almost anything except sit still. His heroic virtue—that is to say, his superiority to adults—lies in his freedom from conventional ways of thinking and acting: *all* social habits, from manners to creeds, are regarded as false or hypocritical or both. All emperors are really naked. Alice, surely, must come to the average American as a shock.

To begin with, she is a "lady." When, puzzled by the novelty of Wonderland, she asks herself if she could have changed into some other child, she is quite certain what sort of child she does *not* want to be:

"I'm sure I can't be Mabel, for I know all sorts of things, and she, oh, she knows such a very little . . . . I must be Mabel after all, and I shall have to go and live in that poky little house, and have next to no toys to play with . . . . No, I've made up my mind about it: if I'm Mabel, I'll stay down here."

Among grownups, she knows the difference between servants and mistresses:

"He took me for his house-maid," she said to herself as she ran. "How surprised he'll be when he finds out who I am." . . .
"The governess would never think of excusing me lessons for that. If she couldn't remember my name, she'd call me 'Miss' as the servants do."

And when the Red Queen advises her: "Speak in French when you can't think of the English for a thing—turn out your toes as you walk— and remember who you are!"—she knows that the answer to the question, "Who am I?" is really: "I am Alice Liddell, daughter of the Dean of Christ Church."

What is most likely to bewilder an American child, however, is not Alice's class-consciousness, which is easy to miss, but the peculiar relation of children and grownups to law and social manners. It is the child-heroine Alice who is invariably reasonable, self-controlled, and polite, while all the other inhabitants, human or animal, of Wonderland and the Looking-Glass are unsocial eccentrics—at the mercy of their passions and extremely bad-mannered, like the Queen of Hearts, the Duchess, the Hatter, and Humpty Dumpty, or grotesquely incompetent, like the White Queen and the White Knight.

What Alice finds so extraordinary about the people and events in these worlds is the anarchy which she is forever trying to make sense and order out of. In both books, games play an important role. The whole structure of *Through the Looking-Glass* is based on chess, and the Queen of Hearts' favorite pastime is croquet—both of them games which Alice knows how to play. To play a game, it is essential that the players know and obey its rules, and are skillful enough to do the right or reasonable thing at least half the time. Anarchy and incompetence are incompatible with play.

Croquet played with hedgehogs, flamingos, and soldiers instead of the conventional balls, mallets, and hoops is conceivable, provided that they are willing to imitate the behavior of these inanimate objects, but, in Wonderland, they behave as they choose and the game is impossible to play.

In the Looking-Glass world, the problem is different. It is not, like Wonderland, a place of complete anarchy where everybody says and does whatever comes into his head, but a completely determined world without choice. Tweedledum and Tweedledee, the Lion and the Unicorn, the Red Knight and the White, must fight at regular intervals, irrespective of their feelings. In Wonderland, Alice has to adjust herself to a life without laws; in Looking-Glass Land, to one governed by laws to which she is unaccustomed. She has to learn, for example, to walk away from a place in order to reach it, or to run fast in order to remain where she is. In Wonderland, she is the only person with self-control; in Looking-Glass Land, the only competent one. But for the way she plays a pawn, one feels that the game of chess would never be completed.

In both worlds, one of the most important and powerful characters is not a person but the English language. Alice, who had hitherto supposed that words were passive objects, discovers that they have a life and will of their own. When she tries to remember poems she has learned, new lines come into her head unbidden, and, when she thinks she knows what a word means, it turns out to mean something else.

> *"And so these three little sisters—they were learning to draw, you know—"*
> *"What did they draw?"* . . .
> *"Treacle—from a treacle well. . . ."*
> *"But they were in the well."*
> *"Of course they were: well in."* . . .
>
> *"How old did you say you were?"*
> *"Seven years and six months."*
> *"Wrong! You never said a word like it!"* . . .
>
> *"You take some flour."*
> *"Where do you pick the flower? In a garden or in the hedges?"*
> *"Well, it isn't picked at all: it's ground."*
> *"How many acres of ground?"*

Nothing, surely, could be more remote from the American image of the pioneering, hunting, prepolitical hero than this preoccupation with language. It is the concern of the solitary thinker, for language is the mother of thought, and of the politician—in the Greek sense—for speech is the medium by which we disclose ourselves to others. The American hero is neither.

Both of Alice's "dreams" end in a state of developing chaos from which she wakes just in time before they can become nightmares:

> *At this the whole pack rose up in the air, and came flying down upon her; she gave a little scream, half of fright and half of anger, and tried to beat them off, and found herself lying on the bank with her head in the lap of her sister. . . .*

> *Already several of the guests were lying down in the dishes, and the soup ladle was walking up the table towards Alice's chair, and beckoning to her impatiently to get out of its way.*
> *"I can't stand this any longer!" she cried, as she jumped up and seized the table-cloth with both hands: one good pull, and plates, dishes, guests and candles came crashing down together in a heap on the floor.*

Wonderland and Looking-Glass Land are fun to visit but no places to live in. Even when she is there, Alice can ask herself with some nostalgia "if anything would ever happen in a natural way again," and by "natural" she means the opposite of what Rousseau would mean. She means peaceful, civilized society.

There are good books which are only for adults, because their comprehension presupposes adult experiences, but there are no good books which are only for children. A child who enjoys the *Alice* books will continue to enjoy them when he or she is grown up, though his "reading" of what they mean will probably change. In assessing their value, there are two questions one can ask: first, what insight do they provide as to how the world appears to a child?; and, second, to what extent is the world really like that?

According to Lewis Carroll, what a child desires before anything else is that the world in which he finds himself should make sense. It is not the commands and prohibitions, as such, which adults impose that the child resents, but rather that he cannot perceive any law linking one command to another in a consistent pattern.

The child is told, for example, that he must not do such-and-such, and then sees adults doing precisely that. This occurs especially often in the realm of social manners. In well-bred society, people treat each other with courtesy but, in trying to teach their children to be polite, their method of instruction is often that of a drill sergeant. Without realizing it, adults can be rude to children in ways which, if they were dealing with one of their own kind, would get them knocked down. How many children, when they are silenced with the command, "Speak when you're spoken to!" must have longed to retort as Alice does:

"But if everybody obeyed that rule, and if you only spoke when you were spoken to, and the other person always waited for you to begin, you see that nobody would ever say anything."

It would be an exaggeration to say that children see adults as they really are, but, like servants, they see them at moments when they are not concerned with making a favorable impression.

As everybody knows, Dodgson's Muse was incarnated in a succession of girls between the ages of eight and eleven. Little boys he feared and disliked: they were grubby and noisy and broke things. Most adults he found insensitive. At the age of twenty-four, he wrote in his diary:

I think that the character of most that I meet is merely refined animal. How few seem to care for the only subjects of real interest in life!

Naturally, most of his "child-friends" came from middle- or upper-middle-class English homes. He mentions having met one American child and the encounter was not a success:

Lily Alice Godfrey, from New York: aged 8; but talked like a girl of 15 or 16, and declined to be kissed on wishing good-by, on the ground that she 'never kissed gentlemen'. . . . I fear it is true that there are no children in America.

And the children he understood best were the quiet and imaginative ones. Thus Irene Vanbrugh, who must have been going through a tomboy phase when she met him, says:

He had a deep love for children, though I am inclined to think not such a great understanding of them. . . . His great delight was to teach me his Game of Logic. Dare I say this made the evening rather long, when the band was playing outside on the parade, and the moon shining on the sea?

The question for an adult reader of Lewis Carroll, however, is not the author's psychological peculiarities, but the validity of his heroine. Is Alice, that is to say, an adequate symbol for what every human being should try to be like?

I am inclined to answer yes. A girl of eleven (or a boy of twelve) who comes from a good home—a home, that is, where she has known both love and discipline and where the life of the mind is taken seriously but not solemnly—can be a most remarkable creature. No longer a baby, she has learned self-control, acquired a sense of her identity, and can think logically without ceasing to be imaginative. She does not know, of course, that her sense of identity has been too easily won—the gift of her parents rather than her own doing—and that she is soon going to lose it, first in the *Sturm und Drang* of adolescence and then, when she enters the adult social world, in anxieties over money and status.

But one cannot meet a girl or a boy of this kind without feeling that what she or he is—by luck and momentarily—is what, after many years and countless follies and errors, one would like, in the end, to become.

ALICE

by *Roger Lancelyn Green*

(1960)

DODGSON FIRST MET Alice on April 25, 1856, just before her fourth birthday when he was visiting the Deanery at Christ Church to take a photograph of the Cathedral; "The three little girls were in the garden most of the time, and we became excellent friends." Lorina, the eldest, was seven at this time, and Edith was two, while their brother Harry, whom Dodgson had already met and was to tutor for a little while, was nine. The friendship grew and continued for almost ten years, though Dodgson never got on well with either the Dean or Mrs. Liddell; he seldom visited at the Deanery, except to see the children, and he certainly never stayed with the Liddells at Llandudno, as legend has it that he did. Entries in his diary show that his visits to the Deanery were usually timed to coincide with Mrs. Liddell's absence from home. The children, however, visited him in his rooms fairly frequently, sometimes accompanied by their governess, Miss Prickett, who was nicknamed "Pricks," and who may have been the original of the Mouse in *Wonderland*, since the history lesson beginning "William the Conqueror whose cause was favoured by the Pope . . ." is an actual quotation from Havilland Chepmell's *Short Course of History* (1862), pages 143-4, which was one of their lesson-books.

Dodgson told many stories to the three little girls before the famous picnic which produced the main part of *Alice in Wonderland*:

"We used to sit on the big sofa on each side of him," remembered Alice in 1932, "while he told us stories, illustrating them by pencil or ink drawings as he went along. . . . He seemed to have an endless store of these fantastical tales, which he made up as he told them, drawing busily on a large sheet of paper all the time. They were not always entirely new. Sometimes they were new versions of old stories; sometimes they started on the old basis, but grew into new tales owing to the frequent interruptions which opened up fresh and undreamed-of possibilities."

Among these stories was "A Mad Tea-Party," in which the three children appear as the little girls who lived in the treacle well, Elsie being "L.C." (Lorina Charlotte), Lacie an anagram of "Alice," and Tilly being short for "Matilda," which was Edith's nickname. "Pig and Pepper" may also have been one of these stories, since Cheshire Cats were in Dodgson's mind at the time, following a correspondence in *Notes and Queries* (of which he was an eager reader) on the origin of the expression "To grin like a Cheshire Cat." He must have followed with amusement the various old—and odd—explanations unearthed by the learned in their vain attempts to explain the phrase. Do Cheshire Cats grin because Cheshire is the only County Palatine? Or were snarling armorial leopards (of which the Red Cat of Brimstage may be one) painted on so many inn signs in Cheshire made more like grinning cats by painters who had never seen a leopard? Or was Cheshire cheese made into the shape of a cat before being sent for export to Bristol? Or was it simply that the young ladies of Cheshire (referred to as "The Cheshire Cats" by their cousins in the next county, "The Lancashire Witches") were noted for the breadth of their smiles?

Dodgson did not enter into the controversy, but he noted that it was not getting anywhere.

"Would you tell me please, which way I ought to go from here?"
"That depends a good deal on where you want to get to," said the Cat.
"I don't much care where," said Alice.
"Then it doesn't matter which way you go," said the Cat.
"—So long as I get somewhere," Alice added as an explanation.
"Oh, you're sure to do that," said the Cat, "if you only walk long enough."
Alice felt that this could not be denied. . . .

The Cheshire Cat correspondence having faded away, leaving only the grin—still unaccounted for—Dodgson, with a passing thought for an even older phrase, "A cat may look at a king," was ready to begin wondering how "As mad as a hatter" originated. The tea party may have been a fairly mad one in Dodgson's rooms when, according to Alice, he would say, "Now then, it's a rainy day, let's have some tea." Ordinary afternoon tea had not yet come into fashion, but Dodgson's suggestion would be timed to coincide with the children's "tea" at 6 P.M.—hence the hour at which the Mad Hatter's watch had stopped. When Miss Prickett was not available, the children were escorted by their nurse who, we can well imagine, was apt to drop off to sleep like any Dormouse.

"When we went on the river for the afternoon with Mr. Dodgson," recorded Alice, "which happened at most four or five times every summer term, he always brought out with him a large basket full of cakes, and a kettle, which we used to boil under a haycock, if we could find one. On rarer occasions we went out for the whole day with him, and then we took a large basket with luncheon—cold chicken and salad and all sorts of good things. One of our favourite whole-day excursions was to row down to Nuneham and picnic in the woods there. . . .
"The party usually consisted of five—one of Mr. Dodgson's men friends as well as himself and us three. His brother [Wilfred] occasionally took an oar in the merry party, but our most usual fifth was Mr. Duckworth, who sang well. . . ."

On June 17, 1862, an important expedition took place. Dodgson's two eldest sisters, Fanny and Elizabeth, and his Aunt Lucy Lutwidge were staying in Oxford as his guests, and he took them on an all-day picnic on the river, with Robinson Duckworth, who was then a young don at Trinity, to help him row. "Ina, Alice and Edith came with us." They set

out at twelve-thirty, got to Nuneham by two, and landed there to have
dinner and walk in the park, before starting back at half past four.

About a mile above Nuneham heavy rain came on, recorded Dodgson
in his diary.

*After bearing it for a short time I settled that we had better leave the
boat and walk; three miles of this drenched us all pretty well. I went on
first with the children as they could walk must faster than Elizabeth, and
took them to the only house I knew in Sandford, Mrs. Broughton's, where
Ranken lodges. I left them with her to get their clothes dried, and went
off to find a vehicle. . . . We all had tea in my rooms about 8:30, after
which I took the children home.*

Just over a fortnight later, Dodgson and Duckworth took the three
children on another river expedition, upstream this time, and for the
afternoon only. It was on July 4, and is probably the most famous picnic
that has ever taken place.

Duckworth and I made an expedition up *the river to Godstow with
the three Liddells; we had tea on the bank there, and did not reach
Christ Church again till quarter past eight. . . . On which occasion,* he
added later, *I told them the fairy-tale of* Alice's Adventures under
Ground, *which I undertook to write out for Alice.*

"The story was actually composed and spoken *over my shoulder* for
the benefit of Alice Liddell," wrote Duckworth. "I remember turning
round and saying, 'Dodgson, is this an extemporary romance of yours?'
And he replied: 'Yes, I'm inventing as we go along.' I also remember how,
when we had conducted the three children back to the Deanery, Alice
said, as she bade us good-night, 'Oh, Mr. Dodgson, I wish you would
write out Alice's Adventures for me!' . . ."

And Alice Liddell recorded, "I think the stories he told us that afternoon must have been better than usual, because I have such a distinct
recollection of the expedition, and also, on the next day I started to pester
him to write down the story for me."

On the next day, sure enough, Dodgson records that he set out for
London and by chance traveled with the Liddells, and he added, concerning the story, "Headings written out on my way to London."

And the story itself? *I distinctly remember,* wrote Dodgson, *how,
in a desperate attempt to strike out some new line in fairy-lore, I had sent
my heroine straight down a rabbit-hole, to begin with, without the least
idea what was to happen afterwards.*

Having got Alice down into the hall underground, Dodgson harked back to the disastrous expedition to Nuneham of two weeks previous—when, as likely as not, Alice, in the midst of their discomforts, had burst into tears and been accused of causing the flood by her crying, while one of the party may have remarked that it was "raining cats and dogs," at which odd expression the children might have protested that, if so, they hated cats and dogs.

They were indeed a curious party that assembled on the bank, wrote Dodgson in his original version, *the birds with draggled feathers, the animals with their fur clinging close to them—all dripping wet, cross and uncomfortable. The first question of course was how to get dry: they had a consultation about this, and Alice hardly felt herself at all surprised at finding herself talking familiarly with the birds, as if she had known them all her life. Indeed, she had quite a long argument with the Lory, who at last turned sulky, and would only say 'I am older than you, and must know best,' and this Alice would not admit without knowing how old the Lory was, and as the Lory positively refused to tell its age, there was nothing more to be said.*

After this, the Mouse gave its history lesson; but even Havilland Chepmell did not prove dry enough for the purpose.

"In that case," said the Dodo solemnly, rising to his feet, "I move that the meeting adjourn, for the immediate adoption of more energetic remedies—"
"Speak English!" said the Duck. "I don't know the meaning of half those long words, and what's more, I don't believe you do either!" And the Duck quacked a comfortable laugh to itself. Some of the other birds tittered audibly.
"I only meant to say," said the Dodo in rather an offended tone, "that I know of a house near here, where we could get the young lady and the rest of the party dried, and then we could listen comfortably to the story which I think you were good enough to promise to tell us," bowing gravely to the Mouse.
The mouse made no objection to this, and the whole party moved along the river bank, (for the pool had by this time begun to flow out of the hall, and the edge of it was fringed with rushes and forget-me-nots) in a slow procession, the Dodo leading the way. After a time the Dodo became impatient, and, leaving the Duck to bring up the rest of the party, moved on at a quicker pace with Alice, the Lory and the Eaglet, and soon brought them to a little cottage, and there they sat snugly by the fire, wrapped up in blankets, until the rest of the party had arrived, and they were all dry again.

After this the Mouse proceeded with its tale—"It *is* a long tail, certainly," said Alice, looking down with wonder at the Mouse's tail, which was coiled nearly all round the party. (Was Dodgson remembering his early poem—"It was a tail of desperate length"—or was Aunt Lucy Lutwidge wearing so long a boa that she had wrapped it round the three children when the rain began?)

The "Tale" was different from the final one which tells what "Fury said to a mouse," but after it Alice made the same injudicious remarks about Dinah—the tabby cat at the Deanery, "my special pet"—and when she was left alone, she

began talking to herself again as usual, "I do wish some of them had stayed a little longer! and I was getting to be such friends with them—really the Lory and I were almost like sisters! and so was the dear little Eaglet! And then the Duck and the Dodo! How nicely the Duck sang to us as we came along through the water; and if the Dodo hadn't known the way to that nice little cottage, I don't know when we should have got dry again. . . ."

The fun of the story was increased by the realization that the Lory was Lorina and the Eaglet was Edith, while Dodgson ("Do-do-dodgson" when he stammered) was the Dodo and Duckworth was the Duck. "The Duck from the Dodo," wrote Dodgson in the copy of the facsimile of *Alice's Adventures under Ground* which he gave to Duckworth in 1887.

Duckworth's songs were a great feature of the expeditions and the children learned to sing "Sally come up," the minstrel song by T. Ramsey and E. W. Mackney which was parodied in the story:

> *Salmon come up! Salmon go down!*
> *Salmon come twist your tail around . . .*

And not long afterwards when Dodgson visited them at the Deanery to write in the books for collections of crests (including their own, which sported three leopards' faces, or—the Cheshire Cat of heraldry; and probably the Gryphon of Wales, as well as the Lion and the Unicorn in the Royal coat of arms) he listened to them singing J. M. Sayles's "Beautiful Star":

> "Beautiful star in heav'n so bright
> Softly falls thy silv'ry light,
> As thou movest from earth so far,
> Star of the evening, beautiful star,
>   Beau-ti-ful star,

> Beau-ti-ful star,
> Star-of the eve-ning,
> Beautiful, beautiful star."

This became "Beautiful Soup" very readily, after the Gryphon and the Mock Turtle had danced the Lobster Quadrille while singing "Salmon come up!" But between these two adventures Alice had twice tried to recite the poems which Miss Prickett taught them in the schoolroom: "How doth the little busy bee," by Isaac Watts, and Robert Southey's "You are old, father William," both of which suffered a Wonderland change in the process.

Even the story as first written down was not all told on July 4, for on August 6, Dodgson wrote in his Diary,

In the afternoon Harcourt and I took the three Liddells up to God-stow, where we had tea; we tried the game of "The Ural Mountains" on the way, but it did not prove very successful, and I had to go on with my interminable fairy-tale of Alice's Adventures. *We got back soon after eight, and had supper in my rooms, the children coming over for a short while. A very enjoyable expedition—the last, I should think, to which Ina is likely to be allowed to come—her fourteenth time.*

It was certainly the last expedition that year, for the Liddells went off next day to their summer home at Llandudno. On November 13, Dodgson "began writing the fairy tale for Alice, which I told them July 4, going to Godstow—I hope to finish it by Christmas." But it was not actually finished until early in February, 1863, and he was not able to finish the illustrations in the beautifully written copy for Alice until September of the year after.

The story without pictures, however, was to be seen at the Deanery in 1863, and there one day the novelist Henry Kingsley, who was visiting the Dean, chanced to pick it up, and, once started, could not lay it down until he had finished. He urged Mrs. Liddell to persuade the author to publish it; but Dodgson was doubtful, and did not want to risk losing money over it. However, he consulted Duckworth, who read over what had been written and assured him that the book would succeed, if only he could persuade some good artist to illustrate it, and suggested John Tenniel, who drew excellent cartoons of animals in *Punch* and had recently illustrated *Aesop's Fables.*

Dodgson, however, was still uncertain whether a story composed extempore for three particular children, and based moreover on their

own experiences, from picnics on the Thames to unusual games of croquet and cards at the Deanery (he had the rules for his new *Court Circular* printed in 1860, and for *Croquet Castles* in 1863), could appeal to
other children. As a final test he lent the story (probably in his own
rough copy) to George Macdonald, who had already written several
delightful fairy tales such as "The Light Princess." Macdonald took it
home and his wife read it out loud to the children. "I remember that first
reading well," wrote Greville Macdonald in his *Reminiscences of a Spe-
cialist* in 1932, "and also my braggart avowal that I wished there were
60,000 volumes of it." If Greville, aged six, could be so enthusiastic, and
such an expert as George Macdonald advocated publication, Dodgson
could hesitate no longer, and he at once set about revising and enlarging
the story to make it more suitable for publication.

Out came the more definite references to the picnic at Nuneham, and
also Alice's slighting references to Gertrude and Florence (probably
friends or cousins of her own) to be replaced by Ada and Mabel, who
could not be identified. The Caucus Race was substituted for the warm
fire and blankets at Sandford and a better tail was given to the Mouse;
the Gryphon and the Mock Turtle discoursed at far greater length on the
education of the young—though all their "extras" still paralleled those
which, in default of Miss Prickett, Alice received from outside instructors:
the Drawing-master, though hardly "an old conger-eel"—he was actually
John Ruskin—did come once a week to teach Drawing, Sketching, and
Painting in Oils. Instead of "Salmon come up," the Mock Turtle sang
a parody of "Will you walk into my parlour, said the spider to the fly,"
and Alice was given another recitation meant to be Isaac Watts's " 'Tis the
voice of the sluggard, I heard him complain, 'You have waked me too
soon, I must slumber again.' " At this time Dodgson only gave her four
lines for the first stanza, and for the second merely,

> *I passed by his garden and marked with one eye*
> *How the owl and the oyster were sharing a pie—*

When the songs were set to music in 1870 by William Boyd, Dodgson
added two more lines,

> *While the Duck and the Dodo, the Lizard and Cat*
> *Were swimming in milk round the brim of a hat.*

It was not until 1886, when *Alice* was made into an operetta, that he
wrote the sixteen-line version now generally known, with the last com-

plete line (only cut in the book because the Mock Turtle must still interrupt),

And concluded the banquet by eating the Owl.

The most important additions, however, were the chapters called "Pig and Pepper" and "A Mad Tea-Party," "Who Stole the Tarts?" and "Alice's Evidence." There was no Duchess in *Alice's Adventures under Ground*: the White Rabbit exclaimed, "The Marchioness! the Marchioness! Oh my dear paws! oh my fur and whiskers! She'll have me executed, as sure as ferrets are ferrets!" which was rather awkwardly tacked on to what must have been another story, built up round Dodgson's card game of *Court Circular* by letting him tell Alice: "The Queen's the Marchioness, didn't you know that?"

The Cook, the Cat, and the Mad Tea-Party were waiting to be fitted in from another story, introduced by the Fish-Footmen—perhaps suggested by a "learned" article on talking fish, with an amusing du Maurier illustration in *Punch* for March 22, 1862; and there were G. W. Langford's morbid verses waiting to be parodied as the Duchess's Lullaby,

> Speak gently to the little child!
> Its love be sure to gain;
> Teach it in accents soft and mild;
> It may not long remain.

The elongation of the Trial of the Knave of Hearts from one page to two chapters may have been suggested to Dodgson by his visit to the Assize Court on July 13, 1863, of which he notes that he heard "some very petty cases, but they were interesting to me, as I have seen so little of trials." To increase the "Evidence," the nonsense verses "She's All My Fancy Painted Him," were resuscitated from *The Comic Times* and revised to fit.

That same July, Dodgson was having trial pages of *Alice's Adventures* set up by the Oxford University Press and was still hoping to illustrate the book himself, even going so far as to prepare a block on wood—a half-length of Alice—which Thomas Woolner, the Pre-Raphaelite, looked at and "condemned the arms, which he says I *must* draw from the life."

He was meeting and photographing several artists such as Rossetti and Arthur Hughes that autumn, besides the editor and playwright Tom Taylor, and they are likely to have dissuaded him from continuing with his own attempts as an illustrator. Reverting to Duckworth's suggestion of asking Tenniel to illustrate *Alice*, Dodgson got an introduction from Tom Taylor and called on him on January 25, 1864. Tenniel was interested, asked to see the complete story, and wrote on April 5 to tell Dodgson that he was willing to undertake the task.

As Dodgson could not illustrate his stories himself, he did the next best thing; he employed an expert artist to make the illustrations which he could see in his own mind but lacked the skill to reproduce on paper, paying for the work himself and, so far as possible, "using" the artist as if he were a piece of machinery hired for the purpose. This explains why Tenniel's illustrations are so much a part of the two *Alice* books that no other artist has ever come near to equaling them; the same is also true of *Sylvie and Bruno*, though to a lesser extent, the book being less clearly imagined by the author, and Harry Furniss falling short of Tenniel's skill as an artist. It also explains Tenniel's repugnance to illustrate *Through the Looking-Glass* and his warning to Furniss, "Lewis Carroll is impossible . . . I'll give you a week, old chap; *you* will never put up with that fellow a day longer."

Not only did Dodgson pay for the illustrations to his books, but he paid also to have them printed, merely employing Messrs. Macmillan & Co. to publish them on a commission basis. The work was done by the Clarendon Press at Oxford; the complete book in galley proofs was sent to Macmillan's on December 16, 1864; Tenniel checked his last proofs by the middle of June; the Press printed off two thousand copies and forty-eight were bound up early in July, most if not all of which Dodgson sent out as presents to his friends, young and old, Alice receiving the first copy on July 4, 1865—three years to the day after the original picnic.

Before the book was properly out, however, Tenniel wrote that he was "entirely dissatisfied with the printing of the pictures," and Dodgson —always scrupulously careful to give only of the best—withdrew it from circulation. He sent a letter to all who had received copies asking that they should be returned, and he retrieved in this way thirty-four copies which he gave to children's hospitals where they speedily disintegrated. The fourteen or so copies which chanced to survive from this first four dozen, which constituted the First Issue of the First Edition of *Alice's Adventures in Wonderland*, are now among the most valuable books of the last hundred years, specimens having been known to fetch as much as £5,000 each. The remaining 1,952 were sold (in unbound sheets) to Messrs. Appleton of New York, who issued one thousand with a new title page (dated 1866)—thus making the Second Issue of the First Edition. These title pages were printed at Oxford and supplied with the sheets. Title pages for the remaining 952 copies were subsequently printed in America—thus making the Third Issue of the First Edition. It was also "pirated" in the U.S.A. in serial form, appearing in the December, 1866 and January, 1867 numbers of *Merryman's Monthly*.

Meanwhile, Dodgson had the book reprinted by Messrs. Clay of London, and it was published by Macmillan's early in December, 1865, though it was dated 1866; Dodgson received the first copy on November 9, and Tenniel gave his "approval" later in the month.

This was the Second Edition, of which two thousand copies were printed, and Dodgson calculated that if all copies were sold, he would still be £200 out of pocket, "But if a second 2,000 could be sold it would cost £300, and bring in £500, thus squaring accounts and any further sale would be a gain, but that I can hardly hope for."

By the time of his death some 180,000 copies had been sold, which suggests that he made some £18,000 out of this book alone—the equivalent of £100,000 in today's purchasing values, and that, moreover, at a time when there was virtually no income tax.

Alice's Adventures did not achieve immediate fame, or even great sales according to the modest figures of a century ago. It did not go "out of print" (i.e. when the first four thousand copies were disposed of, and Dodgson's loss over the first edition was balanced by sales) until October, 1866, the first copies of the "5th thousand" reaching him on December 1. And the early reviewers had not treated it as anything out of the ordinary; the *Athenaeum* commented that "Mr. Carroll has labored hard . . . and we acknowledge the hard labor . . . a stiff, overwrought story," and the *Illustrated Times* thought it "too extravagantly absurd to produce more diversion than disappointment and irritation." But the *Pall Mall Gazette* gave it first place among the season's children's books, which included works by Jean Ingelow, William Gilbert, Ballantyne, and Manville Fenn; "This delightful little book is a children's feast and triumph of nonsense . . . never inhuman, never inelegant, never tedious"; "a glorious artistic treasure," wrote the *Reader's* reviewer: "a book to put on one's shelf as an antidote to a fit of the blues."

But it speedily began to creep into literature. Thirty years after its publication, Charlotte, in *The Golden Age*, can tell the story of Alice's adventures to her dolls as if it had been "Cinderella" or "Puss in Boots," the author assuming naturally that every reader knew the book intimately.

As early as August, 1866, Dodgson thought of writing a sequel to *Alice's Adventures* which would use up what he remembered of several more stories told to the three Liddell girls. But considering the illustrations so very important a part of the book, he decided not to begin writing it until he had his artist waiting to illustrate it. The trouble was that Tenniel refused to do it; one book by Lewis Carroll was all, he felt in 1866, that he could stand. So Dodgson made pilgrimage round the artists of the day, beginning with "Dicky" Doyle, who had illustrated *The King of the Golden River* for Ruskin. W. S. Gilbert, then known more for his illustrations to his father's children's stories and his own *Bab Ballads*, was tried; and then Sir Noel Paton, whose paintings of fairies Dodgson admired so much. Paton was too ill to undertake it, and insisted that "Tenniel is *the* man"; and in June, 1868, Tenniel consented to illustrate the projected book "at such spare times as he can find."

By August of that year Dodgson was busy writing *Looking-Glass House*, and a chance meeting while staying with his uncle, Skeffington Lutwidge, in Onslow Square solved the question of what Alice should find the greatest difference after passing through the Looking-Glass. A little cousin called Alice Raikes was playing in the garden, and Dodgson called her in. "Would you like to come and see something which is rather puzzling?" he asked, and led her to a tall mirror across the corner of the room.

"Now," he said, giving me an orange, "first tell me which hand you have got that in." "The right," I said. "Now," he said, "go and stand before that glass, and tell me which hand the little girl you see there has got it in." After some perplexed contemplation, I said, "The left hand." "Exactly," he said, "and how do you explain that?" I couldn't explain it, but seeing that some solution was expected, I ventured, "If I was on the *other* side of the glass, wouldn't the orange still be in my right hand?" I can remember his laugh. "Well done, little Alice," he said. "The best answer I've had yet."

I heard no more then, but in after years was told that he said that had given him his first idea for *Through the Looking-Glass . . .*

Not the first idea, of course, but the final twist. For the story originated, as Alice Liddell recorded, in several told to her long before the *Wonderland* picnic, "particularly the ones to do with chessmen, which are dated by the period when we were excitedly learning chess." The Diaries for that period are lost, but we may perhaps assume that the year

was 1859, since in *Through the Looking-Glass* Alice tells Humpty Dumpty
that her age is "seven years and six months"; as she was born on May 4
(the date of the Mad Tea-Party), 1852, this gives November 4 (compare
the boys making the bonfire in Chapter I), 1859.

Dodgson's diary being missing, we cannot check what actually happened that day, but the meeting with the Red Queen in the "Garden of
Live Flowers" and the adventure of the train may date from the occasion
when he visited the three children on holiday in April, 1863. This was at
Charlton Kings, near Cheltenham, "where they were staying with Dean
Liddell's mother, who lived at Hetton Lawn. On April 4, Dodgson
records:

*Reached Cheltenham by 11:30 A.M. I found Alice waiting with Miss
Prickett at the station, and walked with them to Charlton Kings, about
one and a half miles. In the afternoon, we went in a large party in the
carriage up to Birdlip, where Ina, Alice and Miss Prickett got out, and
walked back with me over Leckhampton Hill. Except for the high wind,
the day could hardly have been better for the view; the children were
in the wildest spirits.*

Doubtless those wild spirits demanded a story, and Miss Prickett, or
"Pricks," was the model for the Red Queen—"one of the thorny kind," as
the earlier editions of the book had it—whom Dodgson later described as
"the concentrated essence of all governesses."

Miss Prickett may well have urged her charges to go "Faster! Faster!"
and may even have produced dry biscuits to refresh them—and once again
the important business of education as imparted by her was there to form
the basis for many conversations in the story.

Dodgson spent most of the next day with the Liddells at Hetton Lawn,
and though he left Charlton Kings next day, he rejoined them a week later
on their train journey home. "We had a very merry journey to Oxford
together," he records—and with such a raconteur as a companion, they
may well have expected the train to jump over a brook at any moment!

When Dodgson came to write *Through the Looking-Glass*, he was
making a more conscious literary effort than in writing out the *Adventures
under Ground* for Alice; and he had also time to let his various recollected
stories simmer down. His method of writing seems to have been to collect
scraps which "came" to him and recollections of stories which he had told,
besides suggestions growing out of books, pictures, and even topical

events which would have meaning for Alice and her sisters while seeming mere fancy to the ordinary reader.

For a topical example, Henry Luke Paget, later Bishop of Chester, who was an undergraduate at Christ Church about 1870, used to recall that "Alice, for instance, can buy two eggs cheaper than one at the Sheep's shop. 'Only you must eat them both,' said the Sheep, and a Christ Church undergraduate knew that if he ordered one boiled egg he was served with two, but one was invariably bad."

Perhaps another idea, that for the Anglo-Saxon Messengers with their appropriate "attitudes," came from a performance at the Christ Church theatricals on December 5, 1863 of Robert Brough's burlesque *Alfred the Great*, in which a particular point was made of the Anglo-Saxon setting; both Dodgson and the Liddell children were in the audience.

Far more important than this, however, was the "Stanza of Anglo-Saxon Poetry" that Dodgson had written at Croft at the end of 1855, which ran,

> 'Twas bryllyg, and the slythy toves
>   Did gyre and gimble in the wabe;
> All mimsy were the borogoves;
>   And the mome raths outgrabe.

In this version, which is preserved in *Mischmasch* and was first published by Collingwood in *The Lewis Carroll Picture Book* in 1899, the stanza is followed by learned notes parodying those in an actual text, giving the meanings of the strange words. This was obviously impossible to transfer as it stood to *Through the Looking-Glass*, but the meanings must be given somehow; Dodgson accordingly introduced Humpty Dumpty with his appropriate Nursery Rhyme and developed him into the kind of burlesque professor who could properly give Alice a lecture on etymology. This also gave the opportunity for the introduction of the theory of "portmanteau" words—which does not occur in the notes to the 1855 "Stanza of Anglo-Saxon Poetry." In fact, the real portmanteau words occur in the rest of the "Jabberwocky" poem, which was written at a different time (the date, unfortunately, is not preserved) while Dodgson was "staying with his cousins, the Misses Wilcox, at Whitburn, near Sunderland. To while away an evening the whole party sat down to a game of verse-making, and 'Jabberwocky' was his contribution."

The party probably included a mutual cousin of Dodgson and the Wilcoxes, the poetess Menella Bute Smedley, and the substance of the poem parodies her much longer versification of a German legend, "The Shepherd of the Giant Mountains," which first appeared in *Sharpe's London Magazine* in March, 1846, with a Griffin in place of the Jabberwock nesting in an incredibly "Gothick" oak tree beneath whose shade, in lieu of the Tumtum tree, a "beamish boy," the Shepherd Gottschalk, waited to slay it with a weapon that might well have been described as "vorpal."

"Jabberwocky" was not the only poem of an earlier date which Dodgson adapted for the new book and invented a character to suit. In *The Train* for October, 1856, appeared his parody of Wordsworth's "Resolution and Independence, or The Leech-Gatherer" called "Upon the Lonely Moor," which he improved into the ballad "A-sitting on a Gate" (to be sung to the tune of Thomas Moore's "I give thee all, I can no more, tho' poor the off'ring be"), and invented the character of the White Knight (as he admitted in 1893) "to suit the speaker in the poem."

Other ideas in the book may have originated in verses and pictures in *Punch*, of which Dodgson was an earnest student, and some of the ideas may have been shared with the Liddells and woven into stories during the previous ten years.

"Allow me to disagree with you," says the Plum Pudding, getting up in the dish and bowing to the diner who is about to help himself in the drawing by Edward Bradley ("Cuthbert Bede," author of *Mr. Verdant Green*) on January 19, 1861; Tenniel's cartoon "Law and Lunacy: Or, A Glorious Oyster Season for the Lawyers" (January 25, 1862) revives the saying: "No more sense than an oyster" in a feast that suggests the orgy of the Walrus and the Carpenter. "Ballad from Bedlam" contains such useful hints as:

> The elephant with cheerful voice
> Sings blithly on the spray,

while Looking-Glass Insects may have been an improvement on George du Maurier's collections of "Specimens not yet included in the Collection at Regents Park" in June and August, 1869, which include The Umbrella Bird, The Scissor-Wing Brush-Tail Razor-Bill, and the Tromboniferous Windbird—which have to be seen to be believed.

Literature also played its part, usually subconsciously, if the White Queen owes anything to Mrs. Wragg in Wilkie Collins' *No Name* or the White Knight to Hudibras—or the opening passages about Alice, Dinah, and the kittens to a parody of Dickens' *Cricket on the Hearth* in *Black-*

wood's Magazine, November, 1845 (as Kathleen Tillotson suggests in the
Autumn, 1950, number of *English*); far more obviously in "The Garden
of Live Flowers" which follows Section xxii of Tennyson's *Maud,* particularly the stanza,

> There had fallen a splendid tear
>   From the passion-flower at the gate.
> She is coming, my dove, my dear;
>   She is coming, my life, my fate.
> The red rose cries, "She is near, she is near";
>   And the white rose weeps, "She is late";
> The larkspur listens, "I hear, I hear";
>   And the lily whispers "I wait."

The passionflower gave way to the tiger lily when the religious origin
of its name was pointed out to Dodgson, but otherwise all the flowers may
be found in the poem. But the Garden may have been invented on a late
visit to the Liddells, whose younger sisters were Rhoda (Rose), born
1860; and Violet, born 1864—of whom the Tiger lily might well say: "You
keep your head under the leaves, and snore away there, till you know no
more what's going on in the world, than if you were a bud."

It must not be thought that either of the *Alice* books is derivative;
they are both original with the absolute originality of sheer genius. All the
various "originals" and suggestions served as so many sparks to touch off
the sleeping gunpowder of Dodgson's imagination.

Alice *and the* Looking-Glass *are made up almost wholly of bits and
scraps, single ideas which came of themselves,* wrote Dodgson in April,
1887, after the two books had been made into an operetta by Henry Savile
Clarke. *In writing it* [Alice's Adventures under Ground] *out, I added
many fresh ideas, which seemed to grow of themselves upon the original
stock; and many more were added when, years afterwards, I wrote it all
over again for publication; but (this may interest some readers of* Alice
*to know) every such idea and nearly every word of the dialogue came of
itself. Sometimes an idea comes at night, when I have had to get up and
strike a light to note it down—sometimes when out on a lonely winter
walk, when I have had to stop, and with half-frozen fingers jot down a
few words which should keep the new-born idea from perishing—but
whenever or however it comes,* it comes of itself. *I cannot set invention
going like a clock, by any voluntary winding up; nor do I believe that any
original writing (and what other writing is worth preserving?) was ever
so produced. . . .*

And, in reference to *The Hunting of the Snark*, though the answer is equally applicable to *Alice* (by which I designate the two books, *Alice's Adventures in Wonderland* and *Through the Looking-Glass and What Alice Found There*), Dodgson wrote in the same article,

Periodically I have received courteous letters from strangers begging to know whether [it] is an allegory, or contains some hidden moral, or is a political satire; and for all such quesions I have but one answer, "I don't know!" . . .

Furthermore, he wrote in a letter towards the end of his life, also about the *Snark*:

I'm very much afraid I didn't mean anything but nonsense! Still, you know, words mean more than we mean to express when we use them; so a whole book ought to mean a great deal more than the writer meant.

But consciously—and for several skins at least of that fascinating onion, the Subconscious—Dodgson told stories to children, following whatever development came into his logical mind, whatever new twist was given by some sudden question or misunderstanding from his audience, or whatever path a conscious or unconscious literary, dramatic, or visual recollection might lead him to transmuted by the act of creation.

"One thing that made his stories particularly charming to a child," wrote Gertrude Chataway, to whom *The Hunting of the Snark* (1876) was dedicated, "was that he often took his cue from her remarks—a question would set him off on quite a new trail of ideas, so that one felt one had somehow helped to make the story, and it seemed a personal possession. It was the most lovely nonsense conceivable, and I naturally revelled in it. His vivid imagination would fly from one subject to another, and was never tied down in any way by the probabilities of life."

Those who have told impromptu stories to children know how easy and natural it is to weave such fantasies as Dodgson wove, and by what means they are born and grow and suffer sudden and unexpected changes and developments; only our stories are but clay models, and into his the genius of "Lewis Carroll" breathed the breath of life.

Also we, like all subsequent writers, are under his influence. Lewis Carroll has so permeated our thoughts—subconsciously and unknowingly far more than consciously—that we can seldom do more than imitate. *Alice* is so much a part of the cultural heritage of the Western world that it is hard to realize its uniqueness or to see how startlingly new it was.

About *Alice* Dodgson wrote: "I can guarantee that the books have no religious teaching whatever in them—in fact they do not teach anything at all."

To see how utterly different this was from all that had gone before, one has but to read *The Water Babies* (1863), an absolute orgy of self-conscious didacticism in which the fancy moves awkwardly, even guiltily, and the moral purpose is underlined throughout.

Although Catherine Sinclair in *Holiday House* had raised her voice as early as 1839 against the children's books of the period which, in their eagerness to instruct, had outlawed humor and imagination from the nursery, she had not been able to do much herself. Harry and Laura were more like real children than Maria Edgeworth's Rosamund or Matilda could ever be, and a moment's natural naughtiness was not underlined as the first step to hell, as it would have been by Mr. Barlow in Mrs. Sherwood's sin-obsessed *Fairchild Family*. Uncle David could also tell a "Wonderful Story" in which a fairy-tale giant wandered through mazes of delightful nonsense; but even there a definite moral emerged.

But in the forties and fifties the barriers were being broken down just a little; fairy tales were allowed into the more broadminded nurseries; Thackeray flouted convention with *The Rose and the Ring* (1855), though even he was forced to excuse himself in the unsuitable subtitle "A Fireside Pantomime," and the nursery-rhyme collections had been reinforced by the quiet appearance of Edward Lear's *A Book of Nonsense* in 1846, where the "limericks" (though not then so called) were modeled on the booklets in the same verse-form which he had known as a child about 1822.

Nevertheless, these earlier premonitions of the dawn of levity were always at one remove from the child. Either they were set in a fairy world, a world of the past, or else they were kept at a suitable distance by the footlights of verse—as even W. B. Rands does in *Lilliput Levee*, which appeared a year before *Alice's Adventures in Wonderland*. Rands knew something of the wonderland of a child's imagination, but seems not to have had the courage to take it seriously, so that his moments of freedom become a positive burlesque of wishful thinking.

The revolutionary nature of "Lewis Carroll's" achievement cannot be exaggerated. Alice was a genuine child who, instead of tripping her demure way round the parish with the Mays in *The Daisy Chain* or emulating Mary Charlesworth's *Ministering Children,* danced joyously into

Wonderland, turning all Miss Prickett's teachings topsy-turvy, joking with the Duchess about the necessity for there being a moral in every story, and came home to her Victorian nursery without a spot on her character—or a suspicion of having learned anything more serious than the rules of a Caucus Race or the way to cut Looking-Glass cake.

"The directness of such a work was a revolution in its sphere," wrote Harvey Darton in his *Children's Books in England* in 1932. "It was the coming to the surface, powerfully and permanently, the first unapologetic, undocumented appearance in print, for readers who sorely needed it, of liberty of thought in children's books. Henceforth fear had gone, and with it shy disquiet. There was to be in hours of pleasure no more dread about the moral value, the ponderable, measured quality and extent, of the pleasure itself. It was to be enjoyed and even promoted with neither forethought nor remorse."

Harvey Darton further maintains that while "*The Water Babies* is a very fine period piece, almost, indeed, a museum piece, the *Alices* will never be put in a museum, because they will neither die nor grow out of fashion." During the thirty years since he wrote this, *Alice* has moved up in the literary scale and been accepted officially as a classic for the adult— for without question the reader of mature age gets much out of it that is lost upon the child, or perceived in a different way. It is partly as an excuse for this new attitude that critics have tried so hard to prove that Dodgson meant very much more by his two stories than mere lighthearted amusement for children.

With those who believe that an extremely careful and detailed religious, political, or mathematical allegory is intended, it seems hardly necessary to deal. Except in an odd momentary flash such double meanings are not the work of the subconscious mind—and Dodgson's conscious intentions seem hardly open to doubt. The subconscious as explored by the psychoanalysts such as Professor Empson or Dr. Greenacre may yield a few clues as to Dodgson's character and suggest a few possible twists or preoccupations which could have produced certain incidents in *Alice*; but they *were* subconscious and have no direct bearing on the stories. If, however, the adult reader sees them as composed of Freudian symbols, there may be some reluctance in giving them to a child to read; the modern preoccupation with the new and only half-understood science of psychology sometimes tends to see *Alice* as full of horrors, from

Alice's fear of going out like a candle to the Queen's decapitation complex.

It seems unlikely that more than one child in a million will see anything but amusement in *Alice*—and it is impossible to predict the odd child, who might equally have been frightened by the most unexpected thing elsewhere. Tenniel's drawing of Alice with the long neck has been found frightening, and Dodgson himself hesitated over the possible terrors of the Jabberwock. But it might be the White King's threat to Haigha: "If you do that again, I'll have you buttered"—which to one child was the funniest line in either book, just as (to take an actual case) a mother discussing what books frightened children confessed that *Peter Pan* was the terror of her childhood—not because of any of the doings of Captain Hook, but because Mr. Darling lived for a while in the dog kennel!

Setting aside this possibility, it seems only fair to point out that decapitation, change of size, the Dormouse in the teapot, or the Red Knight falling into his own helmet are quite unreal to children and a part of their natural imagination, which can invent for itself and acclaim as riotously funny "horrific" ideas which far outdo the experiences of Red Riding Hood's grandmother or the Myth of Cronos.

That a number of modern children find little enjoyment in *Alice* is not a sign of a more fastidious and humanitarian mind, but of lesser powers of imagination. The modern accent is once again upon the inculcation of facts, as it was in the days before Catherine Sinclair registered the first effective protest against "the reading which might be a relaxation from study becoming a study in itself." The willing suspension of disbelief becomes harder to achieve, and the attempt to do so has become far less common or necessary since there are so many more books—and other occupations—from which today's children may choose.

Alice, moreover, was at its most popular among children when reading aloud was still customary. The ideal age is from four till eight, and often by the time it can be read easily the perfect moment is passed, for—to generalize—the only decade in life during which *Alice* does not appeal is from eight to eighteen. Sophistication has lowered the age limit, which would probably have been at twelve in Dodgson's day; the appeal to the "eighteen-plus" group is by no means new—*Alice* was the rage among undergraduates by the mid-seventies, and the language of "Jabberwocky" became current in public schools at much the same time.

A census carried out by the *Academy* (July 2, 1898) found *Alice* at the top of the list of the ten children's books most in demand, the other nine being, in descending order, *Robinson Crusoe*, Lang's *Fairy Books*, Hans Andersen, *The Water Babies*, Mrs. Molesworth's stories, *Eric, or Little by Little*, *The Jungle Books*, Grimm, and *Treasure Island*. Doubtless fond uncles may have raised the percentage for Farrar and Kingsley, but the list squares well with other contemporary evidence.

The immediate literary effect of *Alice's Adventures in Wonderland* was to let loose the imprisoned waters of levity—which became a positive flood when *Through the Looking-Glass* appeared at the end of 1871.

"*Alice* is always being imitated," complained Andrew Lang in 1895, and Harvey Darton, as late as 1932, noted that "The fault of the many imitators of Lewis Carroll—who are to this day a permanent plague to all editors and publishers of literature for children—is that they force the transition from one nature to the other; they invent, but they have not the logic."

It was Dodgson's logic which gave the particular turn to his humor and supplied him with the tools wherewith to construct his masterpiece; it was his training in formal logic, as Peter Alexander, himself a professional logician, points out, which enabled him to build "a setting within which inconsistency would appear inevitable, and so convincing; or, more precisely, showed him how to *use* a common fairy-tale setting to contain more than any normal fairy tale ever contained." The purely logical sequence of reasoning from an illogical premise—usually a phrase in popular use but used loosely—is well exemplified by the conversation between Alice and the Cheshire Cat on "getting somewhere," or by the discussion with the White King on the hay diet:

> "*There's nothing like eating hay when you are faint*," he remarked to her as he munched away.
> "*I should think throwing cold water over you would be better*," Alice suggested—"*or some sal-volatile.*"
> "*I didn't say there was nothing better*," the King replied, "*I said there was nothing like it.*"

Professor Alexander further points out how wrong Alexander Woollcott was in talking of a discrepancy between "the man who wrote the most enchanting nonsense in the English language," and the "puttering, fussy, fastidious, didactic old bachelor," and comments:

For the will to escape was joined with the ability to escape; an ability which depended on a detailed knowledge of, and interest in, logic. Without Dodgson the pedantic logician, Carroll the artist would have been of considerably less importance; there was no discrepancy.

Dodgson was a consistent figure throughout his life; his habits and idiosyncrasies were all there before *Through the Looking-Glass* was published, they merely grew more pronounced and less accommodating in his later years.

The basis for the methodical exactness of detail which his contemporaries at Christ Church found so irritating was his scrupulous sense of duty: "Oh that I might hear 'Well done, good and faithful servant,'" was an early prayer committed to his diary, but it was a prayer which grew more and more urgent as the allotted span of his earthly life drew towards its end. From this sprang his hypersensitive care over the preparation of his books; his care to give the best he could gave the finish and precision of *Alice*, but also the direct preaching which mars *Sylvie and Bruno* from the literary point of view. This care was known only to himself, but his scrupulous endeavor to give the most perfect result possible on the mechanical side is shown by his withdrawal of the first edition of *Alice's Adventures in Wonderland* because the printing was not up to the highest standard, by his attempt to recall the sixtieth thousand of *Through the Looking-Glass* for the same reason, and by his refusal to publish the first printing of *The Nursery Alice* because the colors were too gaudy. Fearing that copies of a book might be printed too hurriedly in order to meet a sudden demand, he wrote to his publishers,

As to how many copies we can sell I care absolutely nothing; the one only thing I do care for is, that all copies that are sold shall be artistically first-rate.

This thoroughly praiseworthy attitude only became excessive when Dodgson began trying to make everyone else as scrupulously honest as himself, running the Senior Common Room at Christ Church, of which he was curator for almost ten years, on these lines, and writing notes to the postmaster about the dishonesty of having the mail collected a few minutes earlier than the time advertised on the letter boxes, and to the chaplain for reciting the Creed too fast.

His life was ordered with great strictness and method. Early rising, scripture reading before attendance at Chapel (Oxford Cathedral, in the case of Christ Church), lunch of a few biscuits and a glass of sherry so as not to interrupt his work; long walks several times a week for the good of his health; dinner in Hall, but only a short time in the Senior Common Room thereafter; a postprandial snooze firmly negatived, and work again until late at night. Then, when increasing insomnia left the mind apt to wander over trivial or harmful matters, the rigid discipline of Pillow Problems—mathematical and geometrical puzzles that could be worked out on the blackboard of the mind.

The scrupulous care for every detail made letter-writing a major occupation, and Dodgson kept a register from 1861 until a few days before his death which ran to over 98,000 entries with notes and cross-references as described in his pamphlet "Eight or Nine Wise Words About Letter-Writing" (1890).

When going away, he worked out exactly what he would need (just as, before beginning a letter, he chose exactly the right-sized sheet of paper to fill completely), wrapped each article carefully in paper before packing any of them, and sent his luggage in advance (nearly as many trunks as the Baker, one might think!), carrying a small black bag himself. He was also careful to take, in a specially made purse, all the exact sums of money he would need on the journey, each in a separate division ready for use.

In the black bag would be a number of toys and puzzles to produce if he were lucky enough to share a compartment with children, and many child-friendships began in this way. Many more began at the seaside, Dodgson spending a couple of months at Eastbourne each summer after his father's death in 1868, after which his sisters set up house together at The Chestnuts, Guildford, where also he was a frequent visitor.

Little girls met on the shore would be told stories or presented with safety pins before paddling, but there was always the scrupulous application to the parent or guardians before the friendship was well under way. Later in life Dodgson had child visitors—often of the stage-children whom he met after *Alice* was dramatized in 1886—who would stay under the care of his landlady at Eastbourne, or with friends at Oxford.

Dodgson's sentimental relationship with his numerous child-friends has been the subject of some curiosity, not always of a charitable nature. It must be stressed again that the glorious escape from the stammer while in their society was a very strong incentive for Dodgson to seek these friendships; he was simply and honestly happy in the company of children, more so with girls—though earlier in his life there were many small boys among his friends, such as Greville MacDonald, Hallam Tennyson, and Harry Liddell—who were more interested in his tales and puzzles, more orderly and less rampageous, and far better subjects for photography. Dodgson was an artist who never learned to draw, though some charming sketches of children on the beach survive; he had the artist's genuine delight in beauty of form, and without it would not have been the finest photographer of children in the nineteenth century. After having exhausted the possibilities of grouping and costume, it is natural that he should have turned to nude models—always after careful consultation with the parents, and with scrupulous consideration for the child. In 1880, however, some ill-natured gossip must have got about, and Dodgson may suddenly have felt that his interest in nude photography contained the hidden seeds of sin. With his scrupulous honesty and devout sense of duty, he at once gave up photography altogether. But some years later he occasionally drew from the model in the studio of his friend Mrs. Shute, widow of a Christ Church don, and he wrote to Harry Furniss, who was illustrating *Sylvie and Bruno*:

> *I wish I could dispense with all costume, naked children are so pure and lovely, but "Mrs. Grundy" would be furious, it would never do. . . . You must remember that the work has to be seen, not only by children, but by their* Mothers; *and some* Mothers *are* awfully *particular. . . .*

The last photographs were taken in July, 1880, a few months after another source of suspicion to "awfully particular" mothers. Dodgson kissed one of his Oxford child-friends whom he thought was well under fourteen, only to discover that she was, in fact, seventeen; he was much upset and consulted his friend Canon Kitchin, who suggested interviewing the girl's father, another don, after which that storm in a teacup blew over.

The kissing of children in that sentimental age was much practiced, and has not gone out completely even now. On the whole, boys were apt to object early to wholesale and promiscuous osculations, while girls accepted them as natural, up to the dividing line, "where the stream and river meet," which was set at fourteen. Dodgson was merely being an adult of his period in bestowing frequent kisses on his child-friends— and he could make capital game of excessive kissing, as is shown in a delightful letter to the child-actress Isa Bowman, who had begged for "Millions of hugs and kisses."

Millions must mean 2 millions at least . . . and I don't think you'll manage it more than 20 times a minute—[a sum follows]. I couldn't go on hugging and kissing more than 12 hours a day; and I wouldn't like to spend Sundays that way. So you see it would take 23 weeks of hard work. Really, my dear child, I cannot spare the time.

It has been suggested that Dodgson fell in love with Alice Liddell, possibly even while she was a child, and was "sent about his business" by Mrs. Liddell, whose ambition to marry all her daughters into the titled aristocracy was a standing joke at Christ Church. This is a wildly unlikely suggestion; the Christ Church undergraduates thought that Dodgson had proposed for Lorina and been rejected—but they had also thought that his interest in the children was a "cover" for a flirtation with Miss Prickett, the governess. Dodgson was unusual to the extent that a grown man's interest in children had to be explained by the average undergraduate in some such way.

Mrs. Liddell may well have felt jealous of Dodgson's influence over her children; he considered her quite right in forbidding Lorina to visit him unchaperoned after the age of thirteen. But she disliked Dodgson for other reasons. One of her protégés was a titled undergraduate, Lord Newry; she wished the rules to be stretched a point to allow him to give a dance, but Dodgson the scrupulous would not allow a golden tassel to sway his fairness of judgment, and he vetoed this when it was brought up at the college meeting. "I have been out of her good graces ever since Lord Newry's business," wrote Dodgson in his diary on October 28, 1862, and Mrs. Liddell's coldness, though lifted a little, closed down even more firmly as time went on. For Dodgson found himself compelled to attack Dean Liddell's administration of college affairs more and more, beginning with an acrimonious correspondence in January, 1864, over the appointment of Junior Students, and going on to the public ridicule of the architectural alterations at Christ Church satirized in *The New Belfry* (1872), *The Vision of the Three T's* (1873), and other of the *Notes by an Oxford Chiel*. Finally, his letters to the *Pall Mall Gazette* in November, 1874, which prevented Liddell's extravagant scheme for building cloisters round Tom Quad, completed the rift.

But long before this Alice had become only a memory; "Alice seems changed a good deal, and hardly for the better—probably going through the usual awkward stage of transition," he noted on May 11, 1865, when she was just thirteen, and this seems to have been almost their last meeting. Even by then the dream-flowers of Wonderland were "Pluck'd in a far-off land"—and Alice soon became a dreamchild herself to whom Dodgson looked back with special gratitude for "the happy summer days" and for the spark which she had struck from his genius which had resulted in *Wonderland* and *Through the Looking-Glass.*

Doubtless a natural pang of jealousy came Dodgson's way now and then as one or another of his favorite child-friends took to herself a husband. Isa Bowman, one of the half-dozen or so who came nearest to usurping Alice's place, remembered how furious he was when she came to announce her engagement, and how he tried to cover it up by snatching the posy from her belt and flinging it out of the window, exclaiming, "You know how I hate flowers!"

But this was the pang of a moment, and he could write wisely and charmingly to an ex-child-friend on her marriage and continue the friendship to her children. During the last ten years of his life he found older girls more congenial, and made several friends from the High School, and also from the newly founded women's colleges. Several of his own nieces were educated in Oxford, and they found him as charming and attentive an uncle as any of his child-friends could have done.

Lewis Carroll

by T. B. Strong

(1898)

IT IS NOT EASY to write of Lewis Carroll adequately. It is natural to expect that so exceptional a mind should have been developed in exceptional surroundings by means of exceptional experiences, and therefore any account of his life that is truthful must be, in some measure, disappointing: for he spent his time within the walls of Christ Church, and the life of an Oxford don is for the most part uneventful; at least, it is not rich in incidents that are likely to attract the general reader. Mr. Dodgson was the product of the old order of things in Oxford. He belonged to the time when places on academic foundations were held, under certain conditions, for life, and when the work required of those who held them was not precisely defined by statute, but was left largely to the discretion of the individual. Mr. Dodgson came up to Christ Church from Rugby in 1850, as a Commoner, according to the old practice, and was made student in 1852 on the nomination of Dr. Pusey. According to the constitution of the House then prevailing, the dean and canons nominated by turns; and the person so nominated held his position for life, provided he remained unmarried and proceeded to Holy Orders. It was to a position of this sort that Mr. Dodgson was nominated. This was shortly before the era of great university changes. It was Mr. Dodgson's fate to live under a series of successive enactments which modified in many ways the old conditions; still, though the nature of his tenure was in some measure affected by them, he remained till his death on the Foundation of Christ Church to which he had been originally nominated by Dr. Pusey.

He was not bound, as we have already said, to any special course of academic study or teaching, but he held from 1855 to 1881 the position of mathematical lecturer. This office was in no way an arduous one, and he had plenty of time left to him in which to pursue his own studies. He was a laborious worker, always disliking to break off from the pursuit of any subject which interested him; apt to forget his meals and toil on for the best part of the night, rather than stop short of the object which he had in view. A person who works in this way is usually dependent on his moods; and if the mood for work rarely visits him, he gets very little done. Mr. Dodgson's paroxysms, though frequent, were, fortunately for him, intermittent. No man could have held out for very long under such a *régime* as his when the fever of work came upon him. But though this passion for violent labor was irregular, he never seemed idle; his mind was original and perpetually busy; and the general average of his working time was high.

In 1860, Mr. Dodgson took Holy Orders as a deacon; he was never ordained to the priesthood. It is difficult to speak of a side of his character in regard to which he was very reserved, but no one who knew him at all intimately could doubt that the old friend who has sketched his character in the *Oxford Magazine* is right in finding the keynote of his life here. His ministry was seriously hindered by native shyness, and by an impediment in speech which greatly added to his nervousness. And the fact that he was never ordained priest restricted still further the already narrowly limited opportunities of an academic cleric. It prevented, for instance, his being invited to preach before the University in regular course. But though his voice was rarely heard, there was no question as to the deeply religious bent of his life; there is nothing more curious to his friends than to see his name connected in some of the papers with stories turning on the light use of Biblical language. He held this and all such things in severe abhorrence, and he acted out his principles in his life.

A man who separates himself from what is called University business, who pursues a recondite subject at hours that differ widely from those of the majority, can be indeed solitary in Oxford. To a large extent, especially in his later years, Mr. Dodgson did live as a recluse. There must be many people in Oxford who did not know him by sight, and still more who never spoke to him. To all these it must have been a marvel that such books as the *Lewis Carroll Series* and the works on mathematics should have come from one retiring academic don. But those who knew him ceased to find it puzzling. There was always the same mind displayed in his talk. When he was playful or inclined to be paradoxical he could be as irresistibly funny as any of the characters in his books. The things he said in conversation do not lend themselves to description. He talked readily and naturally in connection with what was going on around him; and his power lay, as so often in the books, in suddenly revealing a new meaning in some ordinary expression, or in developing unexpected consequences from a very ordinary idea. Jokes like these require a long explanation of the circumstances to make them intelligible. They are not like the carefully elaborated impromptu which is easily handed about, being specially prepared for exportation. In the same way, Mr. Dodgson was always ready to talk upon serious subjects; and then, though he restrained his sense of humor completely, he still presented you with unexpected and frequently perplexing points of view. If he argued, he was somewhat rigid and precise, carefully examining the terms used, relentless in pointing out the logical results of any position assumed by his opponent, and quick to devise a puzzling case when he wanted to bring objections against a rule of principle. But his skill lay rather in tracing consequences than in criticizing fundamental assumptions; and he was apt at times to exaggerate the value of side issues.

When all this has been said of Mr. Dodgson, and when we have noted his unfailing courtesy to those with whom he was brought in contact, we have given some account of the impression made by him upon his colleagues. The circumstances of Oxford life lend themselves to reserve, as we have already said; and the man who chooses to pursue a student's life chooses a very uneventful one. The appearance and disappearance of the undergraduates mark the chief difference in the year—the difference between Term and Vacation. To those who are tutors or lecturers, Term brings an access of educational work; to those who are not, but who, like Mr. Dodgson in his later years, pursue their studies in their own way, the presence or absence of the undergraduates is a mere detail. When they are in residence, dinner is in Hall, and a gown is necessary; when they are away, dinner is in Common Room, and gowns are not worn. And dinner is the time when the student emerges into society. An equable life in Oxford, varied by these differences, interrupted by an occasional visit to London to take some child-friend to the theater, or by the summer visit to Eastbourne, and the visit to his home at Christmas, was Mr. Dodgson's habit for many years. Such a course of living does not suggest much to the biographer, but it may be very happy, though it is uneventful, and it gives opportunities for great friendships. Oxford life is greatly the poorer by Mr. Dodgson's death.

It is impossible to deal with the life of a student without considering the value of his written work. In so doing, the present writer is limited by his lack of mathematics to the works published under the name of Lewis Carroll. There seems to be a general agreement that in the most successful of these, Mr. Dodgson rose to the point of genius. In all such matters it must be difficult to lay down the principles which explain the success. There is no question about the fact. Children are delighted with the books, and still more, perhaps, people who have passed the age of childhood. To have secured the ear of both these classes is success beyond, perhaps, what the author originally expected. If we must say what seems to us a conspicuous feature about the works, it is this: the most successful passages in the *Alice* books, the passages which recur most often to the memory, are the dialogues. And the secret of their attractiveness is, in large measure, the sudden and unexpected direction given in them to ordinary thoughts and phrases. Ordinary conversation is built up very largely of phrases which are used conventionally. Their exact meaning is hardly thought of, and they are used without question. Their ordinary use is often not the only possible one, but they are so familiar that it is only the ordinary usage that occurs to the mind. Mr. Dodgson has shown the existence of all sorts of pitfalls and surprises round the ordinary course of conversation. If he had done it badly, if he had exaggerated and lost proportion, his work would have been set aside as foolish. But he has so woven his eccentric interpretations into the atmosphere of a dream, and so fitted them into the circumstances of his narrative, that they not only produce their effect when they are read, but remain in the mind afterwards.

"I'm sure I'll take you with pleasure!" the Queen said. "Twopence a week, and jam every other day."

Alice couldn't help laughing, as she said, "I don't want you to hire me —and I don't care for jam."

"It's very good jam," said the Queen.

"Well, I don't want any to-day, at any rate."

"You couldn't have it if you did want it," the Queen said. "The rule is, jam to-morrow and jam yesterday—but never jam to-day."

"It must come sometimes to 'jam to-day,'" Alice objected.

"No, it can't" said the Queen. "It's jam every other day, to-day isn't any other day, you know."

"Take some more tea," the March Hare said to Alice, very earnestly.

"I've had nothing yet," Alice replied in an offended tone, "so I can't take more."

"You mean you can't take less," said the Hatter; "it's very easy to take more than nothing."

A great part of the dialogue flows on in a similar style to this, and the result is that it combines the appearance of familiarity with continual surprise. *The Hunting of the Snark* especially seems to us to depend for its effect upon the combination of familiar language with unexpected meanings. The story goes on and seems comprehensible, though it really leads nowhere. It is very amusing in such passages to watch the gigantic struggles of the intrepid man who translated *Alice in Wonderland* into German. He succeeds well on the whole with the songs, even with such a song as that belonging to the Lobster Quadrille; but one cannot help wondering at times what the Germans make of the dialogue; its shifts and turns come off stiffly in that tongue. *Through the Looking-Glass* has, so far as we are aware, foiled the efforts of the translator. The present writer has seen a German version of the song "Jabberwocky" by the late Dean Scott, of Rochester, but the number of new words in the second of the *Alice* books makes it practically impossible in any other language than its own. In connection with these, it is due to Lewis Carroll to remark that the word *chortle* has found a place in the new English Dictionary edited by Dr. Murray. Its rapid adoption into so scientific a work seems to show that it supplied a felt want in the language.

The verisimilitude which the dialogue lends to the whole story makes the more definitely imaginative parts of the books tolerable. The whole is worked into a complete unity, and the reader lives in the scenes described. It is on the side of mere innovation that Lewis Carroll passes into perilous regions. This comes out very clearly in *Sylvie and Bruno*. Here the author has become somewhat self-conscious; he describes his methods of work in his preface, and sets his readers problems in the criticism of the text. The whole is much less compressed than the earlier works; he trusts less to sudden surprises in familiar regions of thought and more to pure imagination. The rapid passage from the dream-world to that of ordinary life destroys the unity of the story, and, if the truth must be told, the tendency to exhortation spoils its spontaneity. The earlier books derived their charm from their complete artistic unity. The reader is carried along without any disturbance of his point of view from beginning to end, and charmed all the way. But *Sylvie and Bruno*, though there are many passages in it which only Lewis Carroll could have written, is incoherent as a whole, and never seems, like the others, inevitable.

There is another section of Mr. Dodgson's work of which comparatively little is known outside of Oxford. We have said that the author lived a recluse life and took little part in University business, but he occasionally broke silence, when a subject that interested him was under discussion, by writing a squib. There are six of these small pamphlets in existence, now very rare. They were published at various times singly, and were collected under the general title of *Notes by an Oxford Chiel*. Two of them are concerned with the alterations made in Christ Church, when the Cathedral and Great Quadrangle were restored. Two are concerned with financial discussions connected with the Museum. These, though they contain many delightful passages, are obscure to the general public. The other two represent Mr. Dodgson's contribution to two questions which agitated the world in London and elsewhere, as well as in Oxford. One of these—called "The Evaluation of Π"—deals with the controversy over the salary of the late Professor Jowett; and the other—called "The Dynamics of a Parti-cle"—gives an account of the famous election campaign, at the end of which Mr. Gladstone ceased to represent the University in Parliament. (These were first printed in 1865.) The style of humor which prevails in these is of a distinctly academic type, and the events satirized in them do not survive, in all their detail, in the memory of the present generation. Hence the time has almost come when a new edition, if such were made, would have to contain notes and an introduction. But they are among the best of Mr. Dodgson's productions. The method of the "Dynamics" consists as before in unexpected turns and surprises, only the language employed is not that of ordinary conversation, but the definitions of Euclid and other such things, in some cases slightly parodied. The following definitions[1] will illustrate the character of the work:

I. Plain superficiality is the character of a speech, in which any two points being taken, the speaker is found to lie wholly with regard to those two points.

III. When a Proctor, meeting another Proctor, makes the votes on one side equal to those on the other, the feeling entertained by each side is called Right Anger.

IV. When two parties, coming together, feel a Right Anger, each is said to be complementary to the other (though, strictly speaking, this is very seldom the case).

V. Obtuse Anger is that which is greater than Right Anger.

This last definition, and some other passages from these papers, are occasionally quoted still; but for the most part Mr. Dodgson's comments have shared the oblivion into which the controversies which evoked them have fallen.

It remains to say a few words about the logical works which have appeared under the name of Lewis Carroll. It is perhaps a matter for surprise that these were not, like the mathematical books, published under Mr. Dodgson's real name. Why they were classed with the *Lewis Carroll Series* the present writer does not know; it certainly did not mean that the author treated them lightly; he meant them very seriously indeed. He was firmly convinced that the ordinary logical methods were inadequate to the performance of much work fairly to be expected of the mind; and he was confident that his own principles, besides affording an agreeable exercise for the intellect, were of great scientific value. It is difficult to share this conviction. It is true that the diagrams and mathematical formulae are often extraordinarily ingenious, but the assumption which was at the bottom of the whole speculation will not bear investigation. In the *Logic* Mr. Dodgson carried to the most violent excess his habit of developing unexpected results and unnoticed inferences. He tried to give words a sharply defined meaning, as if they were mathematical symbols, and strove to systematize the various inferences which could be drawn from them. A word to him not only had its direct positive meaning, but also conveyed negative information in various directions. And all this had to be drawn out and taken into account in his system. Besides this principle of analysis, Mr. Dodgson was ruled by a great belief in formulae in which letters (as in algebra) took the place of words. This confidence naturally led him to think of sentences as mere forms, of which the concrete meaning was insignificant. Thus, if any one were to attempt to solve the complicated problems which are set at the end of *Symbolic Logic*, he would find that the actual propositions occurring in them are quite irrelevant. Any propositions would do as well, whether they had a rational meaning or not, provided they contained the requisite number of symbols, or of words treated as symbols.

In this part of his work (and we believe in his mathematical books also) Mr. Dodgson's great originality of mind was his chief danger. He read comparatively little of the works of other logicians or of mathematicians who had dealt with the same subjects as himself. He preferred to evolve the whole out of his own mind without being influenced by others. There was gain in this, but there was also loss. If he saved himself from being misled by others, he also deprived himself of the value of their work, which would both have saved him trouble and warned him of mistakes. He dealt with these scientific matters as he had dealt with the ordinary language of conversation, in his own way and from his own point of view. The one process produced *Alice*, the other the *Symbolic Logic*. And if the latter is a failure as a Logic, it is surely because a gift like his of eccentric originality lends itself but poorly to rigid analysis and systematic exposition.

It is impossible to do justice in a sketch like this to any mind of impressive originality, and the peculiar circumstances of Mr. Dodgson's life, together with the very unusual character of his genius, do not make the task easier. Those who knew him and mourn his loss are able to read between the lines in his books, and see there the working of the mind they knew; for, as we have said, the cast of his thought was very much the same in everything that he approached; the humor of *Alice* and the other books was one manifestation of an original and perhaps somewhat eccentric genius. And those who know him only through his books have a real knowledge of him; they are not looking at a mere fanciful product of his leisure, though they learn from others how natural it seemed that a clever, simple-hearted, and religious man should express himself in books for children of all ages.

Lewis Carroll

by *Virginia Woolf*

(1939)

THE COMPLETE WORKS of Lewis Carroll have been issued by the Nonesuch Press in a stout volume of 1293 pages. So there is no excuse—Lewis Carroll ought once and for all to be complete. We ought to be able to grasp him whole and entire. But we fail—once more we fail. We think we have caught Lewis Carroll; we look again and see an Oxford clergyman. We think we have caught the Reverend C. L. Dodgson—we look again and see a fairy elf. The book breaks in two in our hands. In order to cement it, we turn to the *Life*.[1]

But the Reverend C. L. Dodgson had no life. He passed through the world so lightly that he left no print. He melted so passively into Oxford that he is invisible. He accepted every convention; he was prudish, pernickety, pious, and jocose. If Oxford dons in the nineteenth century had an essence, he was that essence. He was so good that his sisters worshiped him; so pure that his nephew has nothing to say about him. It is just possible, he hints, that "a shadow of disappointment lay over Lewis Carroll's life." Mr. Dodgson at once denies the shadow. "My life," he says, "is free from all trial and trouble." But this untinted jelly contained within it a perfectly hard crystal. It contained childhood. And this is very strange, for childhood normally fades slowly. Wisps of childhood persist when the boy or girl is a grown man or woman. Childhood returns sometimes by day, more often by night. But it was not so with Lewis Carroll. For some reason, we know not what, his childhood was sharply severed. It lodged in him whole and entire. He could not disperse it. And therefore as he grew older this impediment in the center of his being, this hard block of pure childhood, starved the mature man of nourishment. He slipped through the grown-up world like a shadow, solidifying only on the beach at Eastbourne, with little girls whose frocks he pinned up with safety pins. But since childhood remained in him entire, he could do what no one else has ever been able to do—he could return to that world; he could re-create it, so that we too become children again.

In order to make us into children, he first makes us asleep. "Down, down, down, would the fall *never* come to an end?" Down, down, down we fall into that terrifying, wildly inconsequent, yet perfectly logical world where time races, then stands still; where space stretches, then contracts. It is the world of sleep; it is also the world of dreams. Without any conscious effort dreams come; the white rabbit, the walrus, and the carpenter, one after another, turning and changing one into the other, they come skipping and leaping across the mind. It is for this reason that the two *Alices* are not books for children; they are the only books in which we become children. President Wilson, Queen Victoria, the *Times* leader writer, the late Lord Salisbury—it does not matter how old, how important, or how insignificant you are, you become a child again. To become a child is to be very literal; to find everything so strange that nothing is surprising; to be heartless, to be ruthless, yet to be so passionate that a snub or a shadow drapes the world in gloom. It is so to be Alice in Wonderland.

It is also to be Alice through the Looking-Glass. It is to see the world upside down. Many great satirists and moralists have shown us the world upside down, and have made us see it, as grown-up people see it, savagely. Only Lewis Carroll has shown us the world upside down as a child sees it, and has made us laugh as children laugh, irresponsibly. Down the groves of pure nonsense we whirl laughing, laughing—

> *They sought it with thimbles, they sought it with care;*
> *They pursued it with forks and hope . . .*

And then we wake. None of the transitions in *Alice in Wonderland* is quite so queer. For we wake to find—is it the Reverend C. L. Dodgson? Is it Lewis Carroll? Or is it both combined? This conglomerate object intends to produce an extra-Bowdlerized edition of Shakespeare for the use of British maidens; implores them to think of death when they go to the play; and always, always to realize that the "true object of life is the development of *character*. . . ." Is there, then, even in 1293 pages, any such thing as "completeness"?

Lewis Carroll's

Gay Tapestry

by Alexander Woollcott

(1939)

ON THE FOURTH OF JULY, 1862, the Reverend Charles Lutwidge Dodgson, a young Oxford don who was then, and for nearly half a century remained, Mathematical Lecturer of Christ Church, took the day off and went a-rowing with the small daughters of the Dean. That eventful picnic was duly noted in his neat and interminable diary that night. The entry runs thus:

I made an expedition up the river to Godstow with the three Liddells; we had tea on the bank there and did not reach Christ Church until half-past eight.

But at that time he did not deem one subsequently enhanced detail of the day sufficiently important to be worth chronicling. He said nothing of the fairy tale he began to spin "all in the golden afternoon" there in the shadow of the hayrick to which the four Argonauts retreated from the heat of the sun. It was a tale about just such a little girl as the gravely attentive Alice Liddell who used to prod him when he ventured to let lapse for a time this story of another Alice falling down a rabbit-hole into the world of the unexpected. In response to such proddings, he carried the story along on that and other afternoons and finally committed it to manuscript as *Alice's Adventures under Ground*. Somewhat expanded, this was published three years later under the *nom de guerre* of Lewis Carroll and under the title of *Alice's Adventures in Wonderland*.

In the sixty years that have passed since then, this gay, roving dream-story and its sequel have seeped into the folklore of the world. It has become as deeply rooted a part of that folklore as the legend of Cinderella or any other tale first told back in the unfathomable past. Not Tiny Tim, nor Falstaff, nor Rip Van Winkle, nor any other character wrought in the English tongue seems now a more permanent part of that tongue's heritage than do the high-handed Humpty Dumpty, the wistful Mad Hatter, the somewhat arbitrary Queen of Hearts, the evasive Cheshire Cat, and the gently pathetic White Knight.

The tale has been read aloud in all the nurseries from Oxford town to the ends of the Empire. And there is no telling how many copies of it have been printed and sold. For when it was new, there was no binding law of international copyright and it was as much the prey of all the freebooters in America as was a somewhat kindred work of genius that came out of England a few years later—the nonsensical and lovely thing called *Pinafore*.

And the *Alice* books have known no frontier. If you poke about in the bookstalls on the Continent, you will stumble inevitably on *Alice's Abenteuer in Wunderland*. Or *Le Aventure d'Alice nel Paese Meraviglie* (with illustrations, of course, by Giovanni Tenniel). You might even run into *La aventuroj de Alicio en Mirlando* which, if you must know, is life down a rabbit-hole as told in Esperanto. And you are certain to come upon *Les Aventures d'Alice au Pays de Merveilles* with one of the puns of the incorrigible Mock Turtle (Fausse-Tortue) rendered thus unrecognizable:

"La maitresse était une vieille tortue; nous l'appelions chélonée."

"Et pourquoi l'appeliez-vous chélonée, si ce n'était pas son nom?"

"Parcequ' on ne pouvait s'empêcher de s'écrier en la voyant: Quel long nez!" dit la Fausse-Tortue d'un ton fâché; "vous-êtes vraiment bien bornée!"

Then the *Alice* books have been employed as scenarios for controversy. A long bibliography of such satires as *Alice in Kulturland* or *Malice in Blunderland* would indicate as much. The tale of Alice's adventure down the rabbit-hole and through the looking-glass is still a very source book for withering anecdotes in the House of Commons or malignant cartoons in *Punch*; and even so sedate an orator as Woodrow Wilson, in speaking once of the ceaseless vigilance and aspiration required of a progressive, compared himself to the Red Queen, who, you will remember, had to run as fast as her legs would carry her if she wanted so much as to stay in the same place.

Plays have been wrought from the stuff of the Alice story. Some of these in London have been ambitious harlequinades. Irene Vanbrugh, for instance, could tell you how Lewis Carroll once watched her play the Knave of Hearts. More often, they have been sleazy, amateurish ventures, an outlet for the exhibitionism of grownups, who would then have the effrontery to say they were doing it to please the kiddies.

Even the symphony orchestras know Alice; for the chatter of the flowers in the looking-glass garden, the thunder of "Jabberwocky," the hum of the looking-glass insects, and the wistfulness of the White Knight have all been caught up in the lovely music of Deems Taylor. The artists have discovered it; and the book has even undergone the sometimes painful experience of being illustrated by Peter Newell.

Indeed, everything has befallen *Alice,* except the last thing—psychoanalysis. At least the new psychologists have not explored this dreambook nor pawed over the gentle, shrinking celibate who wrote it. They have not subjected to their disconcerting scrutiny the extraordinary contrast between the cautious, prissy pace of the man and the mad, gay gait of the tale he told. They have not embarrassingly compared the Reverend Charles L. Dodgson with the immortal Lewis Carroll, two persons whom he himself never liked to see together.

One discrepancy between them has always been a subject of amused reflection—a discrepancy not unfamiliar to a generation which knows that one of its own most hilarious clowns is (in what is sometimes confusedly called real life) the professor of political economy at McGill University.

It was the dual nature which, when Lewis Carroll was asked to contribute
to a philosophical symposium, compelled the Mathematical Lecturer of
Christ Church to reply coldly:

> *And what mean all these mysteries to me*
> *Whose life is full of indices and surds?*
> $$x^2 + 7x = 53$$
> $$= \frac{11}{3}$$

It was the discrepancy which once proved so embarrassing to him in
his relations with his Queen. Victoria had been so good as to be delighted
with Mr. Dodgson's photographs, for you may be sure that the then
Prince of Wales, when he visited Oxford, did not get away without some
samples of Mr. Dodgson's adroitness with a camera. Victoria even went
so far as to say that Albert would have appreciated them highly. Then,
when *Alice* was published and won her heart, she graciously suggested
that Mr. Dodgson dedicate his next book to her. Unfortunately for Her
Majesty, his next book was a mathematical opus entitled *An Elementary
Treatise on Determinants.*

But the discrepancy which would more deeply interest those given to
a new research into old lives lies in the fact that the man who wrote the
most enchanting nonsense in the English language—a just description,
surely, of the *Alice* books and *The Hunting of the Snark*—was a puttering, fussy, fastidious, didactic bachelor who was almost painfully humorless in his relations with the grown-up world around him. You can see
that much unconsciously revealed in the fatuous biography written a few
months after Lewis Carroll's death in 1898 by his oblivious and too
respectful nephew, who was awed by what he called the "purity and
refinement" of his uncle's mind. That the shadow of a disappointment fell
athwart the uncle's life, his nephew did detect; but he was the kind of
biographer who would go on to say: "Those who loved him would not
wish to lift the veil from these dead sanctities."

You must picture Lewis Carroll as living precisely in his quarters in
the Tom Quad at Christ Church, all his life neatly pigeonholed, all the
letters he wrote or received in thirty-seven years elaborately summarized
and catalogued, so that by the time he died there were more than 98,000
cross-references in the files of his correspondence. He was the kind of
man who kept a diagram showing where you sat when you dined with
him and what you ate, lest he serve you the same dish when you came

again. He was the kind of man who, when an issue of *Jabberwocky,* the
school paper of a Boston seminary, published a coarse anecdote from
Washington's Diary, wrote to Boston a solemn rebuke of such indelicacy.
He was the kind of man who gravely stipulated that no illustrations for
a book of his be drawn on Sunday and who could indite the following
reproach to a friend of his:

*After changing my mind several times, I have at last decided to ven-
ture to ask a favour of you, and to trust that you will not misinterpret my
motives in doing so.*

*The favour I would ask is, that you will not tell me any more stories,
such as you did on Friday, of remarks which children are said to have
made on very sacred subjects—remarks which most people would recognize as irreverent, if made by grown-up people, but which are assumed
to be innocent when made by children who are unconscious of any irreverence, the strange conclusion being drawn that they are therefore innocent when repeated by a grown-up person.*

*The misinterpretation I would guard against is your supposing that
I regard such repetition as always wrong in any grown-up person. Let me
assure you that I do not so regard it. I am always willing to believe that
those who repeat such stories differ wholly from myself in their views of
what is, and what is not, fitting treatment of sacred things, and I fully
recognize that what would certainly be wrong in me, is not necessarily
so in them.*

*So I simply ask it as a personal favour to myself. The hearing of that
anecdote gave me so much pain, and spoiled so much the pleasure of my
tiny dinner-party, that I feel sure you will kindly spare me such in future.*

Above all, he was the kind of man who, in publishing his *Pillow
Problems* (part of his series of *Curiosa Mathematica*), recommended
these exercises in mental arithmetic not only as an agreeable diversion
for a sleepless couch but, more especially, as a way of driving out the
skeptical thoughts, the blasphemous thoughts, and "the unholy thoughts,
which torture with their hateful presence the fancy that would fain be
pure."

And yet in all the anthology of the gentlest art compiled by Mr. Lucas,
there are no letters more charming or more frivolous than those which
Lewis Carroll wrote to any one of the little girls in whose presence only
he was a truly free spirit and at whose courts he was happy to play jester
all his days in the land. Calverley, Ruskin, Millais, Tennyson, the Rossettis, Ellen Terry, these pass by in the long procession of his friends; but
the greater part of his thought and his genius and his devotion was given

to the children who one by one succeeded Alice Liddell in the garden of
his friendship. He met them in railway carriages (for he always carried
a few puzzles in his pocket against such chance encounters) and he
scraped acquaintance with them on the beach, being well supplied always
with safety pins in case they wanted to go in wading. His letters to them
would run like this:

November 30, 1879

*I have been awfully busy, and I've had to write heaps of letters—
wheelbarrows full, almost. And it tires me so that generally I go to bed
again the next minute after I get up: and sometimes I go to bed again
a minute before I get up! Did you ever hear of any one being so tired as
that?* . . .

Or like this:

December 26, 1886

My dear E——,—*Though rushing, rapid rivers roar between us (if you
refer to the map of England, I think you'll find that to be correct), we
still remember each other, and feel a sort of shivery affection for each
other.* . . .

Or like this:

December 27, 1873

My dear Gaynor,—*My name is spelt with a "G," that is to say
"Dodgson." Any one who spells it the same as that wretch (I mean of
course the Chairman of Committees in the House of Commons) offends
me* deeply, *and for ever! It is a thing I can forget, but never can forgive!
If you do it again, I shall call you "'aynor." Could you live happy with
such a name?*

*As to dancing, my dear, I never dance, unless I am allowed to do it
in my own peculiar way. There is no use trying to describe it: it has to be
seen to be believed. The last house I tried it in, the floor broke through.
But then it was a poor sort of floor—the beams were only six inches thick,
hardly worth calling beams at all; stone arches are much more sensible,
when any dancing, of my peculiar kind, is to be done. Did you ever see
the Rhinoceros and the Hippopotamus, at the Zoölogical Gardens, trying
to dance a minuet together? It is a touching sight.*

*Give any message from me to Amy that you think will be most likely
to surprise her, and, believe me,*

Your affectionate friend,

Lewis Carroll

Lewis Carroll's case was stated in his own words in one comment on
Alice. He wrote:

The why of this book cannot, and need not, be put into words. Those for whom a child's mind is a sealed book, and who see no divinity in a child's smile would read such words in vain; while for any one who has ever loved one true child, no words are needed. For he will have known the awe that falls on one in the presence of a spirit fresh from God's hands, on whom no shadow of sin, and but the outermost fringe of the shadow of sorrow, has yet fallen; he will have felt the bitter contrast between the selfishness that spoils his best deeds and the life that is but an overflowing love. For I think a child's first attitude to the world is a simple love for all living things. And he will have learned that the best work a man can do is when he works for love's sake only, with no thought of fame or gain or earthly reward. No deed of ours, I suppose, on this side of the grave, is really unselfish. Yet if one can put forth all one's powers in a task where nothing of reward is hoped for but a little child's whispered thanks and the airy touch of a little child's pure lips, one seems to come somewhere near to this.

The discrepancy between that solemn dedication and the irresponsible laughter of the book it referred to would, I fear, arouse the most animated curiosity in the clinic of a Dr. Edward Hiram Reede or the library of a Lytton Strachey. They can be pardoned an acute interest in the inner springs of any fellow man who has fallen into thinking of all life as a process of contamination and who, as Newman said of young Hurrell Froude at Oxford, has "a high, severe idea of the intrinsic excellence of virginity." But those of us whose own memories of childhood are inextricably interwoven with all the gay tapestry of *Alice in Wonderland* would rather leave unexplored the shy, retreating man who left so much bubbling laughter in his legacy to the world.

On the

ALICE

Books

by *Walter de la Mare*

(1932)

... BOTH STORIES have a structural framework—in the one playing cards, in the other a game of chess, the moves in which Dodgson only to some extent attempted to justify. These no doubt suggested a few of his chief characters, or rather their social status; but what other tale-teller could have made Carroll's use of them? All that he owed to the device of the looking-glass, except that it is one which has perplexed and delighted child, philosopher, and savage alike, is that the handwriting in the story is the wrong way round, and that when Alice wished to go forwards she had to walk backwards—a method of progression that is sometimes of

service even in life itself. Both stories, too—and this is a more question-
able contrivance, particularly as it introduces a rather sententious elder
sister—turn out to be dreams; and one little girl I know of burst out crying when the final awakening came.

All this, however, affects the imaginative reality—the supreme illusion
—of the *Alices* no more than its intricate chronology and knowledge of
the law affect that of *Wuthering Heights*, and these have been proved
to be unassailable. In reading the Carroll stories, that is, we scarcely
notice, however consistent and admirable it may be, their ingenious
design. And that is true also of *As You Like It.* Quite apart from any
such design, at any rate, they would still remain in essence perhaps the
most *original* books in the world. Indeed, the genius in Carroll seems to
have worked more subtly than the mind which it was possessed by
realized. It is a habit genius has.

Then again, the Queen of Hearts, he said himself, was intended to be
"a blind and aimless Fury," the Red Queen was to reveal "the concentrated essence of all governesses," the Mad Hatter was once a don, the
White Queen strongly reminded him of Mrs. Wragge in Wilkie Collins'
No Name, and the White Knight was intended to characterize the speaker
in Wordsworth's "Resolution and Independence." But if he had been
merely as successful as *that,* where would these immortals be now? The
reason is in service to the imagination, not vice versa. "Please never *praise*
me at all," Dodgson entreated a child who had written to him about the
Alices. "I just feel myself a trustee, that is all." So might Nature herself
reply if one commended her for the inexhaustible versatility of design
revealed in her hippopotamus, her camel, her angelfishes, and her flea!

So too with the *Snark.* "I am very much afraid," wrote Dodgson, "I
didn't mean anything but nonsense. . . . But since words mean more than
we mean to express when we use them . . . whatever good meanings are
in the book I am very glad to accept as the meaning of the book"—a
remark which is not only modest and generous but well worth pondering.

The intellectual thread, nonetheless, which runs through the *Alices*
is the reverse of being negligible. It is on this that their translucent beads
of fantasy are strung, and it is the more effective for being so consistent
and artfully concealed. As in the actual writing of poetry the critical
faculties of the poet are in a supreme and constant activity, so with the
Alices. Their "characters," for example, in all their rich diversity, are in
exquisite keeping with one another. It may too have been due not to

design but to happy accident (a remark that applies to Lear's limericks but not to most books aimed at the young, however wide they may fall of the mark) that though both books were written for children, the only child in them, apart from an occasional infant, is Alice herself. The Mad Hatter is perennial forty, the Carpenter is of the age of all carpenters, the Red King is, say, the age Henry VIII was born, while the Queens and the Duchess—well, they know best about that.

Alice herself, of course, with her familiar little toss of the head, with her serene mobile face, courteous, amiable, except when she *must* speak up for herself, easily reconciled, inclined to tears, but tears how swiftly dashed away; with her dignity, her matter-of-factness, her conscientiousness, her courage (even in the most outlandish of circumstances) never to submit or yield; and with one of the most useful of all social resources, the art of changing a conversation—what a tribute she is not only to her author but to Victorian childhood! Capable, modest, demure, sedate, they are words a little out of fashion nowadays; but Alice alone would redeem them all. And even if now and then she is a trifle superior, a trifle *too* demure, must not even the most delicate of simple and arduous little samplers have its wrong side?

She might indeed have been a miniature model of all the Victorian virtues and still have fallen short if it were not for her freedom from silliness and her saving good sense—a good sense that never bespangles itself by becoming merely clever. However tart and touchy, however queer and querulous and quarrelsome her "retinue" in Wonderland and in Looking-Glass Land may be—and she all but always gets the worst of every argument—it is this sagacity of mind and heart that keeps her talk from being merely "childish" and theirs from seeming grown-uppish, and, in one word, prevents the hazardous situation from falling into the non-nonsensical. She wends serenely on like a quiet moon in a checkered sky. Apart, too, from an occasional Carrollian comment, the sole medium of the stories is *her* pellucid consciousness: an ideal preached by Henry James himself, and practiced—in how different a setting—in *What Maisie Knew*.

It is this rational poise in a topsy-turvy world (a world seen upside-down, as M. Cammaerts says, and looking far more healthy and bright) that gives the two tales their exquisite balance. For though laws there certainly are in the realm of Nonsense, they are all of them unwritten laws. Its subjects obey them unaware of any restrictions. Anything may happen there except only what can't happen *there*. Its kings and queens are kings and queens for precisely the same reason that the Mock Turtle is a Mock Turtle, even though once he was a real Turtle—by a divine right, that is, on which there is no need to insist. A man there, whether he be Tweedledum or the Carpenter or the White Knight, apart from his being a gentleman so perfect that you do not notice it, is never "a man for a' that," simply because there isn't any "a' that." And though "morals" pepper their pages—"Everything's got a moral if only you can find it"— the stories themselves have none. "In fact," as Carroll said himself, "they do not teach anything at all."

Instead, they stealthily instill into us a unique state of mind. Their jam—wild strawberry—*is* the powder—virgin gold dust—though we may never be conscious of its cathartic effects. Although, too, Carroll's Nonsense in itself, in Dryden's words, may be such that it "never can be understood," there is no need to understand it. It is self-evident: and indeed may vanish away if we try to do so. Precisely the converse is true of the sober-sided order of nonsense. The longer we ponder on that, the more hollowly the tub resounds, the drabber grows the day. The *Alices* lighten our beings like sunshine, like that divine rainbow in the skies beneath which the living things of the world went out into radiance and freedom from the narrow darkness of the Ark. And any mind in their influence is freed the while from all its cares. Carroll's Wonderland indeed is a (queer little) universe of the mind resembling Einstein's in that it is a finite infinity endlessly explorable though never to be explored. How blue are its heavens, how grass-green its grass—its fauna and flora being more curiously reviving company not only than those of any but the pick of *this* world's but than those of almost any other book I know. And even for variety and precision, from the Mad Hatter down to Bill the Lizard, that company is rivaled only by the novelists who are as generous as they are skilled—an astonishing feat, since Carroll's creations are not only of his own species but of his own genus.

Just, too, as in the talk in the *Alices* we realize the meaning of a remark made by a writer in the old *Spectator*: "Nothing is capable of being well set to music that is not nonsense," contrariwise, to invert a reference to the law in the *Antiquary*, what sounds like flawless sense in them may be flawless *nonsense* for all that. "*Must* a name mean something?" was Alice's first question to Humpty Dumpty. "Of course it must," said Humpty Dumpty with a short laugh. "*My* name means the shape I am. . . . With a name like yours, you might be any shape, almost."

Whose is the nonsense here, Humpty Dumpty's or the London Directory's—where Smith may be grocers, Coopers haberdashers, and Bakers butchers? And what (on earth) would any man look like if he looked like a Wilkinson, a Marjoribanks, or a John James Jones? Charles Dickens alone could say. Then again, Humpty Dumpty's "Let's go back to the last remark but one" (an unfailing resource in any heated argument), his "If I'd meant that, I'd have said it," his *"One* can't, perhaps, but *two* can," and his righteous indignation with a person who doesn't know a cravat from a belt—well, not even a Lord Chief Justice in a black cap could be more incisive and more to the rational point.

What, too, even from a strictly conventional point of view, is unusual, unpractical, amiss in the Duchess's kitchen? She is gracing it with her presence, and these are democratic times; she is nursing her baby, and *noblesse oblige;* and the kitchen is full of smoke, which Victorian kitchens often were. What do we expect in a kitchen? A cook, a fire, a cat, and a cauldron with soup in it. It is precisely what we get—and, to give it flavor, someone has been a little free with the pepper. The cook, it is true, is throwing frying pans and saucepans at her mistress, but nowadays there's many a lady in the land who would forgive the fusillade if only she could secure the cook. As for the Duchess's remarks, they are as appropriate as they are peremptory. And do we not expect the highborn to be a little highhanded? Alice enquires why her cat grins like that.

> "It's a Cheshire cat," she says, "and that's why."
> Alice smiled that she didn't know cats could grin.
> "They all can," said the Duchess, "and most of them do."
> Alice didn't know of any that did.
> "You don't know much," said the Duchess, "and that's a fact."

She goes on to remark that the world would be much improved if everybody in it minded his own business; and the only defect in that little grumble is that it is a counsel of perfection. Surely, too, when cosmological explanations of "how the earth rotates on its axis" are about, one's sole resource is to chop off somebody's head.

As for the lullaby the Duchess sings as she sits—long-coated, broadgrinned infant in lap—in that marvelous headdress, square knees apart, dour and indomitable, it preaches justice in the first stanza and proves her personal practice of it in the last:

Speak roughly to your little boy,
  And beat him when he sneezes:
He only does it to annoy,
  Because he knows it teases.
                    CHORUS
              Wow! wow! wow!

I speak severely to my boy,
  I beat him when he sneezes;
For he can thoroughly enjoy
  The pepper when he pleases!
                    CHORUS
              Wow! wow! wow!

Such discipline—those nursery *wows*—may sound a little harsh in the kindergartens of our own baby-ridden age, but it was on this basis Victorian mothers brought up the pioneers of our Empire!

So far, so practical. But it must not be forgotten that this "large kitchen" into which nine-inch Alice had so unceremoniously intruded belonged to a little house in a wood only about four feet high, nor that the Duchess's grunting infant as soon as it breathes the open air in Alice's arms turns placidly into a small pig. And that, except metaphorically, children don't do. Not in real life, that is. Only in *dreams*.

And it is here that we stumble on *the* sovereign element in the *Alices*. It consists in the presentation of what is often perfectly rational, practical, logical, and, maybe, mathematical; what is terse, abrupt and pointed, in a state and under conditions of life to which we most of us win admittance only when we are blessedly asleep. To every man his own dreams, to every man his own daydreams. And as with sense, nonsense and un-sense; as with me, you and a sort of us-ishness; as with past, future and the all-and-almost-nothing in between; so with Greenwich time, time and *dream*time; with good motives, bad motives and dream-motives; self, better-self and dream-self. Dreaming is another state of being, with laws as stringent *and* as elastic as those of the world of Nonsense. And what dream in literature has more blissfully refreshed a prose-ridden world than the dream which gently welled into Dodgson's mind that summer afternoon, nearly seventy years ago, when, sculls in hand and eyes fixed on little Alice Liddell's round-orbed countenance, the Lewis Carroll in him slipped off into Wonderland?

Who can say what influences one silent consciousness may have upon another? May it not be to some magical suffusion and blending of these two, the mathematician's and the child's, that we owe the *Alices?* Even the technical triumph of the two books consists in having made what is finally declared to be a dream actually and always *seem* to be a dream. Open either of them at random; ask yourself any one of the questions on the page exposed; endeavor to find an answer not merely as apt and pungent as are most answers of the *Alice* order, but one that will at the same time fret by not so much as a hair's breadth the story's dreamlike crystalline tissue; and then turn back to the book for *Carroll's* answer. That alone, though a trivial one, will be proof enough of the quality of his genius.

And what of the visionary light, the color, the scenery; that wonderful seascape, for example, in "The Walrus and the Carpenter," as wide as Milton's in "Il Penseroso"—the quality of its sea, its sands, its space and distances? What of the exquisite transition from one setting on to another in a serene seductive discontinuity in—for but one example—the chapter entitled "Wool and Water"? First the little dark shop and the hunched-up placid old sheep, with her forest of knitting needles, who but an instant before was the White Queen; then the cumbrous gliding boat on that queer glutinous water, among the scented rushes—"dream rushes" that melt away "almost like snow" in Alice's lap; and then, without the faintest jar, back into the little dark shop again—Platonic original of all little dark shops. All this is of the world of dreams and of that world alone. The *Alices* indeed have the timelessness, the placelessness, and an atmosphere resembling in their own odd fashion not only those of the *Songs of Innocence* and Traherne's *Meditations,* but of the medieval descriptions of paradise and many of the gemlike Italian pictures of the fifteenth century. This atmosphere is conveyed, as it could alone be conveyed, in a prose of limpid simplicty, as frictionless as the unfolding of the petals of an evening primrose in the cool of twilight; a prose, too, that could be the work only of a writer who, like John Ruskin, had from his earliest years examined every word he used with a scrupulous attention:

It succeeded beautifully. She had not been walking a minute before she found herself face to face with the Red Queen, and full in sight of the hill she had been so long aiming at.

"Where do you come from?" said the Red Queen. "And where are you going? Look up, speak nicely, and don't twiddle your fingers all the time."

Alice attended to all these directions, and explained, as well as she could, that she had lost her way.

"*I don't know what you mean by* your *way,*" *said the Queen:* "*all the ways about here belong to* me—*but why did you come out here at all?*" *she added in a kinder tone.* "*Curtsey while you're thinking what to say. It saves time.*"

Alice *wondered a little at this, but she was too much in awe of the Queen to disbelieve it.* "*I'll try it when I go home,*" *she thought to herself,* "*the next time I'm a little late for dinner.*"

"*It's time for you to answer now,*" *the Queen said, looking at her watch:* "*open your mouth a little wider when you speak, and always say 'your Majesty.'*"

"*I only wanted to see what the garden was like, your Majesty——*"

"*That's right,*" *said the Queen, patting her on the head, which Alice didn't like at all:* "*though, when you say 'garden,' I've seen gardens, compared with which this would be a wilderness.*"

Alice *didn't dare to argue the point, but went on:* "*—and I thought I'd try and find my way to the top of that hill——*"

"*When you say 'hill,'*" *the Queen interrupted,* "*I could show you hills, in comparison with which you'd call that a valley.*"

"*No, I shouldn't,*" *said Alice, surprised into contradicting her at last:* "*a hill ca'n't be a valley, you know. That would be nonsense——*"

The Red Queen shook her head. "*You may call it 'nonsense' if you like,*" *she said,* "*but I've heard nonsense, compared with which that would be as sensible as a dictionary!*"

Alice *curtseyed again, as she was afraid from the Queen's tone that she was a little offended: and they walked on in silence till they got to the top of the little hill.*

For some minutes Alice stood without speaking, looking out in all directions over the country—and a most curious country it was.

A most curious country it *is*—how silent, how solitary, how remote—and yet one incomparably less so than that is the memory and imagination of this strange meditative queen, all of whose "ways" beyond any manner of question *belong* to *her!* What relation any such region of the world of dreams has to the world of our actual, who can say? Our modern oneiromantics have their science, but the lover of the *Alices* is in no need of it. What relation any such dream-world has to some other state of being seen only in glimpses here and now might be a more valuable but is an even less answerable question. In any case, and even though there are other delights in them which only many years' experience of life can fully reveal, it is the child that is left in us who tastes the sweetest honey and laves its imagination in the clearest waters to be found in the *Alices*.

How the books fare in translation—in Hebrew, in Chinese, in Irish, for example—I am, alas, unable to say. Since, however, their species of nonsense is purely their own, we must not too complacently flatter ourselves that it is also wholly English, quite apart from its being how oddly verdant an oasis amid what we are pleased to contemn as such quantities of Victorian sand. To be too solemn about it, to turn these tiny classics into an intelligence test and their Alice into an examination paper, would, as Mr. Chesterton has warned us, be little short of a miracle of Georgian stupidity. Any such perils defied, may that nonsense in all its varieties continue to blossom like the almond tree: the oaks of the forest will flourish nonetheless bravely in its floral company. Indeed, there are times and crises in affairs not only personal, but public, political, and even international, when the following tribute from M. Cammaerts may first serve for a solace and then for a solemn warning:

"The English," he says, "speak, in an offhand way, of possessing a Sense of Humor or of not possessing it, little realizing that this sense, with the meaning they attach to it, is almost unique in the world, and can be acquired only after years of strenuous and patient effort. For many foreigners, Einstein's theories present fewer difficulties than certain limericks. . . ."

Than certain limericks! We can at need, that is, while still we keep the mint, dole out these precious coppers whensoever the too, too intellectual alien proves intractable, while for our own precious island currency we can treasure the gold of the crystal-watered land of Havilah—Carroll's and the *Alices'*. And if at any time in the solitude of our hearts we ourselves need an unfaltering and unflattering critic, which is not unseldom, there is always the Cheshire Cat.

Escape Through the Looking-Glass

by *Florence Becker Lennon*

(1945)

*Then it really has happened
after all! And now, who am
I? I will remember, if I can!
I'm determined to do it!*

. . . *Looking-Glass* is a masterpiece—only a shade less than *Wonderland* —but it already exudes the ripe flavor of approaching decay and disintegration into the cruel (on paper) and unusual Mr. Dodgson and the sentimental-religious Louisa Caroline, as one of the Oxford parodists signed "The Vulture and the Husbandman."

A certain grimness and harshness of *Through the Looking-Glass* derive from the Red Queen and her consort. The plot is Berkeleyan and horrible—"Who dreamed it?" If Alice dreamed it, then the Red Queen was really one of Dinah's kittens, and the Red King merely a chess piece —but suppose it was the Red King's dream?

The chess game, instead of Reds and Whites, might be divided into Lefts and Rights, with Carroll on the Left side. The Red King, Queen, and Knight are all strong and disagreeable characters; the White royalty, weak and ridiculous, but amiable. Was Archdeacon Dodgson—as the righteous representative of established order—strong, unreasonable perhaps, though hardly disagreeable? The Red Queen's rules of behavior are the rules of a right-handed world interpreted by a left-handed child, who feels he is asked to do everything backwards. Hence the idea of going the other way to reach the top of the hill, and of running hard without getting anywhere. If the dream is the Red King's, the world belongs to father; if it is Alice's dream, little Charles has a place in the world. Every child has such fantasies—the wonder is to have remembered them in the twilight state before sleep, and to have been able to write them down before they faded.

This chess game, so much—perhaps so consciously—like Life (as Carroll would write it), is played on several planes, has several interpretations, and no definitive triumph. Although Carroll claims it is a complete game, Mr. Madan[1] says "it is not up to chess standard, and had no normal checkmate." The White Knight does win permission to escort Alice to the last brook. Does this mean "Carroll's Alice-self finds that the left way is the right way"? Professor Harry Morgan Ayres, who recognizes the White Knight as Carroll's spokesman, finds it significant that he is the only one with the courtesy and wit to help a lost child—"the one 'creature' in all the two books that shows a touch of human affection for the little girl."[2]

Dr. A. L. Taylor, in his ingenious book, *The White Knight*, has a good deal to say about Carrollian games. He thinks of the chess game as seen from the standpoint of the pawn, who does not grasp the whole picture. None of the pieces does; even the Queens, who can see more of the board, don't know:

To understand one's part in a game of chess, one would have to be aware of the room and the unseen intelligence which is combining the pieces.
The moves of the two Queens are inexplicable to Alice because of a limitation in her powers. . . . But if the length of the board is time, the breadth of the board must be time also, a kind of time known only to mathematicians and mystics: the kind of time we call eternity.
When she became a Queen she could see both ways. At the end she comes to the door with the Visitors' Bell on one side and Servants' Bell

on the other—she had gone full circle in time, which, unknown to her, was a little planet like that in *Sylvie and Bruno Concluded,* in which "the vanquished army ran away at full speed, and in a very few minutes found themselves face to face with the victorious army, who were marching home again, and who were so frightened at finding themselves between two armies that they surrendered at once."

The book has one grim defeat in the trappings of victory. Humpty Dumpty demonstrates *Looking-Glass* methods by analyzing "Jabberwocky." The youth slays the Jabberwock—is the author trying to tell himself, by writing the poem backwards, that this is a disastrous victory? What drove Charles back into himself and his childish memories? Was it not his acceptance of ordination without resolving his doubts? For him, taking orders was, implicitly, giving in to his father. No one, reading the elder Dodgson's letter, would say he exercised no tyranny over his son.

The letter shows how stern the Archdeacon was under his gentleness. His grandniece, who recalled little else about him, said that he had "decided ideas" about his children's character development.[3] A mere lifted eyebrow, in a home keyed to sensitive response, is more urgent than infinite beatings in a more happy-go-lucky environment. How could anyone revolt against the Canon, with his charm, his faultless altruism, his perfect fatherhood?

Even less could Charles revolt against his mother, the vague, the gentle, the good, with the soft voice that was never raised. Charles was the eldest son, probably the favorite. He had the energy to attempt revolt, but loyalty blocked him. His loved ones and the whole social system were against him. He has left brave and heartening documents of his struggle against distortion, locked in the velvet-lined iron maiden of his period, and his caricatures of that iron maiden helped later generations to master her. Nobody knows how many middle and late Victorians found life more bearable because of the *Alice* books, or how often Carroll's gallows humor helped other sensitives to bear the cross, or even to wriggle out from under it in a good-natured way. Yet the timeless quality of *Looking-Glass,* as of *Wonderland,* rests not on the neurosis of a man or of an age, but on the genius that illuminates our essential nature.

An admirer gushed, "Mr. Dodgson is broad—as broad as Christ."[4] He shared other characteristics with Christ too; at least the Christ of the nineteenth-century stained-glass attitudes. One interpretation of the Christ story is that he [Dodgson] crucified his infantile jealousy of his father and love of his mother by renunciation (Hamlet, Oedipus). Carrying the renunciation to its logical end, he gave up everything, including life. Whether that was the historic Christ is not the question here. But for millions of persons, for two thousand years, the cross has symbolized this very renunciation of jealousy and power, and the crucifixion of the animal natural man, beginning with his infant desire to supplant his father.

Dr. Greenacre[5] sees the same problem. She says:

> . . . the search is for a love which will avoid or control all aggressiveness and hostility, and with it all sexuality; a love in which natural human instinctual pressures will be converted into duty, obligation, denial, and sanctity, in which conscience will take the place of instinct, and will sacrifice freedom of thought as well as of action.

Charles left his father enthroned. In *Sylvie and Bruno* it was as true king of Elfland. In *Through the Looking-Glass*, the Red King's dream may be considered as requiring abject submission to the father, the potent king who could annihilate the other characters simply by awakening. Charles surrenders everything—except his sense of humor. The unpleasantness of the Red King in no way represents the charming Canon Dodgson, but may show how Charles felt in his early childhood about his father's power. The conflict in his nature comes out all through the chess game, with the characters split into Reds and Whites. The Reds are fierce and irritable, the Whites gentle and sheepish—literally sheepish in the White Queen's metamorphosis. In the attempt to separate out pure forms, the opposites always encroach. An artist who travels too far toward "purity" always produces horrors too, and whoever, dissatisfied with the rainbow scheme of nature, tries to achieve whiteness, is startled to see black shadows at his heels.

The attempt to curb his youthful revolt also did strange things to Charles. The younger generation, knocking at the door, is not usually too disturbed at the older generation's shudders (or bluster). But Charles, who describes the proper feeling for God (perhaps for his earthly father too) as a sort of dread—not fear, but respect and love tempered with reverence—lacked the courage to make the final thrust and dethrone his father. "Jabberwocky" is not so much a parodied epic as an epic in reverse. The hero does slay the monster, but not with the ring of the true victor—and he is welcomed by his parent, instead of by a beautiful maiden. To such a pass is Beowulf-Siegfried fallen. In *The Hunting of the Snark*, the hero is eaten by the monster.

The hero is supposed to attain to the maiden and to the throne of the old king. But the most Charles was able to become, in *Through the Looking-Glass*, was—a queen. He was no more capable of kingship than Edward the Eighth. Despite the reinstatement of Bruno's father as King of Elfland, Bruno will never make a king either.

In a sense, "Jabberwocky" and *The Hunting of the Snark* are the same poem. Carroll says so himself, indirectly—he says *The Hunting of the Snark* is laid on "an island frequented by the Jubjub and Bandersnatch— no doubt the very island where the Jabberwock was slain." His stifled impulses toward self-assertion and toward the normal sex life kept sending him weird messages, of which these two poems are about the clearest. Since "Jabberwocky" was written several years before the book, he had time to perfect the intricately camouflaged sex symbolism—but then he proceeded to give himself away, first in Humpty Dumpty's explanations, and later in the introduction to *Snark*, where he explains "and the bowsprit got mixed with the rudder sometimes." Originally he planned to use the Jabberwock for the frontispiece of *Looking-Glass*, but finally substituted the White Knight, after sending a questionnaire to thirty mothers of little girls.

It has been hinted that his sex symbolism, and therefore presumably his sex life (in the mind—for no one claims he had any other sort), remained on an immature level. But it seems that he made at least one attempt to escape from celibacy into matrimony. If there was such an attempt, it was frustrated, and must have left him permanently discouraged; there is no intimation of a second. That the attempt, or the falling in love, occurred between the telling of the first *Alice* story in 1862 and the printing of the second late in 1871 is suggested by the increased sentimentality and the increased shadow in the latter. His first defeat was his acceptance of ordination; his second, less certainly documented as to names, dates, and reasons, was surely his failure to achieve a satisfactory adult love-relationship. The second defeat shows in a certain asperity of the *Looking-Glass* creatures—those that are not on the "sweet" side.

Several signposts point to disintegration: moments when the author steps out of character and reminds the reader that it is a dream, as in the boat ride, when the rushes fade so quickly, and he announces that, being dream-rushes, they must fade even faster than real ones. In transcribing *Alice's Adventures under Ground* into the published version, he carefully deleted all such passages. In fact, therein lies his invention of a whole new genus of literature, in which "psychological facts" are treated as objective fact—in which coexistence in the mind implies ability to coexist objectively. The dead, the unborn, the nonexistent, talking animals, humans in impossible situations—all are taken for granted, and the dream is not disturbed.

To *Alice* and its calm transference of the preposterous and magical into the everyday, can be traced such books as David Garnett's *Lady into Fox*, Christopher Morley's *Thunder on the Left*, James Hilton's *Lost Horizon*, the works of Robert Nathan, A. A. Milne, and many others. Gertrude Stein and James Joyce were Carrollian adepts. Works of imagination had existed before, but the special technique of the dream was Dodgson's own invention. Swift, for instance, takes pains to explain everything in *Gulliver*. Even *A Midsummer Night's Dream*, which has been called the first nonsense book in English, carefully prepares the groundlings for miracles to come. But the utter simplicity of the opening of *Alice* is disarming, and no explanations are required.

Alice was beginning to get very tired of sitting by her sister on the bank and of having nothing to do: once or twice she had peeped into the book her sister was reading, but it had no pictures or conversations in it, "and what is the use of a book," thought Alice, "without pictures or conversations?"

There, in one paragraph, is the protagonist, her age and temperament, the setting, and the mood. The next paragraph mentions parenthetically that the hot day "made her feel very sleepy and stupid," and introduces the White Rabbit. By paragraph three the Rabbit has taken the watch out of its waistcoat pocket and started down the rabbit-hole, and in paragraph four Alice is down after it. Just in that easy, insinuating way our dreams bring us truths from *l'autre monde*. The method, once learned, became a part of our literary technique, and we forgot where we learned it, just as we forgot that the King's Messenger was the first to say, "As large as life and twice as natural."

Dodgson knew his technique, but he slipped a second time in *Through the Looking-Glass*, where Alice listens to the White Knight's parting song, while the sunset falling on his hair makes a picture that she remembers in afteryears. This is more definite and more sentimental than the few transitions of the sort he permitted himself in *Wonderland*, which remains a flawless work of art because of the balanced tensions between the many threads of his nature. By 1871 the webbing had begun to give and sag a bit.

Through the Looking-Glass, like *Wonderland*, is an infinite onion, with many layers. After all, Carroll was a philosopher, which means he transmuted his experiences into something beyond life. It is not for nothing that Eddington referred five times to *Through the Looking-Glass* in his *Nature of the Physical World*, or that writers on relativity, semantics, and other modern paths up the mountain frequently use Carrollian quotations for signposts. As a mathematician he was a great poet. Under the guise of nonsense he shows the ephemerality and unimportance of our most cherished categories, including time and space, and his social criticism is present by implication. The pacifists of 1914 might have described the soldiers fraternizing in the trenches in terms of the wood where things have no names. The stern categories called them back to the logical-nonsensical business of murdering one another as the fawn that trustfully allowed Alice to put her arms around its neck inside the wood emerged suddenly, exclaiming, "Why—I'm a fawn—and you're a human child!"

Space is annihilated in the garden of live flowers. Alice and the Red Queen were

running hand in hand, and the Queen went so fast that it was all she could do to keep up with her: and still the Queen kept crying "Faster! Faster!" but Alice felt she could not go faster, though she had no breath left to say so.

The most curious part of the thing was, that the trees and other things round them never changed their places at all: however fast they went, they never seemed to pass anything. "I wonder if all the things move along with us?" thought poor puzzled Alice. And the Queen seemed to guess her thought, for she cried "Faster! Don't try to talk!"

The Queen continues to hurry her along.

"Are we nearly there?" Alice managed to pant out at last.

"Nearly there!" the Queen repeated. "Why, we passed it ten minutes ago! Faster!"

When they stop, Alice leans against a tree, which to her surprise is the tree they had stood under before they started running.

"Well, in our *country," said Alice, still panting a little, "you'd generally get to somewhere else—if you ran very fast for a long time as we've been doing."*

"A slow sort of country!" said the Queen. "Now, here, you see, it takes all the running you can do, to keep in the same place. If you want to get somewhere else, you must run twice as fast as that!"

Carroll seems to have been anticipating twentieth-century New York. This is a wholly original sort of thinking, now made familiar by Einstein, but in the nineteenth century just coming slowly to birth, here and there, in the minds of scattered philosophers. Carroll upsets everything, tests everything, and does not hesitate to change the frames of reference.

A later chapter subjects time to the same procedure.

"Living backwards!' Alice repeated in great astonishment. "I never heard of such a thing!"

"—but there's one great advantage in it, that one's memory works both ways." . . .

"What sort of things do you remember best?" Alice ventured to ask.

"Oh, things that happened the week after next," the Queen replied in a careless tone. "For instance, now" she went on, sticking a large piece of plaster on her finger as she spoke, "there's the King's Messenger. He's in prison now, being punished: and the trial doesn't even begin until next Wednesday: and of course the crime comes last of all."

"Suppose he never commits the crime?" said Alice.

"That would be all the better, wouldn't it?" the Queen said, as she bound the plaster round her finger with a bit of ribbon.

Next the Queen shouts that her finger is bleeding. Then her brooch flies open, and finally she pricks herself. She is now perfectly calm, having bound up her finger, bled, and screamed.

Carroll started playing around with time when he wrote his early essay, later given as a lecture, before the Ashmolean Society, "Where Does the Day Begin?" Then, in *Wonderland,* the unfortunate Hatter has insulted Time, so that it is always six o'clock, with no time to wash the tea things. The idea develops in *Sylvie and Bruno,* on the Professor's native planet where everything is different, and whence he brings the Outlandish watch with the reversal peg. Does the extreme regimentation of Charles's own life suggest a repressed desire to be temperamental and unpunctual? He just missed the complete absurdity of Kant, whose neighbors in Königsberg set their watches by his regular afternoon walk; but he succumbed to the tyranny of time in fact, while trying to escape it in theory. A true Carrollian solution.

How often he lets off steam by permitting some horror *almost* to happen, then diverting it to something commonplace! Suggesting that the Red King might have dreamed the whole world, he permits Alice to waken and find the Red Queen reduced to a kitten, implying the same of the King. But the choicest and subtlest shock to be found anywhere, even in Carroll, is Humpty Dumpty's remark to Alice.

> *"Seven years and six months!" Humpty Dumpty repeated thoughtfully.*
> *"An uncomfortable sort of age. Now if you'd asked my advice, I'd have said, 'Leave off at seven'—but it's too late now."*
> *"I never ask advice about growing," Alice said indignantly.*
> *"Too proud?" the other enquired.*
> *Alice felt even more indignant at this suggestion. "I mean," she said, "that one can't help growing older."*
> *"One can't, perhaps," said Humpty Dumpty; "but* two *can. With proper assistance, you might have left off at seven."*
> *"What a beautiful belt you've got on!" Alice suddenly remarked.*

It is so subtly done that many readers fail to realize just what is implied by "proper assistance." Perhaps Greville Macdonald did not think through Carroll's argument that he, Greville, would be better off with a marble head, because then he would not have to have his hair combed. There was the letter, too, that Charles wrote his sister: "If I had shot the Dean I could not have had more said about it!"

Is some childhood reminiscence behind his speaking of seven and a half as an "uncomfortable age"? His own transition from thinking of himself as Bruno to thinking of himself as Alice seems to have occurred between five and seven. As the Gentleman in White Paper said to Alice, "So young a child ought to know where she's going, even if she doesn't know her own name." Charles himself must have been in the wood where things have no name. Or did a Caterpillar or a Wood Pigeon ever ask him who he was?

And who was Alice in the second book? In part, of course, she was still Charles Dodgson. And in part she was a new Alice, Alice Raikes, whose father, a distant connection of the Dodgsons, was Postmaster General, and whom Carroll met quite by chance.

He was visiting an uncle who lived in Onslow Square, South Kensington. One day, strolling in the gardens and watching some children at play, he heard one addressed as "Alice." He introduced himself to her, saying, "So you are another Alice. I am very fond of Alices." Then he asked all the children into his uncle's house, to show them "something rather puzzling." He gave Alice an orange, and asked her which hand she was holding it in.

"My right hand," said Alice.

There was a long mirror across one corner of the room. He said, "Go and look at the little girl in the glass over there and tell me which hand she is holding the orange in."

Alice stood before the glass and slowly said, "She is holding it in her left hand." He asked her how she could explain that. She thought a moment and then said, "Supposing I was on the *other* side of the glass, wouldn't the orange still be in my right hand?"

This was perfect. Dodgson laughed and said, "Well done, little Alice, it's the best answer I've had yet." He told friends that this episode gave him the idea of a "'Looking-Glass Country' where everything would be reversed," and to that extent Alice Raikes entered the *Looking-Glass*. But Alice Liddell was there too. The period between the two Alices may correspond with the period mentioned by Mrs. Skene, when Charles interrupted his visits to the Liddell family, because, she said, of a difference arising from his extreme sensitiveness. The nostalgic poem [in the preface to *Looking-Glass*] seems to date the breach:

> *I have not seen thy sunny face,*
> *Nor heard thy silver laughter:*

it begins. It ends:

> *It shall not touch, with breath of bale,*
> *The pleasance of our fairy-tale.*

Pleasance is an unusual word. It is also Alice Liddell's middle name; further, he closes *Through the Looking-Glass* with an acrostic on her full name.

Other threads bind the two books. The King's Messengers, Hatta and Haigha, are our old friends Hatter and Hare, from the Mad Tea-Party. Tenniel lets us in on the secret, showing Hatta still with his cup of tea and sandwich, and hat that was neither his nor stolen—a high hat such as Dodgson commonly wore. Hatta is just out of jail, where he has been living on oyster shells since the trial. Professor Harry Morgan Ayres presents some ideas about secondary sources for the names Hatta and

Haigha. He also reproduces some drawings from the Junian codex in the Bodleian, to which both Carroll and Tenniel must have had access, giving plausible sources for the "Anglo-Saxon attitudes."

Following Shane Leslie, Taylor[6] thinks the Tweedles are High and Low Church, and their struggle is the Oxford Movement:

> Strife is the pattern throughout; strife in and about the church; the spirit of Guy Fawkes Day is symbolized in the first chapter and the nursery rhymes were chosen to fit into the strife-pattern. . . .
> "Rattle" and "ritual" are almost the same word. . . . But it was Low Church which spoiled High Church's rattle or ritual. . . . The monstrous crow which ended their mock-heroics is the threat of disestablishment, which certainly did cause the English Church to sink its differences.

All these topical interpretations are of interest, and lend depth to the weaving. Perhaps they are all true. But somehow the pearl of every one of Lewis Carroll's books is the poem at its heart.

Carroll's philosophy became steadily more conscious and more concentrated, from *Wonderland* to *Looking-Glass,* from *Looking-Glass* to *Sylvie and Bruno,* with its moralistic detours. But, as his philosophy became more conscious, it also grew more concentrated, drier, and less nutritious. Still in his best vein, but unlike anything in *Wonderland,* is this half-dreamy, half-waking episode from *Looking-Glass:*

> *"Things flow about so here!" she said at last in a plaintive tone, after she had spent a minute or so in vainly pursuing a large bright thing that looked sometimes like a doll and sometimes like a work-box, and was always on the shelf next above the one she was looking at,*

like J. W. Dunne's receding rainbow.[7]

Comparing this with Alice's soliloquy when she was falling down the rabbit-hole reveals a more mature, less naïve mind—but Dodgson's emotions did not mature to correspond; he aged without mellowing. The Tweedle brothers are a special university type—querulous, meticulous, infantile, quarrelsome. Alice asks for guidance out of the wood and is answered with irrelevant and trifling animosities, boasting, cowardice—all the vices of the desk soldier. Oxford was biting into Dodgson's bone and he was biting back.

Both Martin Gardner[8] and Dr. Taylor have modern scientific explanations for Alice's remark to the kitten that Looking-Glass milk might not be good to drink. Gardner refers it to the left-handed stereoisomers, and suggests Looking-Glass milk might be antimatter, and both it and Alice might explode on contact. "For after all, except in size, Alice does not change at all in her strange journey."

Taylor refers to Pasteur's discovery in 1846 of polarized crystal, left-handed and right-handed tartaric and paratartaric acid. "Pasteur also noted the universe was dyssymetric."

Gardner refers Alice's difficulties with the vanishing goods on the shop shelves to the vanishing electron. His *Annotated Alice* is a useful and beautiful book, with only one flaw—he has made it a book for adults because he believes the *Alice* books have lost their audience of children!

Dinah, whose ectoplasm, the Cheshire Cat, escorted Alice through *Wonderland,* is still behind the scenes. She is the mother of the two kittens that metamorphose into the two queens, and at the very end Alice suggests that Dinah was Humpty Dumpty, "however, you'd better not mention it to your friends just yet, for I'm not sure." Humpty Dumpty is a long way from the humorous, graceful, evanescent Cheshire puss. In fact, he is the essence of materialism—his fall shakes the woods from end to end. And contentious—was there ever the like? His explanation of the portmanteau words is too well known to quote, but it is commonplace that they have enriched the language and penetrated the dictionary and the law courts.

Tenniel took the trouble to make the Lion and the Unicorn likenesses of Gladstone and Disraeli, as his cartoons of the two alternating Prime Ministers in *Punch* demonstrate. This lends point to Alice's passage with the King:

> *"Does—the one—that wins—get the crown?" she asked, as well as she could, for the run was putting her quite out of breath.*
> *"Dear me, no!" said the King. "What an idea!"*

So much for politics—and much more in two paragraphs than the many labored pages in *Sylvie and Bruno.*

Carroll covers "civilized warfare" in the tournament between the Red and White Knight:

> *"I wonder, now, what the Rules of Battle are," she said to herself, as she watched the fight, timidly peeping out from her hiding-place. "One Rule seems to be, that if one Knight hits the other, he knocks him off his horse; and if he misses, he tumbles off himself. . . ."*

The White Knight is the gem of *Through the Looking-Glass.* He is the only character in the book with any sweetness of temper; although he falls off his horse and makes the ridiculous upside-down inventions of a left-handed person trying to live right-handed, he shows Alice-Charles the way out of the wood, which none of the others had the sense or the courtesy to do.

Taylor seems to have been the first to notice that

The principle which eluded the White Knight was of course gravity. The word gravity is carefully avoided during the whole of this chapter, but he looked a little grave, and more than once he remarked gravely. The pun has no existence for him or Alice. . . . As a planesman or inhabitant of the surface, "balance" was an idea he had failed to grasp.

His theory is that the Knight is like an animal trying to understand the human world from his flatland basis, who believes he has no chance, as we have no chance, of reasoning about the universe. . . . Dr. Taylor believes the White Knight stands for pure science and the Aged, Aged Man for applied science.

Looking-Glass ends with the coronation and banquet. The awakenings in the dream books grow more nightmarish each time, from the first Alice mildly brushing the leaves off her face, through *Looking-Glass* Alice shaking the Red Queen into a kitten after the dreadful banquet, to a still more dreadful one in *Sylvie and Bruno Concluded*, where everything shakes and changes, ending with Prince Uggug's transmogrification into a porcupine.

The dream did not belong to the Red King, because the Red Queen becomes a kitten; the kindly old bumble-headed Don Quixote, the White Knight, shows Alice out of the wood—she is crowned and becomes a Queen herself. The story has a happy ending, but it is hardly a happy story. The black shadow of Jabberwock hangs over it from the earliest pages: Jabberwock, standing for failure, in the sense of burying and betraying some at least of the ten talents. Escape is no longer so complete or so satisfying as in *Wonderland*, though the moment when Alice steps through the gauzy looking-glass never loses its thrill.

Perhaps it was part of Carroll's plan for his books to end weakly. The alternative is "came the dawn," or the wind-up of *Sylvie and Bruno*. *Through the Looking-Glass* could have finished with the characteristic remark of the White Queen, that Hatta is in jail, being punished; the trial will come next Wednesday, "and of course the crime comes last of all."

"Suppose he never commits the crime?" said Alice.
"That would be all the better, wouldn't it?" the White Queen said.

There sits Hatta, looking for all the world like Charles Dodgson in one of his doleful moments, meditating on the uncommitted crime for which he is incarcerated in Oxford, in his reverend collar and high hat, puzzling over Bruno's problem of spelling LIVE backwards. . . .

II
As
Victorian
and Children's
Literature

From

"Children's Books,"

a review of

ALICE'S
ADVENTURES
IN WONDERLAND

by Anonymous

(1865)

SOMEHOW WE DO NOT feel as if the writers of books for children had made any great advance on the author of *Philip Quarll* or those who provided Mr. Newbery, of St. Paul's Churchyard, with the matter of his "gilt books," how pretty, how strange, and fairylike in their gaudy Dutch paper binding! It may be a superstitition, but *The Perambulations of a Mouse,* thumbed and got by heart by the firelight, in the days when we were tiny, has not been exceeded by any late product of ingenuity addressed to the small people of today.

One notable and delightful exception to our remark, however, is to be found in Herr Andersen's stories. . . . On the quaintness and pathos of the author—only approached or excelled by those of Hawthorne—we need not descant anew. . . .

Alice's Adventures in Wonderland. By Lewis Carroll. With Forty-two Illustrations by John Tenniel (Macmillan & Co.).—This is a dream-story, but who can in cold blood manufacture a dream, with all its loops and ties, and loose threads and entanglements and inconsistencies, and passages which lead to nothing, at the end of which Sleep's diligent pilgrim never arrives? Mr. Carroll has labored hard to heap together strange adventures and heterogeneous combinations, and we acknowledge the hard labor. Mr. Tenniel, again, is square and grim and uncouth in all his illustrations, howbeit clever, even to the verge of grandeur, as is the artist's habit. We fancy that any real child might be more puzzled than enchanted by this stiff, overwrought story.

From

"Literature

for the Little Ones"

by Edward Salmon

(1887)

THE LAST QUARTER of a century has been rich in marvels for the nursery. Whilst a literature has sprung up for the older boys and girls, that for babes, or rather the small boys and girls, has acquired a tone and undergone developments which carry it altogether beyond anything previously written. In 1863, Kingsley published *The Water Babies*, and, a year after, Tom Hood was delighting the world with such works as *The Fairy Realm, The Loves of Tom Tucker and Bo-Peep, Funny Fables for Little Folks,* and *From Nowhere to the North Pole*. With all his rollicking humor, there was in Tom Hood an undercurrent of satire which hardly fitted him to be regarded, even in those books which he penned especially for them, as a successful writer for children. *From Nowhere to the North Pole* is a work apparently designed to expose the petty tyrannies of which the little ones are guilty in such important matters to them as toys and sweetmeats. Hood aimed at making his work readable equally to the parent and child. In this he somewhat missed his mark.

It requires an older intellect than one of eight or ten years to appreciate the fun of the Hall of Idle Inventions, and similar shots at human failings and weaknesses which appear in this book. Among these "idle inventions" is a machine for making poetry. Only those who know that Hood opposed vehemently all his life imperfect meters and bad rhymes will see his point. "Poetry," the machinist says, "is not meant to be understood," and hence such lines as the following, turned out by the "Latest Invention for Writing Poetry by Machinery," accomplish their purpose:

A Song

Merrily roundelay happiness blue,
Sicily popular meet tumtiddy,
Popinjay Calendar fiddle-strings grew,
Capering mulberry feet tumtiddy.

The extraordinary adventures which Frank undergoes, as a consequence of sleeping on a stomach too full of plum cake, are best told by himself when he is accused of fibbing.

"It's not fibs," he says; "I was invited to Fairydom by Prince Silverwings, and I've been in the Insect World and in Teumendtlandt, and in Quadrupedremia, and among the Gingerbreadians, and before the Lord Chief Justice in Air; and I've seen the Learned Frog, and visited the bottom of the sea, and lodged with a hermit crab at number 42, Submarine Villas; and I've been taken prisoner by the Wild Wallpaperites, and then I was carried off to the North Pole by the iron in my blood; and I should have been gobbled up by monsters if Noah had not come in the ark and rescued me."

Tom Hood's works were, and are still, deservedly popular, but they can hardly be called so in the circles for which he intended them.

Between Tom Hood and Mr. Lewis Carroll—to call Mr. D. C. Lutwidge[1] by his famous *nom de plume*—there is more than a suspicion of resemblance in some particulars. *Alice's Adventures in Wonderland* narrowly escapes challenging a comparison with *From Nowhere to the North Pole.* The idea of both is so similar that Mr. Carroll can hardly have been surprised if some people have believed he was inspired by Hood. Both books deal with the contorted events which figure in a child's dream, and both may be almost equally well described by some lines from the introductory verse of *Alice's Adventures in Wonderland* addressed to those who in fancy pursue

> *The dream-child moving through a land*
> *Of wonders wild and new,*
> *In friendly chat with bird or beast,*
> *And half believe it true.*

Though *Alice's Adventures in Wonderland* and *Through the Looking-Glass* are, of course, undeniably clever and possess many charms exclusively their own, there is nothing extraordinarily original about either, and certainly the former cannot fairly be called, as it once was, the most remarkable book for children of recent times. Both these records of Alice's adventures would be but half as attractive as they are without Mr. John Tenniel's illustrations. Of the two books, *Through the Looking-Glass* is the more humorous, chiefly owing to the fact that, after Alice has climbed through the mirror, everything is reversed, and that to reach a point it is apparently necessary to walk away from it. Mr. Carroll is an irrepressible punster. *Through the Looking-Glass* contains a pun which is particularly good. Alice is introduced to a leg of mutton. She immediately asks the Red Queen if she shall cut her a slice. "Certainly not," answers the Red Queen; "it isn't etiquette to cut any one you've been introduced to." In *Alice in Wonderland* the funniest idea is the little heroine's telescopic physique. Mr. Carroll's style is as simple as his ideas are extravagant. This probably accounts for the fascination which these stories of a child "moving under skies never seen by human eyes" have had over the minds of so many thousands of children and parents.

To Mr. George Macdonald belongs the credit due to a really original writer. . . .

ALICE
IN WONDERLAND

in Perspective

by Elsie Leach
(1964)

CONFRONTED WITH *Alice in Wonderland,* the adult reader does not quite know what to think. He senses that it is an original work of the imagination, with meaning for adults as well as for children. He dismisses as a fantastic diversion for children the plot line—what little there seems to be —and the character of Alice, and he appropriates the witty dialogue as though it were intended for him alone. Thus the part which is quite peripheral to the meaning of the book—divorced from character and action— he makes central in his appreciation.

At least this is essentially the approach of the modern critics of *Alice.*

A professional philosopher concentrates on the logical fallacies and prin-ciples illustrated in *Alice* and points to Dodgson's concern with philo-sophical concepts of time, justice, and personal identity. The student of semantics has long enjoyed his own *Alice in Wonderland,* though he finds *Through the Looking-Glass,* especially Humpty Dumpty's remarks, a richer text than the first book. One reader maintains that *Alice* and its companion book are allegories of the intellectual struggles of mid-Victorian Oxford: the Oxford Movement, the *Essays and Review* con-troversy, and the Huxley-Wilberforce debate. They "are books for children in much the same sense as *Gulliver's Travels* is a book for children." Another reader uses *Alice* and Dodgson's other writings to psychoanalyze the author. And although William Empson has read the book more seri-ously and carefully than the others, he too focuses on what the book has in it for him. He insists on the Freudian implications of the work, and in describing it, distorts to prove his point.[1]

What Dodgson was doing in *Alice in Wonderland* can be seen if the reader compares the book to standard fare written earlier for children. Though collections of folk tales, such as the Taylor translation of *House-hold Tales* (1823) and the Dasent translation of *Norwegian Popular Stories* (1859), were available for children, few authors chose to model their stories upon the fairy tale or to incorporate fairy-tale elements into new narratives for children. Hans Christian Andersen's fairy tales were published first in 1835 and translated into English by 1846, but no English writer had yet emulated his practice. Thackeray's *The Rose and the Ring* (1854) is a spoof of the fairy tale from a common-sense, adult position, not an enthusiastic exercise of the liberated imagination. English books written for children were supposed to be realistic in order to provide essential instruction in religion and/or morality, that the child might become a virtuous, reasonable adult. But unlike earlier English writers, Dodgson used a number of characteristics found in fairy tales, and his tentative title, *Alice Among the Elves,* suggests that he recognized the fact himself. As a matter of fact, there *are* no elves in his book, but there are changes in size and transformations (the baby into a pig), haughty royalty (albeit playing cards), an abundance of talking animals, and such details as magic objects and the tiny golden key opening the door into the garden. Perhaps it is not irrelevant that his heroine is the small child turned out into a magical world as in so many folk tales. Of course, *Alice* differs from the folk tale in that the heroine's antagonists are not clearly defined as "black" villains or villainesses, and no magical formula guides her to triumphant vindication. But the similarities to the fairy tale help mark the book as a departure from the norm of contemporary stories written for children.

The choice of fairy-tale elements is just one indication that in writing *Alice* Dodgson rejected the rational approach of earlier writers for children, that is, their insistent appeal to the reason of their readers. Nothing could be more antirational than Dodgson's narrative, for he chose a *dream* situation as central (and this dream is no orderly allegory). Conscious exercise of reason is not apparent in the situations which occur or in Alice's particular attempts to cope with them. The narrative thread itself is seemingly lost in the vagaries of Alice's adventures; they are not dictated by the usual rewards-punishments or challenge-response plot structure. In fact, one of the difficulties of the book for some readers is its lack of conventional orientation. It is doubtless fitting that the scene in court (in both senses of the phrase) should come last, but Alice's "progress" cannot be described in meaningful, social, spatial, temporal, or moral terms.

The character of Alice herself is a bit puzzling, even to the modern child, because it does not fit a stereotype. How much more unusual she must have seemed to Victorian children, used to girl angels fated for an early death (in Dickens, Stowe, and others), or to impossibly virtuous little ladies, or to naughty girls who eventually reform in response to heavy adult pressure. Margery of the famous *Goody Two Shoes* (still popular in Dodgson's time) is a female Horatio Alger, wise and mature in her infancy, a mouthpiece for the author's rational abhorrence of superstitious belief in ghosts and witchcraft, and a successful climber of the social ladder. The heroine of Maria Edgeworth's *Frank and Rosamond*, one of the better books for children in the early nineteenth century, recognizes and shuns her own immature behavior after the kindly probing and reasonable questioning of her parents, much as Emma Woodhouse finally recognizes her folly upon the prompting of Mr. Knightley.[2] But Alice is neither naughty nor overly nice. Her curiosity leads her into the initial adventure and most of the later ones of the book, yet she is not punished for it, nor does she regret what she has done. On the other hand, we are not left with the feeling that Alice's experiences have been especially rewarding either. Alice feels great bewilderment and distress when she shoots up rapidly after sampling the cake labeled "Eat Me" and tries to establish her identity by reviewing, in her words, "all the things I used to know": multiplication tables, geography, the improving verse, "How doth the little busy bee." Nothing comes right. Her earlier experience is no help to her, and her education has not prepared her for *this* experience.

Indeed, one of the most striking features of the book, especially if one reviews what was standard fare for children of the time, is the strong reaction *against* didacticism which so many of the episodes illustrate. Dodgson's parodies of the instructive verse which children were made to memorize and recite ridicule its solemnity and the practice of inflicting it upon the young. Isaac Watts's "How doth the little busy bee" becomes the amiably heartless "How doth the little crocodile," and his highly edifying "The Sluggard" is rendered as a nonsensical narrative about a lobster. Alice's "Father William" is hardly the venerable patriarch of Southey's poem. Some of the characters Alice meets order her to "stand up and repeat" such poems as a test of her memory, and in other ways too they display the usual adult preachy officiousness. The Caterpillar, for example, is very abrupt and irritable with Alice, and orders her to keep her temper. Not five minutes later, the polite Alice inadvertently offends him by expressing dissatisfaction with her present height of three inches. He draws himself up to his full three inches and loses *his* temper. However, a more obvious example of unreasonableness is the Duchess. At her first meeting with Alice, the Duchess has been rude and violent, but perhaps because of her fear of beheading she is wonderfully mellowed when Alice encounters her during the croquet game. In her own kitchen she indulges in baby-beating and brutal candor. "If everybody minded their own business," the Duchess said, in a hoarse growl, "the world would go round a deal faster than it does." Thus she answers Alice's exclamations about the barrage of pots and pans.

At the croquet ground she is all sweetness, though not necessarily a bearer of light. When Alice comments politely, "The game's going on rather better now," the Duchess replies,

"'Tis so, . . . and the moral of that is—'Oh, 'tis love, 'tis love, that makes the world go round!'"
"Somebody said," Alice whispered, "that it's done by everybody minding their own business!"
"Ah well! It means much the same thing, . . . and the moral of that is—'Take care of the sense, and the sounds will take care of themselves.'"
"How fond she is of finding morals in things!" Alice thought to herself.

In this episode, the Duchess's motto is "Everything's got a moral, if only you can find it," and she becomes more and more extravagant and non-sensical in her application of axioms to everything Alice says and does. When Dodgson makes a ridiculous character like the Duchess praise and practice moralizing in this manner, he clearly indicates his attitude toward didactism directed against children. I wonder whether he had consciously in mind the comment in *Little Goody Two Shoes* that Margery had the art of moralizing and drawing instructions from every accident, as when the death of a pet dormouse gave her the opportunity of reading them (the children) a lecture on the uncertainty of life, and the necessity of being always prepared for death.[3]

Not only is the Duchess inconsistent, unpleasant, and pointlessly didactic, but she is of no help to Alice in her predicament. Nor are the other characters Alice meets, with the exception of the amiable Cheshire Cat, the only one to admit he is mad; they snap at her, preach to her, confuse her, or ignore her. They behave to her as adults behave to a child—they are peremptory and patronizing. Only the eccentric Cat accepts her as an equal. In the guise of dream fantasy, *Alice* states the plight of a little girl in an adult world. Throughout the book Dodgson describes sympathetically the child's feelings of frustration at the illogical ways of adults—their ponderous didacticism, and contradictory behavior. They aren't consistent and they aren't fair. And their puzzling use of language is one very important manifestation of their bullying and condescension; it is primarily a mode of self-exposure rather than an exercise in logic and semantics. The underlying message of *Alice,* then, is a rejection of adult authority, a vindication of the rights of the child, even the right of the child to self-assertion. Though the Queen is the most threatening of the figures Alice meets, Alice dares to contradict her at their first meeting and later, at the trial, she alone has the courage to call the Queen's bluff. Contrast with this Margery's easy accommodation to her great difficulties as a child. Margery succeeds by becoming more adult—more sensible and rational—than most of the adults of *Little Goody Two Shoes.* She lectures *them* on their follies and superstitions. The child-adult conflict of *Alice* gives direction to the heroine's adventures and controls all the notable features of the work— the kind of character Alice is, her relationships with the other characters, the texture of the dialogue, and the placement of the incidents. Thus the work can be read as a meaningful whole, and its meaning is not very esoteric after all.

The ALICE Books
and the Metaphors of
Victorian Childhood

by Jan B. Gordon
(1971)

> The child is the interpreter of the People. Rather, he is the
> People with their inborn truth before they become deformed,
> the People without vulgarity, without uncouthness, without
> envy, inspiring neither distrust nor repulsion. Not only does
> the child interpret the People, he also justifies and exonerates
> them in many things. . . . No, childhood is not merely an age
> or a degree in life, it is the People, the innocent People.
> (Michelet, *Le Peuple*, Part II, chapter IV)

ALICE's *Adventures in Wonderland* begins with a gesture of boredom:
little Alice, having lost interest in a story being read her by an older sister,
begins her journey in pursuit of a White Rabbit. But, significantly, adventure is possible only after turning one's back upon civilization and its
joyless values, symbolized here by the volume "without pictures or conversations." Little wonder that Dodgson, whose stuttering inability to
pronounce his own surname gave rise to one of the tale's most memorable
characters, should have taken such care in supervising Tenniel's illustrations and their synchrony with the conversations. Perhaps he was going as

far as humanly possible to prevent the *Alice* books from having the same
effect upon children as the volume from whose sonorous rhythms his
heroine flees on the initial page. And, although his achievement has been
translated into over a hundred languages and dialects, *Alice in Wonderland* and *Through the Looking-Glass* have not been unqualified successes
at preventing all potential Alices from following their own White Rabbits
into their own dream-world.

Of course, the distinction I am attempting to make is obvious enough:
languages and dialects belong to an adult communication circuit, whereas
the realm of childhood has its own internal form of communication, less
dependent upon linguistic translation, Freudian reduction, sophisticated
experiments with chess moves, or subtle parodies upon Victorian political
leaders. Happily, children engage in none of those activities. The *Alice*
books' very appeal to adults, and particularly literary critics, may well
account for the indifference with which so many children greet their pages
until they are well beyond Alice's age. There is a paradox in all this:
notably, that an adult who, because of traditional respect for its legendary
greatness or the desire to inculcate its morality, elects to read *Alice's
Adventures in Wonderland* to a child before bedtime, may well prompt a
sudden flight into dreamland. Lewis Carroll had the reputation, while an
Oxford don at least, of drawing pictures of the few students who turned
up at his lectures, yawning at him—and later, distributing the finished
artifacts to his class.[1] Such is self-consciousness of a high order. My argument in this essay is heavily weighted toward what I think to be a
neglected view of Carroll's achievement: that these two companion
volumes, veritable landmarks of Victorian literary history, are decadent
adult literature[2] rather than children's literature.

The growth of the fairy tale as a distinctive literary genre occurs quite
late historically. And at least one of the best-known pioneers of the form,
Grimm, paralleled his study of the magically real world of the child with
the equally magical world of linguistics, where somewhat similar sensa-
tional events occur: gemination; the instant loss of prefixes and suffixes;
and transformed vowels and consonants. The relationship between the
development of language and the growth of the child has always been
close, particularly in Victorian England where the very concept of development was almost a myth, the kind of myth that often accompanies
pragmatic, progress-oriented temperaments. Darwin's voyage, the *Bildungsroman* tradition that shapes so many Victorian novels (and the use

of fairy tales like "Jack the Giant Killer" and "Cinderella" in Dickens' variants upon that tradition), new scientific notions regarding the conservation of energy (that Freud was later to incorporate into his theory of displacement), and projects like the Oxford English Dictionary all testify to the way in which succession, inheritance, historicism, and development permeated the Victorian mind. If one of the characteristics of the fairy tale is the use of ritual to evoke a magic spell that will expand boundaries to such an extent as to make a myth, the adult parody proceeds in the opposite direction: its "problem" is to use magic to recapture the ritual with all of its spontaneous, preverbal play. In the process, the adult hopes to move from myths of childhood (where children function as metaphors) to participation in the ritual itself. Instead of a magic mirror that opens up upon an enlarged world, the adult sees himself hideously transformed. The innocence of the fairy tale and the horror of the Gothic tale are reverse sides of the same Victorian coin; one involves the success of magic whereas the other, as exhibited in *Frankenstein* and *Dracula*, involves the misappropriation of magic by science and, consequently, the failure to regress, except voyeuristically.

Not the first, but surely a representative use of the child as a metaphor in the early nineteenth century, occurred when Pitt was besieged by a group of industrialists complaining about a temporary tax surcharge used to finance the wars against Napoleon. The additional levy had placed the manufacturers in a squeeze between labor costs and gross profits, and they sought a reduction in the minimum wage for healthy male labor. In declining their request for relief from government wage regulation, Pitt commented, "Take the children!"[3] Even the young, whose age exempted them from conscription, were not to escape the loss induced by battle. It was a cruel way of equating children and adults, and made explicit a tendency already exhibited in late eighteenth-century English genre painters who, following the suggestions inherent in Reynolds' *Discourses*, had often clothed their children in the heavy draperies of the "grand manner"—a garb that makes them indistinguishable from their elders.

It is a reminder that the nineteenth-century concept of childhood is, in certain respects, not dissimilar from that of the child who had the misfortune of being born prior to the Renaissance. It is not that progeny were not appreciated or their needs not ministered to, but that the child was not assigned a special category distinct from adulthood much before the seventeenth century. Philippe Ariès brilliantly demonstrates in his *L'Enfant et la familiale sous l'ancien regime* that, prior to the late Renaissance, children up to the age of seven had little personal identity, a characteristic surely attributable to the high rate of infant mortality.[4] Since families were accustomed to producing many more infants than would normally be expected to survive childhood, the infant could not really be considered as a potential adult until he had survived the dangerous early years. Survival itself became the qualifier for adult life. In Western Europe, the Reformation and the Counter Reformation would seem to have been largely responsible for imposing a separate and special status upon the child, initially by insisting on the innocence of childhood (and thus the necessity for an assumed separation from the adult world). Its status as a sort of emotional and moral limbo exempt from the world of knowledge of sexual good and evil meant that the child's life was given its own norms and functions. Of course, from another perspective, this shift amounts to a fall into self-consciousness, since every child thus comes to participate more directly in the rhythms of an allegory in which he assumes or is given the role of the Innocent. The metaphoric transformation of every child into a potential Christ broadens the base of the faith by bringing the Savior closer to every man; it accomplishes much the same thing as does the vernacular rendering of the liturgy.

If every infant, however, comes to participate symbolically in the life of Christ, then sacrifice is the inevitable outcome. But between the Renaissance and the occasion of that sacrificial act in the nineteenth century, there arose a new moralization of society's treatment of the child, as could be expected from any heightened allegory. And this moralization by which the new status of the child was defined had a number of immediate institutional effects: the growth of a separate toy industry during the early seventeenth century and the discovery of the advantages of separate rooms for children in the houses of the bourgeoisie. Both would suggest a significant shift in the consciousness of the role of the child within a particular culture.

Although advances in hygiene and a somewhat altered role of the child in the drama of man's relationship with his God are partially responsible, the student of the concept of childhood would doubtlessly look beyond the Reformation to the rise of capitalism. The role of the commercial bourgeoisie in the formation of the modern family was essentially spatial, as Michel Foucault has suggested.[5] Before the sixteenth or seventeenth centuries, life was more communal than private, a circumstance that was true not only among the regular population, but among the court aristocracy, who conceived of life as a constant public self-representation. It was the urban middle classes who first promulgated an ideal of the family as a self-contained, autotelic unit, shut away from public view.[6] Private property and the private status of the child *naturally* reinforced each other, to such an extent that the English adopted a mixture of both, the "kinder-garten," to match the luxuriance of those other well-manicured eighteenth-century gardens. It was an apt introduction to the age that, from Locke to Rousseau, was to consider the psychological requirements of the state of childhood as well as the childhood state. The child was given his own *space,* and the first children's literature, as highly didactic and doctrinaire as it was, arose during the beginning of the eighteenth century as the sole mode of entertainment in that "world apart."

Perhaps this bequest to children of themes common to all of society took place in several stages. The demand of the Reformation, that the Church modify the old fund of the "miraculous" that had nourished medieval literature and the liturgy, meant that the extraordinary tales of Morgane the Fairy, Melusine, and Artigall suddenly became vulnerable. The medieval verse chronicle and chivalry cycles merged with the tradition of oral folklore and were preserved by popular storytellers who frequented fairs and marketplaces. This popular reworking of themes common to medieval romance, although essentially rural in its orientation and in the medium of delivery, became the literature of the upper classes, at least until the beginning of the eighteenth century. Ariès has suggested that the young valets, foster brothers, and nurses who were the child's companions in the early years always told the same transposed oral fables to the young nobles and bourgeois, providing a consistent link with a culture that was essentially rural and miraculous long after the child's parents had turned to other literary forms. The upper classes had ceased to be exposed to this mixture of old wives' tales, hagiography, and fairy tales that comprised the first children's literature, largely because of the increasing popularity of the novel. And that which, prior to the novel, had been a literary staple, became a "scrap" for the child—a tale told before bedtime. Perrault's *Contes du temps perdu,* which appeared in 1697, thus creates a literature designed specifically for children. But perhaps the most interesting feature of this evolution is what it tells us about the psychology of childhood: notably, that long before the abandoned child had become a consistent figure in nineteenth-century fiction, the eighteenth-century child was enjoying an abandoned literature.

If one had to choose the image most closely associated with the Victorian novel, the orphan would rank high on any list. Although statistics are by no means conclusive, there would appear to have been no greater percentage of orphans among the middle classes that provided the bulk of the audience for the nineteenth-century novel than at any other time in British history. Although child abuses were rampant during the Victorian period, phenomena corresponding to workhouses and chimney sweepers, and surely as malevolent, could be found during almost any period of history. Obviously the child without parental guidance or support exists partially on a metaphoric level. Surely, to probe the popularity of the emblem is to find out how the concept of the child invaded the consciousness of the Victorian era. Although space does not allow a complete exposition of this occurrence, the orphan clearly came to symbolize all the discontinuities that faced the age. As Walter Houghton has astutely observed in *The Victorian Frame of Mind*, the problem of locating a point of origin was one of the continuing struggles of the years 1832–1901. Once Chambers and Lyell, two geologists, had challenged the theological idea of a Creation in a single instant of time with their Uniformitarian thesis, Victorian England was quite literally cast adrift upon the seas of time. If the earth had been created not at some "still point" two billion years prior to the nineteenth century, as theologians had insisted, but was in fact the result of a continuing process of sedimentation that was still going on, then there was no effective escape from a continuing generation—not even in the illusion of *Genesis*. The impact of the *Voyage of the Beagle* was not entirely dissimilar, since the concept of the fortuitous mutation implied a certain lack of any orderly progression from a Creation in the past. All those species on the Ark were not the boundaries of Divine Will, but rather a broad base from which creations were still taking place—some of which survived to replace their ancestors in the struggle for existence on earth. The menagerie that moves through *Alice's Adventures in Wonderland* clearly exists in a post-Darwinian tent, and new species can be called into existence merely by a mutation in the child's imagination or as a function of her size. They are the products of an anthropomorphic intelligence.

The child adrift in the city, as, for example, Dickens' Little Jo of *Bleak House* or someone perhaps slightly older, as Dorothea Brooke in George Eliot's *Middlemarch,* was a symbol for treating the effects of development and process in Victorian England. Having no surname, such children were the people without a past, not unlike those new species with whose generic Latin names Darwin busied himself. So many of the characters in nineteenth-century British novels are looking for origins, trying to locate a point from which they can date their existence. Casaubon, looking for the key to all mythologies, is perfectly suited to Dorothea Brooke because he is investigating historically what Dorothea Brooke is trying to live and what Tertius Lydgate is attempting to examine scientifically in his study of the origins of cell structure and their breakdown—particularly, to locate a point of human beginnings in an age that came to see all beginnings as merely another fiction in the saga of development. One way of "living" one's disconnectedness is to imagine existence itself as an alienated activity, and the child searching for foster parents is almost an *exemplum* of that psychic state.

Another manifestation of this same tendency is the effort of Victorian novelists to detach fictional activity in time. So often, novels are set prior to the occasion of their actual authorship: *Middlemarch* is removed from 1871–72 to the eve of the First Reform Bill (1832); Hardy's *The Mayor of Casterbridge,* set back to the years immediately following the passage of the First Reform Bill; and Meredith's *Diana of the Crossways,* set back from the1880's to the 1840's, the period marked by a sequence of collapses wrought by speculation in rail shares. To make fiction so obviously historical has also an inverse effect: it makes history, and hence origins, a fiction.

The *Alice* books are no exception. Characteristically Victorian in his blurring of beginnings, Carroll, whose stuffy preference for perfection has made him an object of adoration to bibliophiles for a century, was apparently so unhappy with the first edition that the publication of *Alice's Adventures in Wonderland* was delayed until 1866. The tale itself was initially told at the famous boating party of three little girls and two British dons on July 4, 1862. That "golden afternoon," as described in Carroll's introductory poem, was actually, as we now know thanks to historical research, not so pastoral as its author would have us believe, but "wet and rather cool." But the mind that searches for a point of origins always hypostasizes it as pastoral and the pastoral mode seldom accommodates itself to the vagaries of British weather. The shower that had overtaken the group on an earlier expedition on June 17 obviously inspired the pool of tears. But the date specified in the story itself is precisely fixed at May 4, Alice Liddell's tenth birthday. Since the heroine of *Through the Looking-Glass* is seven and a half just six months later, her adventures should, were we dealing in historical reality rather than fiction, be dated at 1859—the year Darwin shocked Victorian England by making its quest for origins an almost impossible task without the leap of faith. The significance of Alice's pursuit of time into a subterranean world beneath the layering of the earth's surface reverberates through the nineteenth century.

The predominating structure of the nineteenth-century novel, from *Mansfield Park* to *A Portrait of the Artist as a Young Man*, often seems to involve something like the Cinderella myth. Lionel Trilling's "young man from the provinces," whose growth and education is the subject matter of so many Victorian novels, is often a stray waif or wanderer who is rescued by being taken into one of those Victorian houses in the mode of Heathcliff, David Copperfield, or Bella Wilfer in *Our Mutual Friend*. The person who had been the object of the rescue then is miraculously transformed into a saint whose sacrificial gesture rescues others. And, as a reward, he is given rule of the castle or what is left of it after the Tories have been dispossessed. What is less clear is whether or not the transformed questor lives happily ever after. One suspects that such is part of the unfinished nature of every journey in the nineteenth century, and that the inheritor of Victorian spaces may turn out to be just as tyrannical as those who originally rescued him and set him to work. All those novels lent their names by houses—*Wuthering Heights, Waverly, Bleak House, Mansfield Park, Howards End*, to name just a few—have a way of being either domesticated into horrible middle-class apartments or degenerated into the whispering, echoing ghosts born from an incest with the past and manifested as the Gothic. If, indeed, this pattern is an inevitable feature of the novel in the nineteenth century, then the shift from Alice's journey in the *Adventures in Wonderland* to her posture in *Through the Looking-Glass* is more comprehensible: domestication within a veritable mansion of mirrors is the consequence of the search for meaning and identity. And Looking-Glass House is as much a part of the nineteenth century as the mirroring portraits that stare out at Dorian Gray and Stephen Daedalus at the conclusion of their respective labyrinthine journeys.

But to say all this is to say that the concept of the Victorian child marks a substantial shift from the eighteenth-century notion of childhood. That special status which had been afforded the child in *Emile* or Perrault's *Contes* seems to have been denied by the Victorians. As previously noted, so much mid-Victorian genre painting continues the tendency to be seen in the late eighteenth and early nineteenth centuries of clothing children in the garb of their elders. The judicial system, which had formerly placed the juvenile offender within a separate court system, now made the child subject to the workhouse and the prison. There are records of children in their teens being hung for petty crimes in the 1850's. Rather than attempting to protect children with special legislation, as the eighteenth century had done, the Victorian child was actually afforded the protection of minimum-hour and minimum-wage legislation *after* adults had already been awarded the same luxury. And, perhaps most significantly for the *Alice* books, Michel Foucault, in *Madness and Civilization*, argues that the nineteenth-century conception of a person judged insane appropriated the unfortunate individual to the status of childhood. Madness came to be regarded as a corollary of failed development, rather than a condition of animality, as it had been in the eighteenth century.[7] This was yet another way of equating the child and the adult in the period; it meant no special protection, no *in loco parentis*, on the part of institutions. This transformation of the child, from infancy to adolescence, is nowhere better illustrated than in Hardy's *Jude the Obscure*, where a doomed infant is referred to as "Little *Father* [italics mine] Time."

To do away with childhood is, of course, to relieve parents of an important obligation; it makes every child an orphan in role whether he is in fact or not. And it means that every parent participates only vicariously in the upbringing of the child. To make every child a "little adult" has two disturbing effects: first, every adult participates in childhood fantasy freely, since there are no longer any barriers separating subject and object; and second, there is the threat of real damage to the family structure, since every individual's adaptation becomes a function of the conditions of his adoption. The orphaned child is, in effect, an exile not only from beginnings (and hence time, the dimension of *Alice's Adventures*), but family relationships (and hence space, the chess-board logistics of *Through the Looking-Glass*). This may well account for the amazing abundance of children's literature in the nineteenth century, which exceeds the output of any comparable period since the Middle

Ages. What is denied in fact has a way of appearing in our fictional fantasy.

A quick reading of Froebel's *The Education of Human Nature* or Herbart's *Science of Education*, two popular books on the education of the child in Victorian England, reveals a sad burden.[8] The role of the parents is minimized in the growth of the child because he is not seen to have an identity prior to the age of seven, the argument being that before that age, in Froebel's words, "the mind has not triumphed over the needs of the body." Twenty-five years later, Freud was first to suggest that such a triumph takes place only at an enormous cost and may not be one of the benevolent gifts of social evolution, but in fact may be a step backward—repression. One wonders whether Alice's attempt during her *Adventures* to constitute a social family among the animals is not the burden of Victorian exile. She is constantly attempting to discover her destiny by examining the will of each animal she encounters. It is as if to find out what was expected of her were crucial to defining her sense of self:

> "Well! What are you?" said the Pigeon. "I can see you're trying to invent something!"
> "I—I'm a little girl," said Alice, rather doubtfully, as she remembered the number of changes she had gone through, that day.
> "A likely story indeed!" said the Pigeon, in a tone of the deepest contempt.

Alice learns that few animals have wills as demanding and inflexible as those in the upper world of adults. Her identity is absolutely variable and conditioned by perspective rather than by the a priori demands of her governess. The resulting disorientation amounts to a dislocation that, from one point of view, is an individual fall; from another it is the whole world of humans that has fallen. The escape provided by the dream from the book being read her by her sister in Chapter One of the *Adventures* leads to a world that, though dissimilar from the adult world above ground, quickly becomes filled with adult institutions, including obnoxious tea parties and trials. Wonderland is clearly no utopia, as a number of critics have insisted, but rather quickly assumes the same illogic and estrangement as the realm in which most humans exist. Petty jealousies and vindictive outbursts just as surely come to characterize the life of the garden, and there is little that Alice can do to prevent such an evolution. Although the first book has all the trappings of romance, including a quest for identity, a magic garden, magical transformations, and the luxuriance of perpetual springtime and a perpetual beginning, it ends with a trial, and there are no trials in utopias. It is strangely reminiscent of Carroll's experience upon seeing a sign that he thought read "Romancement," only to discover, upon getting closer, that it actually said "Roman cement." So much for what happens to romances!

To escape human willfulness, either deliberately, as in flight from one's past beginnings, or defensively, through the mask of boredom that provides a barrier to further brutalization, is always a worthy goal. But there is some real question about the success of such a venture. Even as Alice falls down the rabbit-hole, she seems to bear the burden of domestication, placing the marmalade jar in its appropriate compartment as if trying to maintain some vestige of order in a locale where disorder seems to be the rule. But the attempted flight from the effects of prior wills and commandments is perhaps, after the orphan, the most popular theme of Victorian verbal and visual art. So many of the orphans are bound by the testaments and codicils of guardians, which dictate the ward's potential marriage partner or the range of his occupation: Jarndyce *vs.* Jarndyce in *Bleak House*; old Featherstone's two wills in *Middlemarch*; the legacy of the title character in Trollope's novel *The Warden*; and Forster's linking of the inheritance of estates with the question of England's future. Clearly the will is, like so much vicarious participation in the nineteenth century, an effort to control destiny from another world beneath the surface. Those illustrations of deathbed scenes that grace the frontispieces of so many chapters in Victorian fiction and history are surely part of a last effort of the mortally ill to reconstruct a fictional family that he has created rather than had thrust upon him. And, similarly, Alice must learn that one escapes from one's familial past only temporarily, that the tedium imposed by the adult world is repeated among the children and their animals voluntarily as a way of establishing identities. Sadly, Alice discovers through the vehicle of the dream that the trial, or the reading of a will, or the determination of a guardian with which so much Victorian experience began, is a constantly repeated feature of human development. Her adventures end in the courtroom where mere whimsy determines guilt *after* sentence—which is to say that she concludes her journey at the same location from which so many nineteenth-century novels commence: a quite fortuitous and fictional judgment day. This might help to explain why Alice, while in Wonderland, is always attempting to discover how to *begin*, while simultaneously worried about how her dream is going to *end*:

> *How she longed to get out of that dark hall, and wander about among those beds of bright flowers and those cool fountains, but she could not even get her head through the doorway; "and even if my head would go through," thought poor Alice, "it would be of very little use without my shoulders. Oh, how I wish I could shut up like a telescope! I think I could, if I only knew how to begin."*

But on the very next page, the opposite concern is voiced:

> *First, however, she waited for a few minutes to see if she was going to shrink any further: she felt a little nervous about this; "for it might end, you know," said Alice to herself, "in my going out altogether, like a candle. I wonder what I should be like then?" And she tried to fancy what the flame of a candle looks like after the candle is blown out, for she could not remember ever having seen such a thing.*

Alice, like so many Victorian children, is initially aware of abandonment, of being trapped somewhere between *beginnings* and *endings* without the necessary map. She is a character in an epic with its defining time of *in medias res*, its catalogue of animals rather than ships, and its generic division into twelve books. And the first thing that Alice does is to cry, and then to talk to herself in soliloquy. It is that act, not the abrupt alterations in shape, which convinces the little girl that this realm is ruled by a double standard. The solitude of alienation induces a sudden transformation during which Alice becomes unsure whether she exists as subject or object:

> *"Come, there's no use in crying like that!" said Alice to herself rather sharply. "I advise you to leave off this minute!" She generally gave herself very good advice (though she seldom followed it), and sometimes she scolded herself so severely as to bring tears into her eyes; and once she remembered trying to box her own ears for having cheated herself in a game of croquet she was playing against herself, for this curious child was very fond of pretending to be two people. "But it's no use now," thought poor Alice, "to pretend to be two people! Why, there is hardly enough of me left to make* one *respectable person!"*

Alice's first response, then, is an act of self-reflectiveness, a recognition that a fall is also a *lapsus* in its ontological sense—a disintegration of the self into complementary components. She discovers that solitude is a short-lived condition, and the defensive posture that the self assumes is itself a mode of self-multiplication. What happens to Alice on the individual level is not substantially different from what takes place when she enters an estranged environment; sacred spaces quickly become filled up with animals and flowers that almost seem to be self-generating. She no sooner arrives in utopias than she humanizes them, and she humanizes them by introjecting her own schizoid-ness. It is a condition where convertibility and reversibility are norms: cats eat bats just as bats eat cats; punishment may precede the crime just as surely as following it; and the underground kingdom may parody the rules that govern conduct above Wonderland.

A large part of the "double-ness" that is a structural motif in *Adventures in Wonderland* and *Through the Looking-Glass* is a reflection of Alice's own condition, the result of a discovery that what she had thought to be a quest is but a metaquest, characterized by infinite regress and double-binds. John Fowles's suggestion in *The French Lieutenant's Woman* that *Dr. Jekyll and Mr. Hyde* is practically a psychological guidebook to Victorian England is surely applicable to Alice's quest. The romantic quest for communion with the alien "other" concludes when the self comes to the realization that the alien is but an extension of *it-self*. Hence, a journey that had previously been exterior is transformed into an interior quest upon the realization that outside and inside are the same— that the self (in this case, Alice) humanizes the other during the course of her adventures so that what had been Wonderland becomes a pretty socialized place after all. Hence two predominant patterns in *Alice* would appear related: the confusion between "self" and "other," and the fact that all of her solitary experiences inevitably end when she finds herself in the company of an extraordinary number of hosts. Everything from the pool of tears to the croquet game must be violated with something resembling overpopulation, the last effect of socialization.

One of the first things Alice learns in Wonderland is that punishment for transgression, a constant fear in the topside existence, is just as much a threat to her in the new environment. But rather than crying at the prospect of receiving physical punishment from those who lay down the law, she comes to understand that one is punished to stop the distress of previous punishment, not for any literal sins. Her own tears have resulted in the deep pool in which she finds herself, and yet she fears the further chastisement of being drowned in her own tears:

"I wish I hadn't cried so much!" said Alice, as she swam about, trying to find her way out. "I shall be punished for it now, I suppose, by being drowned in my own tears!"

Like Dostoevski's Underground Man, Alice discovers that retribution involves a scheme of ever-receding termini. In the spaces of Wonderland, one opens doors with keys only to find other doors. This multiplication is a replica of Victorian discipline couched in terms of a psychological domino theory; Froebel's somewhat bizarre development thesis imagined punishment as having a multiplier effect, so that the more swiftly the child is spanked or otherwise rebuked, the more effective is the punishment, since the guilty one feels doubly guilty about displaying tears and hence revealing how effective the initial retribution has been. Alice's education in the first of the two books is acquired as a direct consequence of guilt. Only when she offends one of the animals in this Victorian menagerie by a seemingly innocent expression of preferences, as when she mentions the cat to the mouse without the knowledge of the power politics of Underground, does she acquire knowledge. Carroll is actually making an astute observation on Victorian education, notably that the acquisition of knowledge and guilt over assumed transgression often accompany each other in nineteenth-century theories of development.

The real nineteenth-century fairy tale, from which *Adventures* and *Through the Looking-Glass* depart, had a conspicuously moral, if not didactic, purpose.[9] Perhaps the tale that in plot most nearly resembles the *Alice* books is Christina Rossetti's *Speaking Likenesses* (1874). But that story has a remarkably unpleasant tone, designed to illustrate the evils of antisocial behavior. The heroine, a juvenile named Flora, ruins her own birthday party and, skulking away to pout in a yew-lined forest, finds a mysterious door leading to a great mirror-lined hall, where another party is in progress. Instead of ordinary guests, Flora sees the most grotesque children:

One boy bristled with prickly quills like a porcupine, and raised or depressed them at pleasure; but he usually kept them pointed outwards. Another, instead of being rounded like most people, was faceted at very sharp angles. A third caught in everything he came near, for he was hung round with hooks like fishhooks.

Flora is prevented from eating the delicious food by a domineering birthday queen, and victimized by the other guests in a series of cruel games until finally she and they all build glass towers round themselves.

Insults and missiles are hurled, and Flora awakes screaming, to find herself back in the yew alley. Throughout the dream, the moral is brought home with an almost repellent repetition. Since selfishness is the basis of Flora's naughtiness, Christina Rossetti makes each loathsome dream-child exercise its own deformity for self-gratification. There is, for example, a typically Victorian game called Self Help, in which little Flora is ironed and goffered by Angles. Scarcely the equivalent of what Samuel Smiles talked about, this "game" would seem to be an illustration of the vices to which one is exposed in any self-gratifying activity. It is clear that the only way for the child to express her repressed sense of selfhood is by asserting herself, and the mode of assertion is mutual torment. And, like Carroll, Christina Rossetti raises the problem of sequels on the last pages:

And I think if she lives to be nine years old and gives another birthday party, she is likely on that occasion to be even less like the birthday queen of her troubled dream than was the Flora of eight years old; who, with dear friends and playmates, and pretty presents, yet scarcely knew how to bear a few trifling disappointments. . . .

Speaking Likenesses illustrates two of the most characteristic features of nineteenth-century children's literature: the tendency to gloat over the physically grotesque, and a marked insistence upon the efficacy of punishment as *therapy*. If the mentally ill were regarded as children in the nineteenth century, there is also the sad hint that all misbehaving children were ill; Catherine Sinclair, in *Holiday House*, was to state this notion most succinctly: "Punishment is as sure to do us good when we are naughty as physic when we are ill."

Charles Kingsley, in *The Water Babies* (1863), was similarly interested in the educative value of punishment. The book is essentially one of the many accounts of a child learning to be good as he matures. Characteristically following the Cinderella pattern, Tom leaves the dark abode of the chimney sweeper's body and receives his education as a water baby in the sea under the stern rule of a Mrs. Bedonebyasyoudid. She holds weekly sessions chastising wrongdoers, on the principle of an eye for an eye. Since the punishment is a natural consequence of the sin, it always fits the crime. The real purpose of *The Water Babies* is to give an account of the education of the child from the waif to an honest English gentleman. But for Kingsley, systematic schooling was not the answer; it results in the kind of creatures Tom encounters on the Isle of

Tomtoddies who have been turned into garden vegetables, "all heads and no bodies." Since a healthy mind must be balanced by a healthy body during this period of muscular Christianity, corporal punishment was seen to be as valuable as questions and problems. Tom's growth is related in three distinct stages: life in the river, where he is unconfined and allowed to exercise natural curiosity; then the period with the water babies, a time of painful moral training during which selfishness must be purged; and lastly, the journey to seek Mr. Grimes, during which the youth learns active goodness. It is this stage that perfects his character, that makes him fit for grace. In both Christina Rossetti's and Kingsley's stories, the plot line is linear, involving a pilgrimage from naughtiness to goodness, from transgression to redemption. But the final product is always a child that has become an adult, and hence is capable of retrospectively viewing and comprehending the meaning of the allegory.

Alice's Adventures in Wonderland, however, is a far more sophisticated volume that transcends the limitations of so much Victorian children's literature while at the same time posing new problems. Since many of the events are repeated *ad infinitum,* there is some question whether there is one experience rather than a series of hurdles. There would appear to be no progression in successive stages of maturity; even at the outset, Alice seems pretty grown up, taking great care to note location and to tidy up the pantry as she falls into the golden world. Since she continually repeats the same or similar mistakes (usually unwittingly insulting some animal by referring to a predator or a predatory set of values), it could be said that Alice may not mature at all during the course of her explorations. Like most heroines in Victorian children's literature, hers is the problem of identity. Once thrust into a strange kingdom, a relativism of size and language forces her to be literally at sea, even when she has climbed out of the pool of tears. And as previously noted, the problem of identity is inextricably bound up with the difficulty of locating a point of origin. Her comment, "if I only knew how to begin," applies equally to aliens, orphans, people at the beginning of initiation rituals, and, of course, storytellers. The only things we really know for sure about Alice's past are that she has been bored by her sister's incessant reading, and that the reading diet has resembled, not just a little, the type of children's literature written by Rossetti, Kingsley, and Hood; and that her responses are initially colored by her victimization at the hands of their art:

It was all very well to say "Drink me," but the wise little Alice was not going to do that in a hurry. "No, I'll look first," she said, "and see whether it's marked 'poison' or not"; for she had read several nice little stories about children who had got burnt, and eaten up by wild beasts, and other unpleasant things, all because they would not remember the simple rules their friends had taught them. . . .

Rather than typical children's literature, with its pattern of repressive violence, *Alice's Adventures* is a self-conscious response to the absence of self. It takes little psychology to understand the dynamics of introjection, that the child oppressed by such literature quickly identifies with the aggressor in order to avoid further violence. One suspects that this pattern may well be responsible for the disappearance of the concept of childhood during the nineteenth century that has been discussed before in more detail. Unfortunately, it is typically a process by which an excess of brutality is always reinforced when masochism becomes sado-masochism. The only way to escape violence is either to pretend to be bored or to adopt the identity of the "other," both of which have the effect of doing away with one's sense of one's own identity.

This may well account for the merging of two genres in mid-Victorian England: the Gothic horror tale and children's literature. If children become monsters in the manner in which I have suggested, then one mode of brutalization is as effective as the other. The most amazing feature of, say, Dickens' treatment of children, is how quickly they are transformed into monsters. Even Oliver Twist's surname forces the reader to appropriate the twisting condition normally associated with creatures more closely akin to the devil! One effect of this identification with evil adults as an act of protection is that the only way of approaching child-hood is by way of the opposite of satanic monstrosities—namely, the golden world of an edenic wonderland whose pastoral dimension gives it the status of a primal scene. Like the Victorian use of wills and the rapid increase in the production of pornography in mid-Victorian England, however, that golden world is a place of vicarious participation, an acknowledgment that the more real world of childhood has disappeared. Empson's idea in "The Child As Swain," that Alice's experience amounts to a Fall, is an oversimplification; the Fall is an a priori condition of the *Alice* books, not a description of their action.

When Alice discovers that the Mouse has enemies, she asks for an account of his "history," by which she refers to the rodent's autobiography.

What she gets, as promised, is "a long and sad tale" that is printed in the shape of a tail. And, confusing history and story, the Mouse in effect gives us the entire plot of *Adventures in Wonderland*: It begins with a meeting in a house and concludes with litigation in a courtroom. Such is to say that Alice learns little experientially, and comes finally to distrust her senses altogether, since two different sets of standards govern the exterior world in Wonderland and the earth's surface. She does, however, gain knowledge from another kind of adventure, the aesthetic adventure. Her entire world underground comes to exist as a collage of stories: pigeons are saying "a likely *story* indeed"; the Caterpillar replies to Alice's puzzling question by giving her a rhymed account of the life of Father William that is the "story" of his own furry existence, only slightly transposed; and the Footman at the house of the Duchess repeats his remarks "with variations." Yet, when Alice is asked to give an account of her own life during the Mad Tea-Party, she is unable to oblige her curious hosts:

> "*Suppose we change the subject,*" *the March Hare interrupted, yawning.* "*I'm getting tired of this. I vote the young lady tells us a story.*"
> "*I'm afraid I don't know one,*" *said Alice, rather alarmed at the proposal.*
> "*Then the Dormouse shall!*" *they both cried.* "*Wake up, Dormouse!*" *And they pinched it on both sides at once.*

All along, Alice learns that she must acquire an aesthetic sensibility, and somewhat self-consciously recognizes that she must become an artist in order to share her life with animals. Only when she makes public the private soliloquy of the first chapter can she distance herself from the confinement of corrupted utopias. One of the accomplishments of art is the idyllic transformation of the past, whatever one's present perspective may be:

> "*It was much pleasanter at home,*" *thought poor Alice,* "*when one wasn't always growing larger and smaller, and being ordered about by mice and rabbits. I almost wish I hadn't gone down that rabbit-hole— and yet—and yet—it's rather curious, you know, this sort of life! I do wonder what can have happened to me! When I used to read fairy tales, I fancied that kind of thing never happened, and now here I am in the middle of one! There ought to be a book written about me, that there ought! And when I grow up, I'll write one—but I'm grown up now,*" *she added in a sorrowful tone:* "*at least there's no room to grow up any more* here.*"

Alice must become an artist, transforming the outer or "green world" into the enclosed, autotelic pleasure dome of *Through the Looking-Glass.* Haigha and Hatta of *Looking-Glass* are clearly the Hare and the Hatter that had previously resided in Wonderland. The latter story takes place indoors in autumn; its predecessor, characteristically, takes place outdoors in the spring. And Alice is able to dissolve the Looking-Glass for herself and her kitten with the hypnotic formula: "Let's pretend." Never was there such contrived artifice in *Alice.* In the first book, the reader is more interested in Alice's adventures, in what happens to her on a relatively experiential level. On the second trip, we tend to accept her and to look around with her, as if we were in that other transformed nature in Victorian England, the Crystal Palace. The excursion has moved from time to space, from an impressionistic, almost fortuitous cluster of events that seem unique to a more static outlook. In *Through the Looking-Glass* the somewhat arbitrary preferences of the geometrician who laid out the landscape and manipulates the chessmen loom large. As Harry Levin has wisely observed,[10] the events of the second kingdom, like that of most attempts to transform the natural world, are given the dimension of something that has happened before and will happen again and again. Tweedledum and Tweedledee will fight; the Lion and the Unicorn will be ridden out of town; and Humpty Dumpty will continue to re-enact his disappearing *act.* But, most importantly, we are aware that his movements are an "act," a dramatization of what has gone before. The garden in Wonderland is more like that tended by Keats's gardener, Fancy, who, in "Ode to Psyche,"

> . . . e'er could feign,
> Who breeding flowers, will never breed the same.

Alice's Adventures in Wonderland stands to *Through the Looking-Glass* as play stands to artifice. The flowers in *Through the Looking-Glass* appear to be magic plants precisely because that is the only way by which the adult can enter the child's world. The two volumes are by no means the same book, and the fact that so many critics treat them as identities just illustrates one of the things Alice must learn—that primitive experiences do not have sequels except as vicarious modes of participation. At the conclusion of *Adventures in Wonderland*, Alice Liddell's sister, Lorina, also falls asleep—and dreams. And that vision is the vision of her younger sister having become an artist:

Lastly, she pictured to herself how this same little sister of hers would, in the after-time, be herself a grown woman; and how she would keep, through all her riper years, the simple and loving heart of her childhood; and how she would gather about her other little children, and make their *eyes bright and eager with many a strange tale, perhaps even with the dream of Wonderland of long ago. . . .*

This is a child who participates in the dream of her sister having become an artist, and by retelling the tale of Wonderland, democratizes and domesticates the experience of the kingdom. That tale which Alice tells is quite clearly *Through the Looking-Glass*, where, at the trial, the entrapment and attempted confession of growing up become, in the adult space, a chess game. Although there is a connection between the two (both represent the arrested movement symbolized in the word "checkmate"), games are the sequels of experience, an attempt to pattern the random, spontaneous movement of earlier adventures.

Like so many children, then, Alice begins her adventures in response to the brutality of the children's fairy tale only to become herself the teller of the story to the next generation. Like so much of the language in the two books, that motif is itself tautological. But the fairyland has suffered in the transformation, for it now can be approached only as "once upon a time," not, as in *Adventures in Wonderland*, by following the time rabbit! It is a transformation similar to the larger patterns operative in nineteenth-century literature as a whole. If the period begins with the image of a child in prison, it concludes with the adolescent having improved nature by turning his mind to unnatural arts.[11] St. Stephen commences his escape from the Daedalian labyrinth by opening his confession with the words, "Once upon a time, and a very good time it was. . . ." But as we read further in *A Portrait of the Artist as a Young Man*, we discover that Stephen's coming into consciousness is related self-reflexively; he has been told the tale of his origins by someone else. For "Once upon a time" does not exist *from within* the children's world, but only from the voyeuristic gaze of the adult storyteller who has become an artist, as the most convenient way of recapturing time past.

Wilde, Lang, Macdonald, and other *fin-de-siècle* dandies were each to testify to the disappearance of childhood by their interest not only in writing children's literature, but by actually living in the polymorphous perverse world of the presexually aware child. *Alice's Adventures in Wonderland* is a *Bildungsroman*, but *Through the Looking-Glass* is a

Künstlerroman, a genre wherein the child's apprenticeship is now indistinguishable from his existence-as-art. But turning life into art is itself a kind of horror story. And the jaded dandy, Carroll included, resembles, not just a little, the bored child. In their themes and development, the *Alice* books are as encompassing of the Victorian period as the image of the Queen of the pack of playing cards, the Queen whose dispossessed children, scattered over the face of Europe, came back to haunt the future of England in the next generation just as surely as did Alice's story.

ALICE

by Robert Graves

(1925)

WHEN that prime heroine of our nation, Alice,
Climbing courageously in through the Palace
Of Looking-Glass, found it inhabited
By chessboard personages, white and red,
Involved in never-ending tournament,
She being of a speculative bent
Had long foreshadowed something of the kind,
Asking herself: "Suppose I stood behind
And viewed the fireplace of Their drawing-room

From hearthrug level, why must I assume
That what I'd see would need to correspond
With what I now see? And the rooms beyond?"

Proved right, yet not content with what she had done,
Alice decided to increase her fun:
She set herself, with truly British pride
In being a pawn and playing for her side,
And simple faith in simple stratagem,
To learn the rules and moves and perfect them.
So prosperously there she settled down
That six moves only and she'd won her crown—
A triumph surely! But her greater feat
Was rounding these adventures off complete:
Accepting them, when safe returned again,
As queer but true—not only in the main
True, but as true as anything you'd swear to,
The usual three dimensions you are heir to.
For Alice, though a child, could understand
That neither did this chance-discovered land
Make nohow or contrariwise the clean
Dull round of mid-Victorian routine,
Nor did Victoria's golden rule extend
Beyond the glass: it came to the dead end
Where empty hearses turn about; thereafter
Begins that lubberland of dream and laughter,
The red-and-white-flower-spangled hedge, the grass
Where Apuleius pastured his Gold Ass,
Where young Gargantua made whole holiday . . .
But farther from our heroine not to stray,
Let us observe with what uncommon sense—
Though a secure and easy reference
Between Red Queen and Kitten could be found—
She made no false assumption on that ground
(A trap in which the scientist would fall)
That queens and kittens are identical.

III
Comparisons
with
Other Writers

Lewis Carroll and T. S. Eliot as Nonsense Poets

by *Elizabeth Sewell*

(1958)

He thought he saw a Banker's Clerk
    Descending from a bus:
He looked again, and found it was
    A Hippopotamus.

I saw the 'potamus take wing.

It was Chesterton, that man of marvelous perception and often perverse practice, who announced in 1904 that Nonsense was the literature of the future. It was a brilliant guess. Even now, however, when it is clear that he was right, when the trials in *Wonderland* and the *Snark* have become prototypes of real trials from Reichstag to McCarthy, and much of our literature—poetry and criticism—and most of our philosophy is shaped on Nonsense principles, people are slow to recognize its importance, or that of Lewis Carroll. Carroll is no *lusus naturae* but a central figure, as important for England, and in the same way, as Mallarmé is for France.

Nonsense is how the English choose to take their Pure Poetry, their *langage mathématique* or *romances sans paroles*: their struggle to convert language into symbolic logic or music. It is a serious struggle, but taken this way it need not appear so. Nonsense? A mere game, of course. This is characteristic of us. We like, you might say, to play possum in these matters.

with words a logical universe of discourse meticulously selected and controlled; within this playground the mind can then manipulate its material, consisting largely of names of things and numbers. The process is directed always towards analyzing and separating the material into a collection of discreet counters, with which the detached intellect can make, observe, and enjoy a series of abstract, detailed, artificial patterns of words and images (you may be reminded of the New Criticism) which have their own significance in themselves. All tendencies towards synthesis are taboo: in the mind, imagination and dream; in language, the poetic and metaphorical elements; in subject matter, everything to do with beauty, fertility, and all forms of love, sacred or profane. Whatever is unitive is the great enemy of Nonsense, to be excluded at all costs.

The pure practice of Nonsense demands a high degree of asceticism, since its very existence in the mind depends on limitation and infertility. Nonsense is by nature logical and antipoetic. The Nonsense poet, therefore, faces a constant paradox of self-denial. Something of the effects of this can be seen in the work of three great Nonsense practitioners, Mallarmé, Carroll, and Mr. T. S. Eliot.

Mallarmé devoted his life, at great cost, to this paradox, becoming in the course of it an ascetic, atheistic, secular saint of letters. Neither Carroll nor Mr. Eliot was content to do this, and in their attitude and literary production they can be seen to resemble one another, their progressions describing similar curves, perhaps characteristic of great Nonsense men: they begin with strict Nonsense of a high order, but then, chafing at the game's restrictions, they desire to include some or all of those elements of real life—human relationships, the body, sex, love, religion, growth and development in the natural world—which Nonsense rules out. The desire is noble but it disintegrates the game. Mallarmé in the end cunningly escapes the paradox by progressing to thinking about thinking, in *Un coup de dés*, allowing himself a dangerously beautiful if shadowy ship and ocean and a sudden miraculous precipitation of stars, yet keeping the overall figure of dice-play, which is numbers and a game, and so could be Nonsense still. The Eliot-Mallarmé connection is close, Mr. Eliot himself providing clues to it in "Lines for an Old Man" and "Little Gidding"; but the Eliot-Carroll connection is closer. With Carroll we move from pure Nonsense in the *Alices* through *The Hunting of the Snark* to *Sylvie and Bruno*, and with Mr. Eliot from *The Waste Land* and the poems of the Sweeney period through the *Four Quartets* to the late plays. Carroll is the best interpreter we have for Mr. Eliot, and *Old Possum's Book of Practical Cats*, Mr. Eliot's overt Nonsense work, is not a chance production, the master in a lighter mood. It is integral to the whole body of his work, and a key to his poetry and his problem.

Mr. Eliot couches his own autobiography in Nonsense terms, but at one remove, for he parodies Lear's *Autobiography* into "How unpleasant to meet Mr. Eliot!" He is an extensive parodist, as Carroll was, and in each case this is a device for handling what might otherwise be dangerous for Nonsense. It is a matter of affirming and denying, and in his autobiography Mr. Eliot affirms and denies Nonsense in its relation to himself. He has told us that he drew from *Alice in Wonderland* that rose garden with which the first of the *Four Quartets* opens, leading into the image of the rose which pervades and closes the last of them. In his 1929 essay on the Dante he so greatly reveres, he says that we have "to pass through the looking-glass into a world which is just as reasonable as our own. When we have done that we begin to wonder whether the world of Dante is not both larger and more solid than our own." Nonsense goes deep in Mr. Eliot. One does not describe one's life, even ironically, construct an image system in serious poetry, or interpret an honored poet in terms of something one considers trivial. It is we who would be at fault in seeing Nonsense so. What Mr. Eliot is doing here is working at the dilemma of his vocation as a Nonsense poet. The *Four Quartets* epitomize the problem. They are religious poems; yet one of their main images comes from classical Nonsense, the Wonderland rose which becomes the *Paradiso* rose, drawn in its turn from a poet to understand whom, according to Mr. Eliot, we have to go through the looking-glass. And Nonsense as a pure systematic art form of mind and language excludes both poetry and religion.

Lewis Carroll, much less of a poet than Mr. Eliot but no less devoted a churchman, faces the same problem. He had, however, two advantages:

first, he had an official status in the matter; second, he was luckier in his period. He had a triple identity, as the Reverend Charles Dodgson, as a professional mathematician and symbolic logician, and as a Nonsense writer. The last two, closely allied as they are, were allowed to meet; the first was sealed off, at least up till the *Sylvie and Bruno* period. And the age in which he lived, a pre-Freudian era in which more modern meanings of "repressions" or "integration" were unknown, made possible such a separation and that which resulted from it—the perfection of the *Alices.* (The *Snark* is already much more ambiguous.) It is a pattern that Mr. Eliot might almost envy, if only for its true Nonsense quality. He, in his Nonsense autobiography, describes his own features as being "of clerical cut,"[1] and it is remarkable how character after character in the plays is impelled towards Holy Orders. Harry in *Family Reunion* departs for "a stony sanctuary and a primitive altar"; Celia in *The Cocktail Party* joins an order, "a very austere one," and is martyred; Eggerson in *The Confidential Clerk* announces that Colby Simpkins will soon be entering the Church; and in *Murder in the Cathedral* the protagonist is archbishop, saint, and martyr already. Mr. Eliot's difficulty is that nowadays religion and other such vital subjects cannot conveniently be affirmed and then closed off. One has to be Nonsense man, poet, and churchman all at once. Carroll's hippopotamus, secure in its Nonsense bounds, can remain of the earth, earthy; but Mr. Eliot's has got into the poetry and has somehow to be got into heaven. Yet despite the superficial differences between them, to us readers it is a great help to have one such quadruped by which to measure a second, and Carroll is the best point of reference we have for understanding Mr. Eliot.

Anyone interested in drawing minor parallels between earlier Eliot poems and the *Alices* will find material ready to hand: the reminiscence of the Frog Footman in "Portrait of a Lady" ("I shall sit here . . ."); the executioner who haunts "Sweeney Agonistes" among the playing cards as he does the Queen's croquet game; the echo, also in "Sweeney," of the riddle of the Red King's dream, "If he was alive then the milkman wasn't"; the reversals or full stops of time in the two writers; the endless tea-party, interminable as the Hatter's, in "Prufrock," "Portrait of a Lady," "Mr. Apollinax," "Hysteria," "A Cooking Egg," *The Waste Land,* where the typist comes home at teatime; the first scene of *Family Reunion,* Skimbleshanks in *Old Possum,* till only the tea leaves are left in "The Dry Salvages"; and so on. These are not uninteresting, but they are very minor affairs. It is in the major poems, as it should be, that Carroll and Non-sense begin to be really helpful.

The Waste Land is comparable to the *Alices* and to them alone, as Mr. Eliot's nearest approach to pure Nonsense practice. He admits certain elements into his subject matter—myth, love, the poetry and beauty of the past—which are dangerous, but he employs classic Nonsense techniques to control them. Thus, the fragmentation in the poem is not to be regarded, in this light, as a lament on our modern condition. It is the Nonsense poet's way of analyzing his subject matter into discrete parts, "one and one and one" as the Red Queen says,[2] to make it workable in Nonsense terms. The same is true of the sterility the poem deals with. This, too, is the Nonsense poet carefully setting up the conditions necessary for the exercise of his special art. To hold the whole poem together, the two classic Carroll frameworks are employed, playing cards and chess, the digits and moves of a game substituted for those dangerous and un-Nonsense entities, human relationships. The Nonsense rules procure the necessary working conditions—detachment of mind from subject matter, analysis of material, manipulation of patterns of unfused images. Into this careful systematics, highly intellectual as Nonsense is, even potentially subversive material can be fitted and held, and the result is probably Mr. Eliot's masterpiece.

With the *Four Quartets*, the situation is made more difficult by what is now the poet's increasing emphasis upon unitive subjects, particularly love and religion. We need here, as points of reference, the *Alices* and the *Snark*, with a glance forward to *Sylvie and Bruno*. The overall Nonsense control of *The Waste Land* has gone; in its place we have Nonsense pro-cedures still operating, but used now as defenses against particular dangers. We will consider four of these: poetry, words in their nonlogical functions, and the two central images, roses and dancing.

Traditional forms of poetry are admitted into the *Quartets* from time to time, with their complement of metaphor and nonlogical speech so antithetical to Nonsense. When they appear, however, they tend, as in the *Alices*, to be pounced on and immediately subjected to critical analysis. See Part II of "East Coker," for instance, where the passage "What is the late November doing" is followed at once by

> That was a way of putting it—not very satisfactory.
> A periphrastic study in a worn-out poetical fashion.

So Alice says to the Caterpillar after repeating some verses, "Not quite right, I'm afraid. . . . Some of the words have got altered," and receives the reply, "It is wrong from beginning to end." Poetry is dangerous to Nonsense, even if unsatisfactory, even if parodied, and it is as well to reduce it to criticism at once. No one interested in the present hypertrophied condition of literary criticism should overlook the importance of the Caterpillar and Humpty Dumpty as spiritual ancestors of this development.

Words, the materials of poetry with their aura of figures and dreams, are perilous too. Mr. Eliot's description of his own conversation, restricted so nicely to What Precisely, acknowledges the Nonsense rule: words must be rigorously controlled lest dream and poetry creep in. So "Burnt Norton" says that words decay with imprecision, will not stay in place, will not stay still, to which Humpty Dumpty adds, "They've a temper, some of them, particularly verbs." In "East Coker" comes the phrase "the intolerable wrestle with words and meanings," and the complaint that one has only learned to get the better of words for the thing that one no longer has to say; but the obligation is to master the words, as Humpty confirms, "The question is, which is to be master, that's all." A poet may be in part at least subject to his words; a Nonsense poet never. Only at the end of "Little Gidding" are the words allowed out to dance, and even then they have to be formal, exact, precise. So we come to dancing and roses, the two great Dante images for heaven which are also Nonsense images in Carroll and Eliot poetry.

A rose is about as dangerous an image for Nonsense as could be imagined. It implies an immense range of living company—beauty, growth, the body, sex, love. Roses in Nonsense will need special treatment, and Carroll begins to operate on his immediately, with pots of paint wielded by playing-card people or animated numbers. Mr. Eliot adopts a different but no less effective technique, sterilizing his rose in his turn, at the beginning and end of "Little Gidding," with ice and fire which cancel one another out and wipe away with them the living notion of the rose, leaving only a counter or cipher, suitable for Nonsense, behind.

Lastly, there is the dance, a dangerously living and bodily image too. Carroll's attitude to it is always insecure. The cavorting Mock Turtle and Gryphon are clumsy and tread on Alice's feet; three times round the mulberry bush is enough for Tweedledum and Tweedledee. Carroll's most revealing dance occurs in one of his letters, where he compares his own dancing to a rhinoceros and hippopotamus executing a minuet together. Carroll is the reluctant dancing hippo. Mr. Eliot is a reluctant dancer also in the *Quartets,* even though dancing is the way to heaven. The dance is constrained: "At the still point, there the dance is," restricted as the circling round the Mad Hatter's table or the crocodile walking up his own forehead in *Sylvie and Bruno.* The best comment on this inhibition of free movement comes in the *Snark.* "In my beginning is my end or say that the end precedes the beginning," it runs in "East Coker" and "Burnt Norton," and the Bellman, familiar with this condition, describes it as being "snarked," a state when "the bowsprit got mixed with the rudder sometimes." Movement in Nonsense is admitted only to be annulled, if the control and pattern are to be preserved.

Where then can we go now? It seems only towards *Sylvie and Bruno, The Cocktail Party, The Confidential Clerk.* There is already a surprising similarity between Part II of "The Dry Salvages,"

> Where is there an end of it, the soundless wailing,
> The silent withering of autumn flowers

and so on, and the prose-poem with which *Sylvie and Bruno* ends, with its chilly mists and wailing gusts over the ocean, its withered leaves of a blighted hope, and the injunction, to the hero sailing for India, "Look Eastward!" as the Eliot poem bears us on to Krishna and Arjuna. Yet this is not Mr. Eliot's last word as Nonsense poet. He will talk about love and God and heaven in the later *Quartets* and plays, as Carroll does in *Sylvie and Bruno Concluded,* but this is not the answer, nor the way in which the hippopotamus can enter heaven. Mr. Eliot's answer is more direct and much more surprising; one hesitates, with any writer calling his book *Old Possum,* to suggest that it seems also largely unconscious. He implies that the way for a Nonsense poet to reach heaven is by Nonsense itself; and so we have *Old Possum's Book of Practical Cats.*

Cats and Nonsense writers agree well together, in life and in books. Cats are images for the body and for woman (so Grishkin) but in appeasable form. It is possible that cats are also images for God, in miniature. Mr. Empson suggests that the Cheshire Cat represented God, and I believe that the GREAT RUMPUSCAT (Mr. Eliot's capitals) might do so too. "Gerontion," after all, speaks openly of Christ the tiger. But here there is no menace, Mr. Eliot can permit himself liberties Carroll never took, and sly theological eddies wander through the *Possum* book, in "Old

Deuteronomy," or the cat's three names, one of which is ineffable. In this so-called minor work can be found all the love and charity which cause Mr. Eliot, as Nonsense poet, so much trouble in the rest of his poetry, but released and reconciled. Here, too, sin is behovely ("I could mention Mungojerrie, I could mention Griddlebone") but all shall be well; and there is set moving in "The Song of the Jellicles," at long last and in spite of all impediments and far beyond any of the supposedly more poetic works, a dance so free and loving and joyful, yet quiet and half-secret, that it is a clear image of heaven and an invitation thither.

Since there is in any case a ball in preparation here, and it seems the merest accident that Mr. Eliot left one thing out of this, his most beautiful Nonsense poem, may I make the omission good and offer, in recognition and gratitude, a rose for the Jellicles.

On Lewis Carroll's
ALICE
and her White Knight
and Wordsworth's
"ODE
ON IMMORTALITY"

by Horace Gregory

(1944)

What though the radiance which was once so bright
Be now for ever taken from my sight,
  Though nothing can bring back the hour
Of splendour in the grass, of glory in the flower;
      We will grieve not, rather find
      Strength in what remains behind;
      In the primal sympathy
      Which having been must ever be . . . .

—STANZA X, *Ode on Intimations of Immortality
from Recollections of Early Childhood.*

"Then you keep moving round, I suppose?" said Alice.

"Exactly so," said the Hatter: "as the things get used up."

"But what happens when you come to the beginning again?" Alice ventured to ask.

"Suppose we change the subject," the March Hare interrupted, yawning. "I'm getting tired of this. I vote the young lady tells us a story."

"I'm afraid I don't know one," said Alice, rather alarmed at the proposal.

"Then the Dormouse shall!" they both cried. "Wake up, Dormouse!"

IT IS IN LIKE MANNER, and with no intentional disrespect to literature itself, that each generation from Pindar's day to this changes the subject slightly and tells its story. I would like to suggest that even the Dormouse's story as it was told on a fine mid-Victorian afternoon is not entirely irrelevant to the subject of Wordsworth's "Ode on Immortality." We remember that the Dormouse spoke of three sisters who had been living at the bottom of a well (to be exact, it was a treacle well) and that they drew (they had been learning how to draw) all manner of things from it, everything that began with M, such as mouse-trap, and the moon, memory and muchness: and today, as we reread the "Ode," memory and muchness disturb us most, and from these we progress toward Wordsworth's moon, who with delight looked round her when the heavens were bare.

If one rereads the poem for the sake of recapturing the associations it once held, it is likely to contain memories which its long title half-unconsciously revives; and none of us, I think, can hold Wordsworth or the "Ode" wholly responsible for this phenomenon. For most of us the earliest reading of the poem had its beginning in a school classroom, with Wordsworth read (as Alice's Gryphon might well recall) at odd moments between the study of those superior branches of learning which include Ambition, Distraction, Uglification, and Derision. My own recollection of the "Ode" is surrounded by the images of a boys' preparatory school, where, behind a desk, a young, thin, nervous, red-headed Scotsman sat— and it was he who instructed us in English poetry, basketball, and tennis. I remember him reciting Shakespeare and the "Jabberwocky" with a recklessness that matched his leaps and rushes on the concrete tennis court—and in his reading of Wordsworth's "Ode," he accented a touch of malice (which all of us shared in the reciting the poets of the Lake school) by a slight exaggeration of his Edinburgh burr: one could hear it clearly as he read aloud:

> Our birth is but a sleep and a forgetting:
> The Soul that rises with us, our life's Star,
>   Hath had elsewhere its setting
>   And cometh from afar. . . .

As one heard the *rrs*, the atmosphere increased its tension, for it was part of our unspoken agreement not to laugh aloud at Wordsworth's famous "Ode." Without knowing why, we felt immensely superior to the image of the lank and gray-haired, long-nosed, elderly poet whose head leaned with a weak, womanish tilt out of the darkness of a photo-plated engraving which faced the title page of Wordsworth's *Poetical Works;* it was an unvoiced pact among us to read him with an air of prep-school skepticism, and to justify our attitude by frequently reciting:

> "O mercy!" to myself I cried,
> "If Lucy should be dead!"

Yet we could not dismiss him utterly; for the "Ode" was almost certain to turn up in awkward places: its title would reappear in questioning footnotes in schoolbook anthologies of English verse and scrawled in chalk up on the classroom blackboard. From a sense of duty to his students (and the power exerted by college entrance boards), our instructor persisted in the revival of the "Ode" on mimeographed sheets of paper that were rapidly circulated around the room during the weighted silence of a moment which always precedes a written examination. Who wrote it and what did the poem mean, and what, O what, was Wordsworth's philosophy? This last we agreed, if not completely understood, was called "Pantheism," and was of heavier substance than anything that went by the name of philosophy in the poetry of Shelley, Keats, or Byron, and one could prove it (if I remember correctly) by contrasting two skylark poems in which it was shown that Shelley lost himself in Nature, while Wordsworth, in a trying hour, was found. It was agreed that Wordsworth somehow achieved salvation and, if less attractive than Byron or Coleridge, was out of danger—was safe and not to be questioned in open controversy; it was as though Wordsworth's recollections of childhood had begun at the very moment when the pleasures of our own had vanished. From a last reading of his "Ode" one went to college, leaving the memories of "The Solitary Reaper," "The Reverie of Poor Susan," "To a Skylark," "I Travelled Among Unknown Men," and fragmentary stanzas of "Resolution and Independence" floating and yet heard distinctly within the recesses of the inner ear.

To speak of Wordsworth and his "Ode" again today is like asking oneself the question that Alice ventured: "But what happens when you come to the beginning again?" So much has happened to Wordsworth and ourselves that a true beginning is difficult to find: one road winds backward to the first decade of the nineteenth century in which the "Ode" was written; another to what we mean when we speak of poetry at all; and still another to Alice herself and to her childhood, which was over-shadowed by the unnamed presence of Wordsworth among the trees of that dark forest where the White Knight recited his ballad of "The Aged, Aged Man."

Since I confess a predilection for the second and third of three possible beginnings, I shall speak of the first only, as it serves to illuminate the darkness surrounding Alice as "she leant against a tree . . . listening in a half-dream to the melancholy music of the song." The first road recalls a number of familiar images, images of Rousseau and of the Fall of the Bastille; the title page of Blake's *Songs of Innocence*; Mr. Thomas Day's adopted daughter, Sabrina, the educated orphan, whose innate goodness was severely tested by her foster father ("It is said that he dropped hot sealing wax on her arms to inure her to pain, and fired blank cartridges at her petticoats to train her in self-control."); images of Mr. Day's Sanford and Merton, Miss Maria Edgeworth's Lazy Lawrence; and among them that dark-eyed, semitragic child of genius, Hartley Coleridge, of whom it has been so often said that he was the living prototype of the child within the "Ode":

> Behold the child among his new-born blisses,
> A six years' Darling of a pigmy size!

These and a hundred other pictures crowd the scene, filling a decade of unresolved Napoleonic Wars: Miss Austen's precocious girls with clear heads and cool fingers—and everywhere the hope of the world seen in a child's face, the child no longer stained by sin, the guiltless child, and the innocent, even idiot boy believed to possess the secret of human happiness. The reflected likeness of that child may be seen in the pallid, soot-streaked features of Smike and Oliver Twist who followed after; and after them came the pink-cheeked, Maypole dancing figurines of Miss Kate Greenaway; and a distinct resemblance to the child's behavior may be found among the heroes of social novels, ranging their separate ways through the fiction of the twentieth century.

Returning to the "Ode" itself and the moment of its birth, we would agree, I think, that its so-called philosophic generalities had been given the particulars of light, shade, depth, color, and motion in a number of Wordsworth's earlier poems: "Her Eyes Are Wild," "We Are Seven," "The Sparrow's Nest," "The Reverie of Poor Susan," "Michael," and "I Travelled Among Unknown Men" were of the same world that was viewed so hopefully in the opening stanzas of the "Ode." His readers were familiar with its terms; they knew its "Fountains, Meadows, Hills, and Groves," they shared the emotion implied by the use of each abstract noun within the "Ode": each joy, each grief, each bliss, each soul, each glory; and, I think, we may grant that they were as well prepared to read the poem as he was to write it. Even the difficult concept of human immortality was expressed in a language that Wordsworth's early readers (with the aid of his prefatory note) could accept and welcome, and as they redis-covered it within the "Ode," it seemed to fall into place as effortlessly as sunlight upon the earth. So much, then, for our first beginning, which in itself could be expanded into a volume of considerable size and weight. From what we know of the "Ode" and its predecessors, we are reasonably safe in saying that it summed up a number of the beliefs and observations which had been already exposed to light in eloquent passages of "The Prelude" and which had taken form in the first ten stanzas of "Resolution and Independence."

Our second beginning contains a few remarks on the general nature of what we talk about when we speak of poetry at all; and here, I think that if Alice's White Knight were brought in to join us, he would insist that such remarks should be called "warnings." That is not their name, of course; nor does the present occasion speak with the urgency of air-raid alarms and threats, yet something very like a "warning" is sounded every time an interpretation of poetry takes place. Unless one is actually read-ing the poem, hearing it, perceiving it, and is aware (for the time being) of certain hitherto unnamed emotional responses, the warning that one hears is, "What does the poem mean?"—then, a moment later—"Is the poem poetry?" From then onward we can tell you what poetry is called or has been called, but not what it is: I am inclined to think that the Wordsworth who wrote the "Ode" called it "natural piety," and that the White Knight called it "my own invention." The Gryphon and the Mock Turtle (since they were obviously concerned with matters of educational importance) undoubtedly called whatever poems they read by the name of "lessons," and most of us, like Alice, tend to respect such formidable creatures, who had received the best of educations and who wept, who hid their faces in their paws at the slightest recollection of their past experiences. The pity was that lessons lessened from day to day—and that for them there had passed away a glory from the earth.

I, for one, am willing to believe that whatever the something is that is first thought of as poetry and is then given, like the White Knight's ballad, a number of different names—I believe that the kind of poetry we carry seriously in mind—soon acquires a quality that resembles an independent life, a being which springs from and yet finds a place apart from all other things in this imperfect world. As we read it, the poem exists beyond the time and the occasion that prompted its arrival; and there are moments when the poem seems to exist even beyond the gifts, the skills, the ambitions, and intentions of the person who wrote it. There are times when one might almost say that the life of a poem depends upon the varieties of misconception taking place around it; and if we are willing to agree that the play *Hamlet* may be read (quite as one reads the best of Shakespeare's tragedies) as a dramatic poem, surely that example should be a warning to us all. Like Hamlet's father's ghost who walks within it, the play itself still walks the earth to haunt the wariest of its interpreters. Despite the number of footnotes—or is it because of them?—that almost crowd the text of *Hamlet* off the printed page, its central being remains remarkably alive, and while it may be great joy for us to speculate on the names that it may be called, including semantics, psychology, social science, or education, the independent power of life within the play is undiminished.

So it is when we approach any work conceived by human imagination: from the imperfect sources of human life, even from violent action and disorder, a selection of shapes and sounds, color and motion takes place, and we recognize that something has been done which is self-contained and active. These remarks or "warnings" are not, of course, "my own invention"; they have been spoken with far greater accuracy long ago and they may be found by those who have eyes to read them in Homer's story of the creation of Achilles' shield. The shield was an extremely cunning work of art, and its multitudinous figures resembled life so closely that the shield in its entire being seemed a mirror of the very world Achilles and his enemies had known; and we must remember that Achilles wore it to protect his body from a fatal wound. Was the shield self-knowledge? I suspect that is one of the names that it might be called.

But as I turn from Homer back to Wordsworth, and from Words-worth to Alice, I cannot prove that Alice herself had read the whole of the famous "Ode" that asserts the promise of immortality. Others have spoken (and among them, Mr. William Empson) of Alice's perceptive wit in voicing criticism, yet I can say that her interpreter, who disguised himself as "Lewis Carroll," was not unfamiliar with the world of child-hood that the Lake poets celebrated and held before the eyes of their admirers. We know that Carroll's criticism of it was fully conscious (one has but to read the parodies he wrote while an undergraduate at Oxford), but we also know that he accepted the major premise of the "Ode," even the vision, or rather one of those words which begin with M—the memory of the happy moment associated with the past—and if the theme of the "Ode" is closely related to the theme of growing up, certainly the theme of Alice's adventures is of the same character, and is, if anything, illumi-nated by a greater number of precise steps onward from childhood to maturity.

The first expression of Alice's concern about growing up reached its crisis in her interview with the Caterpillar. She was in deep trouble, and she did not, of course, wish to grow up too fast, yet she wished to be more than her three inches high. It was no wonder that the Caterpillar instructed her to recite Robert Southey's "The Old Man's Comforts," an eminently respectable poem that had appeared in the *Youth's Magazine* for February, 1816, and since that time had been memorized by an entire generation of proper children. If her recitation of "Father William" did not recall the image of Wordsworth directly, the memory of Southey recalled him at his weakest, bringing to mind the unhappy "Peter Bell," who, after a wild career, saw goodness in an ass's skin and became an honest man. From him we turn to Wordsworth's "Idiot Boy" and to "Simon Lee" and from "Simon Lee" we return to Robert Southey, the most devoted and least gifted of Wordsworth's three great friends. One remem-bers Dorothy Wordsworth and Coleridge readily enough, but Southey (not without cause) is as readily forgotten, and if it were not for Alice, who would care to read Southey's unconscious parody of Wordsworth's philosophic attitudes? Who would waste his time reading:

> In the days of my youth, I remember'd my God!
> And He hath not forgotten my age.

To these lines Alice quickly replied:

> *Do you think I can listen all day to such stuff?*
> *Be off, or I'll kick you down stairs!*

And then said timidly, "some of the words have got altered": indeed they have, and very lively words they have become. I doubt if any critic of Alice's day would have dared to go half as far as her imperfect memory carried her; and if her words "got altered," they certainly transformed the kindly, senile, sweet old Father William. Was the association also that of another William, a William Wordsworth who succeeded Southey as Poet Laureate, traveling where "other palms are won," beyond the "Ode"; was Father William the elderly poet who made petulant yet shrewd inquiries to an admirer concerning the welfare of his American investments? Perhaps Alice did not intend to go as far as that, yet her remarkably feminine (one almost says "feline") perceptions were aroused, and at the very least, her Father William knew the value of commercial enterprise and the jargon of salesmanship:

> *"You are old," said the youth, "as I mentioned before,*
> *And have grown most uncommonly fat;*
> *Yet you turned a back-somersault in at the door—*
> *Pray, what is the reason of that?"*
>
> *"In my youth," said the sage, as he shook his grey locks,*
> *"I kept all my limbs very supple*
> *By the use of this ointment—one shilling the box—*
> *Allow me to sell you a couple?"*

The altered words had done their work; the recitation was not quite right. Was it fair? was it cruel? was it ethical? Alice herself was not troubled by these questions; her subconscious will had voiced its criticism, and to those who had enjoyed her version of "Father William," all questions of justice and morality were made to seem as irrelevant as the memory of conscious right and wrong within the action of a dream. But the authoritative, masculine Caterpillar, who had been brought up to respect the philosophy of the Lake poets, was sure that she was wrong from beginning to end, and said so.

I shall not attempt to enlarge upon the intentions which inspired flaws in Alice's memory; we know only that she was neither deaf nor blind and that something had happened to Father William between the date of Wordsworth's "Ode" and Alice's arrival on the scene that was none too lovely to contemplate. We also know that Alice's "Father William" had been read and still continues to be read by thousands who had never heard of Southey's "The Old Man's Comforts," and, what is more important, those very readers grow restless and uncomfortable as they read the following lines from Wordsworth's "Ode":

> The Youth, who daily farther from the east
> Must travel, still is Nature's Priest,
> And by the vision splendid
> Is on his way attended. . . .

Surely, the youth in Sir John Tenniel's drawing of Father William's son (and Sir John's illustrations of Alice's adventures are not to be ignored) was a portrait of a singularly dull young man. Was he the Idiot Boy? was he Michael's son? was he Nature's Priest? Perhaps not, perhaps he was none of these, but his likeness to his brothers is scarcely short of being fatal.

Meanwhile, Alice's encounter with the Caterpillar had prepared her for a more important and later crisis in growing up, and here, at last, we come upon her in the dark forest attended by the White Knight, whose foolish face was lit by a faint smile. The White Knight was about to sing his ballad.

"It's long," said the Knight, "but it's very, very beautiful. Everybody that hears me sing it—either it brings the tears into their eyes, or else—"
"Or else what?" said Alice, for the Knight had made a sudden pause.
"Or else it doesn't, you know," replied the Knight.

The old Knight was very kindly, very gentle; he had great difficulty in staying on his horse; he was perhaps the meanest flower of knighthood; he was all too human—and there in the dark forest, and with the Knight reminding us of tears, we almost hear the strains of "Resolution and Independence":

> Thanks to the human heart by which we live,
> Thanks to its tenderness, its joys and fears,
> To me the meanest flower that blows can give
> Thoughts that do often lie too deep for tears.

"Resolution and Independence," which is a far better poem than the "Ode," and which was foreshadowed by the "Ode," closely approached the climax of Wordsworth's poetic life; and if the poem moves in the direction of Wordsworth's maturity, a recollection of it also guides the reader in the direction of Alice with the White Knight at her side at evening in the forest. We are being prepared for the burlesque of "Resolution and Independence" in the White Knight's ballad of an aged, aged man, "the oldest man . . . that ever wore grey hairs."

> *I'll tell thee everything I can:*
>   *There's little to relate.*
> *I saw an aged, aged man,*
>   *A-sitting on a gate.*
>
> *"Who are you, aged man?" I said.*
>   *"And how is it you live?"*
> *And his answer trickled through my head,*
>   *Like water through a sieve.*

By the time the Knight completes the singing of his ballad, we are well past the "Ode," stepping through it to the other side, quite as Alice once walked, or half-climbed, through the Looking-Glass. Meanwhile, Lewis Carroll's criticism of Wordsworth had shifted its position of attack from indirect reference to explicit parody of a particular poem. Across that merest space from the "Ode" to contemplation of the Leech-gatherer (which is almost impossible to measure because it is so near, so far), the first of our beginnings, with its images of Rousseau and the guiltless face of childhood ("A Presence which is not to be put by"), seems to tremble and dissolve as though London Bridge itself were about to fall. But Alice had already heard the crash that followed her conversation with Humpty Dumpty, and the continuous failure of well-intentioned, adult (though sometimes rude) authority no longer troubled her.

If Alice, after her visit with the White Knight, had begun to grow up, it was in spite of and in a totally different way than Father William and the Aged Man approved. What if she had known something of the same world that Wordsworth's "Ode" had opened to other children (and certainly to their parents and schoolmasters) of her day? The words, somehow, were not the same, and the vision of the Lake poets had shifted its perspective—and here we must remember that Alice was a heroine and not a hero. From the White Knight she had learned of what poetry might be called, but her perceptions were becoming critical in the sense that she was soon to have other things than poetry to fill her mind. She had to say good-by to the White Knight, leap to the Eighth Square, and after a moment of dismay, be glad at last to wear a crown upon her head. Her reward was that Queen Victoria thoroughly enjoyed her adventures, for the Queen had known and witnessed the failures of masculine authority and the weaknesses of the speculative, or, as Wordsworth would have said, "the philosophic mind." Surely, her advisers and ministers had changed and fallen since she first came as a girl—scarcely a young woman —to wear the crown. There had been Grey and Melbourne, Palmerston and Peel, Derby and Lord Russell—and as for other changes, that troublesome Reform Bill was like the battle between the Lion and the Unicorn—but the Queen had outlived them all. She had outlived her poet laureates, Southey and Wordsworth—and the arrival of Tennyson would, no doubt, bring other changes. As for a style, a language, a fashion being laughed at, one had only to remember that in the century before Alice had been born, John Gay's *The Beggar's Opera* laughed Italian opera off the London stage.

But after this much is said of Wordsworth and Alice, why was it, granting the usual changes in poetic taste and fashion, that Wordsworth's "Ode" and its successor, "Resolution and Independence," became so vulnerable to Alice's remarks? Unlike Achilles' shield, Wordsworth's "Ode" is by no means self-contained; it tends to fall apart, and even the most casual reader of it notices a change of temper, sensibility, and feeling that divides its opening stanzas from its last. Whatever the causes of this defect may be, surely no poet of Wordsworth's stature ever stumbled so blindly into so many traps as he. The most important of these was his undue speculation in prose on the philosophic sources of his poetry. His own definitions of poetry haunted him for fifty years of his long life, and even now they continue to haunt academic discussions of his remains. Every schoolboy can cheerfully quote and requote his eloquent phrases concerning "the spontaneous overflow of powerful feeling," yet I suspect that Wordsworth's lack of impulsiveness, coupled with the mere desire to "overflow," explains many a dull passage in "The Prelude" and "The Excursion." There can be little doubt that he accepted the role of being a poet with admirable seriousness, and in reading Dorothy Wordsworth's *Grasmere Journal* (1802), one can see that he approached his task with a strenuous immensity of purpose that is unequaled in English literature. In the closing stanzas of the "Ode" and through certain passages of "Resolution and Independence," he proved his ability to make his observation, his experience, his emotions, his insights, and his thinking flow as though they traveled in a single stream, yet his longer poems contained elements of greatness rather than the completed structure of great poetry. We can sight their far distance from the self-contained design of a true poem by contrasting them with "Lycidas" and "Samson Agonistes." Did his effort to acquire a "philosophic mind" stand in the way of his development to full maturity? The effort rewarded him with a cloak of authority which became transparent in the merest glance from Alice's candid eye.

In defense of Wordsworth, one can reply that Alice, despite her wit, despite her sharpness, lacked a perception into the tragic aspect of life that Wordsworth saw; she knew terror, but not grief; she had little concern for things outside the ranges of her immediate vision; she was a practical young female, caught, for the moment, in the mortal coils of growing up, and it is doubtful if, in her life beyond her journey through the Looking-Glass, one would find her meditating on the values of poetry.

Admitting that the difficulties of Wordsworth's verse are those of memory and muchness, there are glimpses throughout it of that something, which for me, whatever name it takes, is poetry. For poetry, as I read it, is only incidentally concerned with such abstractions as "the philosophic mind," or history, or science: it need not quarrel with them, it should not quarrel with them—and, on occasion, it should be aware of them to its own advantage. It has been said often enough that literary expression (being what it is) is always vitally concerned with what we call our senses—but here we must not forget our sixth sense, intelligence, for poetry must always contain something to delight the mind. Too often we credit the superior critic (and among superior critics Alice should not be forgotten) with an order of intelligence that is not to be found in poetry; this may be an unspoken hint, but it is implied. Although differences of opinion may be expressed among them, no such division exists between the gifted poet and his commentators. It is intelligence in its heightened sense, and in, I think, the best meaning of the term, that enters all poetry worthy of our attention; it implies an awareness and a sensibility reflected in the poem itself, and however subconscious or deliberate its offices may be, it imposes those limitations that are sometimes separately regarded as poetic form; it is sensible of ethics and of the devotional spirit, and for the individual poet as well as the reader of his poetry it sometimes illuminates the darkened path toward a true knowledge of mankind.

Since this discussion threatens to expand beyond all thought of Wordsworth's "Ode" and Alice, I fear I shall return to all three of my beginnings; and it is time (if the March Hare still has his watch) for someone else to tell a story.

Did Mark Twain Write "ALICE'S ADVENTURES IN WONDERLAND"?

by George Lanning

(1947)

WHO WROTE *Alice's Adventures in Wonderland?* There would seem to be no dispute on this point. Yet, two individuals have spent considerable time assembling evidence to prove that Charles Dodgson did not write this book and its sequel, *Through the Looking-Glass*. They maintain that the pseudonym "Lewis Carroll" conceals quite another personality from that of the austere, scholarly mathematics professor. This evidence they have published in a lengthy monograph called *The Most Remarkable Echo in the World*. They are H. M. and D. C. Partridge. In their book they state definitely that Samuel Clemens and not Charles Dodgson is the man behind the Carroll pen name, and they discuss some rather striking similarities between the work of the two authors which they believe bear out their contention. The reasons they give for this deception are several: first, Twain was a prolific writer who realized that an author can do severe damage to his reputation if he publishes too much in a given length of time (presumably he already had slated several books for publication when the idea for *Alice* occurred to him); second, he wanted *Alice* to be judged on its merits alone, not on the reputation of its author; and third (and perhaps most important), he loved a mystery, he loved confounding critics with the seeming paradox of a mathematician who wrote satirical fantasy on the side.

Mark Twain, unlike many writers, worked closely with the illustrators of his books; the Partridges claim that there was a good, particular reason for this. In the illustrations for several of his works, they tell us, there are clues to his authorship of *Alice*. In *Following the Equator*, for instance, is an illustration titled "Australian Bells." These bells appear sprawling down the page in the same way that the type pattern of the story "A Caucus-Race and a Long Tale" appears in *Alice's Adventures in Wonderland*. The Partridges believe that, through close collaboration with the artist, Twain endeavored to give his readers a clue to his identity as "Carroll" by recalling to their minds the unmistakable type pattern of the "Caucus" story.

There are other instances of this collaboration.

In the first edition of Twain's *The Gilded Age* is an illustration in which a girl is seen leaning against a table, her head bowed over a white kid glove; the mate to the glove is on the floor, and beside it lies a fan. In Chapter IV of the book about Wonderland is this passage (the White Rabbit is speaking):

> *"Oh my fur and whiskers! She'll get me executed, as sure as ferrets are ferrets! Where can I have dropped them, I wonder!" Alice guessed in a moment that it was looking for the fan and the pair of white gloves, and she very good-naturedly began hunting about for them, but they were nowhere to be seen. . . .*

Another clue the Partridges have found in the same book, this time in the text, appears on the last page. Twain wrote:

> "Alice"—even the same name is used—"sat by the open window in the room, looking out upon meadows where the laborers were cutting the

second crop of clover. . . . She was thinking.
 "She said, 'They will never know.' "

Alice's remark, if we are to accept the Partridges' premise, is unfortunately correct: they have not known—they have not even guessed, most of them—that there was the slightest connection between Mark Twain and the man who was presumably the creator of *Alice*. (Yet, as the authors point out, Twain lived in England for some time. And this fact, they feel, disposes of the argument that, after all, Dodgson narrated these stories long before publication to the daughters of Canon Liddell. For there is no proof that Dodgson told them. On the contrary, one summer's eve, when Twain was living in England, he took a trip up the river and changed places with the scholar, and then *Alice* was born. The eager little girls to whom the magic stories were told [by Twain] became conspirators in the deception.)

In the first English edition of *Alice's Adventures in Wonderland*, in the first illustration for Chapter VIII, the initials M. T. and S. C. appear on the Five of Spades. These are not, of course, the initials either of John Tenniel, the illustrator, or of Dodgson. They *are* the initials of Mark Twain-Samuel Clemens. This edition was published in England in 1865, by Macmillan and Company, and was ordered suppressed. The reason given was that the author and the illustrator objected to the poor quality of the woodcuts. But, in later editions, neither pair of initials is visible in the picture, from which fact the Partridges leave us to draw whatever conclusion we choose.

The authors feel that it is also significant that throughout his life Charles Dodgson stated that he had no interest in works not bearing his own name; furthermore, he was known to have said, upon at least one occasion when confronted by an ardent fan, that "My name is Dodgson and *Alice's Adventures* was written by Lewis Carroll."

Mark Twain, the Partridges state, never imagined that his ruse would be as effective as it was, for he wrote later, in *Sketches New and Old*:

I really had no desire to deceive anybody, and no expectation of doing it. Yet I purposely hoped to make it obscure—and I did. But I was too ingenious. I mixed it up rather too much; and so all that description as a key to the humbuggery was entirely lost.

Another time, he wrote:

Tomorrow I mean to dictate a chapter which will get my heirs &

assigns burned alive if they venture to print it this side of A.D. 2006—which I judge they won't. The edition of A.D. 2006 will make a stir when it comes out. I shall be hovering around taking notice, along with other dead pals.

It is entirely probable, say the Partridges, that part of the "stir" resulting from this edition of 2006 will be the revelation that it was from the pen of Mark Twain-Samuel Clemens, and not from that of Charles Dodgson, that *Alice* emerged. Until that time, we who remain skeptics are left considering this most immortal and enigmatic of literary documents with fresh interest and curiosity, for the question remains, absurd and tantalizing: Who *did* write *Alice's Adventures in Wonderland* and *Through the Looking-Glass?*

ALICE

Meets

the Don

by John Hinz

(1953)

EARLY in *Don Quixote* the hero and his squire chance upon some goat-herds' huts. Famished and exhausted, they glut themselves with chunks of goat's meat "as big as their Fists," washed down with huge drafts of wine. The Knight must express his thanks—nor, an audience at hand, is he ever unwilling to speak. "And now Don Quixote having satisfy'd his Appetite, he took a Handful of Acorns, and looking earnestly upon 'em; O happy Age, cry'd he, which our first Parents call'd the Age of Gold!" Here follows one of the most remarkable passages in all literature, a Marvell-ous description of earth's lush bountifulness in "that holy Age" when

. . . Men, for their Sustenance, needed only to lift their Hands, and take it from the sturdy Oak, whose spreading Arms liberally invited them to gather the wholsome savoury Fruit; while the clear Springs and silver Rivulets, with luxuriant Plenty, offer'd them their pure refreshing Water. . . . As yet no rude Plough-share presum'd with Violence to pry into the pious Bowels of our Mother Earth, for she without Compulsion kindly yielded from every Part of her fruitful and spacious Bosom, whatever might at once satisfy, sustain and indulge her frugal Children.

It was a Wordsworthian age too, for

. . . Lovers then express'd the Passion of their Souls in the unaffected Language of the Heart, with the native Plainness and Sincerity in which they were conceiv'd and divested of all that artificial Contexture, which enervates what it labours to enforce . . . .

It was, moreover, this Golden Age when man was child of Nature, an age of innocence:

. . . Imposture, Deceit and Malice had not yet crept in. . . . Justice . . . was equally and impartially dispensed; nor was the Judge's Fancy Law, . . . the modest Maid might walk where-ever she pleas'd alone, free from the Attacks of lewd lascivious Importuners.

Finally, the Don brings his talk to bear on modern times and, invariably, himself:

. . . But in this degenerate Age . . . no Virtue can be safe, no Honour be secure . . . . Thus that Primitive Innocence being vanish'd . . . there was a necessity to oppose the Torrent of Violence: For which Reason the Order of Knighthood-Errant was instituted. . . .

We are breathless at the close; the rapture, the delicious phraseology disconcerts us. Here are echoes not only of Marvell and Wordsworth, but of Ovid and Vergil. The Don, indeed, resembles that messiah whose coming Vergil seemed to predict: a child who should rule all the earth, make tame the wild beasts, bring back the Golden Age. "Know, Sancho," declares the intrepid hero to his cringing squire when they encounter, a little later, the fulling-mill hammers, "I was born in this Iron Age to restore the Age of Gold . . . ." Clearly from these goatherds, from this simple repast and eloquent rhapsodizing of nature's erstwhile benevolence, *Don Quixote* is sprung from the pastoral tradition, as William Empson has observed in his *Some Versions of Pastoral*. It is not pure pastoral, to be sure, but rather pastoral mixed with heroic, *mock-heroic*—an ever-shifting combination of the two to puzzle and tantalize the reader. "For though it don't make you laugh outright, it may chance to make ye draw in your Lips, and shew your Teeth like a Monkey," grins Cervantes. The final chapter of Mr. Empson's book concerns another puzzling and provoking work, abounding in madness and wisdom, dealing with another Golden Age: Lewis Carroll's *Alice in Wonderland* and *Through the Looking-Glass.*

But the kinship between Alice and the Don lies deeper than a shared convention. In the gallery of immortal literary portraiture they look rather like a fond, if eccentric, uncle and his precocious niece. Nor on closer scrutiny can the resemblance be casually dismissed. How basic, complex, even conscious the relationship is can perhaps most clearly be seen in the light of Don Quixote's impassioned speech—set off, one recalls, by a handful of acorns.

In that Golden Age of Don Quixote's oration, when the earth was yet young and agreeable, animals of course could speak, as Chaucer slyly assures us at the outset of the "Nun's Priest's Tale":

> For thilke tyme, as I have understonde,
> Bestes and briddes koude speke and synge.

Naturally, then, when Don Quixote and Sancho, while at dinner in a meadow under a shady tree with the Canon and his company, see a goat-herd speaking chidingly to his goat ("the Creature seemed to understand him . . . and looked up in his Face as if she wou'd let him know that she minded what he said"), the loquacious Knight for once says nothing, though the company—and especially the Canon—are much amused. Instead, the Don listens gravely to the goatherd's explanation: "Gentle-men," said he, "I wou'd not have you think me a Fool, because I talk so seriously to this senseless Animal, for my Words bear a mysterious Mean-ing; I am indeed, as you see, Rustical and Unpolish'd . . . ."

Doubtless Don Quixote understands what it is to speak seriously to a senseless animal: he has to reason with Sancho. The rustic and unpolished goatherd, he readily perceives, is Nature's child, one to whom "bestes and briddes koude speke." If Wordsworth later chose for his subject matter "humble and rustic life . . . because, in that condition, the essential pas-sions of the heart . . . speak a plainer and more emphatic language," he only mimicked the Don. That Alice, still trailing clouds of glory, should be able freely to converse with birds and animals and think little of the matter need occasion us no surprise. She is a child, unpolished and unspoiled, whose words bear a mysterious meaning, a living microcosm of that Golden Age. It is only because we understand and believe this that we can listen so gravely to the impossible conversations, feeling with Alice that it is quite natural to hear her "talking familiarly with them, as if she had known them all her life."

The Don too is a child. Childlike is his terrible naïveté, his heroic innocence, his elevation and high seriousness. He believes and so exacts unquestioning belief from others. Of the charms of his unseen Dulcinea he cries to the merchants, the eternal merchants, "Had I once shew'd you that Beauty . . . What Wonder would it be to acknowledge so notorious a Truth? The Importance of the thing lies in obliging you to believe it, confess it, affirm it, swear it, and maintain it, without seeing her. . . ." Faith is itself a virtue to the sure and simple, to the child. Seeing is not believing; rather, to believe is at last to see. Not infrequently Don Quixote echoes Christ.

Only as a child, perhaps, may one view the world as orderly and whole. Perhaps only then the great chain is complete, and everything knows its rightful place. In *Alice*, when all the animals ask at the end of the great Caucus Race, "But who is to give the prizes?" the dear, extinct Dodo (Dodgson, the name suggests, disguising himself as an "old fossil") points to Alice, saying, "Why, she, of course." The animals themselves, Mr. Empson has pointed out, recognize who and what she is, this human child, and most fittingly it is the Dodo, that foolish evolutionary relic, who says so.

To an adult, beset by doubts and misgivings, this simple, all-embracing perspective is lost. The ancients' exhortation to "know thyself" becomes an impossible prescription. What place in the cosmic pattern of things is there, say, for a poor middle-aged hidalgo? But a knight-errant Don Quixote, who has "lost the Use of his Reason" but gained in its stead an infant calm and limitless faith, can boldly assert "I know very well who I am." And Alice, whose dignity and composure must disconcert many of the strange creatures who are forever shouting at her and ordering her about, asks herself "Who in the world am I? Ah, *that's* the great puzzle!"

But there are more particular and obvious parallels between Alice's adventures and the Don's. Consider, first, how both suddenly awake in a strange world such as dreams are made of. Alice is sitting drowsily with her sister "when suddenly a white rabbit with pink eyes ran close to her," chattering to itself and nervously consulting a pocket watch. She starts to her feet, runs after it, unhesitatingly follows it down a large rabbit-hole (a thing the Freudians will never forgive her), where she encounters that terrifyingly topsy-turvy world. Or, in *Through the Looking-Glass*, she is "sitting curled up in a corner of the great armchair, half talking to herself and half asleep" when she is struck with the odd notion of entering the room which appears to be on the other side of the mirror over the chimney piece. The glass melts away at her touch, and suddenly she is in the Looking-Glass world, where left is right and everything seems to work exactly contrary to what she has learned to expect. Likewise the Don, a middle-aged gentleman of meager means, "by sleeping little and reading much" of the novels of chivalric romance, becomes suddenly obsessed with the idea of being himself a knight-errant, of setting out, mounted and costumed, on some dangerous quest of knightly honor. Instantly the real world is transformed for him: inns are castles, wenches are virgins, windmills are giants. A strange fancy seizes hold of a child-mind, the daft knight's and the little girl's, casting over it the spell of a dream.

Consider of what similar stuff these dreams consist. Cervantes describes Don Quixote's dream world thus:

A world of disorderly Notions, pick't out of his Books crouded into his Imagination; and now his Head was full of nothing but Inchantments, Quarrels, Battles, Challenges, Wounds, Complaints, Amours, Torments, and abundance of Stuff and Impossibilities; insomuch, that all the Fables and fantastical Tales which he read, seem'd to him now as true as the most authentick Histories.

This list of particulars agrees almost completely with Alice's: for "Inchantments" recall the fantastic changes in size Alice undergoes, the vanishing cat, the shop that becomes a boat; for "Battles" and "Challenges" recollect Tweedledee and Tweedledum, the Lion and the Unicorn, the White Knight and the Red; for "Quarrels" open to any page in *Alice*—there was never such a quarrelsome book. So it goes through all the "abundance of Stuff and Impossibilities." If the Don's dream-world is peopled with the characters of chivalric romance, Alice's is peopled with characters from Mother Goose—Humpty Dumpty, the Queen of Hearts, and others.

"When I used to read fairy tales, I fancied that kind of thing never happened, and now here I am in the middle of one!" exclaims Alice.

The "Fables and fantastical Tales" of the Knight correspond to the fables and fairy tales of the child.

Of course Cervantes' book includes characters drawn from the real world, from the author's experience—peasants and goatherds, barbers and curates. But then, Carroll's book is filled with Oxford "characters," as Professor Ayres observed: Tweedledum and Tweedledee, the eternal schoolboys; the Gryphon and the Mock Turtle, the old university grads; and so on. Guy Boas traced out the Oxford pattern in *Alice* even further: the Caterpillar and Alice represent the tutor and the undergraduate; the Oxford don dyspeptic is the Caterpillar; the don lugubrious, the Mock Turtle; the don nervous, the White Rabbit; the don inventive, the White Knight; the don magnificent, Humpty Dumpty—everything but the Don Quixote.

The world in which both Alice and the Don find themselves is, moreover, exceedingly hostile. It is forever seeking to trick and destroy them. The disagreeable people Alice meets torment and puzzle her; they are rude; they insult; they make the most atrocious puns. The Mad Tea-Party is filled with such:

> *"Take some more tea," the March Hare said to Alice, very earnestly.*
> *"I've had nothing yet," Alice replied in an offended tone: "so I can't take more."*
> *"You mean you can't take less," said the Hatter: "it's very easy to take more than nothing."*

Or, when listening to the Dormouse's story about three sisters who lived at the bottom of a treacle well and were learning to draw—treacle, of course—Alice ventured to ask a question:

> *"But I don't understand. Where did they draw the treacle from?"*
> *"You can draw water out of a water-well," said the Hatter; "so I should think you could draw treacle out of a treacle-well—eh, stupid?"*
> *"But they were in the well," Alice said to the Dormouse, not choosing to notice this last remark.*
> *"Of course they were," said the Dormouse: "well in."*

Alice is soon dizzy trying to follow the semantic flip-flops:

> *"Really, now you ask me," said Alice, very much confused, "I don't think—"*
> *"Then you shouldn't talk," said the Hatter.*
> *This piece of rudeness was more than Alice could bear: she got up in great disgust and walked off . . . .*

Don Quixote too must endure a thousand jokes, must be the victim of numberless conspiracies. The innkeeper, whom he has mistaken for the lord of a manor, decides "to make Sport that Night, resolv'd to humour him in his Desires" and puts the simple Don up to spending all night watching over his arms heaped in a horse trough. The Barber and the Curate, to cure their friend of his folly, stop up the door of his library, staunchly maintaining afterwards with the housekeeper, who is in on the deception, that there never has been such a room. The elaborate mockeries that the Duke and Duchess perpetrate occupy so large a part of *Don Quixote* and are so many and notorious they need scarcely be mentioned. Either the world is terrified at the madman, or it laughs at him.

Were ever two books more filled with madness? It is the theme that underlies both, constantly writhing and twisting to the surface. Wonderland is bedlam, the Cheshire Cat assures Alice:

> *"In* that *direction," the Cat said, waving its right paw around, "lives a Hatter: and in* that *direction," waving the other paw, "lives a March Hare. Visit either you like: they're both mad."*
>
> *"But I don't want to go among mad people," Alice remarked.*
>
> *"Oh, you can't help that," said the Cat: "we're all mad here. I'm mad. You're mad."*

They are: the Hatter, the March Hare, the Footman, the Queen of Hearts, the White Queen, the White Knight . . . all of them. "It's really dreadful," Alice mutters to herself, "the way all the creatures argue. It's enough to drive one crazy!"

The madness of *Don Quixote* is as pervasive as that of *Alice*, if basically different: in one the world is sane, the central character mad; in the other, the world is deranged, the central character rational. There is insanity elsewhere in *Don Quixote*—in the fits of Cardenio, for example—but it all comes to focus in the person of the Don himself. The situation in one book is that in the other seen in the looking-glass—contrariwise. And, as sometimes happens in looking in such a glass, we become confused. Is it actually the Don who is mad, the world which is sane? Isn't there something quite mad in Alice's sweet reasonableness? If, like the Canon, we stand "amaz'd at Don Quixote's methodical and orderly Madness," how are we to regard Alice's orderly and methodical sanity? Alice's seeming sanity and the Don's seeming madness have, moreover, a common result: they utterly alienate each from the "real" world about them. The Don's unreality constantly evokes wonder: "They'd look upon him, and admir'd him as a Man of another World." So the Unicorn looks on Alice a long time "with an air of the deepest disgust" before asking, "What—is—this?" He can scarcely believe she is real. "I always thought," he declares, "they were fabulous monsters!" So real, on the other hand, are Don Quixote's illusions, that practical, earthy Sancho comes to believe them himself. "At my return," he tells his wife, "thou shalt find me some Earl, or the Governor of some Island; ay, of one of the very best in the whole World . . . ." When Tweedledee tells Alice she is only "a sort of thing" in the Red King's dream, the question arises as to what would happen if he should wake.

> "Well, it's no use your talking about waking him," said Tweedledum, "when you're only one of the things in his dream. You know very well you're not real."
> "I am real!" said Alice, and began to cry.
> "You won't make yourself a bit realler by crying," Tweedledee remarked: "there's nothing to cry about."
> "If I wasn't real," Alice said—half laughing through her tears, it all seemed so ridiculous—"I shouldn't be able to cry."
> "I hope you don't suppose those are real tears?" Tweedledum interrupted in a tone of great contempt.

The question becomes curiouser and curiouser.

In the perverse world in which they find themselves, Alice and the Don are also utterly dependent on their own resources. The Don's romantic ideals bear no relationship to the "real" world; Alice's education seems all askew—the multiplication table tricks her; her geography is all backwards; when she recites her lessons, the words are all changed. Both fortunately have resources upon which to fall back, resources which are peculiarly powerful and much alike. Alice, according to a later essay by Lewis Carroll, was intended to be portrayed as "trustful, ready to accept the wildest impossibilities with all that utter trust that only dreamers know." Don Quixote too may be epitomized by these words, and it is in fact this same simple innocence which shields them both. It raises them above the things that always threaten not only to destroy them but, worse, their spirits. It is the source of that good-humored dignity which clings to them throughout the direst calamities, clothing them with an unassuming nobility, an integrity that must ultimately triumph.

The Knight, in his very first adventure, meeting two strumpets at the door of an inn (which he mistook for the gate of some huge castle), addresses them gravely and with courteous respect. "When they heard themselves stiled *Virgins*, a Thing so out of the Way of their Profession, they would not forbear laughing outright . . . ." In the first of an almost endless series of incidents, Don Quixote is scorned, his innocence mocked, his courtesy abused. Yet such is the terrible power of innocence that in just a few moments they are quietly and rather respectfully helping him remove his armor, listening attentively, though without understanding, to his speeches. "The two Females, who were not used to such rhetorical Speeches, could make no Answer to this; they only ask'd him whether he would eat any thing?" They play Magdalene to his Christ.

When, in Wonderland, the Caucus Race is over and the animals look to Alice to give the prize (it is her first encounter with these strange creatures), they imply in this gesture a certain superiority in her. Despite the initial peevishness of the Mouse and Alice's quarrel with the Lory, it is she who conquers them. She more than survives all the trials to which she is subjected—including the last great trial. They insult her, they may confuse her momentarily, but they can never subdue her. She throws them off with a characteristic toss of the head; her innocence shields her, as the Knight's shields him. She lives in that Golden Age, to return at last to Don Quixote's speech, when "Justice . . . was equally and impartially dispensed; nor was the Judge's Fancy Law," when ". . . the modest Maid might walk where-ever she pleas'd alone . . . ."

Finally, the story of Don Quixote and that of Alice end, as they must, in the same fashion—with the end of the dream. Both, like life, accelerate toward the close. A chapter near the end of *Don Quixote* is entitled "How Adventures Crouded So Thick and Threefold on Don Quixote, that They Trod Upon One Another's Heels." "Off with her head!" screams the fierce Red Queen. Suddenly both Alice and the Don burst out of their dream-world—wakening, disillusionment, and death. Both must at last look on Camelot, and the looking-glass cracks.

Don Quixote, returning home for the last time with Sancho and coming to an inn, sees it for what it is. When he is home, he falls into a deep sleep from which he awakens with his reason restored. "My Judgement is return'd clear and undisturb'd . . . ," he declares. His friends take this to be merely a new twist of his madness. "No more of that, I beseech you," he begs, ". . . pray Gentlemen, let us be serious." Like a good Catholic, he makes his last confession to the Curate, dictates his will to the Scrivener, lives three days more, and the Don, "a good natur'd Man, and of so agreeable a Behavior, that he was not only belov'd by his Family but by every one that knew him," dies.

Alice dies too—not physically perhaps, not the Alice who awakens, but the innocent, naïve, trusting Alice of the dream. That Alice is surely dead. If, as is often said, *Alice* is about the difficult and confusing process of growing up (the child shouted at, lectured, poked, examined, disciplined—and somehow, in spite of it all, becoming an adult), then the child in Alice perishes when she becomes sophisticated, self-conscious. "Who cares for *you*?" said Alice (she had grown to her full size by this time). "You're nothing but a pack of cards!" She is no longer innocent. She has eaten the fruit of the tree of knowledge, whose taste, as Milton says, is mortal.

But the greatest likeness between Alice and the Don lies not in parallels but in proportions. What common arrangement of elements, what blend of the tragic, comic, and heroic gives them their peculiar and characteristic savor? Certainly, first, they are both complex. This is not to say they are difficult to read; on the surface they are plainly enough written. They have the strange quality, however, shared by only a select few books—such as *Gulliver's Travels*—of being readable on several levels at the same time and without confusion. They resemble (if the comparison is not too hoary) a series of boxes nesting one within the other, each progressively more difficult to open and yielding a more valuable favor. And, as in any great work of art, the inmost can never quite be reached.

The outside box we can open almost as children: *Alice* is a child's story, a fantasy, a book of delightful nonsense; and *Don Quixote* is the comic, broadly humorous account of a foolish knight and his ridiculous squire. The next box is perhaps that which contains the two stories as satire: *Alice* becomes a satire on growing up and, obliquely, a tract on education; *Don Quixote* is a burlesque on chivalric romance—the level at which Byron understood it. Within this (and it may be that these boxes open in a different sequence to different readers) *Alice* is a commentary on Oxford; *Don Quixote*, here and there, on the Spain of his day. *Alice* is said to be crammed with mathematical allegory and whimsical logic. Both, Mr. Empson discovers, are versions of pastoral.

The very germ of both books, the content of the elusive last box, is the author himself. *Alice* and *Don Quixote* are autobiographical—not as that term may be applied to any piece of literature, but in a very special and significant sense: failure. Cervantes, who was, he thought, a failure at fifty, an impoverished writer of pastoral and chivalric romances which brought him neither fame nor satisfaction, creates for his single great masterpiece an impoverished gentleman "nigh fifty years of Age" who is driven mad by reading just such romances and strives in the person of a knight-errant to "purchase everlasting Honour and Renown." The "Knight of the Woeful Figure," one suspects, is the author; the story of the daft and noble knight for whose true virtue and courage the world has no reward is the story of Cervantes himself. Perhaps its effect was intended to be cathartic—the Knight is a fool indeed to believe that the wages of integrity and labor are fame in this world. But no man can really despise himself and continue to live. As the story of Don Quixote de la Mancha progresses, Cervantes reveals himself; the vitriolic caricature becomes gradually a sympathetic portrait; the fool turns into the wise man; the assassination is, in the end, an errand of mercy.

There are glimpses of Carroll to be found in scattered parts of *Alice*— in the Dodo, for example, or even in Alice's person now and again. But the only substantial self-portrait comes almost at the end of *Through the Looking-Glass*, in the figure of the ridiculous White Knight, who almost certainly is modeled after Don Quixote. It is he who, when Alice is about to be captured by the Red Knight, dashes in to save the lady in distress. "You will observe the Rules of Battle, of course?" he asks the Red Knight before they prepare to fight—he is as meticulous as the Don ever was to observe the conventions and rituals of chivalry. After the savage and foolish encounter ("It was a glorious victory, wasn't it?" he asks), Alice offers to help him off with his helmet—it is very awkward to remove—and abruptly we recall the kindness of the wenches to Don Quixote, their strange and benevolent defender.

"Now one can breathe more easily," said the Knight, putting back his shaggy hair with both hands, and turning his gentle face and large mild eyes to Alice. She thought she had never seen such a strange-looking soldier in all her life.

He resembles Don Quixote in many other ways, in the way he is dressed, for example: "He was dressed in tin armour, which seemed to fit him very badly...." He has a fondness, too, for making speeches:

"The great art of riding," the Knight suddenly began in a loud voice, waving his right arm as he spoke, "is to keep—" Here the sentence ended as suddenly as it had begun, as the Knight fell heavily on the top of his head....

He is forever inventing things which bear no relationship to the real world about him—as Don Quixote invents castles and virgins and giants. He has anklets on his horse's feet to guard against the bites of sharks. He prudently carries with him a box for clothes and sandwiches—as Don Quixote resolved to take along, after his first misadventure, money and clean shirts—but to keep out the rain he hangs it lid down. Under his folly, though, as under Don Quixote's, is a good and kindly purpose—and a part of the author himself.

Probably the warmest, most gently affectionate passage in either *Alice* book is the following:

Of all the strange things that Alice saw in her journey Through the Looking-Glass, this was the one that she always remembered most clearly. Years afterwards she could bring the whole scene back again, as if it had been only yesterday—the mild blue eyes and kindly smile of the Knight—the setting sun gleaming through his hair, and shining on his armour in a blaze of light that quite dazzled her—the horse quietly moving about, with the reins hanging loose on his neck, cropping the grass at her feet—and the black shadows of the forest behind—all this she took in like a picture, as, with one hand shading her eyes, she leant against a tree, watching the strange pair, and listening, in a half-dream, to the melancholy music of the song.

Here Lewis Carroll tries to stay for a moment Alice's ever-accelerating journey. She is in the Seventh Square now; one more and she becomes a queen—and the Reverend Mr. Dodgson must lose another of his child-friends. She is still too innocent to understand what it means to the lonely, gentle, and foolish White Knight; he understands only too well.

"You've only a few yards to go," he said, "down the hill and over that little brook, and then you'll be a Queen—But you'll stay and see me off first?" he added as Alice turned with an eager look in the direction to which he pointed. "I shan't be long. You'll wait and wave your handkerchief when I get to that turn in the road! I think it'll encourage me, you see."

She does wait, of course, though perhaps somewhat impatient to get on.

"I hope it encouraged him," she said, as she turned to run down the hill: "and now for the last brook, and to be a Queen! How grand it sounds!"

It is difficult to say, finally, whether *Don Quixote* and *Alice* are essentially comic or tragic. If it is true that comedy tends to make all things equal, the high low and the low high, then, to that extent, they are comic. "For it may be said of Knight-Errantry, as of Love," Don Quixote tells Sancho, "that it makes all Things equal." The leveling process continues inevitably in both books: Don Quixote is humbled, Sancho is exalted; the fierce creatures are nothing but a pack of cards, and Alice is a queen. Or if we say the comic spirit manifests itself in endless and diverting conversation, then also they are comic. Few books are so packed with interesting talk. Bergson ascribed comedy to "rigidity," a certain "mechanical elasticity" in action or character—of which, he said, citing the Don, the absent-minded individual is a favorite example and the somnambulist, the supreme. Here, too, we would have to consider both books comic—though Bergson would admit no benevolence into his definition, and benevolence is at the very heart of *Alice* and *Don Quixote*.

But all these remarks avoid the particular quality which sets off Alice and the Don and gives them their unique and piquant flavor. They are, I suppose we shall have to agree, comic—but they are also heroic. Not mock-heroic, genuinely heroic. That is why we cannot laugh at them, as Bergson would have us, without feeling. You do not laugh at what you have learned to revere. Do we not admire Alice's heroism and the Don's? They have indomitable courage; they persevere against frightful odds; they are determined never to submit or yield. If, then, they contain something of their creators, we ought not to be surprised.

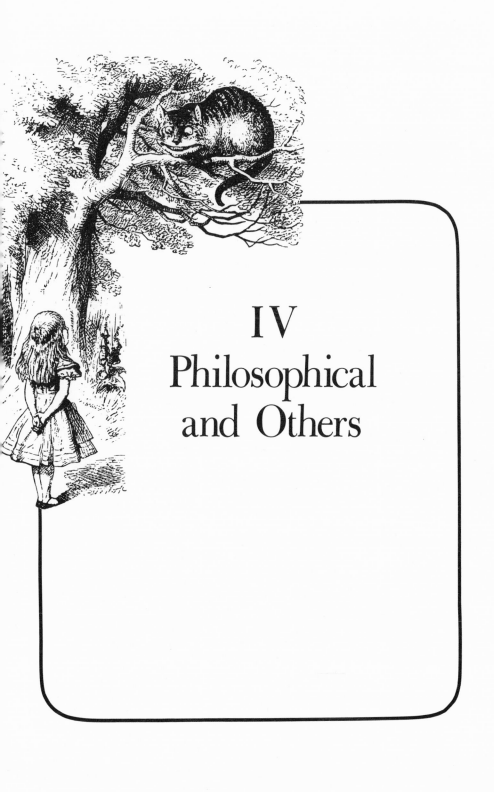

IV
Philosophical
and Others

The Philosopher's

ALICE
IN WONDERLAND

by Roger W. Holmes

(1959)

HAVE YOU EVER seen Nobody? What would your world be like if objects had no names? Can you remember what will happen week after next? How many impossible things can you believe before breakfast—*if* you hold your breath and shut your eyes? These questions transport us to the world of Lewis Carroll: to Wonderland, with the White Rabbit and the Mock Turtle and the pool of tears and the Mad Hatter's tea-party; to the Looking-Glass country, with its Garden of Insects and the Jabberwocky and the Walrus and the Carpenter and shoes and ships and sealing wax and cabbages and kings. They also transport us to the realm of Philosophy.

Alice's Adventures in Wonderland and *Through the Looking-Glass* belong most obviously and particularly to children, whether in nurseries or bomb shelters. We can never forget Mrs. Miniver reading aloud to her children while enemy planes roared overhead:

Lastly, she pictured to herself how this same little sister of hers would, in the after-time, herself be a grown woman; how she would keep, through all her riper years, the simple and loving heart of her childhood; and how she would gather about her other little children, and make their *eyes bright and eager with many a strange tale, perhaps even with the dream of Wonderland of long ago; and how she would feel with all their simple sorrows, and find a pleasure in all their simple joys, remembering her own child-life, and the happy summer days.*

Few who step through the magic mirror into the Looking-Glass country realize that its landscape is a chessboard and its events part of a chess problem: "White Pawn (Alice) to play, and win in seven moves."[1] Still fewer know that both Wonderland and the Looking-Glass country belong to the logician and the philosopher as much as to parents and children. These regions are crowded with the problems and paraphernalia of logic and metaphysics and theory of knowledge and ethics. Here are superbly imaginative treatments of logical principles, the uses and meanings of words, the functions of names, the perplexities connected with time and space, the problem of personal identity, the status of substance in relation to its qualities, the mind-body problem.

Sometimes Lewis Carroll presents his readers with an amusing logical absurdity, as when the Duchess in *Alice's Adventures in Wonderland* produces, "Never imagine yourself not to be otherwise than what it might appear to others that what you were or might have been was not otherwise than what you had been would have appeared to them to be otherwise" in her attempt to "put more simply" her exhortation to Alice to "be what you would seem to be." Or he merely touches ideas playfully, as in the Cheshire Cat's proof that he is mad:

[Alice] "And how do you know that you're mad?"
"To begin with," said the Cat, "a dog's not mad. You grant that?"
"I suppose so," said Alice.
"Well, then," the Cat went on, "you see a dog growls when it's angry, and wags its tail when it's pleased. Now I growl when I'm pleased, and wag my tail when I'm angry. Therefore I'm mad!"

This may not be good logic, but it has philosophic implications.

Sometimes Carroll finds an unforgettable illustration of a major principle. We know that if all apples are red, it does not follow that all red things are apples: the logician's technical description of this is the non-convertibility *simpliciter* of universal proportions. The Hatter at the famous tea-party has just proposed the provokingly incomplete riddle about the raven and the writing desk. The March Hare says to Alice:

"Do you mean that you think you can find out the answer to it?"
"Exactly so," said Alice.
"Then you should say what you mean," the March Hare went on.
"I do," Alice hastily replied; "at least—at least I mean what I say—that's the same thing you know."
"Not the same thing a bit!" said the Hatter. "Why, you might just as well say that 'I see what I eat' is the same thing as 'I eat what I see'!"
"You might just as well say," added the March Hare, "that 'I like what I get' is the same thing as 'I get what I like'!"
"You might just as well say," added the Dormouse, which seemed to be talking in its sleep, "that 'I breathe when I sleep' is the same thing as 'I sleep when I breathe'!"
"It is the same thing with you," said the Hatter.

The Dormouse goes back to sleep, but logic comes to life.

Most often Carroll uses the absurd hilarity of Wonderland to bring difficult technical concepts into sharp focus; and for this gift teachers of logic and philosophy have unmeasured admiration and gratitude. One need not try to do division with Roman numerals to appreciate the value of including the zero among numbers, even though zero counts nothing. In the related field of logic the null class, the class without members, is as useful but more difficult to explain. The class of female presidents of the United States is a genuine class, but as a simple matter of empirical fact it is as of 1959 a class without members. Lewis Carroll reminds us that we often refer to this curious but important logical entity. The White King is waiting for his messengers and asks Alice to look along the road to see if they are coming:

"I see nobody on the road," said Alice.
"I only wish I had such eyes," the King remarked in a fretful tone. "To be able to see Nobody! And at that distance too! Why, it's as much as I can do to see real people, by this light."

This is amusing and, without benefit of logic, it is also confusing. When the messenger finally arrives, several pages later, confusion is doubly confounded:

"Who did you pass on the road?" the King went on. . . .
"Nobody," said the Messenger.
"Quite right," said the King; "this young lady saw him too. So of course Nobody walks slower than you."
"I do my best," the Messenger said in a sullen tone. "I'm sure nobody walks much faster than I do!"
"He can't do that," said the King, "or else he'd have been here first."

"Nobody" may stand for no person, but you had better be careful how you talk about him!

The logician in Lewis Carroll was fascinated by words. In the poem about the Jabberwocky, "Twas brillig and the slithly toves/did gyre and gimble in the wabe . . . ," words are used as portmanteaus; Humpty Dumpty explained: "mimsy" meant both *miserable* and *flimsy*, packing in two meanings at once. Of all words, name-words have given the philosopher and the logician most trouble. No one (remember him?) knew this better than Lewis Carroll. Alice has just boasted to the Gnat that she can name the insects:

"Of course they answer to their names?" the Gnat remarked carelessly.
"I never knew them to do that."
"What's the use of their having names," the Gnat said, "if they won't answer to them?"
"No use to them," said Alice, "but it's useful to the people that name them, I suppose. If not, why do things have names at all?"

Why, indeed? Medieval philosophers fought bitterly about this. Alice seems to be a Nominalist, suggesting that names are tags by which we can conveniently denote objects without having to point. But a few pages later she comes to the Wood-where-things-have-no-names and quickly discovers what the Medieval Realists knew: that names have a connotation as well as a denotation. She meets a fawn and, since the fawn cannot in this magic place remember that Alice is a "child," he allows her to pet him and put her arm around his neck, as in the famous illustration by Tenniel. As soon as they reach the edge of the wood the fawn darts away in fright. So names are more than tags: they convey information. Such a wood evokes fascinating philosophic speculation. Suppose we could remember no names. Not only would it be impossible to communicate with anyone about objects except by pointing, but also we should be unable to generalize and should have to rely entirely on conditioned responses. The fawn might still be afraid of Alice *if* it had experienced children; but Alice could have no rational knowledge, could not be human in the usual sense.

Humpty Dumpty is a Realist when he asks Alice what her name means.

> "Must *a name mean something?" Alice asked doubtfully. "Of course it must," Humpty Dumpty said with a short laugh: "my name means the shape I am—and a good handsome shape it is, too. With a name like yours, you might be any shape, almost."*

But our egghead friend shows a Nominalist tendency a little later when the advantage of Un-birthdays comes under discussion and he points out how nice it would be to get Un-birthday presents 364 days of the year rather than birthday presents only once. "That's glory for you," he says.

> "*I don't know what you mean by 'glory,'" Alice said.*
> *Humpty Dumpty smiled contemptuously. "Of course you don't—till I tell you. I mean 'there's a nice knock-down argument for you!'"*
> *"But 'glory' doesn't mean 'a nice knock-down argument,'" Alice objected.*
> *"When I use the word," Humpty Dumpty said in a rather scornful tone, "it means just what I choose it to mean—neither more nor less."*
> *"The question is," said Alice, "whether you can make words mean so many different things."*
> *"The question is," said Humpty Dumpty, "which is to be the master— that's all."*

A little later Humpty Dumpty gets impatient and uses the word "impenetrability" to mean, "We've had enough of that subject, and it would be just as well if you'd mention what you mean to do next, as I suppose you don't mean to stop here all the rest of your life." When Alice observes that that is a great deal to make one word mean, our learned egg closes the argument by saying: "When I make a word do a lot of work like that I always pay it extra. You should see them come around to me on a Saturday night, for to get their wages, you know." The problem raised here is of the first importance to philosophy. *May* we, like Humpty Dumpty, make our words mean whatever we choose them to mean? One thinks of a Soviet delegate using "democracy" in a UN debate. May we pay our words extra, or is this the stuff that propaganda is made of? Do we have an obligation to past usage? In one sense words are our masters, or communication would be impossible. In another, we are the masters; otherwise there could be no poetry.

The most complex discussion of the function of words takes place between Alice and the White Knight when the latter offers to sing Alice a song. This passage is a classic. The Knight announces that the name of the song "is called 'Haddock's Eyes' " and the following famous conversation ensues:

> "Oh, that's the name of the song, is it?" Alice said, trying to feel interested.
> "No, you don't understand," the Knight said, looking a little vexed. "That's what the name is called. The name really is "The Aged Aged Man.' "
> "Then I ought to have said 'That's what the song is called,'?" Alice corrected herself.
> "No, you oughtn't: that's quite another thing! The song is called 'Ways and Means': but that's only what it's called, you know!"
> "Well, what is the song, then?" said Alice, who was by this time completely bewildered.
> "I was coming to that," the Knight said. "The song really is 'A-sitting On A Gate. . . .' "

The issues it raises are technical and abstract, but not without excitement. Pause and analyze the situation which the White Knight describes. There are two things involved, the name of the song and the song itself. Of the name it can be said a) what the name *is*, b) what the name *is called*. And of the song itself it can be said a) what *the song* is, and b) what *the song* is called.

Start with the name. John Keats is named *John,* but this is not necessarily what the name is called. If I were to introduce Keats ("This is John Keats"), I should be doing two things. In the first place I should be giving his name, and in the second I should be telling what symbol we use for his name in English. On the Piazza Espagna in Rome there is a tablet saying that a certain *Giovanni* Keats died in an adjacent building. Surely "Giovanni" is what Italians *call* Keats's first name! Does it not follow that "John" is what Keats's countrymen call it? What *is* his name? John? Giovanni? Johann? Ian? Or something to which all these refer? You might be perplexed if asked whether you enjoyed the music of Joseph Green, but this recalls the composer of *La Traviata* quite as surely as Giovanni Keats is the author of the "Ode on a Grecian Urn."

The perplexity about Keats can be resolved patriotically by assigning the symbol used in the country of birth as *the* name. Keats's given name is John; all others are what the name is called by *Auslanders*. But what about common nouns? A thing like a twenty-four-hour interval has no birthplace, no country. It is variously referred to as "day" or "*jour*" or "*Tag*" or "*giorno*" or any of a large number of symbols. What about the name itself of what we call "d-a-y"? Clearly it has no name. But *it itself* is called "day" or "*jour*" or whatnot and we are immediately in the White Knight's second major division: things and what things are called. If we are to believe the White Knight, we can be sure that classes of things, such as twenty-four-hour periods, are not called by their names!

The word "call" is ambiguous. We call a person by name or nickname: if I had known Keats intimately I might *call* him "Jack." In another sense I describe him to someone else; then I *call* him "England's greatest romantic poet" or "one whose name is writ in water." The first illustrates what a name is called, and is the arbitrary assigning of a tag to an individual. The second is an example of what a thing is called, and how information is conveyed. You might say that Keats was so many inches tall; he could then be called a man of such-and-such a stature. You might call a day a period of so many minutes, or a pebble on the beach of Time. Here is essentially the difference between a dictionary and an encyclopedia: the one gives information about names, the other provides data about things. Except, as the White Knight made clear, the items in a dictionary are not properly names at all!

We come, finally, to the thing itself. And here Lewis Carroll was definitely pulling our leg. The White Knight said that the song he was singing *was* "A-sitting On A Gate"—but remember that that was not its name! It was not even what the thing was called—a sad song or a lengthy one. What could it be, if it is neither the name of the song nor a description of the song? It could only be *the thing itself*. The nearest we can come to it is to point or shout—"this" or "that" or "Hey, you!" Recall the Beaver in *The Hunting of the Snark*, who had forgotten his name.

> *He would answer to "Hi" or to any loud cry,*
>   *Such as "Fry me!" or "Fritter my wig!"*
> *To "What-you-may-call-um!" or "What was his name!"*
>   *But especially "Thing-um-a-jig!"*

To be consistent, the White Knight, when he had said that the song *is* . . . , could only have burst into the song itself. Whether consistent or not, the White Knight is Lewis Carroll's cherished gift to logicians.

One more passage in *Through the Looking-Glass* delights the logician. The White Queen has just told Alice she is exactly one hundred and one, five months, and a day.

> *"I can't believe that!" said Alice.*
> *"Can't you?" the Queen said in a pitying tone. "Try again: draw a long breath, and shut your eyes."*
> *Alice laughed. "There's no use trying," she said, "one* can't *believe impossible things."*
> *"I daresay you haven't had much practice," said the Queen. "When I was your age, I always did it for a half-hour a day. Why, sometimes I've believed as many as six impossible things before breakfast."*

Can one believe impossible things? If I told you I had seen an eagle whose markings were an exact replica of the America flag, you might say, "Impossible!" But you would be wrong. Such a bird is only improbable. You could believe in the existence of such a creature any time of day if the evidence were sufficiently persuasive—and it might be. But if I told you I had in my pocket a fine example of a round square, you would again say, "Impossible!" and this time you would be right. No matter how long you hold your breath, or how early you make the effort, it is both true and significant that you cannot believe impossible things. Much can be said about this built-in rejector of the illogical. Without it we should be as desperately zany as the White Queen.

The wealth of material which Lewis Carroll presents for the illuminating of philosophy is almost without end. In Wonderland, for example, a baby turns gradually into a pig. Could there be a more telling illustration of the importance of causes, or of their significance? Wonderland was also a place where it was always teatime. The Mad Hatter had recited a poem at the Queen's party and she had shouted that he was murdering time ("Off with his head!") and ever since then it had remained six o'clock. Can one discuss time as a metaphysical dimension without reference to this party? And the Looking-Glass country had its peculiarities too. For one thing, time went backwards—but more about time later. It was also a place where space presented problems. When Alice walked into the garden from the Looking-Glass house she discovered that she could only get to a hill which she saw in the distance by walking in the opposite direction. Alice had a hectic encounter with the Red Queen when she learned that they must run as fast as they could to stay in one place, and twice as fast to get anywhere else. These instances, like many in the *Mary Poppins* books, raise questions of the nature of the world in which we live and are a delight to the student of metaphysics. Dorothy Thompson devoted one of her best columns to the trial of the Jack of Hearts in the final chapter of *Alice's Adventures in Wonderland*, showing with devastating effect its similarities to legal procedures in Hitler's Germany, and raising one of the philosopher's favorite subjects, Justice. Alice wondered what happens to the flame of a candle when the candle is put out, while she was shutting up like a telescope during her first adventure in Wonderland, wondered whether she would go out altogether—"like a candle." The Pre-Socratics enjoyed that problem. What *does* happen to the flame?

Some of the philosophic problems are perennial. In her bewilderment at the sudden changes in her size and the conversations with a unique rabbit who wore a vest and gloves and carried a watch, Alice asks herself, "Who in the world am I? Ah, *that's* the great puzzle." And it is one of the greatest of philosophic puzzles, the problem of personal identity. Alice began thinking over all the children she knew that were of the same age as herself, to see if she could have changed for any of them. She could not be Ada, for Ada's hair went in such long ringlets (Materialism). She could not be Mabel, for Alice knew all sorts of things and Mabel knew so very little (Idealism). Multiplication table? $4 \times 5 = 12$. $4 \times 6 = 13$. Oh dear! Geography? London is the capital of Paris, Paris is the capital of Rome. *That's* all wrong. "How doth the little—crocodile." None of this was right: she could not be Mabel. Alice came to the comforting conclusion that she would not do anything her grownups commanded until they could tell her who she was. Here is domestic subversion for which philosophy is the only cure.

The Cheshire Cat offers perplexities. You will remember that he possessed an ability unique among cats. He could disappear, leaving his smile behind. Shades of all discussions of substance and its accidents! Here is a smile without a head. The animal has the fascination of a nightmare: he belongs to a different universe. This feline had another disturbing practice: it would appear and disappear—gradually—starting with the tip of its tail and ending with its smile, or vice versa. This is not so alarming. We belong to such a world. We have seen dry ice disappear; we have seen crystals come into existence. The disappearing stunt is mentioned because it provides later in the Wonderland book an argument amusingly similar to William James's famous illustration of the meaning of Pragmatism.

If a man walks around a tree on which there is a squirrel who never turns his back on the man, does the man walk around the squirrel? The Cheshire Cat has been bold enough to offend the King and the King asks the Queen to have it removed, whereupon she applies her universal panacea, "Off with his head!" When Alice arrived on the scene a considerable argument was under way involving the King, the Queen, and the executioner. The Cat's head, minus body, was an interested spectator.

The executioner's argument was that you couldn't cut off a head unless there was a body to cut it off from: that he had never had to do such a thing before, and he wasn't going to begin at his time of life.

The King's argument was that anything that had a head could be beheaded, and that you weren't to talk nonsense.

The Queen's argument was that, if something wasn't done about it in less than no time, she'd have everybody executed all round. (It was this last remark that had made the whole party look so grave and anxious.)

William James would have solved this problem by defining the meaning of "behead," as he so helpfully centered attention on "walk around" in the case of the squirrel. The Cheshire Cat unphilosophically dodged the issue by disappearing altogether, leaving the King and the executioner running wildly up and down while the rest of the party went back to the croquet game.

Alice's Adventures in Wonderland contains fewer references to philosophy than does *Through the Looking-Glass*. After the success of the former, Lewis Carroll may have been more conscious of his approach in the sequel. It would be stretching a point to find Plato's moral universe in the Duchess's annoying habit of prefacing each of her remarks with "And the moral of *that* is. . . ." And it would be unfair to lay stress on the Mock Turtle's remark that no wise fish would go anywhere without a porpoise. When Alice asked about this, the Mock Turtle replied, "Why if a fish came to *me*, and told me he was going for a journey, I should say 'With what porpoise?'" Read a teleological metaphysics into this if you wish. But when in *Through the Looking-Glass* the White Knight has fallen off his horse for the *n*th time and is resting peacefully head-downwards, talking with Alice:

"How can you go on talking so quietly, head downwards?" Alice asked, as she dragged him out by the feet and laid him in a heap on the

bank. The Knight looked surprised at the question. "What does it matter where my body happens to be?" he said. "My mind goes on working all the time."

he shows himself loyal to the Cartesian dualism of Mind and Body, though he has reservations of which Descartes would not have approved: "In fact, the more head-downwards I am, the more I keep inventing things." As, for example, the pudding made out of blotting paper and gunpowder and sealing wax. Surely the advantage of the head-downwards position for inventing things argues an interaction theory.

Another passage of major philosophic interest from the *Looking-Glass* book has to do with dreams. Tweedledum and Tweedledee and Alice are watching the Red King, who is sleeping fit to snore his head off, as Tweedledum remarked:

> *"He's dreaming now," said Tweedledee, "and what do you think he's dreaming about?"*
> *Alice said, "Nobody can guess that."*
> *"Why, about you!" Tweedledee explained, clapping his hands triumphantly. "And if he left off dreaming about you, where do you suppose you'd be?"*
> *"Where I am now, of course," said Alice.*
> *"Not you!" Tweedledee retorted contemptuously. "You'd be nowhere. Why, you're only a sort of thing in his dream!"*
> *"If that there King was to wake," added Tweedledum, "you'd go out—bang!—just like a candle."*
> *"I shouldn't!" Alice exclaimed indignantly. "Besides if I'm only a sort of thing in his dream, what are you, I should like to know?"*
> *"Ditto," said Tweedledum.*
> *"Ditto, ditto!" cried Tweedledee.*

The Red King performs the function of God in the philosophy of Bishop Berkeley, for whom the tree in the forest exists when there are no humans to perceive it. To be is to be perceived, ultimately in the mind of God—or the Red King. When Lewis Carroll plays with Idealism in this manner, its difficulties are aptly revealed:

> *He shouted this so loud that Alice couldn't help saying, "Hush! You'll be waking him, I'm afraid, if you make so much noise."*
> *"Well, it's no use your talking about waking him," said Tweedledum, "when you're only one of the things in his dream. You know very well you're not real."*

Here we are at the central problem of philosophy, the problem of the

nature of reality, and confronted, as all philosophers are, with the threat
of the subjectivity of knowledge (the ego-centric predicament). How
can I be sure of the reality of anything except my experiences? Alice
invokes a well-recognized criterion of distinguishing between reality and
dreams:

> *"I am real!" said Alice, and began to cry.*
> *"You won't make yourself a bit realler by crying," Tweedledee*
> *remarked; "there's nothing to cry about."*
> *"If I wasn't real," Alice said—half laughing through her tears, it all*
> *seemed so ridiculous—"I shouldn't be able to cry."*
> *"I hope you don't suppose those are real tears?" Tweedledum inter-*
> *rupted in a tone of great contempt.*

If we all exist in the mind of Berkeley's God, just as Alice and Tweedledum and Tweedledee existed in the slumbering mind of the Red King,
tears will exist in God's mind also—and in the Red King's dream. Tweedledum was so good a philosopher as to see that Bishop Berkeley has the
final word here.

Alice thought she had a good point. Dreams are usually less orderly
than waking experiences: in fact, the fascination of dreams is that laws
are broken with delightful unexpectedness. Fundamentally, this is the
fascination underlying both of Lewis Carroll's books, for in both Alice
wakes up from sleep in the final chapter. In a dream, Alice argued,
crying might not produce tears (though the reader remembers that it had
produced a whole pool of them in Wonderland!), and, since there were
tears, she might not be part of the Red King's dream. But what if dreams
are orderly? Is there escape from this subjectivism? The problem is
ancient and has many facets. We leave it suspended in doubtfulness as
Lewis Carroll left it and as it has been left, I believe, by the entire
history of philosophy.

Lewis Carroll is at his best when he considers time. The Looking-
Glass country was a place in which time moved backwards. Through a
playful reference to memory, he approaches the curious character of
Looking-Glass punishment:

> *"What sort of things do you remember best?" Alice ventured to ask.*
> *"Oh, things that happened the week after next," the Queen replied*
> *in a careless tone. "For instance, now," she went on, sticking a large*
> *piece of plaster on her finger as she spoke, "there's the King's Messenger.*

He's in prison now, being punished; and the trial doesn't even begin till next Wednesday; and of course the crime comes last of all."

"Suppose he never commits the crime?" said Alice.

"That would be all the better, wouldn't it?" the Queen said, as she bound the plaster around her finger with a bit of ribbon.

Alice felt there was no denying that. "Of course it would be all the better," she said, "but it wouldn't be all the better his being punished."

"You're wrong there, at any rate," said the Queen. "Were you ever punished?"

"Only for faults," said Alice.

"And you were all the better for it, I know!" the Queen said triumphantly.

"Yes, but then I had done the things I was punished for," said Alice, "that makes all the difference."

"But if you hadn't done them," the Queen said, "that would have been better still, better, and better, and better."

Alice was sure there was a mistake somewhere. It reminds one of the story about the irate father who spanked his son for fighting. When the boy insisted he had not been in a fight the father replied, as he continued to apply the hairbrush, that even if he had not been in one that day he was sure to be in one soon. Unless we take this parent's alarming attitude toward "punishment," we are as much disturbed as Alice about punishment coming before the crime. How could the Mikado make the punishment fit the crime in such a world?

It just does not make sense. Punishment exists in a Bergsonian time-with-direction. As everyone knows who has seen movies run backwards, most human actions so lose their significance when reversed as to appear hilarious. One of the standard amusements in the nickelodeon days was to run backward a film of a man eating steak. Bergson had much to say about memory: he must have been amused at the Queen's remark that she remembered best things that happened the week after next. Past and future are not interchangeable, as is clearly illustrated later in the story, when Alice and the King and the Lion and the Unicorn sit down to enjoy a cake which Alice is asked to cut:

Alice had seated herself on the bank of a little brook, with the great dish on her knees, and was sawing away diligently with the knife. "It's very provoking!" she said, in reply to the Lion. "I've cut several slices already, but they always join on again!"

"You don't know how to manage Looking-Glass cakes," the Unicorn remarked. "Hand it around first, and cut it afterwards."

This sounded nonsense, but Alice very obediently got up, and carried

*the dish around, and the cake divided itself into three pieces as she
did so.*

*"Now cut it up," said the Lion, as she returned to her place with the
empty dish.*

Alice sat down puzzled, not only because she had no cake herself, but
also because it would be extremely difficult to cut no cake. Even our old
friend the null class does not help in this situation. The cutting of a cake
is an action that looks greedily to the future; reverse it and you get nonsense as well as no cake. Bergson is vindicated.

While we are considering time, there is one Looking-Glass event that
deserves special attention. It has to do with the plaster that the White
Queen had applied to her finger while she was expounding the theory of
punishment in her world. Alice was interrupted in her objections to this
theory by the screams of the Queen:

*"Oh, oh, oh!" shouted the Queen, shaking her hand as if she wanted
to shake it off. "My finger's bleeding! Oh, oh, oh!"*

*Her screams were so exactly like the whistle of a steam-engine that
Alice had to hold both her hands over her ears.*

*"What is the matter?" she said, as soon as there was a chance of
making herself heard. "Have you pricked your finger?"*

*"I haven't pricked it yet," the Queen said, "but I soon shall—oh,
oh, oh!"*

*"When do you expect to do it?" Alice asked, feeling much inclined
to laugh.*

*"When I fasten my shawl again," the poor Queen groaned out, "the
brooch will come undone directly. Oh, oh!" As she said the words the
brooch flew open, and the Queen clutched wildly at it, and tried to clasp
it again.*

*"Take care!" cried Alice. "You're holding it all crooked!" And she
caught at the brooch, but it was too late: the pin slipped, and the Queen
had pricked her finger.*

*"That accounts for the bleeding, you see," she said to Alice with a
smile. "Now you understand the way things happen here."*

*"But why don't you scream now?" Alice asked, holding her hands
ready to put over her ears again.*

*"Why I've done all the screaming already," said the Queen. "What
would be the good of having it all over again?"*

If one denies the Vitalistic significance of a bleeding wound and its
repair, this particular incident is more curious than impossible. One *might*
live in a world in which the screams and the pain came before the pin
prick. Here is reversible time, the time Mechanists insist on, strange only

because misunderstood. Within this temporal framework one must elimi-nate purposeful significances, such as catching at a brooch *in order to* pin it. But such a world is possible: certain philosophers from Democritus through Spinoza to the present have recommended it. The world of the self-dividing cake is not.

One final temporal reference has also to do with the poor disheveled White Queen, who couldn't keep her shawl straight and who had got her brush so tangled in her hair that Alice had to retrieve it for her. Alice said she thought the Queen should have a lady's maid to take care of her:

> *"I'm sure I'll take* you *with pleasure!" the Queen said. "Twopence a week, and jam every other day."*
>
> *Alice couldn't help but laughing, as she said, "I don't want you to hire me—and I don't care for jam."*
>
> *"It's very good jam," said the Queen.*
>
> *"Well, I don't want any* today, *at any rate."*
>
> *"You couldn't have it if you* did *want it," the Queen said. "The rule is jam tomorrow and jam yesterday—but never jam* today."
>
> *"It* must *come sometime to 'jam today,'" Alice objected.*
>
> *"No, it can't," said the Queen. "It's jam every* other *day; today isn't any other day, you know."*
>
> *"I don't understand you," said Alice. "It's dreadfully confusing!"*

And so it is. The difficulty is partly the result of one of Lewis Carroll's favorite devices in entertaining children, the play on words. It is also in part the philosophic problem of knowing when the present becomes the past and the future the present. It is the problem with which James was concerned when he described time as shaped like a saddle. It is the problem that bothers the Idealist when he realizes that he can never know the present: to know it is to make it an object of our thinking and hence to put it into the past. Can the present ever be known? Can we ever have jam in the todayness of tomorrow? By its nature tomorrow must come; also, by its very definition, it can never come. The Queen promises Alice jam, but tells her in the same words that she can never have it! Here is one of the famous paradoxes connected with time.

The delight afforded by Lewis Carroll to logicians and philosophers, as well as to children and parents, is rare and brilliant and inexhaustible. You will enjoy rereading *Alice's Adventures in Wonderland* and *Through the Looking-Glass* and finding other riches. You would do well, for example, to consider the Dormouse's wonderful story about the three sisters who lived at the bottom of a treacle well—and were well in. They were learning to draw and "they drew all manner of things—everything that begins with an M, such as mouse-traps, and the moon, and memory, and muchness." Have you ever tried to draw memory or muchness? A whole aesthetic theory could begin with this text. Or you might try Alice's encounter with the Wonderland Caterpillar. Or the extraordinary conversation between Alice and the White Queen and the Red Queen at the Looking-Glass banquet.

And do not stop with these two books. The world of Lewis Carroll is more extensive than most travelers in it realize. Less familiar, though unforgettable once visited, is the wild region of the Snark and the Boojum and the Bellman's problem with the bowsprit that got mixed with the rudder sometimes, in *The Hunting of the Snark*. The more conventional land of the story of *Sylvie and Bruno* and the amusing architecture of Lewis Carroll's logic exercises are now seldom included in an itinerary. There is even a vacation spot for students of government, the little-known "The Dynamics of a Parti-cle," involving plain superficiality, obtuse anger, and acute anger (the inclination of two voters to one another whose views are not in the same direction); a world in which a speaker may digress from one point to another, a controversy be raised about any question and at any distance from that question. *Parti-cles* are divided into genius and speeches, and a *surd* is a radical whose meaning cannot be exactly ascertained. Lewis Carroll, when he stepped back into the real world, was Charles Dodgson, who taught mathematics to men and logic to women at Oxford. A serious contribution to the field of logic is characteristically entitled "What the Tortoise Said to Achilles."

When Alice told her sister all her strange adventures, her sister said:

"It was a curious dream, dear, certainly; but now run to your tea; it's getting late."
So Alice got up and ran off, thinking while she ran, as well she might, what a wonderful dream it had been.

None more wonderful. If this essay has any "porpoise" it is to send you, the reader, to the pleasures of philosophy and logic by way of the unique fascination of Lewis Carroll. And do not get caught in the elusiveness of Alice's jam. Do not promise yourself the delights of philosophy tomorrow. Enjoy them now: take Lewis Carroll down from the shelf tonight.

WONDERLAND

Revisited

by Harry Levin

(1965)

IN THE twentieth century's commemoration of the nineteenth, we have reached the centennial of Alice. Not uncharacteristically, the date has been somewhat blurred. The author, whose fussiness has endeared him to bibliophiles, was dissatisfied with the first edition, so that *Alice in Wonderland* was not publicly issued until 1866. Moreover, if we wish to celebrate the occasion on which the tale was first told, we must look back to that famous boating party of three little girls and two dons on July 4, 1862. That "golden afternoon," as Lewis Carroll describes it in his introductory poem, was actually—as modern research has discovered—"wet and rather cool." Fancy has been at work from the very outset. The rain that had overtaken the same group of five picnickers during an earlier expedition on June 17 seems to have inspired the pool of tears, wherein Alice's sisters Lorina and Edith are immortalized as the Lory and the Eaglet, while their companions Duckworth and Dodgson appear as the Duck and the Dodo. But the date specified in the story is May 4, Alice Liddell's tenth birthday; and, since the heroine of *Through the Looking-Glass and What Alice Found There* is exactly seven and a half just six months later, perhaps her adventures should be predated at 1859.

At all events, the fantasy has now lasted one hundred years. What is more surprising, it has withstood the stringent test of translation into forty-seven languages (by the reckoning of Dr. Warren Weaver, whose collection, ranging from Finnish to Swahili and from Chinese to Esperanto versions, should harbor an independent interest for cultural anthropologists). Excerpts have been quoted in, and out of, every conceivable context. Clearly the *Alice* books must embody certain archetypes, they must touch off some of the deeper responses of human consciousness, in order to have penetrated so far beyond their immediate period and culture. Yet, looking back to them from our present distance, we may also note that they were deeply embedded in their mid-Victorian matrix, that they remain as distinctively English as their heroine's name. Now, the English have no monopoly on nonsense—or, for that matter, on common sense. However, it may be no accident that they have excelled so conspicuously in both. It may be that the one is the price paid for—or else the bonus gained from—the other, that a hard-working sense of practicality gets its recreation from the enjoyment of absurdity. The nonsense of Lewis Carroll has been defined by a French fantast, André Breton, as "the vital solution to a profound contradiction between the acceptance of faith and the exercise of reason."

It was the voice of reason that spoke through the tongue of Edmund Burke, when he remarked: "Though no man can draw a stroke between the confines of night and day, yet darkness and light are on the whole tolerably distinguishable." What could be more pragmatic, more empirical, more thoroughly British? Yet such reasoning could never have satisfied the Reverend Charles Lutwidge Dodgson. From his adolescent magazine, *The Rectory Umbrella,* to his Oxford lecture, "Where Does the Day Begin?", he preoccupied himself with precisely this problem, and stood ready to pursue the sunrise around the world in order to prove his

point that such distinctions were wholly arbitrary. No wonder we experience some hesitation in putting a finger on Alice's anniversary! We live
by those convenient strokes which separate night from day, sleeping from
waking, and madness from sanity. But imagination, poetic or scientific—
and in Dodgson's case it was both—cannot afford to take anything for
granted. It is continually entertaining the most improbable assumptions,
following *non sequiturs* through to their logical consequences, or—like
Dodgson—hopefully working out *pi* to an ever larger number of decimals.
Speculating in his diary, he asked himself:

*Query: when we are dreaming and, as so often happens, have a dim con-
sciousness of the fact and try to wake, do we not say and do things which
in waking life would be insane? May we not then sometimes define
insanity as an inability to distinguish which is the waking and which the
sleeping life? We often dream without the least suspicion of unreality.
"Sleep hath its own world," and it is often as lifelike as the other.*

If this be madness, it is closely allied to the genius of *Hamlet,* and
there is pith in the Gravedigger's observation that the Prince has been
sent to England because "there the men are as mad as he." The Cheshire
Cat should not shock us when it observes of Wonderland: "We're all mad
here. I'm mad. You're mad." The Cheshire Cat itself seems sane enough,
so detached from the frenetic proceedings it comments upon that it fades
away to a mere head and finally a phosphorescent grin. But if it ends by
becoming a mouthpiece, a mascot, a kind of tribal totem for British
humor in its imperturbable discernment of oddities, then the episode that
follows affords us a glimpse of Oxford—a mad, an endless tea-party, with
pointless anecdotes and answerless riddles and feline small talk, presided
over by two certified madmen, a Hatter modeled on a local character and
a Hare whose watch has stopped at six o'clock. Teatime is over, but nothing seems to lie ahead. Three little girls stay forever at the bottom of
a treacle well, in the interrupted story of the Dormouse. That "Ancient
City," which Dodgson refers to directly in his original manuscript, has
constituted an ideal breeding ground for the cultivation of licensed
eccentricity and for the humorous interplay between select intelligence
and encrusted observance.

When Dodgson characterized himself as the Dodo, the reduplicated
syllable echoed his stammer even while pronouncing his own surname,
and the extinct bird attested his incompatibility with larger and freer
worlds. When "Lewis Carroll" won unique and sudden fame, his donnish

self refused to acknowledge the pseudonym that he had contrived by twisting and reversing his first two names. As conservative in politics as he was
orthodox in religion, he was attached for almost fifty years to Christ
Church, which is a cathedral as well as a college. An unordained cleric,
a prim hobbyist, a shy devotee of lost causes and parlor tricks, he passed
through a completely institutionalized career. Professionally he was—from
what we gather—a mediocre mathematician and a dull teacher, supremely
unconcerned with undergraduates and rather difficult in the Common
Room. "There never *was* such a place for things not happening," he complained of Oxford to one correspondent. To another—another little girl—
he confided: "But the great difficulty is that *adventures don't happen!* Oh,
how *am* I to make some happen, so as to have something to tell to my
darling Enid?" The adventures in his otherwise uneventful life were his
friendships with hundreds of little girls, an avocation which we are
inclined to view as either insipid or suspect.

All his other hobbies—games, puzzles, contraptions, album-leaves,
holiday trips, and, not least, storytelling—were directed single-mindedly
toward that end. Since he was remarkably skillful as a portrait photographer, photographic exposure seems to have taken the place of carnal
seduction at the happy climax of these courtships. His flirtations sometimes met with rebuffs from mammas and governesses, and he confessed
to a cousin with wistful bravado that he lived "on the frowns of Mrs.
Grundy." But there was not much cause to be alarmed. His inamoratas
were too prepubescent to have interested Humbert Humbert (though it is
worth noting that Vladimir Nabokov's first book was a Russian translation
of *Alice in Wonderland*). The biographical record, which is stuffy if not
sticky, lends itself to the cruder naïvetés of the psychoanalysts. Its symbolic effect on Carroll's writing has been summed up in two or three suc-
cinct pages by William Empson—who, as a Cambridge man, was in a
special position to elucidate an Oxonian case history. Mr. Empson's essay,
though slightly distorted by the effort to fit it into his thesis on pastoral
convention, is the most illuminating study we have of Lewis Carroll, for
all the bibliographers, antiquarians, and analytic philosophers who have
made an oracle of him.

The light it throws upon Dodgson's motivation, though by no means
irrelevant, is incidental. In some notes for an unpublished article on dress
in the theater (now in the Houghton Library at Harvard), Dodgson
wrote: "Base of argument lies in relations of *sex*, without which purity

and impurity would be unmeaning words." One cannot overlook the sexual charge in his celibate cult of his little darlings; but the outcome, by definition, seems rather pure than impure. He once planned to edit a *Girls' Own Shakespeare,* in which he proposed to purify the text of such gross expressions as Bowdler had not excised. The demure Eros of Lewis Carroll was a Victorian ideal of delicacy, feminine yet neither female nor effeminate. We may appreciate it better if, recalling his miserable school days at Rugby, we compare Alice with Tom Brown, and with that admixture of cant and brutality which passed for what the Victorians liked to call manliness.

> *Speak roughly to your little boy,*
> *And beat him when he sneezes . . .*

In the endeavor to make things happen, the escape from the monotonous quadrangle of his own existence, Dodgson's chosen companion—indeed, his surrogate—was the Dean's daughter, the second one, the one who kept tossing her head back to keep her hair out of her eyes and, when her sisters asked him for a story, hoped "there will be nonsense in it."

Alice, "Child of the pure unclouded brow," with her eager, expressive face, her long, straight hair, and her pinafore that adapts to so many sizes, is the eternal ingénue who combines Miranda's reaction to the wonders of a brave new world with Daisy Miller's resolve not to miss the tourist attractions. No novelist has identified more intimately with the point of view of his heroine. Except for parenthetical comments, which occur less and less frequently, the empathy is complete. "The sole medium of the stories is her pellucid consciousness," as Walter de la Mare has pointed out; this forms the medium for as elegant an exercise in the Jamesian technique of narration as *What Maisie Knew.* Since Alice is in the habit of talking to herself, there can be a good deal of monologue. When she falls silent, the narrator, like a good contemporary of Flaubert, can employ *le style indirect libre:*

> *Down, down, down. Would the fall never come to an end? "I wonder how many miles I've fallen by this time?" she said aloud.*

Alice began by tiring of her sister's book because it had no pictures or conversations in it. Her chronicles are not lacking in those amenities. Each adventure brings a conversation with a new and strange vis-à-vis.

As for the pictorial presentation, it is an integral part of the author's design. He started with his own sketches, chose his illustrator with the utmost concern, and worked with Tenniel in the most indelible of collaborations. Consequently, there is little description in Dodgson's prose. It is all the more convincing because he simply assumes that the sights are there, and that we visualize them through the eyes of his beholder. Instead of describing the Gryphon, he enjoins us parenthetically: "If you don't know what a Gryphon is, look at the picture." Picture and text join forces to align the reader's awareness with that of Alice. Her inherent responsiveness is controlled by the consistent gravity of demeanor imposed upon her by the inhabitants of Wonderland. After the aimless competition of the Caucus Race, when she is compelled to supply the prizes for everybody, including herself:

Alice thought the whole thing very absurd, but they all looked so grave that she did not dare to laugh; and, as she could not think of anything to say, she simply bowed, and took the thimble, looking as solemn as she could.

So it is that children learn to supress their native instinct for laughter in the company of adults. "He talks just as if it was a game!" says Alice of the Red King. But, though it may be a game for her, he is in dead earnest.

Alice soon gets used to the tone of desperate seriousness in which she is greeted by all the creatures she meets, with the exception of the Cheshire Cat, and we get used to the plethora of exclamation points. She is sustained through their dead-pan dialogues by the sense of wonder, the sort of curiosity that animates great poets and scientists. "Curious" is the adjective with which she responds again and again. "Curiouser and curiouser!" is her apt, if ungrammatical, response to the sequence of events. "It was a curious dream," she tells her sister afterward, and that motif is taken up repeatedly in *The Nursery Alice*, the version that Dodgson rewrote for "Infants from Nought to Five." He did not hesitate to tell them how to react:

Once upon a time, there was a little girl called Alice: and she had a very curious dream.
Would you like to hear what it was that she dreamed about?
Well, this was the first thing that happened. A White Rabbit came by, in a great hurry; and, just as it passed Alice, it stopped, and took its watch out of its pocket.
Wasn't that a funny thing? Did you ever see a Rabbit that had a

watch, and a pocket to put it in? Of course, when a Rabbit has a watch,
it must *have a pocket to put it in; it would never do to carry it about in*
its mouth—and it wants its hands sometimes, to run with.

In this elementary reduction, which may serve to emphasize the sophisticated artistry of the work itself, the Rabbit does not talk at all and none
of the conversations is reported. The *textus receptus,* by accepting the
apparent naturalness of the situation, gains credence for its basic pre-
posterousness. Alice's reactions are delayed. With her, we behold no more
at first than a White Rabbit with pink eyes:

> *There was nothing so* very *remarkable in that; nor did Alice think it so*
> very *much out of the way to hear the Rabbit say to itself, "Oh dear! Oh*
> *dear! I shall be too late!" (when she thought it over afterwards, it occurred*
> *to her that she ought to have wondered at this, but at the time it all seemed*
> *quite natural); but when the Rabbit actually* took a watch out of its
> waistcoat-pocket, *and looked at it, and then hurried on, Alice started to*
> *her feet, for it flashed across her mind that she had never before seen a*
> *rabbit with either a waistcoat-pocket, or a watch to take out of it, and,*
> *burning with curiosity, she ran across the field after it, and was just in*
> *time to see it pop down a large rabbit-hole under the hedge.*

In an article on the dramatic adaptation, Dodgson made clear that the
contrast between the audacity and directness of Alice and the nervous
shilly-shallyings of the White Rabbit was intended to stress the invidious
comparison between youth and age. Significantly, since he is so worried
about his costume, and since he heralds the whole adventure for Alice,
the Rabbit is dressed as a herald when he makes his last appearance.
Without lingering over the prenatal symbolism of the rabbit-hole or the
pool of tears, we may observe that Alice's principal problem—determining
her relationship with the others—is the question of size. This, in turn,
becomes a question of eating and drinking, properly or improperly, as
every child has been reminded so often that the reminder punctuates the
very rhythm of infancy. Alice's enlargements and diminutions are stimulated by a magical succession of eatables and potables. Like Gulliver,
she finds herself out of scale with her fellow beings; but she is less concerned with Lilliputians or Brobdingnagians than with her own person
and growth: "I never ask advice about growing." Dodgson himself has
drawn a haunting illustration of Alice cramped within the Rabbit's
house. "How puzzling all these changes are!" she exclaims.

Confused by such dizzying transformations—in short, by nothing more or less than the physiological metamorphoses of girlhood—she undergoes what modern psychologists would term an identity crisis. "Who are *you?*" the Caterpillar asks. In spite of its assurance, no caterpillar can be quite sure who *it* is, after all. "Who in the world am I?" Alice asks herself. Can she be Ada or Mabel? Or is she the White Rabbit's housemaid, Mary Ann? And would some other name confer on her a different personality? "Remember who you are," the Red Queen commands. Yet there may be some advantage, the Gnat whispers, in losing one's name. When Alice's neck grows so long that—in a pigeon's-eye view—she looks like a serpent, the Pigeon asks: "*What* are you?" She replies, rather doubtfully, "I—I'm a little girl." We can hardly blame the Pigeon for retorting: "A likely story indeed!" When she finds herself in the imaginary sphere of the Unicorn, it is he who calls her a fabulous monster. But suspended disbelief is willing to strike a bargain: he will believe in her, if she believes in him. The Lion wearily inquires whether she is animal, vegetable, or mineral. But the Messenger has already presented her credentials: "This is a child! . . . It's as large as life, and twice as natural!"

One of the most touching episodes, and possibly the profoundest, takes place in the wood where things have no name. This is truly that *selva oscura* where the straight way is lost, that forest of symbols whose meanings have been forgotten, that limbo of silence which prompts a cosmic shudder. Less traditionally, since Dodgson was among the pioneers of symbolic logic, it could represent—in W. V. Quine's phrase—"the gulf between meaning and naming." There Alice comes across an unfrightened fawn, who momentarily allows itself to be stroked. Happily they coexist for a time, undivided by identities or classifications. But the moment of self-recognition introduces a shock of alienation.

"What do you call yourself?" the Fawn said at last. Such a soft sweet voice it had!

"I wish I knew!" thought poor Alice. She answered, rather sadly: "Nothing, just now."

"Think again," it said: "that won't do."

Alice thought, but nothing came of it. "Please, would you tell me what you call yourself?" she said timidly. "I think that might help a little."

"I'll tell you, if you'll come a little further on," the Fawn said. "I can't remember here."

So they walked on together through the wood, Alice with her arms clasped lovingly round the soft neck of the Fawn, till they came out into another open field, and here the Fawn gave a sudden bound into the air, *and shook itself free from Alice's arm. "I'm a Fawn!" it cried in a voice of delight. "And, dear me! you're a human child!" A sudden look of alarm came into its beautiful eyes, and in another moment it had darted away at full speed.*

A universe where the self has no labels or signposts to go by, in Dodgson's account, seems less estranging than a familiar environment which casts us in suspicious and hostile roles. Just as Hawthorne's faunlike protagonist regains the language of the birds and beasts when he returns to the countryside, so childhood has the faculty of communicating with nature spontaneously. Adulthood, on the other hand, superimposes its artifice, and Alice's experiences run increasingly counter to nature.

Seeking to avoid the Queen of Hearts' displeasure, her three gardeners paint her white rose trees red. The Queen's peculiar game of croquet, by using flamingos and hedgehogs as mallets and balls, reduces animal life to the inorganic. Alice likewise converses with the flowers, thereby allowing Dodgson to burlesque a pathetic fallacy echoed from Tennyson's *Maud.* Her royal mentors end by putting her on social terms with the inanimate objects that make up the bill of fare at the banquet: "Alice—Mutton: Mutton—Alice." Her relations with the animals are far from idyllic. Though they are never *he* or *she* but always neuter, most of them are highly anthropomorphic. They argue with her, exhort her to mind her manners, and order her around for all the world as if they were grown people. They seem to bear less resemblance to the benign household pets of Sir Edwin Landseer than—as Madame Mespoulet has shown—to the satirical caricatures of J. J. Grandville, who had provided some notable illustrations for the beast fables of La Fontaine. Lewis Carroll's bestiary is post-Darwinian in its vistas of universal struggle for survival, from the obsolescent Dodo to the suppressed guinea pigs. "Do cats eat bats?" Alice muses, or "Do bats eat cats?"

No matter. All species prey and are preyed upon, and the domesticated are worse than the wild ones. The predatory crocodile replaces the busy bee, from the *Divine Songs for Children* of Isaac Watts,

And welcomes little fishes in,
With gently smiling jaws!

So many of her poems, as Alice retrospectively realizes, have been about fishes or other forms of sea food. The impasse of communication, the exchange of ultimata, and the warfare between two mutually antagonistic realms of creation are haltingly and laconically rendered in "I sent a message to the fish." Doubtless the most memorable of these piscatories is the affecting ballad of the Oysters' betrayal, "The Walrus and the Carpenter"; for the stage version of *Alice* Dodgson was persuaded to soften this stark tragedy with an afterpiece, wherein the ghosts of the Oysters exact a nightmarish revenge upon their sleeping destroyers. Alice's mythical mount, the Gryphon, though it might well claim heraldic connections, chats with her in the vulgar idiom of a hackney coachman. His partner, the Mock Turtle, is a spurious animal, a sort of zoological back-formation; but it is a genuine dish and may therefore sing, with the greatest propriety, its lugubrious song to the evening soup—originally the evening star.

Alice's unflagging and versatile appetite leads to certain embarrassments in her encounters. Yet she proves tactful enough to stop herself from admitting that her previous acquaintance with lobsters and whitings has been on the dinner table and not in the ballroom. Her shrinkages have taught her to look at matters from the other side, from the animals' vantage point. She may scorn to be three inches tall, which the Caterpillar naturally thinks is "a very good height indeed." But she learns the hard way from her initial mistake of boasting about her cat Dinah, which hurts the Mouse's feelings and drives the birds away. Cats and kittens, conceivably because of their totemic relation with human beings, are set apart from their fellow creatures ("creatures" being the term that, for Dodgson, embraces both birds and animals). When the offended Mouse consents to tell its tale, this turns out to be a typographical oddity, a calligrammatic poem in the shape of a mouse's tail. The villain is another pet, the dog Fury, who with cold-blooded brutality undertakes to be prosecutor, judge, and jury, like the Snark in the Barrister's Dream. Alice gains a taste of what it feels like to be under such jeopardy when, in her miniature state, she is nearly crushed by a monstrous puppy—a realization made vivid by Dodgson's hatred of dogs.

The fulfillment of the Mouse's caveat is the trial scene. Here the tables are turned, in the sense that the jurors are twelve good creatures and true. One of them is Bill the Lizard again, just as ineffectual with his squeaky pencil as he was in going down the chimney; but, at least, he can write. Alice gains the upper hand again by re-enacting a mishap of a week before, when she had upset a goldfish bowl at home; the re-enactment exemplifies how the dreamwork has been conditioned by daily actualities. Through her divagations she has been sustained by the vision of a delightful garden and her hope of attaining the right size to enter it. Entrance to it is implicitly equated with growing up, which is bound to be somewhat disillusioning. When she eventually gets there, instead of dallying among the fountains and flower beds, she is pressed into service for the crazy croquet game. There have been some previous intimations—the Rabbit, the Duchess, the Fish and Frog Footmen—that, when she reached that enchanted terrain at last, she would find it the precinct of high society. The ugly Duchess, erstwhile so formidable in her own kitchen, has become an affable dowager, who measures an increase of height by resting her chin on Alice's shoulder and insists on pointing out a moral in everything Alice says. How tiresome can they be, these grownups?

In the manuscript, there is but a single matriarchal figure, who bears the compound title "Queen of Hearts and Marchioness of Mock Turtles." Noting in retrospect that this queen is "a sort of embodiment of ungovernable passion—a blind and aimless Fury," Dodgson reminds us of the Mouse's warning against the litigious dog Fury, and of the rage that now and then breaks out in his "frumious" (i.e. fuming and furious) personages. The Queen's habitual ukase, "Off with his head!", is the peremptory exercise of grown-up authority. Her face-card features scarcely reveal the rounded lineaments of Victoria Regina, yet Alice could never have set forth upon her adventures from any other realm than a constitutional matriarchy. In *Through the Looking-Glass*, she is shuttled back and forth by two matrons even more sharply differentiated in Dodgson's intentions: the White Queen, who is "all helpless imbecility," and the Red Queen, who is "the concentrated essence of all governesses." The final examination through which they must put her, before she can become a queen in her own right, has its counterpart in the prior volume, when Alice is sent to be interviewed by the Mock Turtle, and recognizes—with due allowance for sea change—the curriculum that she has studied at day school.

Thence we are wafted not back to the garden party but to the culminating trial: a recapitulation of events and a convocation of characters to which Alice reacts with no Kafka-esque passivity. The charge as stated in the nursery rhyme, the theft of tarts, seems to be a breach of the domestic proprieties. We never reach the second stanza, where the Knave gets punished like a mischievous boy undergoing parental discipline. For Alice has been growing steadily—"a very curious sensation"—until, when she takes the witness stand, she towers above the denizens of Wonderland. She is no longer the spectator but the cynosure. Before she had met anyone, she could soliloquize: "Oh dear, what nonsense I'm talking!" The thin-skinned Mouse could expostulate with her: "You insult me by talking such nonsense!" But it is the others, more and more, who insult her by talking nonsensically. At their first encounter in the garden, "crimson with fury," the Queen of Hearts had ordered Alice's decapitation, and Alice had retorted boldly: "Nonsense!" Having now attained full stature, she repeats the retort with emphasis: "Stuff and nonsense!" When the Queen repeats her furious sentence, Alice dispels the whole nonsensical phantasmagoria with the sensible exorcism: "You're nothing but a pack of cards!"

She is a little girl once more when she awakens, and she must retraverse her adolescence by another route in the sequel. There we soon find her contradicting the Red Queen: "That would be nonsense——" To which the Red Queen majestically replies: "*I've* heard nonsense, compared with which that would be as sensible as a dictionary!" At a parallel stage to the exorcism of the card pack, the second finale, Alice qualifies for her crown by the Queens' catechism: "What dreadful nonsense we *are* talking!" At her coronation, once more she tells the phantoms off and brushes them away, pulling out the tablecloth from under them and stirring the hall into pandemonium—as, Mr. Empson conjectures, Dodgson would so have liked to have done with the high table at Christ Church. We must stay with Alice, however. Consciously she seems to rouse herself, as we do when our wish-dreams threaten to turn into nightmares. Deliberately she shakes the diminishing Red Queen until the figure dwindles into her black kitten. This has all been a dream, too, like the first one, which ended with Alice's older sister Lorina drowsing off into her own dream of Wonderland, and with the soft noises of the river bank providing their oneiric sound effects. "There ought to be a book written about me, that there ought!" of which Alice has been conscious from the beginning.

Her second dream propels her farther into the stratosphere of metaphysical speculation, where she is informed that she is nothing but a figment of the Red King's dream. Awakening, she speculates with her kitten as to who was the dreamer and which the reality. "He was part of my dream, of course—but then I was part of his dream, too!" After the disappearance of the Lion and the Unicorn, she all but dismisses them as a dream within a dream, when she notices the plate for their plum cake at her feet and meditates an existential challenge.

"So I wasn't dreaming, after all," she said to herself, "unless—unless we're all part of the same dream. Only I do hope it's my dream, and not the Red King's. I don't like belonging to another person's dream," she went on in a rather complaining tone: "I've a great mind to go and wake him, and see what happens!"

The Hunting of the Snark has been philosophically interpreted as a fruitless search for the Absolute; the ultimate object of man's quest is foredoomed to vanish away softly and silently; it was the last line of the "Agony" that occurred first to the agonizing poet: "For the Snark *was* a Boojum, you see." Q.E.D. Theirs not to reason why. Just what a Snark might happen to be and why the ill-sorted crew should ever have embarked on the ill-fated undertaking are never explained; and, though the dénouement is not unexpected, it is all the more horrible because it remains unspecified. That self-evident "you see" is the hollowest of ironies. *Sylvie and Bruno* carries Dodgson's mood of subjective idealism toward the evanescent conclusion of Shakespeare and Calderón. "Is life itself a dream?" the narrator wonders. And the terminal acrostic of *Through the Looking-Glass* concludes: "Life, what is it but a dream?"

The stuff of dreams is as illusory as those scented rushes which lose their fragrance and beauty when Alice picks them. Yet Dodgson catches the cinematographic movement of dreams when the grocery shop, after changing into the boat from which she gathers the dream-rushes, changes back into the shop which is identifiable as an Oxford landmark. The next phase is the egg on the shelf, which becomes Humpty Dumpty on his wall. The narration, with its corkscrew twists, carefully observes the postulate that Dodgson formulated in his serio-comic treatise, "Dynamics of a Parti-cle": Let it be granted that a speaker may digress from any one point to any other point." Alice proceeds by digression through Wonderland, since it does not really matter which way she goes. In the Looking-Glass land, which is regulated by a stricter set of ground rules, she is forced to move backward from time to time. Dodgson had given himself his *donnée* by sending her down the rabbit-hole "without the least idea what was to happen afterwards." What extemporaneously followed seemed to consist, as he subsequently recounted it, "almost wholly of fits and scraps, single ideas which came of themselves." Though it may have been obsession which gave them a thematic unity, it was artistry which devised their literary form.

Symmetrically, each of the two books comprises twelve chapters. Both of them conflate the dream-vision with the genre known as the *voyage imaginaire;* in effect, they merge the fairy tale with science fiction. The journey, in either case, is not a quest, like *The Hunting of the Snark*—or that logbook it almost seems to parody, *Moby Dick*. Rather, it is an exploration—underground, in the first instance, and so originally entitled *Alice's Adventures under Ground*. This relates it to a wealth of symbols for the claustral limits of the human condition, from Plato to Dostoevski. Falling can betoken many things: above all, the precondition of knowledge. Subterranean descent can land in an underworld, be it Hell or Elysium or the other side of the earth, the Antipodes, which Alice malapropistically calls "the Antipathies"—not so exact an opposite to our side as the Looking-Glass country, but a topsy-turvydom of sorts, like Butler's *Erewhon*. As we approach it, it seems to be a juvenile utopia, what with its solemn games and half-remembered lessons and ritualized performances of nursery rhymes. Before we leave it, it becomes an unconscious *Bildungsroman*, projecting and resisting the girlish drama of physical and psychological development. "What do you suppose is the use of a child without any meaning? [fumes the Red Queen.] Even a joke should have some meaning—and a child's more important than a joke, I hope."

As for the looking-glass, that has been a traditional metaphor for narcissistic self-absorption, for art's reflection of nature, and—more abstractly —for the reversal of asymmetric relationships. Scientific commentators may see in it an adumbration of up-to-date physical theory regarding particles and antiparticles. Much more prosaically, it might be suggested that any child who grew up in a semidetached house, and had played in the adjoining house, would take as a matter of course the reversed arrangements of rooms. Dodgson, who liked to write backward, wanted to have some pages of his book printed in reverse. His fondness for inverting standard patterns is humanly personified in the mirror-image twins, Tweedledum and Tweedledee. For him, *Alice's Adventures in Wonderland* had been a discovery, an improvisation, a series of serendipities; whereas *Through the Looking-Glass*, seven years later, was faced with the

usual difficulty of sequels. It made up in systematic elaboration for what
it lost in spontaneous flow. If it is less organically imagined, it is replete
with brilliant paradoxes, some of which do anticipate modern science. On
these aspects especially, Martin Gardner has compiled a lucid and suggestive commentary in his *Annotated Alice,* to which I must express a
comprehensive debt of gratitude.

Inasmuch as surprise is of the essence, there is little recurrence from
book to book. We hardly recognize the Hare and the Hatter of Wonderland when they are metamorphosed into the messengers Haigha and
Hatta of the *Looking-Glass.* The later story takes place indoors during the
autumn; its predecessor took place outdoors in the spring. Alice has been
impelled underground by a swift train of circumstances; she dissolves the
looking-glass, for herself and her kitten, with the hypnotic formula: "Let's
pretend." She is more self-conscious on her first trip, and we are more
interested in what happens to her. On her second, we tend to accept her
and to look around with her, as if we were accompanying her through
Disneyland or the World's Fair. The shift from identity to duality is a
transference from self to otherness. The presiding figures from the game
of cards are as remote as epic deities until the end of Part I. Their counterparts from chess are more regularly present throughout Part II, which
is framed by a chess problem—not a very deliberate one. Alice becomes a
pawn, replacing the Queen's daughter Lily, and looks ahead to being
queened; whereas—except for her disappointed wish to arrive at the
garden—her earlier wanderings, through cavernous passages and quasi-
Elysian fields, had no set destination.

The excursion shifts from time to space, from an impressionistic con-
tinuum to a more static outlook, as she crosses the chessboard landscape.
Above its checkered topography looms the presence of the geometrician
who laid it out and manipulates the chessmen. What is happening has
happened before and will happen again, at predictable intervals as long
as folklore persists. Tweedledum and Tweedledee will fight; the Lion and
the Unicorn will be drummed out of town; Humpty Dumpty will fall
from his wall and, though not reconstructed by all the King's horses or
men, will somehow be enabled to re-enact the performance. Now, all fairy-
lands, utopias, paradises, and other imagined worlds—whatever improvements they may have to offer—are bound to draw their inspiration from
the one world that their imaginer knows at first hand. It would be unlikely
if Dodgson's creations were not liberally sprinkled with local and topical

allusions. Sir John Tenniel, who was mainly a political caricaturist, occasionally injected an overt touch: in his drawing of the Lion and Unicorn we discern the features of rival candidates, the Earl of Derby and Disraeli. The latter also seems to have posed for the traveler dressed in white paper, peculiarly appropriate for a Prime Minister, who sits opposite Alice in the railway carriage.

This locale, a favorite with Dodgson, invites a passing glance at nineteenth-century technology. The chorus of voices that Alice hears, while a passenger, chants a commercial refrain where everything is evaluated at one thousand pounds. Since the train is going the wrong way, according to the guard, it escapes to the domain of fancy from the workaday world to which it belongs. Dodgson would try to encompass those two worlds, together with a pious romance, a whimsical tract, and divers other polarities, within the two volumes of *Sylvie and Bruno.* Therein, by means of psychic transitions, the narrative is systematically transposed from the Commonplace to the Marvelous—from Outland, the regime of conspiratorial adults, "Through the Ivory Gate" to Elfland, the preserve of cloying juveniles. The happiest feature of this ambitious scheme is a device which is used to modulate from one plane to the other. At the transitional moment, a Mad Gardener sings a song whose pattern becomes familiar:

> *He thought he saw an Elephant*
> *That practised on a fife:*
> *He looked again, and found it was*
> *A letter from his wife.*
> *"At length I realise," he said,*
> *"The bitterness of Life!"*

If Dodgson had been a romanticist, his daydream might have turned that conjugal letter—that grimly realistic slice of life—into a missive from a fair stranger. Instead—and this is what spells the difference between romance and nonsense—life is made less bitter by the spectacle of a tootling elephant. The transformation is made explicit by the Professor, who is the Carrollian mentor of Sylvie and Bruno, when he persuades the Gardener to unlock, for the three of them, what is tantamount to the gate of fantasy:

> *He thought he saw a Garden-Door*
> *That opened with a Key:*
> *He looked again, and found it was*

A Double Rule of Three:
"And all its mystery," he said,
"Is clear as day to me!"

Alice thought she saw a host of chimeras. She looked again, and found
it was only a pack of cards or a set of chessmen. There is nothing, of
course, so extraordinary in that. Dodgson's achievement was to prolong
her reveries, and to lend their figments every appearance of solidity.
Occasional echoes recall to us those matter-of-fact details from Alice's
waking life—the fishes, the fire irons—which have been transmuted into
fantasies. Unlike those of *Sylvie and Bruno,* wherein the two states are
kept apart, her imaginative processes blend them together. "So many out-
of-the-way things had happened lately that Alice had begun to think that
very few things indeed were really impossible." That state of mind in
which everything seems possible can be maintained by preserving the
conventions in the most absurd situations. Alice practices making a
curtsy, like a properly brought-up little girl, even while she is falling
down the rabbit-hole. In one of Dodgson's magazine sketches, his hero
thought he saw a signboard advertising "Romancement." He looked again,
and was informed that two words had inadvertently been run together:
that the sign advertised a much humbler and harder commodity, namely
"Roman Cement." Meanwhile, a displaced word could act as an incanta-
tion to conjure up a prospect of Elfland.

This transfiguration of commonplace objects and familiar landmarks is
largely a verbal process. The slightest variation in spelling or pronunciation can effect a drastic change, but the Cheshire Cat would be equally
unsurprised if the baby turned into a pig or a fig. Alice becomes uncom-
fortably aware that something odd has been happening to her *Weltan-
schauung* when her memorized arithmetic comes out scrambled and her
geography seems to be disoriented. But the real test is—as it should be—
poetry, and the transforming device is parody. Periodically she is called
upon to recite, or else listen to, a selection of gems from the repertory of
the nursery, dimly recognizable but strangely transmogrified. "Some of the
words have got altered" in her recollection of Southey's parable about
Father William, so that the cautionary elder has become an impenitent
prankster, rebuffing the youth's curiosity with a threat to kick him downstairs. This is, by implication, a rebuff to the perpetual questioning from
Alice herself. Watts's verses for infants, which are as oppressively moralistic as the Duchess, are released from their didactic burdens in the

retelling: the ubiquitous lobster turns ventriloquist and obtrudes itself into "The Voice of the Sluggard."

The distinction between sense and nonsense, in the poem read into the record as evidence against the Knave of Hearts, is obliterated by the omission of proper names. As a result, the reader gropes from relative pronoun to relative pronoun in a game of grammatical blindman's buff:

> *They told me you had been to her,*
> *And mentioned me to him . . .*

The resulting disorientation foreshadows the wood of namelessness or Humpty Dumpty's doctrine that names confer meaning. Alice dismisses the poem as meaningless, though the King endeavors to explicate it, not very successfully. On the other hand, the whispering Gnat succeeds in creating new subspecies of insects by extrapolation from names of existing flies. The Rocking-horse-fly and the Bread-and-butter-fly are worthy subjects for Tenniel's unnaturalism. But the artist firmly balked at the author's notion of a wasp in a wig; that was, he objected, "beyond the appliance of art." It is significant that, when Dodgson composed his ballad about the Walrus, he let Tenniel decide whether the deuteragonist should be a carpenter, a baronet, or a butterfly. Since all three were metrically equivalent, and none required rhymes, the choice was left to depend upon their graphic possibilities—no richer, one would think, for an ostreophagous butterfly than for a periwigged wasp. Verbal considerations were secondary to visual for the nonce.

But, as the Dormouse shrieks when its anecdote trails off into nouns beginning with M, "Did you ever see such a thing as a drawing of a muchness!" Ordinarily, the word precedes the thing. *Façons de parler* regain their primitive magic by being taken literally. Thus, to answer the door is to assume that the door has spoken first. Expressions like Time and Nobody cast off their abstractness and take on the misplaced concreteness of personalities. Metaphors such as "feather" and "catch a crab," when Alice is rowing, can be all too easily hypostatized. Puns are means of unexpected propulsion, because they change the subject so abruptly: they switch fortuitously from one theme to another, with trees that bark like dogs or books so tedious that they dry you off when you get wet. The key words, in Alice's recipe for bread, have a misleading significance for the White Queen:

> *"You take some flour——"*

"Where do you pick the flower?" the White Queen asked. "In a garden or in the hedges?"

"Well, it isn't picked at all," Alice explained: "it's ground—"

"How many acres of ground?" said the White Queen. "You mustn't leave out so many things."

Such redundancies must not be left out, if vital information is to be conveyed. The pun, or any other type of wordplay where relevance is determined by the chance of two sounds coinciding, is a standing invitation to absurdity for better or worse. Insofar as it frees us from the responsibility for being rational, it can be a source of relief. One of the unmistakable marks that make the Snark so inevitable a quarry is its general lack of humor and its particular resistance to punning:

> *The third is its slowness in taking a jest.*
> *Should you happen to venture on one,*
> *It will sigh like a thing that is deeply distressed:*
> *And it always looks grave at a pun.*

It seems characteristic of Lewis Carroll that the most touchingly serious of his lyrics should be the acrostic on Alice Pleasance Liddell. Alliteration, as a variant of rhyme, can be meaningful but is often far-fetched. The crew that sails after the Snark is so utterly miscellaneous because it is made up of occupations which alliterate with the Bellman: the Baker, the Butcher, the Broker, the Banker, the Barrister, the Bonnet-maker, the Billiard-marker, the Boots, and the Beaver. Alice shows us how to mix things up by affecting the letter, when she plays the word game, "I love my love with an H." Nonetheless, given the semirationality of the human mind, even a jumbling together of incongruities must be patterned by some principle of order—if only by an initial consonant. The Walrus talks

> *Of shoes—of ships—of sealing-wax—*
> *Of cabbages—and kings—*

and sealing wax is one of the ingredients of the White Knight's pudding (perhaps for personal reasons connected with Dodgson's voluminous correspondence). "It's not easy to be nonsensical," said Marcel Duchamp, the veteran of cubism and surrealism, in a recent interview, "because non-sensical things so often turn out to make sense." Striving for sheer random heterogeneity, one is much more likely to produce an unconscious association of ideas or a deliberate juxtaposition of opposites:

> *And why the sea is boiling hot—*
> *And whether pigs have wings.*

The value of verse, in this respect, is that its formal constraints are constantly pressing toward a dissociation of sound and sense. The serious poet must struggle against the current; the nonsense poet may float along with it, gurgling happily down the stream. And though there are many varieties of nonsense poetry, which Alfred Liede has earnestly surveyed in his two substantial volumes, *Dichtung als Spiel: Studien der Unsinns-poesie an den Grenzen der Sprache,* "Lewis Carroll is the most enigmatic of nonsense poets." The poem that both illustrates and demonstrates the enigma for us is bound to be "Jabberwocky," which—as its title obscurely hints—seems to be a heroic lay about language. Alice has discovered it in a book, at the outset of her second expedition, and it has filled her head with ideas; but she does not comprehend them until the midpoint, when she encounters Humpty Dumpty, whose onomatopetic name fulfills his linguistic theories and asserts his cavalier Nominalism. "The question is," as he expounds it to Alice, "which is to be master—that's all." The ancient nursery rhyme from which he derives his being was once a riddle rhymed in many languages. The answer is a symbol with many meanings, from the egg that germinates life to the fall that shatters it.

Hence he is fully qualified to be Dodgson's philosopher and philologist; from the precarious eminence of his *hubris,* he dominates the problems of interpretation; and, after his lecture to Alice on semantics, he sets forth an exegesis of "Jabberwocky" which is a model for higher and newer criticism:

> *'Twas brillig, and the slithy toves*
> *Did gyre and gimble in the wabe:*
> *All mimsy were the borogoves,*
> *And the mome raths outgrabe.*

Dodgson, at the age of twenty-three, had lettered this opening quatrain in pseudorunic characters into his family periodical *Mischmasch,* under the caption "Stanzas from Anglo-Saxon Poetry," and with a commentary anticipating Humpty Dumpty. It was wise of him to leave the Anglo-Saxon attitudes to the King's Messengers in *Through the Looking-Glass,* since the lines have little in common with Old English, except for the alliterative pairing of "gyre" and "gimble," plus a certain profusion of gutturals. As a matter of fact, the metrical scheme is one which could evoke reverberations from a nearer monument:

> And this is why I sojourn here,
>   Alone and palely loitering,
> Though the sedge is wither'd from the lake,
>   And no birds sing.

Humpty Dumpty puts on a dazzling exhibition of his mastery over words, in glossing the unfamiliar nouns and verbs and adjectives. Some of these are no more than archaisms; others, which interest us more, are neologisms; and the most interesting, among the latter, are those composites which Dodgson invented and patented as portmanteau words for the diction of dreams.

Leaving them opaque, together with the "very curious-looking creatures" that they denote, we are swept along by the firm syntactic and rhythmic structure, which frames the ineffable adventure and makes it perfectly credible, whatever it may mean. That outline is reinforced if, experimentally, we substitute obvious phrases for obscure ones:

> 'Twas April, and the heavy rains
>   Did drip and drizzle on the road:
> All misty were the windowpanes,
>   And the drainpipes outflowed.

Lacking the dim suggestiveness of those slithy toves and mome raths, this is much too flat and prosy; but it indicates, with diagrammatic sharpness, how the exotic colors have been applied within the conventional contours. Let us intensify the experiment by pitching it in a more apocalyptic key:

> 'Twas doomsday, and the rabid curs
>   Did yelp and yodel in the void:
> All strident were the trumpeters,
>   And the big guns deployed.

This approaches nonsense again, since the very rigidities of syntax and meter—the need to meet formal requirements while sustaining a certain tone, but not necessarily advancing any thought—make nonsense very difficult to avoid and sense extremely easy to neglect. James Joyce, Humpty Dumpty's professed disciple, did not relax these rigidities when he wrote *Finnegans Wake* in prose; rather, he extended them, since his distortions of speech were posited upon correct inflections and set rhythms. Dodgson's surprises, like Joyce's, depend on the calculated subversion of well-established expectations. Order has been artfully deranged to create the illusion of chaos.

"Jabberwocky," despite the double talk of its somnambulistic vocab-·ulary, conforms to all the conventions of balladry. Childe Roland to the dark tower comes; Jack ends by killing the Giant; and, if the Snark proves a Boojum, it is not permitted to vanish away. Grappling with the name-less terrors that menace us all, Dodgson might have boasted, like his insomniac Baker:

> *I engage with the Snark—every night after dark—*
> *In a dreamy delirious fight . . .*

The White King is similarly obsessed with Bandersnatches, who can never be caught or stopped, but who would seem to be lesser evils than the Jabberwock. The slaying of that dread apparition marks a rite of passage for the beamish boy, whoever he may be. Tenniel depicts him sturdily planted, like David before Goliath, confronting a dragonlike foe who is not less terrifying because—like our timid friend, the White Rabbit—he is wearing a waistcoat. The picture was conceived and executed as a frontis-piece to *Through the Looking-Glass.* However, it proved so horrendous that Dodgson feared it might frighten his child-readers. Accordingly, he went to the other extreme; after conducting a private poll among their mothers, he decided to replace the hobgoblin with a good genius; and so the book opens with Tenniel's equestrian portrait of the "gentle foolish face" and the ingeniously cumbersome panoply of the White Knight, accompanied by a pedestrian Alice.

Her belated champion deserves the honor; for he is the kindliest of her guides and advisers, indeed, the truest hero of her story; and it is their encounter, we are told, that she will always remember most clearly. After the preparatory rounds between Tweedledum and Tweedledee and between the Lion and the Unicorn, there is a climactic battle when the Red Knight cries "Check!" and the White Knight somehow manages to rescue Alice, with the noise of fire irons clanking against the fender not far away. With the loping move of the knight in chess, falling off his horse every pace or two, he escorts her to the square where queenship awaits her. Their farewell is as poignant as Dante's from Vergil at the upper boundaries of Purgatory. But the Knight has a closer precedent in Don Quixote, whom he emulates with his uncertain horsemanship and his headful of chimerical plans. His memorable song, which functions as a

Alice Liddell as "The Beggar-Maid," 1858, aged 6,
photographed by Charles L. Dodgson

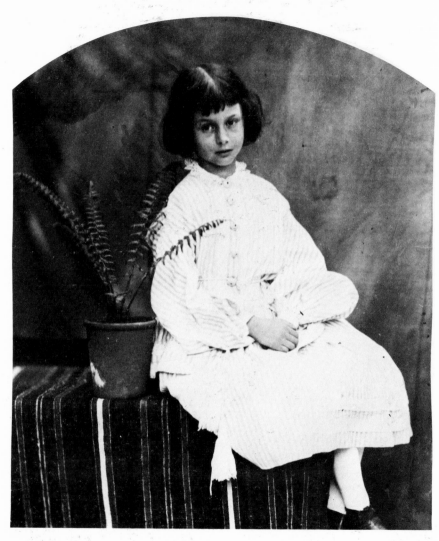

Alice Liddell in 1859,
photographed by Charles L. Dodgson

Alice (*left*) and her older sister Lorina

The Liddell sisters: Edith Mary (the Tertia of ALICE'S ADVENTURES);
Lorina Charlotte (Prima); Alice Pleasance (Secunda),
photographed by Charles L. Dodgson

In the Deanery garden, Christ Church, Oxford, home of the Liddells,
photographed by Charles L. Dodgson

Charles L. Dodgson's study at Christ Church, Oxford,
photographed by Charles L. Dodgson

Charles L. Dodgson, holding his camera lens,
photographed by O. G. Rejlander

Sir John Tenniel

kind of cadenza to the work as a whole, parodies Wordsworth's "Resolution and Independence," where the dejected poet is revivified by the example of the old leech-gatherer plying his humble trade on the lonely moor. An earlier version of Dodgson's burlesque had been separately published, and he drew the character of the Knight to suit the speaker in it. Therefore it is a portrait within a portrait. As Mr. Gardner suggests, Dodgson set up a looking-glass across from his looking-glass.

The image reflected from the one to the other ad infinitum is thus a self-caricature: Dodgson as Lewis Carroll as the White Knight as the speaker of the poem as its interlocutor,

> *an aged aged man,*
> *A-sitting on a gate.*

Dodgson admitted as much in a later memoir, "Isa's Visit to Oxford," when he referred to himself as "the Aged Aged man." No doubt many voices in the two stories are primarily his own: the grumpiness of the Caterpillar, the amusement of the Cheshire Cat, the pedagogy of Humpty Dumpty. In the amiable eccentric who sings the song—and even more in the useless ingenuities, the wool-gathering projects, and the endearing crotchets of its quixotic protagonist—Dodgson has offered us his *apologia pro vita sua*. Virginia Woolf discerned that he had preserved a child within him intact; meanwhile his outer self had become a pedant, who measured everyone's words with a literalness which exposed the contradictions by which they lived; yet, in the dialogue between the incongruous pair, childhood took the measure of pedantry. Understandably, the White Knight is disappointed when Alice sheds no tears at his recital. But the game is virtually over. Alice has only to leap across the brook, be crowned, and wake up to a less adventurous actuality. The storyteller, folding his chessboard and putting away the pieces, can voice the satisfaction of a demiurge who has populated a cosmos and set it in motion, with the White Knight's vaunt: "It's my own invention!"

C. L. Dodgson:

The Poet Logician

by *Edmund Wilson*

(1932; revised, 1952)

IF THE Lewis Carroll centenary has produced anything of special interest, I have failed to see it. C. L. Dodgson was a most interesting man and deserves better of his admirers, who revel in his delightfulness and cuteness but do not give him any serious attention. "Frankly, this is to be the book of Lewis Carroll," wrote John Francis McDermott in his introduction to Dodgson's collected verse, published three years ago, "and I have no intention here of allowing Charles Lutwidge Dodgson, a dull and uninteresting person, to intrude in it any more than is absolutely necessary." Richard Herrick, the editor of *The Lewis Carroll Book*, is so determined that we shall see in Dodgson nothing but an exponent of pure nonsense that he does not hesitate to mutilate his work. He reprints, out of *Rhyme? and Reason?*, only the poems that happen to please him; he suppresses, with the exception of a few stanzas, the long and elaborate "Phantasmagoria," for the extraordinary reason that he believes it to have been spoiled by "Carroll's serious interest in psychic matters"; and he lops off the charming and significant epilogue to *Through the Looking-Glass*, without which the book is incomplete:

> *Still she haunts me, phantomwise,*
> *Alice moving under skies*
> *Never seen by waking eyes.*

On the other hand, he includes some very amusing letters and a mathematical fantasia called "A Tangled Tale." The whole book seems thrown together as a hasty publisher's job—there is not even a table of contents —and is typical of the careless handling that Lewis Carroll ordinarily gets.

The truth is that, if Dodgson and his work were shown as an organic whole, his "nonsense" would not seem the anomaly which it is usually represented as being. It is true that on one of his sides he was a pompous and priggish don. He used to write letters to friends the next morning after he had been having dinner with them and beg them never again in his presence to speak so irreverently of Our Lord as they had the evening before, because it gave him infinite pain; and he wrote to the papers in a tone of indignation worthy of Mr. Podsnap protesting against the impiety of W. S. Gilbert in being whimsical about curates on the stage. But even this side of Dodgson should not be kept out of the picture: the *Alice in Wonderland* side has an intimate relation with it. Under the crust of the pious professor was a mind both rebellious and skeptical. The mathematician who invented Alice was one of those semimonastic types—like Walter Pater and A. E. Housman—that the English universities breed: vowed to an academic discipline but cherishing an intense originality, painfully repressed and incomplete but in the narrow field of their art somehow both sound and bold. A good deal of the piquancy of the *Alice* books is due to their merciless irreverence: in Alice's dreaming mind, the bottoms dismayingly drop out of the didactic little poems by Dr. Watts and Jane Taylor, which Victorian children were made to learn, and their simple and trite images are replaced by grotesque and

silly ones, which have rushed in like goblins to take possession. And in
the White Knight's song about the aged man a-sitting on a gate, a parody
of Wordsworth's "Leech-Gatherer," Lewis Carroll, in his subterranean
fashion, ridiculed the stuffed-shirt side of Wordsworth as savagely as
Byron had ever done. Wordsworth was a great admiration of Dodgson's;
yet as soon as he enters his world of dreams, Lewis Carroll is moved to
stick pins in him. This poem in its original form, before it had been
rewritten to adapt it to Alice's dream, had been even more subversive of
Victorian conventions.:

> *I met an aged, aged man*
> *Upon the lonely moor:*
> *I knew I was a gentleman,*
> *And he was but a boor.*
> *So I stopped and roughly questioned him,*
> *"Come, tell me how you live!"*
> *But his word impressed my ear no more*
> *Than if it were a sieve.*

It is curious what ordination as a clergyman of the Church of England
can do to an original mind. The case of Dodgson is somewhat similar to
those of Donne and Swift—though Dodgson was shy and stammered and
never took priest's orders; and he was closer, perhaps, to Swift and Donne
than to the merely whimsical writer like Barrie or A. A. Milne, for Dodgson had a first-rate mind of a very unusual sort: he was a logician who
was also a poet.

The poetry and the logic in Dodgson were closely bound up together.
It has often been pointed out that only a mind primarily logical could
have invented the jokes of the *Alice* books, of which the author is always
conscious that they are examples of faulty syllogisms. But it also worked
the other way: his eccentric imagination invaded his scholarly work. His
Symbolic Logic (which had nothing to do with the subject called by the
same name of which A. N. Whitehead and Bertrand Russell laid the
foundation in their *Principia Mathematica*) contains syllogisms with
terms as absurd as any in the *Alice* books:

> *A prudent man shuns hyenas;*
> *No banker is imprudent.*
> *No banker fails to shun hyenas.*

Dodgson's *Euclid and His Modern Rivals* had nothing to do with non-
Euclidean geometry, but in the section called "A New Theory of Parallels"

of his *Curiosa Mathematica* he grazed one of the conceptions of relativist theory; and is there not a touch of Einstein in the scenes in which the Red Queen has to keep running in order to remain in the same place and in which the White Queen gives a scream of pain before she has pricked her finger?

In literature, Lewis Carroll went deeper than his contemporaries realized and than he usually gets credit for even today. As studies in dream psychology, the *Alice* books are most remarkable: they do not suffer by comparison with the best serious performances in this field—with Strindberg or Joyce or Flaubert's *Tentation de Saint Antoine.* One of Alice's recent editors says that the heroine's personality is kept simple in order to throw into relief the eccentrics and monsters she meets. But the creatures that she meets, the whole dream, *are* Alice's personality and her waking life. They are the world of teachers, family, and pets, as it appears to a little girl and also the little girl who is looking at this world. The creatures are always snapping at her and chiding her, saying brusque and rude and blighting things (as if their creator himself were snapping back at the authorities and pieties he served); and she in turn has a child's primitive cruelty: she cannot help mentioning cats when she is swimming around with the Mouse, and later on, with the birds all around her, she comes out, as if naïvely, with, "Dinah's our cat. And she's such a capital one for catching mice, you can't think! And oh, I wish you could see her after the birds! Why, she'll eat a little bird as soon as look at it!" But though Alice is sometimes brutal, she is always well-bred; and, though she wanders in a world full of mysteries and of sometimes disagreeable surprises, she is always a sensible and self-possessed little upper-class English girl, who never fails in the last resort to face down the outlandish creatures that plague her; she can always bring the dream to an end by telling the King and Queen and the Court that they're nothing but a pack of cards or by picking up the Red Queen and shaking her. She can also be sympathetic and sometimes—for example, with the White Knight—exhibits a maternal instinct, but always in a sensible and practical way. Lewis Carroll is never sentimental about Alice, though he is later on to become so, in the messiest Victorian way, in the *Sylvie and Bruno* books. Yet *Sylvie and Bruno*, too, has considerable psychological interest, with its alternations of dream and reality and the elusive relationships between them. The opening railway journey, in which the narrator is dozing and mixes with the images of his dream his awareness of the lady sitting opposite him, is of an almost Joycean complexity and quite inappropriate for reading to children.

I do not, however, agree with Mr. Herrick, in the case of the *Alice* books, that the *Alice* that grownups read is really a different work from the *Alice* that is read by children. The grownups understand it better, but the prime source of the interest is the same. Why is it that very young children listen so attentively to *Alice,* remember it all so well and ask to hear it again, when many other stories seem to leave little impression? It is surely the psychological truth of these books that lays its hold on us all. Lewis Carroll is in touch with the real mind of childhood and hence with the more primitive elements of the mind of maturity, too— unlike certain other writers who merely exploit for grownups an artificial child-mind of convention which is in reality neither childlike nor adult. The shiftings and the transformations, the mishaps and the triumphs of Alice's dream, the mysteries and the riddles, the gibberish that conveys unmistakable meanings, are all based upon relationships that contradict the assumptions of our conscious lives but that are lurking not far behind them. In the "straight" parts of *Sylvie and Bruno,* Lewis Carroll was mawkishly Victorian to the point of unintentional parody (having produced in "The Three Voices" a masterpiece of intentional parody!), but in the *Alice* books he quite got away from the upholstery and the gloomy institutions of the nineteenth-century world. I believe that they are likely to survive when a good deal of the more monumental work of that world —the productions of the Carlyles and the Ruskins, the Spencers and the George Eliots—shall have sunk with the middle-class ideals of which they were the champions as well as the critics. Charles Dodgson who, in morals and religion, in his attitude toward social institutions, was professedly, as he himself believed, more conventional than any of these, had over them the curious advantage of working at once with the abstract materials of mathematical and logical conceptions and with the irrationalities of dreams. His art has a purity that is almost unique in a period so cluttered and cumbered, in which even the preachers of doom to the reign of materialism bore the stamp and the stain of the industrial system in the hard insistence of their sentences and in the turbidity of their belchings of rhetoric. They have shrunk now, but *Alice* still stands.

I suggest to the Nonesuch Press that it would do well to get out a definitive and comprehensive one-volume edition of Dodgson, like their admirable editions of Blake and Donne. The trouble about such collections as that which Mr. Herrick has edited is that they are intended primarily for children. There is no Charles Lutwidge Dodgson for grownups. *Sylvie and Bruno*, which is never reprinted, ought to be made available; and there ought to be at least as many readers for the *Curiosa Mathematica* and the "Dynamics of a Parti-cle" as for Donne's sermons or Blake's prophetic books. Dodgson's letters should be included, his articles on local events at Oxford and his journal of his trip to Russia; and there ought to be a good memoir. The only biography of Dodgson is a conventional life by a relative published in 1899. No writer, so far as I know, has ever done a serious portrait of him or made a real study of his work.

May 18, 1932

The needs pointed out in this article were very promptly supplied. In 1935, Mr. J. F. McDermott brought out a volume of the miscellaneous writings of Dodgson: *The Russian Journal and Other Selections from the Works of Lewis Carroll;* and in 1937 the Nonesuch Press did publish, as I had suggested, a well-produced omnibus volume, *The Complete Works of Lewis Carroll*, containing almost everything of Dodgson's (the *Russian Journal* is not included) that a non-scholarly person could read. *Some Aspects of Pastoral* by William Empson (American edition called *English Pastoral Poetry*), published in 1935, includes an interesting study of the *Alice* books, which treats the cataclysmic finale of the dinner at the end of *Through the Looking-Glass* as the eruption of a repressed don, exasperated by dining with his colleagues.

The first full-length biography since *The Life and Letters of Lewis Carroll* by his nephew S. D. Collingwood appeared in 1945: *Victoria Through the Looking-Glass: The Life of Lewis Carroll*, by Florence Becker Lennon. This book has its unsatisfactory features. Mrs. Lennon presents her material in rather an untidy way: she nowhere, so far as I can find, for example, gives the date of Dodgson's birth—certainly not in the proper place; and the filling-in of the background, done from this side of the Atlantic, is synthetic and not easily assimilable. But this study is, nevertheless, the best thing that has yet been written about Lewis Carroll. The literary criticism is excellent; the psychological insight sometimes brilliant; and Mrs. Lennon has brought together, from the most scattered and various sources, a good deal of information. The impression that she actually conveys of what Dodgson's existence was like is more convincing than some of her theories. Mrs. Lennon [See p. 66. Ed.] believes that Charles Dodgson was intimidated by his clergyman father, so that he felt himself obliged to take orders and never dared question the creed of the Church. She seems to believe that he might otherwise have developed as an important original thinker. She also worries about what she regards as his frustrated sexual life: if he had only, she sighs, been capable of a mature attachment for a woman which would have freed him from his passion for little girls! (a penchant with which his position as elder brother of seven motherless sisters as well as the strong feminine streak in him noted by Mrs. Lennon must have a good deal to do). What she does not understand, I think, is that Dodgson, in terms of his age and place, was remarkably "well-adjusted." His enjoyment of the Oxford "Studentship," with its relatively agreeable work and exceptionally comfortable quarters, which he won on his graduation, was dependent on his acceptance of celibacy; and there is nothing to show that this irked him much. His admiration and affection for his father seem to have been complete; the rectory in which he grew up was obviously as little as possible like that described by Samuel Butler in *The Way of All Flesh;* and with the Dodgsons the church tradition was strong: Charles's father and mother, who were cousins, had had the same Archbishop for a grandfather. Since reading this biography and Collingwood's memoir, I am less disposed than I was when I wrote the above article to assume that Charles Dodgson was seriously cramped by his role. Mrs. Lennon insists that, in his photographs, he has the look of one "crucified," but she does not produce any evidence that he actually suffered much. There is mockery of course in Alice, who finds herself at odds with the "creatures"; there are, as both Mrs. Lennon and Mr. Empson suggest, outbreaks of contemptuous violence at the ends of the *Alice* books and *Sylvie and Bruno;* but the forces of benevolence and common sense always triumph in what is not merely the conventional Victorian happy ending, as they certainly did in Dodgson's life. The conditions of teaching in an English university in the middle of the nineteenth century may seem to us today unnatural, but all social and professional situations involve their special disabilities, and in the position that Dodgson had chosen he seems to have functioned well. If a part of his intelligence lived underground, if a part of his personality was screened, it is plain that—Mrs. Lennon admits this—Alice would never have gone down the rabbit-hole, would never have walked through the mirror, if this had not been the case. Dodgson's work in mathematics and logic was somewhat eccentric, too, and he sometimes, we are told, proposed problems, just as his stories do, that probed into the depths of their subjects; but in these scientific fields as in fiction he seems to have given the world all that he was capable of. The author of *Sylvie and Bruno* was trying already for more than he could manage. Mrs. Lennon, has, I believe, been the first to point out the exact and complicated parallels between the dreams and the actualities that make this book psychologically interesting (my own references to these above have been added for the sake of completeness since the article was first written), but the novel for grownups is otherwise childish; and in mathematics and logic, according to the expert opinions cited by Mrs. Lennon, he either ignored or had never discovered the more advanced work in these fields, and did not perhaps get even so far as in his exploration of dreams.

It is one of the pioneering merits of *Victoria Through the Looking-Glass* that Mrs. Lennon has looked up these authoritative estimates of Dodgson's mathematical and logical work; and, a poet, she is able herself to provide an expert opinion on his poetry. The only aspect of his varied activity to which she does not seem quite to do justice is his achievement as an artist-photographer; but this subject has been dealt with since in a book called *Lewis Carroll Photographer* by Helmut Gernsheim (1950). Mr. Gernsheim considers Dodgson "the most outstanding photographer of children of the nineteenth century" and, after Julia Margaret Cameron, "probably the most distinguished amateur portraitist of the mid-Victorian era." In this field he was eccentric and perfectionist as he was in everything else. He showed the real reckless artist's passion in his pursuit of his two favorite kinds of subjects: celebrities and little girls. The former he besieged unabashedly, undaunted by occasional snubs and not afraid to arrive before breakfast, with all his apparatus in a cab, so that his prospects would not have a chance to escape. In his search for attractive little girls, he attended such incongruous functions as archery meetings and Freemason's fêtes, and spent part of his vacations at the seaside, supplied always with safety pins in case he should find "a little girl hesitating to paddle in the sea for fear of spoiling her frock." His trophies repaid him for his risks and ordeals. A few of his portraits were reproduced in the Collingwood *Life and Letters*, but these do not give an adequate idea of the interest and scope of these plates. There was, it seems, an enormous body of work, of which twelve albums are known to survive. The sixty-four plates from three of them that Mr. Gernsheim includes in his book show a dramatic sense of personality—in the posing, the arrangement of the backgrounds, and the feeling for facial expression—that one would not have suspected in Dodgson from his letters and his literary work and that reminds one of his love of the theater (which, in taking Holy Orders at Oxford, he made sure that he would not be expected to renounce). Here, humanly appealing and vivid, you have the troubled Elizabethanism of Tennyson; the jaunty, almost rakish bohemianism of Tom Taylor, the editor of *Punch;* the contemptuous independence of Rossetti; the serious and challenging young-womanhood of the eighteen-year-old Ellen Terry; the healthy Victorian attractiveness of Alexander Munro and his wife; and the morbid Victorian intensity of "Mrs. Franklin and her daughter Rose." There is a liveliness and a humor in these pictures that sometimes suggest Max Beerbohm. It is, one supposes, unlikely that Max could have seen these albums at the time he did his drawings of *Rossetti and His Circle,* but the photographs of the Millais's and the Rossettis seem to anticipate these. As for the pictures of children, they, too, are extremely varied and provide a new revelation of Lewis Carroll's special genius for depicting little English girls that is as brilliant in its way as *Alice.*

Last Days

of

ALICE

by Allen Tate

(1948)

ALICE grown lazy, mammoth but not fat,
Declines upon her lost and twilight age;
Above in the dozing leaves the grinning cat
Quivers forever with his abstract rage:

Whatever light swayed on the perilous gate
Forever sways, nor will the arching grass,
Caught when the world clattered, undulate
In the deep suspension of the looking-glass.

Bright Alice! always pondering to gloze
The spoiled cruelty she had meant to say
Gazes learnedly down her airy nose
At nothing, nothing thinking all the day.

Turned absent-minded by infinity
She cannot move unless her double move,
The All-Alice of the world's entity
Smashed in the anger of her hopeless love,

Love for herself who, as an earthly twain,
Pouted to join her two in a sweet one;
No more the second lips to kiss in vain
The first she broke, plunged through the glass alone—

Alone to the weight of impassivity,
Incest of spirit, theorem of desire,
Without will as chalky cliffs by the sea,
Empty as the bodiless flesh of fire:

All space, that heaven is a dayless night,
A nightless day driven by perfect lust
For vacancy, in which her bored eyesight
Stares at the drowsy cubes of human dust.

—We too back to the world shall never pass
Through the shattered door, a dumb shade-harried crowd
Being all infinite, function depth and mass
Without figure, a mathematical shroud

Hurled at the air—blesséd without sin!
O God of our flesh, return us to Your wrath,
Let us be evil could we enter in
Your grace, and falter on the stony path!

V
Church
and
Chess

Lewis Carroll

and the

Oxford

Movement

by Shane Leslie

(1933)

It is proposed to make a submission a little apart from the many wise and learned books and papers which are being written at this time in honor of the centenary of the Oxford Movement. To what extent did Lewis Carroll reflect contemporary ecclesiastical history in his famous works?

The Oxford Movement, according to Dean Hutton, "seemed almost throughout its whole course to stand apart from the literature of the day," but it gave birth to endless University squibs and parodies. At the beginning there was Archbishop Whately's anonymous "Pastoral Epistle from His Holiness the Pope to some members of the University of Oxford" and there was Freeman's description of Ward's degradation in the Senate House, recounted in the resonant meter of Macaulay. But it has never been suggested yet that Lewis Carroll's work reflected the thought and trouble of Oxford between the forties and seventies, and yet with a tithe of the care which Baconians give to the investigation of Shakespeare it can be shown that such was the case.

Alice in Wonderland was published in 1865 and *Through the Looking-Glass* in 1871. Their theological import has been strangely overlooked by students. It must be remembered that by that time the Tractarians had been scattered but the controversies of High, Low, and Broad Church had taken perennial shape. They were uppermost in every Oxford man's mind at the time. It is not profane to suggest that *Alice in Wonderland* may contain a secret history of the Oxford Movement. Lewis Carroll himself lived as a don at Christ Church under the shadow of Pusey. It is remarkable that he added an Easter greeting to the 1876 edition, in which, significantly, he said: "Some perhaps may blame me for mixing together things grave and gay: others may smile and think it odd that any one should speak of solemn things at all except in Church and on a Sunday." Can he be hinting himself that the story itself mingles the grave and the gay? There is nothing to do but to proceed to the search with the blindfold industry of a professor and the open faith of a child.

Alice, to begin with, may be regarded as the simple freshman or everyman who wanders like a sweet and innocent undergraduate into the Wonderland of a Victorian Oxford when everybody was religious in some way or another. The White Rabbit, whom she immediately meets, is the type of simple English clergyman of the day, with his hole fixed like some country rectory. When he takes his watch out of his pocket (a curious proceeding for any rabbit) he strikes a supernatural note immediately. Alice follows him down the rabbit-hole and it will be remembered that on the way down she noticed a jar significantly labeled Orange Marmalade, which was and still is the symbol of old-fashioned Protestantism since the arrival of the immortal king of that name. Alice expected, like St. Augustine, that she would come out at the Antipodes with her feet in the air and walking on her head. She found herself in a low long hall with locked doors: some of these doors were for High people and others for the Lowly. Perhaps this is meant as an allegory for the Church of England. Alice used a tiny golden key (presumably the Key of Holy Scripture) to open the lesser door. The process of becoming High or Low is of course an Anglican acquirement or privilege and when she drinks out of the bottle labeled DRINK ME, she has taken a drink of a doctrine which makes her so small that she can pass through the Low door. On the way she becomes a little metaphysical and wonders what a candle flame is like when it is blown out. This is the everlasting query of the professors concerning the soul after death.

Her next act is to eat a piece off the cake of dogma and that naturally sends her up high again: higher and higher until she frightens the White Rabbit, who runs off in great alarm of the Duchess, who is presumably a symbol of his Bishop!

When Alice picked up the Rabbit's fan, she found herself shrinking and shrinking until she began to swim about in her own tears, the tears of repentance. She meets a mouse, a Church mouse, swimming about like herself and frightens him away by allusions to Dinah her cat. Now, who can Dinah symbolize except the Catholic enemy? "Would you like cats if you were me?" the Mouse asks very naturally. The Mouse pales with passion and she asks Alice to swim ashore to hear her story, "and then you'll understand why it is I hate cats and dogs." If Dinah was Catholic, Alice's terrier, being Scotch, may be expected to be Presbyterian, and reference to it is equally trying to a Church mouse.

The famous races which follow under the Dodo's presidency show the author's tolerant and equable beliefs amounting to universal salvation all round. The Dodo announces: "Everybody has won and all must have prizes," which sounds like another version of "the first shall be last and the last shall be first." The Mouse's tale is a long and a sad one and may perhaps be read as a skit on the lengthy sermons on Predestination which were in vogue until the Oxford Movement brought a cheerier message. It ends at least: "I'll be judge, I'll be jury ... I'll try the whole cause, and condemn you to death." If that is not the gloomy view which Calvinists take of their Deity, it forms a convincing parallel. But it is a sermon all right, for the Mouse says to Alice, "You are not attending."

When Alice finds herself visibly swelling and filling the White Rabbit's parsonage, it is an Irish gardener whom Lewis Carroll introduces in order to show how to face the supernatural with perfect calm. The White Rabbit asks:

> "Now tell me, Pat, what's in that window?"
> "Sure, it's an arm, yer honour." ...

> "An arm, you goose! Who ever saw one that size?
>   Why, it fills the whole window!"
> "Sure, it does, yer honour: but it's an arm for all that."

The Caterpillar, whom Alice finds smoking on the top of a mushroom, must be the symbol of Oxford philosophy, for he gives Alice advice as though he were Dr. Jowett himself. The mushroom must be the Liberalism or Rationalism of the time, and by nibbling its edge Alice can bring herself to a common-sense stature. The King and Queen of Hearts come on the scene to represent the Royal Supremacy or Erastian principle detested of High Churchmen. The angry Queen is the House of Commons and the King is the Lord Chancellor in the Upper House. When the Queen invites the Duchess (who represents Episcopacy) to play croquet, it means joining in an ecclesiastical debate, though a game played with hedgehogs and flamingos is simple compared to the complexities of the English House of Commons debating the knots of Church ritual.

The Cook, who has a prominent place in the Duchess's kitchen, takes little notice of her and is no doubt the independent Dean of the Bishop's Cathedral. In her excitement the Cook does not mind what she hurls at the Duchess and her baby, who represents the Faithful lying in the Bishop's lap. If the Cook is the typical Dean, say Dean Stanley, and the Duchess is Bishop Wilberforce, the Cheshire Cat, who sits aloft and grins, is a likely skit on Cardinal Wiseman. "It looked good-natured, Alice thought: still it had *very* long claws and a great many teeth, so she felt that it ought to be treated with respect." She consults the Cheshire Cat accordingly and learns that nearby there live a Hatter and a March Hare, both of whom in the Cheshire Cat's opinion are mad. The word mad may be taken to mean religious throughout the book. The Cat says Alice is mad herself to have come there. Finally the Cat, like a symbol of the supernatural, vanishes slowly, leaving only that grin of satisfaction with which the Papal Curia have always regarded Anglican affairs.

The March Hare and the Hatter are the types of Low and High Church parsons with their Dormouse of a congregation slumbering between them. The Hatter with his hat is the High Churchman with his biretta, while his famous watch, which tells the day of the month, must be a Church calendar. It fails to be justified by its works alone, in spite of the butter of piety ingenuously added by the March Hare. Alice reaches a beautiful garden, where the time-serving gardeners are trying to paint white roses red to please the Queen. This must be the Garden of Preferment and they are trying to make their colors suit the State. The Queen, who is forever sentencing her subjects to sentences that are never carried out, recalls the futility of the endless Bishops' legislation against the Ritualists. Meanwhile, the Cheshire Cat has returned to watch like an outsider how things turn out. "How do you like the Queen?" it whispers in a low voice. It is the whisper of Wiseman, and the violent attempts of King and Queen to have the Cat executed seem like a memory of the futile legislation against Papal Aggression in 1851, when Parliament passed a bill to cut off Catholic Bishops from their titles. The executioner, summoned in vain, has a resemblance to Lord John Russell, the Prime Minister of the period. The Mock Turtle appears to resemble or symbolize the Victorian Church of England recalling her old history. "Once . . . I was a real Turtle. . . . We went to school in the sea. The master was an old Turtle—we used to call him Tortoise . . . because he taught us." This was surely a hint of the medieval Pope and the *ecclesia docens*. The extras taught at this famous school were French, music, and washing: possibly the three marks of the distinctively Catholic service, a Latin tongue, church chant, and church millenary. The famous song wherein the Whiting tries to inveigle the Snail to join the Lobster Quadrille refers to the scruples of converts. Some launched out to sea and others, like the Snail,

Said he thanked the whiting kindly, but he would not join the dance.
Would not, could not, would not, could not, could not join the dance.

The grand finale was the trial of the Knave of Hearts for the theft of certain tarts, which were described as made of pepper and treacle and therefore not unlike the composition of the Thirty-Nine Articles, which were composed to catch Catholics and yet assuage Protestants:

The Queen of Hearts, she made some tarts,
All on a summer day:
The Knave of Hearts, he stole those tarts
And took them quite away!

The Articles, if they are personified by the tarts, had been manufactured by Parliament, but it was the knavish Ritualist who was so bitterly accused of having removed their natural sense. Against the culprit, both High and Low, both the Mad Hatter and the March Hare were called as witnesses. It is interesting that the King's words to the Knave were exactly those which had once been hurled at Newman and at everybody who had tried to equivocate on the Articles. "You must have meant some mischief or else you would have signed your name like an honest man." The Tractarians like Ward and Newman signed in no honest but (as they called it) in its unnatural sense and this was at the root of Tract Ninety and led to the undoing of Newman and the rout of the whole Movement as a unistreamed Anglican revival.

Through the Looking-Glass was published in 1871. It is more difficult of interpretation but the following table will be found not far from possibilities:

WHITE			RED	
Tweedledum	High Church		*Humpty Dumpty*	Verbal Inspiration
Unicorn	Convocation of Clergy		*Carpenter and Walrus*	Essayists and Reviewers
Sheep	Dr. Pusey			
White Queen	Dr. Newman		*Red Queen*	Archbishop Manning
White King	Dr. Jowett		*Red King*	Canon Kingsley
Aged Man	Oxford Don		*Crow*	Disestablishment
White Knight	Huxley		*Red Knight*	Bishop Wilberforce
Tweedledee	Low Church		*Lion*	John Bull

Looking-Glass life, in which everything appears reversed, is the symbol of the supernatural life. Alice again is the gentle inquirer, who climbs into this strange world outside of time and space. The clock grins at her with the face of a little old man, as though time had become its own laughingstock. The castles on the chessboard are the colleges, the pawns are the followers of different schools of thought. The White King is probably Dr. Jowett of Balliol, who finds that "he writes all manner of things that I don't intend." Jabberwocky can only be a fearsome representation of the British view of the Papacy as held at that time. It is not difficult to slip parody between the lines such as:

"Beware the Papacy, my son,
    The Jaws that bite, the claws that catch!
Beware the Jesuit bird, and shun
    The Benedictine batch!"

He took his Gospel sword in hand,
    Long time the Roman foe he sought—
So rested he by the Bible tree,
    And stood awhile in thought.

The garden of live (but anchored and somewhat backbiting) flowers may stand for the Oxford Academy. The Red Queen approximates to Archbishop Manning when she gives Alice advice for the journey. Nothing could be more precise, contradictory, and self-assured than the Red Queen. She seems to be hinting of Rome when telling of a garden compared to which the Oxford garden would be a wilderness and of hills compared to which the one on which they stood was as a valley. Alice and the Red Queen survey a world divided like a chessboard into dioceses much as the world appeared during the time of the Vatican Council. The spiritual rivalry between Protestant and Catholic is reflected in the phrase "It's a huge great game of chess that's being played all over the world."

Alice starts as a pawn to the White Queen, that is, as a follower of Dr. Newman, but the ultramontane Red Queen, Manning, urges her to go faster and faster, though, strange to say, as it often is in religion, she finds herself where she was when she started. It is a spiritual journey after all that she has made. To quench Alice's thirst, the Red Queen offers her a dry biscuit which seems to symbolize a sermon. In the next square or diocese Alice meets the weird-looking Glass Insects, which vaguely resemble the sects of English religious life.

The Rocking-horse-fly described as "bright and sticky" looks like a good Methodist on circuit. The Snap-dragon-fly, with its head dipped in brandy, must be the extinct two-bottle Orthodox, as they were called in the grand old days before Temperance reform. The Bread-and-butter-fly, living on a diet of weak tea, is too well-known at religious tables to require further explication.

Tweedledum and Tweedledee, living under the same roof, are obviously the High and Low Church quarreling over the new Ritualism, which is disguised as Tweedledum's nice new rattle. Their rivalry is put an end to by the shadow of the black crow, which is presumably Disestablishment.

The Walrus and the Carpenter must be referred to the higher critics who had come into prominence at this time, like Dean Stanley and Bishop Colenso. They manage to make havoc of the confiding young clergy, represented as Oysters. The Walrus and the Carpenter regret the amount of dogmatic sand which is lying about and refer to the seven advanced essayists and reviewers, who in 1860 swept the Church of England clear of a good deal of doctrine in the celebrated lines whose mystical meaning has lain hidden as yet:

"If seven maids with seven mops
Swept it for a half year,
Do you suppose," the Walrus said,
"That they could get it clear?"
"I doubt it," said the Carpenter,
And shed a bitter tear.

When the unfortunate Oysters hurry up

"The time has come," the Walrus said,
"To talk of many things:
Of shoes—and ships—and sealing-wax—"
Of Genesis and Kings
And whether hell is boiling hot
Or Angel folk have wings."

The words in roman are suggested as a variant reading.

Tweedledum and Tweedledee array themselves in the armories of
Scripture and Church councils and do battle, though they have to share
one sword between them. This is because it is the same sword of doctrine. The White Queen may represent Dr. Newman. She has been so
long preparing herself that she is covered with pins, like all the exasperating little points in theology. She offers to take Alice but her rules are
a little ascetical: "jam to-morrow and jam yesterday—but never jam
today." Alice has a conversation with her on looking-glass or spiritual
lines and admits "one *can't* believe impossible things." But the White
Queen proudly tells her, "Why, sometimes I've believed as many as six
impossible things before breakfast." The Sheep whom Alice finds knitting
in the next square with no less than fourteen pairs of needles is our
friend Dr. Pusey knitting his interminable sermons and pamphlets in
the Anglican shop. Wherever Alice sets her eye on a shelf, everything
seems to melt away. "Things flow about here so." Alice at one moment
is about to buy an Easter egg when it turns into the familiar features of
Humpty Dumpty, who sits on the wall of Scripture looking like the
Verbal Inspiration which was dethroned by the Privy Council in 1866
when, it will be remembered, all the King's lawyers and all the King's
men couldn't put Humpty Dumpty back again. The result of Verbal
Inspiration[1] had been that words had to mean whatever the clerical
Humpty Dumpty chose. As he remarked: "Adjectives you can do any-
thing with, but not verbs—however, *I* can manage the whole lot of them!
Impenetrability!" Is Impenetrability Lewis Carrolline for Infallibility?

The Lion and the Unicorn fighting for supremacy reflect John Bull and the Convocation of Clergy struggling for the upper hand, which invariably goes to John Bull. People paid brown bread or tithes to one or white bread or taxes to the other, but were mighty glad to get them and their quarrels drummed out of town.

The White Knight represents Victorian science, or Huxley in his most cocksure and inventive mood. The Red Knight corresponding is his old enemy Bishop Wilberforce, and they arrive in the same square together and both try to make a capture of Alice. This was the famous occasion when Wilberforce and Huxley clashed in 1866 at the meeting of the British Association.

As a grand finale Alice becomes a queen (shall we say becomes a Roman Catholic?), for she ends by feasting between the Red and White Queens Newman and Manning. And for many simple folk this was the end of the Oxford Movement, not without a hint of being somewhat distracted by the rivalries and embittered clashes between the two Cardinals who were seldom on speaking terms.

We suggest that Lewis Carroll had all this and a great deal more at the back of his mind when he wrote his two masterpieces.

THROUGH THE LOOKING-GLASS

by Alexander L. Taylor

(1952)

THE FIRST CHAPTER of *Through the Looking-Glass* was sent to the press "a few days after the publication of 'Phantasmagoria,'[1] which appeared in January, 1869. Dodgson must therefore have been writing, as opposed to jotting down ideas, at least since his removal to Tom Quad. On 19 April, 1870, he wrote to Miss Mary Marshal, "I don't know when it will be finished."[2] It was published in December, 1871. Fortunately Tenniel had relented and did supply the illustrations.

In *Alice's Adventures* Dodgson had ingeniously concealed certain amusing little problems and "leg-pulls." He deliberately cast *Through the Looking-Glass* in the form of an enigma, a form which appealed to his love of innocent deception and which Kingsley had suggested in *The Water Babies*:

> Come read me a riddle
> Each good little man:
> If you cannot read it
> No grown-up folks can.

And if you will read this story nine times over, and then think for yourself, you will find out why. It is not good for little boys to be told everything, and never to be forced to use their wits.

Compare with this the old Sheep's remark: "I never put things into people's hands; that would never do. They must get them for themselves."

In 1888 Dodgson wrote to Nellie Knight from Eastbourne:

I'm rather puzzled which book to send to Sydney. He looks so young for Through the Looking-Glass. *However, he found out one puzzle . . . that I don't remember anyone of his age ever guessing before, so I think it won't be too old a book for him.*

What Sydney made of it as a puzzle is not recorded. No doubt he enjoyed it as a story.

It is not my intention to go through the book squeezing the last drop of meaning from every word. That would take a very long time—supposing it to be possible, which is by no means certain. As Dodgson said in a letter to a friend in America, "words mean more than we mean to express when we use them; so a whole book ought to mean a great deal more than the writer means."[3] Let us, however, examine some of the ideas on which the book is based.

In the first place, he used the time-honored dream-machinery, that medieval framework for allegory and satire, but he used it with a difference. How long does a dream last? By the clock, Alice's dream lasts hardly any time at all. When it begins, Dinah is washing her white kitten and she is still washing it when Alice awakes—if she has ever been asleep. She has been in some kind of trance, like "the vision of the prophet Mahommed, in which he saw the whole wonders of heaven and hell, though the jar of water which fell when his ecstasy commenced had not spilled its contents when he returned to ordinary existence."

In *Bruno's Revenge* (1867), Dodgson had explained what he meant by the "eerie" state. Twenty-six years later, in the Preface to *Sylvie and Bruno Concluded*, he elaborated his views:

> *It may interest some of my Readers to know the theory on which this story is constructed. It is an attempt to show what might possibly happen, supposing that Fairies really existed; and that they were sometimes visible to us and we to them; and supposing also, that human beings might sometimes become conscious of what goes on in the Fairy-world— by actual transference of their immaterial essence, such as we meet with in "Esoteric Buddhism".*
>
> *I have supposed a Human Being to be capable of various psychic states, with varying degrees of consciousness, as follows:*
>
> a) *The ordinary state, with no consciousness of the presence of Fairies;*
> b) *The "eerie" state, in which, while conscious of actual surroundings, he is* also *conscious of the presence of Fairies;*
> c) *A form of trance, in which, while* unconscious *of actual surroundings and apparently asleep, he (i.e. his immaterial essence) migrates to other scenes, in the actual world, or in Fairyland, and is conscious of the presence of Fairies.*
>
> *I have also supposed a Fairy to be capable of migrating from Fairyland into the actual world, and of assuming at pleasure a Human form; and also to be capable of various psychical states, viz.:*
>
> a) *The ordinary state, with no consciousness of the presence of Human Beings.*
> b) *A sort of "eerie" state, in which he is conscious, if in the actual world, of the presence of actual Human Beings, if in Fairyland, of the presence of the immaterial essences of Human Beings.*
>
> *I will here tabulate the passages in both Volumes, where abnormal states occur.*

And he does.

In *Through the Looking-Glass* Alice is in the normal state at the beginning and the end of the story. She is "eerie" in Looking-Glass House and when she has "entered the palace," just before she awakes. In the garden and on the chessboard she is in the trance state.

The chess pieces, too, have their various states. In Looking-Glass House they are unconscious of Alice's presence; that is, they are in "the ordinary state, with no consciousness of the presence of Human Beings." But in the game they are conscious of the presence of Alice's immaterial essence. Near the end of the game the Queens fall asleep and dream of Alice's world. They are presumably in the trance state then. The Red King is in the trance state throughout and the White Knight might be said to be permanently "eerie."

The rather irritating question, "Which dreamed it?" with its Kantian or Berkeleyan overtones, derives from Dodgson's original ending to *Alice's Adventures under Ground:*

> *But her sister sat there some while longer, watching the setting sun, and thinking of little Alice and her adventures, till she, too, began dreaming after a fashion, and this was her dream.*
>
> *She saw an ancient city, and a quiet river winding near it along the plain, and up the stream went slowly gliding a boat with a merry party of children on board—she could hear the voices and laughter like music over the water—and among them was another little Alice, who sat listening with bright, eager eyes, to a tale that was being told, and she listened for the tale, and lo, it was the dream of her own little sister.*

Less original was the looking-glass idea. It cannot be a coincidence that within a year of each other appeared *Through the Looking-Glass* (1871) and *Erewhon* (1872), both about worlds where everything is the mirror-image of what we regard as normal. Yet it is as certain as anything can be that the books were written independently. Kingsley had used a similar idea in *The Water Babies*, where Tom found the Other-End-of-Nowhere much more like This-End-of-Somewhere than he had been in the habit of expecting. And before that there was the Taylor sisters' *Signor Topsy Turvey's Wonderful Magic Lantern; or The World Turned Upside Down* (1810). Yet Dodgson's use of the looking-glass idea was all his own.

The difference between *Erewhon* and *Through the Looking-Glass* is profound. Butler begins realistically, as Swift did in *Gulliver's Travels*, but soon throws aside all pretense and reveals his purpose as satirical. Dodgson pretends throughout to be writing "nonsense." He acknowledges no obligation to stick to one subject but slides from topic to topic by subtle associations of ideas. Nevertheless, meaning is always there, flowing along like a deep, dark river, with the puns and patter as the play of light on the surface.

Again, Butler used his reversals to cast doubts on the moral and ethical standards of Victorian England. His looking-glass was the circle of stone figures at the head of the pass, six or seven times larger than life, of great antiquity and ten in number, our tribal taboos, the Ten Commandments. Dodgson's satire was directed, as on previous occasions, against controversy in religious matters, while his explorations were mainly in that no man's land between mathematics and theology, into which he had already made some short expeditions.

Another basic idea was that of sending his heroine into a game of chess, and for this he had made, as we have seen, some preliminary sketches from life. Drawing from life was a matter of principle with him, and he recommended it in the most explicit manner to all his illustrators, even overruling Tenniel, who said he no more needed a model in front of him than Dodgson needed a multiplication table.

Chess to Dodgson was something far more than a game. As a mathematician he saw the board like a sheet of graph paper on which it is possible to represent almost anything, and as a theologian he saw in the two sides a far more powerful means of expressing the opposing factions in Church and University than any he had previously hit upon.

Let us begin by examining the most striking and original episode in the whole book, the Red Queen running. Alice, it will be remembered, had met her—by walking away from her—in the Garden of Live Flowers. With her she went to the top of the Principal Mountain and saw all the world she was to enter spread out beneath her in the form of a large chessboard.

> "*It's a great huge game of chess that's being played—all over the world—if this is the world at all, you know.*"

Alice longed to join in and would have preferred to be a queen, but at first she could only be the White Queen's Pawn, though the post held good prospects of eventual Queendom.

> *Just at this moment, somehow or other, they began to run.*
> *Alice never could quite make out, in thinking it over afterwards, how it was that they began: all she remembers is, that they were running hand in hand, and the Queen went so fast that it was all she could do to keep up with her: and still the Queen kept crying "Faster! Faster!"*

Stranger still was the fact that "the trees and the other things round them never changed their places at all: however fast they went, they never seemed to pass anything."

No doubt many of the clever and profound things said of this running are perfectly true. It may anticipate Einstein. It may be a spiritual journey which leaves Alice where she started. But the basis of the running is a mathematical trick. In our world speed is the ratio of distance to time: $s = d \div t$. For a high speed, the distance is great and the time small; so many miles per hour. Through the Looking-Glass, however, speed is the ratio of time to distance: $s = t \div d$. For a high speed the time is great and the distance small. The higher the speed, the smaller the distance covered. The faster Alice went in time, the more she stayed where she was in space.

"*Now, here, you see, it takes all the running you can do, to keep in the same place.*"

This is Fechner's variable 't' which became the fourth coordinate of space.

"*Are we nearly there?*" . . .
"*Nearly there!*" the Queen repeated. "*Why, we passed it ten minutes ago! Faster!*"

They had left our space behind and were running in time.

The Queen propped her up against a tree, and said kindly, "You may rest a little, now."
Alice looked round her in great surprise. "Why, I do believe we've been under this tree the whole time! Everything's just as it was."

Note "the whole time." No wonder the clock on the chimney piece had the face of a little old man and grinned at her!

The White Queen, too, was at home in this unfamiliar element, as her "living backwards" shows. In this, Dodgson was using an idea developed by Plato in the *Statesman* and by Fechner in his "Space Has Four Dimensions." Plato's reversal of time involves an earth-shaking convulsion, after which the dead rise from the earth and "live in the opposite order." This, he says, was the fabled golden age. Fechner's is set in the future but is upon the same cosmic scale. "Growing old will cease," he says, "but all life will consist of rejuvenation." He goes further than Plato and returns us all to our grand ancestor Adam in the Garden of Eden, and Adam, with the whole earth and sea and the sun and the stars, into the Oneness of God.

Dodgson's treatment of the idea is quite different, but certainly not less effective. In the simplest possible terms, he states and then illustrates the principle:

"It's a poor sort of memory that only works backwards," the Queen remarked.

"What sort of things do you remember best?" Alice ventured to ask.

"Oh, things that happened the week after next," the Queen replied in a careless tone.

This, of course, follows from the game of chess, as well as the looking-glass oppositeness. If the length of the board is time, then one direction must be forwards and the other backwards. The King's Messenger, for instance, Hatta (the Mad Hatter), is "in prison now, being punished: and the trial doesn't even begin till next Wednesday: and of course the crime comes last of all."

All through this particular *reductio ad absurdum* the White Queen is plastering her finger. Then she screams that it is bleeding, though she has not pricked it yet. She will—and does—when she fastens her shawl again.

"That accounts for the bleeding, you see," she said to Alice with a smile. *"Now you understand the way things happen here."*

"But why don't you scream now?" Alice asked, holding her hands ready to put over her ears again.

"Why, I've done all the screaming already," said the Queen. *"What would be the good of having it all over again?"*

Alice was a pawn. "Lets pretend we're kings and queens," she had said to her sister, but a pawn she had to be. In time, we human beings are the merest pawns. We move in one direction, forward from one moment to the next, as a pawn moves forward from one square to the next. A pawn's world is Fechner's world of one dimension, pure progress, or Hamilton's abstract, ideal, or pure time, like that space which is the object of geometry. Nevertheless, the pawn's world is not a knife edge, a time-line. Alice does not appear to be able to see even the whole of one square all at once, yet she has some knowledge of the square on either side of her. Dodgson is no doubt conventionalizing the taking move, which does affect the square on either side one ahead. Alice is not interested in "taking" anything, unless we count "taking notice." Or Dodgson may be thinking of the fact that pieces are not always set exactly in the center of the square they occupy, but jostle each other a little and overlap into adjoining squares. *"J'adoube."*

At all events, Alice, when she is a pawn, is continually meeting chessmen, red and white, and, according to the key, they are always on the square next to her on one side or the other. To the right, she meets the Red Queen, the Red King, the Red Knight, the White Knight, and, at the end of the board, the Red Queen again. To the left, she meets the White Queen, the White King, and, at the end of the board, the White Queen again. Of what is happening in the other parts of the board she has no knowledge. She sweeps a narrow track, and events more than one square distant to either side, or behind, or ahead of her are out of her world. A certain lack of coherence in her picture of the game is understandable, particularly as it is in an advanced stage when she begins to move.

In the *Lewis Carroll Handbook,* Falconer Madan regrets that "the chess framework is full of absurdities and impossibilities" and considers it a pity that Dodgson did not bring the game, as a game, up to chess standard, as, says Mr. Madan, he could easily have done. He points out that among other absurdities the white side is allowed to make nine consecutive moves, the White King to be checked unnoticed; Queens castle, and the White Queen flies from the Red Knight when she could take it. "Hardly a move," he says, "has a sane purpose, from the point of view of chess."[4] There is also a mate for White at the fourth move (Dodgson's reckoning): W.Q. to K.'s 3rd instead of Q.B.'s 4th. Alice and the Red Queen are both out of the way and the Red King could not move out of check.

Dodgson's own words, in a preface written in 1887, in reply to criticism of this kind, are as follows:

As the chess-problem, given on the previous page, has puzzled some of my readers, it may be well to explain that it is correctly worked out, so far as the moves *are concerned. The* alternation *of Red and White is perhaps not so strictly observed as it might be, and the "castling" of the three Queens is merely a way of saying that they entered the palace; but the "check" of the White King at move 6, the capture of the Red Knight at move 7, and the final "checkmate" of the Red King, will be found, by any one who will take the trouble to set the pieces and play the moves as directed, to be strictly in accordance with the laws of the game.*

Dodgson was not interested in the game as a game, but in the implications of the moves. He could easily have "worked out a problem." He spent a considerable part of his life doing that kind of thing. But in *Through the Looking-Glass* he was otherwise engaged. In the first place, it would be illogical to expect logic in a game of chess dreamed by a child. It would be still more illogical to expect a pawn which can see only a small patch of board to understand the meaning of its experiences. And there is a moral in that. This is a pawn's impression of chess, which is like a human being's impression of life.

Alice never grasps the purpose of the game at all and when she reaches the Eighth Square tries to find out from the two Queens if it is over. None of the pieces has the least idea what it is all about. The Red King is asleep. The White King has long ago abandoned any attempt to intervene. "You might as well try to catch a Bandersnatch." The Red Knight is quite justified in his battle cry of "Ahoy! Ahoy! Check!" but the White Knight, too, leaps out of the wood, shouting "Ahoy! Ahoy! Check!" and he is not giving check at all but capturing the Red Knight. Neither of them has any control over the square on which Alice is situated, yet the Red Knight thinks he has captured her and the White Knight that he has rescued her. Alice cannot argue with either of them but is simply relieved to have the matter settled in a manner favorable to herself.

As for the Queens, they "see" so much of the board that they might be expected to know what is happening fairly well. But, as will appear, their manner of "seeing" is so peculiar that they know less about it than anybody. To understand one's part in a game of chess, one would have to be aware of the room and the unseen intelligence which is combining the pieces. Deprived of any such knowledge, the chessmen have to explain things as best they can. Nor is this a game between two players. To have made it that would have been tantamount to Dodgson's confession that he believed in two separate and opposite Powers about us. He deliberately avoided any such implication.

He based his story, not on a game of chess, but on a chess lesson or demonstration of the moves such as he gave to Alice Liddell, a carefully worked-out sequence of moves designed to illustrate the queening of a pawn, the relative powers of the pieces—the feeble king, the eccentric knight, and the formidable queen whose powers include those of rook and bishop—and finally a checkmate. That is to say, he abstracted from the game exactly what he wanted for his design, and expressed that as a game between a child of seven-and-a-half who was to "be" a White Pawn and an older player (himself) who was to manipulate the other pieces.

"And yet you incessantly stand on your head . . ."
Drawing by Lewis Carroll

Father William. Illustration by Sir John Tenniel

"Drink Me."
Illustration by Lewis Carroll

"Drink Me."
Original sketch by Sir John Tenniel

"Drink Me."
Finished illustration by Tenniel

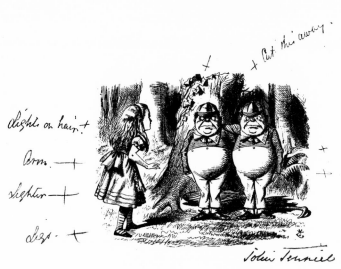

A proof of Tweedledum and Tweedledee,
with Tenniel's instructions for corrections to the engraver

Humpty Dumpty and the Messenger.
Drawing by Lewis Carroll

Tenniel's Humpty Dumpty
and the Messenger

Alice and the Jury.
Sketch by Tenniel

Alice and the Jury.
Finished Tenniel illustration

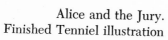

Alice, grown too large for the
Rabbit's house.
Right: Drawing by Carroll;
Below: Tenniel's illustration

on their feet and hands, to make the arches.

The chief difficulty which Alice found at first was to manage her ostrich : she got its body tucked away, comfortably enough, under

her arm, with its legs hanging down, but generally, just as she had got its neck straightened out nicely, and was going to give a blow with its head, it _would_ twist itself round, and look up into her face, with such a puzzled expression that she could not help bursting out laughing : and when she had got its head down, and was going to begin again, it was very confusing to find that the hedgehog had unrolled itself, and was in the act of crawling away : besides all this, there was generally a ridge or a furrow in her way, wherever she wanted to send the hedgehog to, and as the doubled-up soldiers were always getting up and walking off to other

Page of Carroll's original manuscript,
Alice's Adventures under Ground

Only the other day, it will be remembered, Alice had had a long argument with her sister about playing kings and queens. Alice had been reduced at last to saying, "Well, *you* can be one of them, then, and *I'll* be all the rest." Through the Looking-Glass she was "one of them" and the Other Player "all the rest." Perhaps that is how things are. Dodgson certainly hoped so.

Observe the Red Queen about to do her disappearing trick:

"At the end of two yards," she said, putting in a peg to mark the distance, "I shall give you your directions—have another biscuit?"

The biscuit is deliberately used to distract our attention from the fact that these pegs mark out the stages of Alice's pawn-life.

"At the end of three yards I shall repeat them—for fear of your forgetting them. At the end of four, I shall say good-bye. And at the end of five, I shall go!"

She had got all the pegs put in by this time, and Alice looked on with great interest as she returned to the tree, and then began slowly walking down the row.

At the two-yard peg she faced round, and said, "A pawn goes two squares in its first move."

To demonstrate that, she had walked two yards. As a pawn starts from the second square, that takes us to the fourth square on the board. The third peg marks the fifth square, the fourth the sixth, and the fifth the seventh. There is still another square, the eighth, but on that Alice will no longer be a pawn.

"In the Eighth Square we shall be Queens together, and it's all feasting and fun!"

The Red Queen had begun "slowly walking down the row." At the two-yard peg she paused to give Alice her instructions. Alice got up and curtseyed, and sat down again. At the next peg the Queen jerked out some staccato remarks. She did not wait for Alice to curtsey this time, but "walked on quickly" to the next peg, where she turned to say goodbye and then "hurried" on to the last. She was getting up speed. "How it happened, Alice never knew, but exactly as she came to the last peg, she was gone."

What happened we can represent but not really imagine. According to the key, the Red Queen moved away from Alice at an angle across the board (R.Q. to K.R.'s 4th).

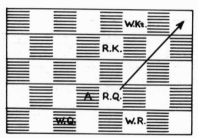

So long as the Red Queen was in the square next to her, Alice could see her and hear her, but when she steamed off in a direction which did not as yet exist for Alice, she simply vanished.

> *Whether she vanished into the air, or ran quickly into the wood ("and she can run very fast!" thought Alice), there was no way of guessing, but she was gone, and Alice began to remember that she was a Pawn, and that it would soon be time for her to move.*

The moves of the two Queens are inexplicable to Alice because of a limitation in her powers. She is unable to conceive of such moves as R.Q. to K.R.'s 4th or W.Q. to Q.B.'s 4th. They can zigzag about the board, sweep from end to end of it if they like, or from side to side. She must laboriously crawl from square to square, always in one direction, with a half-remembered promise to spur her on: "In the Eighth Square we shall be Queens together, and it's all feasting and fun!"

But if the length of the board is time, the breadth of the board must be time also, a kind of time known only to mathematicians and mystics: the kind of time we call eternity.

> For was and is, and will be are but is;
> And all creation is one act at once,
> The birth of light: but we that are not all
> As parts, can see but parts, now this now that,
> And live, perforce from thought to thought and make
> One act a phantom of succession; thus
> Our weakness somehow shapes the Shadow, Time.

What Tennyson put in poetry, Dodgson represented on his chessboard. Alice as she trotted along could see but parts, now the Red King to her right, now the White Queen to her left, but once she became a queen there was a change:

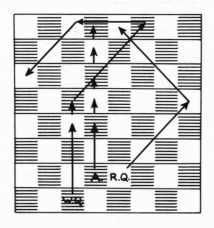

THE
PATHS
OF THE
QUEENS

Everything was happening so oddly that she didn't feel a bit surprised at finding the Red Queen and the White Queen sitting close to her, one on each side: she would have liked very much to ask them how they came there,

(we can follow their moves by the key)

but she feared it would not be quite civil.

She could see them both at once; in the language of psychology, she could attend to a plurality of impressions to which formerly she would have attended in succession.

However, she was by no means sure of herself or her crown as yet, and the Queens put her through her paces:

"In our country," Alice remarked, "there's only one day at a time."

The Red Queen said, "That's a poor thin way of doing things. Now here, we mostly have days and nights two or three at a time, and sometimes in the winter we take as many as five nights together—for warmth, you know."

"Are five nights warmer than one night, then?" Alice ventured to ask.

"Five times as warm, of course."

"But they should be five times as cold, by the same rule—"

"Just so!" said the Red Queen. "Five times as warm, and five times as cold—just as I'm five times as rich as you are, and five times as clever!"

(Note clever and rich as opposites here.)

Alice sighed and gave it up. "It's exactly like a riddle with no answer!" she thought.

It is, however, the answer to the "chess problem," or at any rate, one part of it, the checkmate which, Dodgson said in the 1887 Preface, was strictly in accordance with the laws of the game, while Mr. Madan in the *Handbook* gives him the lie direct: "whereas there is no attempt at one."

According to the key, the position would appear to be:

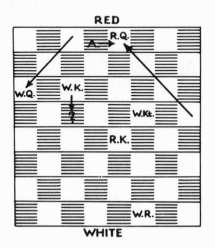

RED / WHITE board with pieces labeled R.Q., W.K., W.Q., W.Kt., R.K., W.R., and A.→

"All sorts of things happened in a moment."

There is therefore something very like a checkmate and a fairly complicated one. The only objection is that the White King must have been in check while the White Queen moved to Q.R. 6th (soup) at Move 10. On the other hand, when Alice was on the Seventh Square she was still a pawn. The White King was behind her and if he had moved to Q.B. 5th she would not have known and he would not have been in check.

As to the succession of the moves, Dodgson admitted that was "perhaps not so strictly observed as it might be." When Alice reached the Eighth Square and became a Queen, she naturally acquired new powers, but not all at once. She could now see from end to end of the board, but her sweep of vision from side to side was limited by the presence of the White Queen on one side and the Red Queen on the other. Whenever the White Queen moved to Q.R. 6th, Alice had to wake up. " 'I can't stand this any longer!' she cried," and as the chess world collapsed in ruins, she seized the Red Queen and accomplished the checkmate.

Dr. Bell, in a footnote to his *History of Mathematics*, makes a two-fisted attack upon Priestley and Dunne for the use they have made of "mathematical" ideas: Mr. Priestley in his time-plays, Mr. Dunne in his dream-philosophy. It is a good thing, Dr. Bell thinks, that the literary world has still not discovered the elliptic functions "whose double periodicity leads at once to a two-dimensional time," expressed, says Dr. Bell, "in the lozenges of a skewed chessboard." On the other hand, he thinks there might be dollars in it.[5] Too late, Dr. Bell! It has been done.

But Dodgson had other reasons for departing from the rules of chess and for avoiding a normal checkmate. These Queens, whose powers in time are far more remarkable than those of the Time Traveller in the "scientific" romance by H. G. Wells, are nonetheless flatlanders. They live—or think they live—on a surface, a time-surface. But the cream of the jest is that their world is no more flat than ours. Like the people of the Middle Ages, they are on a globe and do not know it.

When Alice went Through the Looking-Glass, she went into the room she had just left, the other way round. It was the drawing room and the door was open. She went along the passage, downstairs, and out by the "front door" into the front garden, reversed. In the game of chess she went down the length of the board and at the end came to a door. By this time she was a Queen and could look both ways, forward and back (in time). Which door had she come to, the front door or the back door?

*She was standing before an arched doorway, over which were the words "*QUEEN ALICE*" in large letters, and on each side of the arch there was a bell-handle; one was marked "Visitor's Bell," and the other "Servants' Bell."*

Visitors' Bell: the Front Door. Servants' Bell: the Back Door. Time had gone full circle, or, rather, Alice had gone full circle in time, which unknown to her was a little planet like that in *Sylvie and Bruno Concluded*, on which "the vanquished army ran away at full speed, and in a very few minutes found themselves face-to-face with the victorious army, who were marching home again, and who were so frightened at finding themselves between two armies that they surrendered at once." Her front and back doors—the two ends of the board—were one and the same, in the words of Donne,

> As west and east
> In all flatt maps (and I am one) are one. . . .

In the *New Method of Evaluation* Dodgson had shown that the University, like the Church of England and, in a still wider sense, the whole country, was broken up into two "partial factions." One of these, the Rationalist faction, had as its locus a superficies, and the other, the extreme High Church party, had as its locus a catenary "known as the Patristic Catenary," which he defined as "passing through Origen and containing many multiple points." A catenary is a curve formed by a cord or chain suspended at each end and acted upon only by gravity.

No doubt these notions, working in his mind, helped him towards the idea of the two Queens, those mighty opposites in chess, living on a surface which was actually curved and representing once more two partial factions in the University, the Church or the human mind.

"The Red Queen," said Dodgson, in his "Theatre" article of 1887, "I pictured as a Fury, but of another type: her passion must be cold and calm; she must be formal and strict, yet not unkindly; pedantic to the tenth degree" [I suspect that he wrote n-th here], "the concentrated essence of all governesses!" Clearly, she is on the dogmatic side. She lays down the law to Alice, stresses her title (Apostolic Succession), claims that all the walks belong to her, demands the use of French (Latin services?) and curtsying (genuflection). She is condescending, pats Alice on the head, and has "heard nonsense, compared with which that would be as sensible as a dictionary."

The biscuit which the Red Queen offered Alice as a thirst-quencher might be dry on the Looking-Glass principle, simply as the opposite of a refreshing drink, or it might partake of the woody nature of visible, tangible chess pieces and be made of sawdust; but over and above these meanings, its dryness must be similar to that of the passage read by the Mouse in *Alice*. ("This is the driest thing I know. Silence all round, if you please!") Shane Leslie suggests that the biscuits were sermons, and it is true that the High Church sermons, regarded as of less importance than sacrament, were often perfunctory.

In his general view of the allegory, Shane Leslie is wide of the mark. He identifies the Red Queen as Archbishop Manning and the White Queen as Dr. Newman, who were on the same side in everything of any significance. It is true that they had their disagreements, but to regard the Queens as both representing Catholics reduces the allegory to triviality. The grand opposites of Dodgson's day were Reason and Dogma, and to regard the two sides as anything less fundamental is to underestimate him. Besides, he had already represented these great principles as they worked themselves out in Oxford over the serio-comic business of Jowett's salary, and represented them as superficial in mathematical terms.

"Lastly," said Dodgson in "The Theatre" of 1887, "the White Queen seemed to my dreaming fancy, gentle, stupid, fat and pale; helpless as an infant; and with a slow maundering, bewildered air about her just suggesting imbecility, but never quite passing into it; that would be, I think, fatal to any comic effect she might otherwise produce."

Dodgson repeatedly asserted that he was "no conscious imitator" in the *Alice* books, and so far as the general design is concerned, his claim was just. But certain resemblances to passages in Swift's *Tale of a Tub*, *Battle of the Books*, and *Gulliver's Travels* are too close to be mere coincidence.

"Once upon a time," says Swift in *A Tale of a Tub*, "there was a Man who had Three sons by one Wife, and all at a Birth, neither could the Mid-wife tell certainly which was the Eldest." Wotton's footnote reads: "By these three sons, Peter, Martyn and Jack, Popery, the Church of England, and our Protestant Dissenters are designed" (Martyn: Martin Luther, Jack: John Calvin). Each was left a new coat and a copy of the Will, containing instructions for wearing it. In *Through the Looking-Glass* the coats become shawls; otherwise the White Queen is Jack, the Red Queen Peter.

The White Queen has trouble with her shawl, and Alice has to help her to put it on again while the White Queen looks at her in a helpless, frightened sort of way and whispers something that sounds like "Bread-and-butter, bread-and-butter." Compare this with Jowett signing the Articles for the sake of his tum-tum.

Again, she has been "a-dressing" herself. "Every single thing's crooked," Alice thought to herself, "and she's all over pins!" These pins are no doubt the counterpart of the Red Queen's thorns. The latter was wearing a crown of thorns when Alice met her, only the thorns were turned outward. " 'She's one of the thorny kind,' said the Rose." Because she was a-dressing herself, because every single thing was crooked and she was all over pins, the White Queen must represent the side of the Church which argued, protested, and tried to reinterpret religious ideas by the light of reason—the Protestant side of the Church of England and in particular the Rationalist "mode of thinking."

Alice herself does duty in the allegory for Martin or the Church of England, though she certainly does not represent the Church of England as it was in Dodgson's day. Rather she is the essential quality of the Christian religion—the one all the sects seemed to have forgotten—love.

She took the place of Lily, the White Queen's Imperial Kitten—no doubt the Imperial Church of England which might be expected to result from the first "Pan-Anglican" Conference at Lambeth in 1867. That was why Lily was too young to play and also why she was the child of the King and Queen of Controversy. Alice was the True Church, hoping all things, believing all things, suffering long. In the "Theatre" article, she was to be "loving as a dog" and "gentle as a fawn," courteous

even as though she were herself a King's daughter and her clothing of wrought gold: then trustful, ready to accept the wildest impossibilities with all that utter trust that only dreamers know; and lastly curious—and with the eager enjoyment of Life that comes only in the happy hours of childhood.

Compare with Dodgson's "even as though she were herself a King's daughter and her clothing of wrought gold" his father's words about his ideal Church:

so did He prepare for His Church a covering, hidden within these ordinances for her spiritual nakedness, "a clothing of wrought gold" (Ps. xix, 13) rendering her meet to be brought into the Palace of the Heavenly King.[6]

To have used a real chess problem would have been fatal to the allegory, for it was by no means Dodgson's view that the opposition of the two sides, Red and White, two aspects of the same Church, sprang from the operations of two Hostile Players. On the contrary, the two Queens are really two kittens who come from one cat, Dinah, and Dinah in Tenniel's final illustration is both black and white.

The Queens and Alice were used as mathematical symbols to illustrate certain ideas about time and space. They were also used satirically and allegorically, as described above. In addition there are signs that Dodgson borrowed ideas for the appearance and nature of each character from real persons, and in Alice's case we know the original. It is true that the process of remaking her in accordance with his own ideas and attitude to life has gone far, but we can still recognize the first Alice in the last.

It has been suggested that Dodgson's own parents sat for the portraits of the chess Queens,[7] but I think the Dean and Mrs. Liddell are much more likely models. Dodgson's relations with his father and mother were never anything but happy and normal, whereas a state of emotional tension, in which there was jealousy on both sides, the insolence of office on theirs and the pangs of despised love on his, existed between him and Alice's parents.

The Red Queen was tall, half a head taller than Alice, which was about the Dean's superiority in height to Dodgson. She had heard nonsense, compared to which "that would be as sensible as a dictionary" and it would be difficult for Dodgson or anybody at Christ Church to use the word "dictionary" without thinking of Liddell and Scott. Her coldness, too, her pride and pedantry, suggest the Dean.

There was emphatically no outward resemblance between the White Queen and Mrs. Liddell, who, according to Sir William Richmond, was dark and beautiful.[8] But she was once pinning a dress on Alice when the Prince of Wales burst in unexpectedly and Alice fled. Mrs. Liddell hid her agitation and the Prince did not add to it until about to depart, when he remarked, "Tell Alice I saw her."[9] If Dodgson knew the story, it was the kind of thing to worry him, and may have suggested the situation Through the Looking-Glass, with the figures transposed and Alice pinning on the White Queen's shawl. The allegorical and mathematical ideas would coat the rather dangerous and embarrassing idea of Alice incompletely dressed, as mother-of-pearl coats an irritant within the oyster shell.

Working as he did by associations of ideas, there was no limit to the variety of topics he could introduce. His art was to keep variety from becoming chaotic, to make some unexpected departure lead back to the last remark but one. Why some topics appealed to him and others did not is an enquiry which would take us over the threshold of consciousness and into that dark region where ambiguous forms and uncouth hybrids loom and dwindle. Psychoanalysis, however, is no technique for amateurs. We must be content to follow those trains of thought in which we can perceive intention, and we shall lose little by this, for the intention is fundamental.

There is in existence a photograph just published (1949)[10] but taken by Dodgson in 1858. It shows two of his aunts, the Misses Lutwidge, playing chess. One wears a dark dress and plays black against a dark background; the other, in a checkered or tartan dress, much lighter in tone, plays white against a pale background. The effect is of a battle of light and shade. The disposition of the pieces bears no relation to that in the *Looking-Glass* chess problem, but the germ of the idea is there in the opposed forces. In the course of his chess lessons to Alice, Dodgson transferred the conflict from the players and setting to the chess pieces, in particular to the two Queens. Their powers of movement brought in his mathematics; their opposition suggested the theological controversies of his time, and because he disliked controversy, the Queens also acquired some characteristics from his more personal antipathies.

In Fechner's *Space Has Four Dimensions* the opposites are the Naturalists, who believe only what they see, and the Philosophers, who see only what they believe. The Naturalists, like Dodgson's White Queen, "know only length and breadth —except that is for the astronomers who are forced by the fall of bodies to recognize the third dimension, at least as a hypothesis." In this respect Fechner's astronomers resemble Dodgson's White Knight, whose ballad he rewrote for *Through the Looking-Glass,* adding the lines:

> *Or if I drop upon my toe*
> *A very heavy weight,*

as an illustration of the fall of bodies.

Of all the chessmen, the Knight alone has the power of leaping. This is the symbolism of chess, the horseman's leap expressed by allowing the Knight to move two squares in any direction and one at right angles to that direction—a cross section of a leap. Nevertheless, it makes no difference to the Knight if the intervening squares are packed with friends or foes. He can leap to a vacant square, take an enemy piece, or deliver check over their heads. It is this third dimension which enables him to perform his little miracles, his sudden, unlooked-for interventions in the game.

> *"And really," said Alice,*

referring to the game she had played the previous day, on our side of the Looking-Glass,

> *"I might have won, if it hadn't been for that nasty Knight that came wriggling down among my pieces."*

In Looking-Glass House he was sliding down the poker and balancing very badly. He represents a stage halfway between the Queens, who are flatlanders pure and simple, and Alice, who is a child or Human Being.

It is not necessary to relate the Knight's powers to time-length and time-breadth as in the case of the Queens. Probably Dodgson developed the ideas about the Knight quite separately and fitted them into the general pattern later. However, if it is desired to do so, then his third dimension was the whole of our space.

Of our world he has had only the most tantalizing glimpses, enough to unfit him for his own but not enough to enable him to understand. Yet he is by no means contemptible, this knight in tin armor. He has seen wonders, has even brought back with him odd bits and pieces from *his* Wonderland, which is our common workaday world—beehives and mouse-traps, carrots and fire-irons, outlandish bric-à-brac, whose true nature and purpose are externally beyond him but which he collects hopefully and about which he theorizes happily.

He is Science.

By constantly falling on his head, he has grasped that things never fall upwards, you know, and his experience of rain has confirmed this. Accordingly he turns his box upside down, so that the rain will not wet his things, but alas! his theory is incomplete. He has overlooked the possibility that his things might fall downwards and he has lost them.

Then he has thought of a brilliant scheme for turning himself over in our space—a thing, it is safe to say, no other chessman but a knight could think of doing:

"Now first I put my head on the top of the gate—then the head's high enough—then I stand on my head—then the feet are high enough, you see —then I'm over, you see."
"Yes, I suppose you'd be over when that was done," Alice said thoughtfully: "but don't you think it would be rather hard?"

She means the ground.

"I haven't tried it yet," the Knight said gravely: "so I can't tell for certain—but I'm afraid it would be a little hard."

The charming simpleton is thinking only of the difficulty (for him) of the operation. The consequences to himself have never occurred to him.

Compared to the other inhabitants of the chess world he is a genius, like Newton, voyaging through strange seas of thought alone. His scheme for training hair upwards, like fruit trees, might be impracticable, or it might not. Experiment would have settled the matter, and he was a little dashed by Alice's lack of enthusiasm—but then so few of his schemes had ever met with an enthusiastic reception. In the kingdom of the blind the one-eyed man is thought to suffer from hallucinations.

The principle which eluded the White Knight was, of course, gravity. The word gravity is carefully avoided during the whole of this chapter, but he looked a little grave, and more than once he remarked gravely. The pun had no existence for himself or Alice. His elevated and vertical position on horseback was extremely precarious. Even when sliding down the poker, he balanced very badly. As a planesman or inhabitant of the surface, "balance" was an idea he had failed to grasp. He was unbalanced. But his difficulties were due to no lack of practice. He had had *plenty* of practice—both in mounting and in dismounting.

There is something sublime in his persistence and in his ability to rise above circumstance, to theorize from a head-downward position. Moreover, he had realized that he would probably never be able to stay on horseback without some sort of support and so had invented a helmet in the form of a sugar loaf. This was a conical mass of sugar displayed in confectioners' windows in our grandfathers' day. The White Knight's sugar-loaf helmet was like a large fool's cap and touched the ground all round him. True, he lost himself in it (as one is apt to do in a theory) and the other knight put it on, thinking that it was *his* helmet.

But his cleverest invention was a pudding—during the meat course. It was not cooked in time for the next course, or the next day:

> *"In fact," he went on, holding his head down, and his voice getting lower and lower, "I don't believe that pudding ever was cooked! In fact, I don't believe that pudding ever will be cooked! And yet it was a very clever pudding to invent."*

After the cone, the sphere. He was trying to frame the notion of a solid sphere but his world was flatland. It contained blotting paper which could be bent round into a cylinder or twisted into a cone, but no matter how he stuck it together with sealing wax, he could not make even a hollow sphere out of it, much less a solid one. He even thought of blowing it to pieces with gunpowder and then reassembling the minute fragments. Theoretically, if the fragments were small enough, the feat should be possible. Practically, he had almost abandoned hope of that pudding.

> *"It began with blotting-paper," the Knight answered with a groan.*
> *"That wouldn't be very nice, I'm afraid—"*
> *"Not very nice alone," he interrupted, quite eagerly: "but you've no*

idea what a difference it makes, mixing it with other things—such as gun-powder and sealing-wax. And here I must leave you."

The White Knight's appearance without his helmet is worth noting:

"Now one can breathe more easily," said the Knight, putting back his shaggy hair with both hands, and turning his gentle face and large mild eyes to Alice.

Does not this suggest a dog or a horse, rather than a man? The Knight is being compared to one of the higher animals which has some rudimentary intelligence; an animal which is gentle, unselfish, and uncomplaining. The equation may be stated: man attempting to reason about the universe is like one of the higher animals attempting to understand our world. Both collect data and frame theories. Neither has any chance of understanding the reality. And the symbol by means of which Dodgson demonstrated this profound truth was the knight in chess with his leap over the intervening squares, in the course of which he lost contact with the surface and, however briefly, glimpsed our world.

Of all the strange things that Alice saw in her journey Through The Looking-Glass, this was the one that she always remembered most clearly. Years afterwards she could bring the whole scene back again, as if it had been only yesterday—the mild blue eyes and kindly smile of the Knight—the setting sun gleaming through his hair, and shining on his armour in a blaze of light that quite dazzled her—the horse quietly moving about, with the reins hanging loose on his neck, cropping the grass at her feet—and the black shadows of the forest behind—all this she took in like a picture, as, with one hand shading her eyes, she leant against a tree, watching the strange pair, and listening, in a half-dream, to the melancholy music of the song.

The song was "Upon the Lonely Moor," the parody of Wordsworth's "Resolution and Independence," which Dodgson had sent to *The Train* in 1856, but had partly rewritten and garnished with four new titles. Some of the changes are mere improvements in the verse; for example:

> *He said, "I look for butterflies*
> *That sleep among the wheat"*

is much better than

> *He said, "I look for soap-bubbles,*
> *That lie among the wheat." . . .*

Others seem, if anything, more nonsensical that what he had written at first:

> *But I was thinking of a plan*
> *To dye one's whiskers green,*
> *And always use so large a fan*
> *That they could not be seen.*

However, 'a-sitting on a gate' is a significant attitude for his aged, aged man. If the White Knight's plan of standing on his head on the top bar was likely to prove "hard," it was at least original and showed a desire to go somewhere. Again, the new lines,

> *But I was thinking of a way*
> *To feed oneself on batter,*
> *And so go on from day to day*
> *Getting a little fatter,*

suggest the White Knight trying another method of inventing, or, at all events, producing the sphere, and Dodgson returned to this in his Spherical Professor (*Sylvie and Bruno Concluded*) who finally succeeded in making himself into a perfect sphere and in acquiring sufficient momentum to fly off the earth at a tangent. But the main lines were already laid down in the 1856 version and it seems quite clear to me through all the nonsense that the White Knight is Pure Science and the Aged, Aged Man is Applied Science.

The book, so far from having no moral, is thus a new kind of Morality. The characters are all abstractions and we are prevented from realizing this only by sheer verbal sleight of hand. The symbols are deceptively simple—but so are the properties of a great conjuror. It is the second-rate magician who requires elaborate scaffoldings of chromium-plated tubes and other complicated apparatus. Give Dodgson a ball of wool, a kitten, some chessmen, a looking-glass, and a little girl out of the audience—and watch carefully.

VI
Language
and
Satire

The Poems in ALICE IN WONDERLAND

by Florence Milner

(1903)

FIFTY YEARS AGO the child world was made glad by the appearance of Lewis Carroll's *Alice in Wonderland*. It is a universal story and so belongs to all time. It has never gone out of fashion and never will as long as children love wonder-stories and grownups have young hearts.

But those who read the book when it was first published found in it a delight which the child of today misses. Fifty years ago certain poems appeared in every reader and were read over and over again until the child was stupid indeed who did not unconsciously learn them by heart. Today there is a new fashion in literature. Children are whirled from one supplementary reader to another, conning graceful rhymes and pretty stories all illustrated with artistic pictures, but the old things have passed away.

All the poems in *Alice in Wonderland* are parodies upon these once familiar rhymes. Scattered lines of the poems cling to the minds of older people; they remember being once familiar with them; they recognize the meter and can sometimes repeat two or three opening lines, but the complete poem eludes them, and the author they probably never did know. The children of today do not know the verses at all, and as a parody ceases to be a parody without the original poem as a background, the trouble of gathering these originals seems worth while.

After Alice had fallen down the rabbit-hole and had passed through her first transformation, when she shut up like a telescope until she was only ten inches high and then grew bigger and bigger until "her head struck the roof of the hall," she became confused as to her identity. To make sure of it, she tried to repeat a little poem which everybody in those days knew by heart, and to such children it was very funny when it came all wrong and she says,

> *"How doth the little crocodile*
> *Improve his shining tail,"*

when she thought she was repeating that highly moral poem by Isaac Watts,

Against Idleness and Mischief

How doth the little busy bee
  Improve each shining hour,
And gather honey all the day
  From every opening flower!

How skillfully she builds her cell!
  How neat she spreads the wax!
And labours hard to store it well
  With the sweet food she makes.

In works of labour or of skill,
  I would be busy too;
For Satan finds some mischief still
  For idle hands to do.

In books, or work, or healthful play,
  Let my first years be passed.

That I may give for every day
Some good account at last.

Again, in her conversation with the Caterpillar, Alice told him that being so many different sizes in a day was very confusing, as he would find when he changed into a chrysalis and then into a butterfly. She confessed that she could not remember things and told her experience with "How doth the little busy bee." The Caterpillar, wishing to test the matter, ordered her to say, "You are old, Father William." How well she succeeded will appear from comparing what she said with what she thought she was going to say.

THE OLD MAN'S COMFORTS
AND HOW HE GAINED THEM

Robert Southey

"You are old, father William," the young man cried,
    "The few locks which are left you are grey;
You are hale, father William, a hearty old man;
    Now tell me the reason, I pray."

"In the days of my youth," father William replied,
    "I remember'd that youth would fly fast,
And abus'd not my health and my vigour at first,
    That I never might need them at last."

"You are old, father William," the young man cried,
    "And pleasures with youth pass away.
And yet you lament not the days that are gone;
    Now tell me the reason, I pray."

"In the days of my youth," father William replied,
    "I remember'd that youth could not last;
I thought of the future, whatever I did,
    That I never might grieve for the past."

"You are old, father William," the young man cried,
    "And life must be hast'ning away;
You are cheerful and love to converse upon death;
    Now tell me the reason, I pray."

"I am cheerful, young man," father William replied,
    "Let the cause thy attention engage;
In the days of my youth I remember'd my God.
    And He hath not forgotten my age."

The Duchess's song to the pig baby,

> *Speak roughly to your little boy*
> *And beat him when he sneezes*

is an absurdity in itself, but a much greater one when contrasted with its serious parallel. There is evidently some uncertainty as to the author of this poem, for it occasionally appears as anonymous, but is generally credited as below.

Speak Gently

G. W. Langford[1]

Speak gently! it is better far
   To rule by love than fear;
Speak gently; let no harsh word mar
   The good we may do here!

Speak gently to the little child!
   Its love be sure to gain;
Teach it in accents soft and mild;
   It may not long remain.

Speak gently to the young, for they
   Will have enough to bear;
Pass through this life as best they may,
   'Tis full of anxious care!

Speak gently to the aged one,
   Grieve not the care-worn heart;
Whose sands of life are nearly run,
   Let such in peace depart!

Speak gently, kindly to the poor;
   Let no harsh tone be heard;
They have enough they must endure,
   Without an unkind word!

Speak gently to the erring; know
   They must have toiled in vain;
Perchance unkindness made them so;
   Oh, win them back again.

Speak gently; Love doth whisper low
   The vows that true hearts bind;
And gently Friendship's accents flow;
   Affection's voice is kind.

> Speak gently; 'tis a little thing
> > Dropped in the heart's deep well;
> The good, the joy, that it may bring,
> > Eternity shall tell.

"Twinkle, twinkle, little bat," which the Hatter said that he sang at the concert given by the Queen of Hearts, is the most familiarly suggestive of them all.

Jane and Ann Taylor were two English sisters who wrote together, publishing their poems under such titles as *Original Poems for Infant Minds* and *Hymns for Infant Minds*. Jane was supposed to have written most of them, and this one carries her signature.

The Star

> Twinkle, twinkle, little star,
> How I wonder what you are!
> Up above the world so high,
> Like a diamond in the sky.
>
> When the blazing sun is gone,
> When he nothing shines upon,
> Then you show your little light,
> Twinkle, twinkle, all the night.
>
> Then the traveller in the dark,
> Thanks you for your tiny spark:
> He could not see which way to go,
> If you did not twinkle so.
>
> In the dark blue sky you keep,
> And often through my curtains peep,
> For you never shut your eye
> Till the sun is in the sky.
>
> As your bright and tiny spark
> Lights the traveller in the dark,
> Though I know not what you are,
> Twinkle, twinkle, little star.

Mary Howitt wrote "The Spider and the Fly," the first stanza of which originally read,

> "Will you walk into my parlour?" said the spider to the fly,
> " 'Tis the prettiest little parlour that ever you did spy,
> The way into my parlour is up a winding stair,
> And I've got many curious things to show when you are there."

"Oh, no, no," said the little fly, "to ask me is in vain,
For who goes up your winding stair can ne'er come down again."

This poem has suffered various modifications and several versions appear in print, but the quoted stanza is doubtless from the original one. The beat of the meter is very perfectly kept in the Mock Turtle's "Will you walk a little faster?"

" 'Tis the voice of the lobster," which Alice repeats at the gruff order of the Gryphon, returns to Isaac Watts. Probably no poem in the book is further removed from modern thought and modern literary ideals than this one.

The Sluggard

'Tis the voice of the sluggard; I heard him complain,
"You have wak'd me too soon, I must slumber again."
As the door on its hinges, so he on his bed,
Turns his sides and his shoulders and his heavy head.

"A little more sleep, and a little more slumber;"
Thus he wastes half his days, and his hours without number,
And when he gets up, he sits folding his hands,
Or walks about sauntering, or trifling he stands.

I pass'd by his garden, and saw the wild brier,
The thorn and the thistle grow broader and higher;
The clothes that hang on him are turning to rags;
And his money still wastes till he starves or he begs.

I made him a visit, still hoping to find
That he took better care for improving his mind;
He told me his dreams, talked of eating and drinking;
But he scarce reads his Bible, and never loves thinking.

Said I then to my heart, "Here's a lesson for me,
This man's but a picture of what I might be;
But thanks to my friends for their care in my breeding,
Who taught me betimes to love working and reading."

"Beautiful Soup" is a very funny parody upon a popular song of the time that runs as follows:

Star of the Evening

James M. Sayle

Beautiful star in heav'n so bright,
Softly falls thy silv'ry light,

As thou movest from earth afar,
Star of the evening, beautiful star.

CHORUS:

Beautiful star,
Beautiful star,
Star of the evening, beautiful star.

In Fancy's eye thou seem'st to say,
Follow me, come from earth away.
Upward thy spirit's pinions try,
To realms of love beyond the sky.

Shine on, oh star of love divine,
And may our soul's affection twine
Around thee as thou movest afar,
Star of the twilight, beautiful star.

The most delightful part of the parody is the division of the words in the refrain in imitation of the approved method of singing the song, with its holds and its sentimental stress upon the last word.

Beau—ootiful Soo—oop!
Beau—ootiful Soo—oop!
Soo—oop of the e—e—evening,
Beautiful, beauti—FUL SOUP!

The poem upon which the last parody is based is not as well known as most of the others, the first two lines being the only ones often quoted.

ALICE GRAY

William Mee

She's all my fancy painted her, she's lovely, she's divine,
But her heart it is another's, she never can be mine.
Yet loved I as man never loved, a love without decay,
Oh, my heart, my heart is breaking for the love of Alice Gray.

Her dark brown hair is braided o'er a brow of spotless white,
Her soft blue eye now languishes, now flashes with delight;
Her hair is braided not for me, the eye is turned away,
Yet my heart, my heart is breaking for the love of Alice Gray.

I've sunk beneath the summer's sun, and trembled in the blast.
But my pilgrimage is nearly done, the weary conflict's past;
And when the green sod wraps my grave, may pity haply say,
Oh, his heart, his heart is broken for the love of Alice Gray!

Carroll's first writing followed the wording in the original first version and began:

> *She's all my fancy painted him*
> *(I make no idle boast);*
> *If he or you had lost a limb,*
> *Which would have suffered most?*

But for some unknown reason he dropped the first stanza, beginning with the second, thus obliterating all evident resemblance between parody and original.

The parody is not the highest form of art and not the most skillful form of verse, but Lewis Carroll has done these eight so well that doubtless some of them will live after the originals are forgotten. Even now, in order to search them out, it has been necessary to beat the dust from many a forgotten volume in a library's unmolested corners, but the nonsense rhymes they suggested are jingling upon the tongues of children the wide world over and mingling with their happy laughter.

A Burble
through the
Tulgey Wood
by John Ciardi
(1959)

EVERYONE WHO HAS an emotion and a language knows something about poetry. What he knows may not be much on an absolute scale, and it may not be organized within him in a useful way, but once he discovers the pleasures of poetry, he is likely to be surprised to discover how much he always knew without knowing he knew it. He may discover, somewhat as the character in the French play discovered to his amazement that he had been talking prose all his life, that he has been living poetry. Poetry, after all, is about life. Anyone who is alive and conscious must have some information about it.

And like life, poetry is not uniformly serious. True, poetry is the natural language of man's most exalted thoughts. The rhythmic resemblance between prayer and poetry, for example, can hardly be missed. Yet the more exalted the thought, the more careful the poet must be, for poetic high-seriousness can fall into a burlesque of itself at a touch. William Wordsworth, for all his great powers as a poet, was yet capable of slipping from the intensely serious into the intensely inane. His "Idiot Boy," an intensely serious ballad about the natural unspoiled goodness of a young idiot, can hardly be said to survive such a line as "Burr, burr—now Johnny's lips they burr," a line in which the poet seeks to render soulfully the blubbering of a happy idiot, and falls into bathos. Percy Bysshe Shelley was similarly capable of a kind of labored excess that could turn sublime intention into ridiculous utterance. His "Epipsychidion" sets out to describe ideal love, but few readers today can suppress a smile at the last line: "I pant, I sink, I tremble, I expire!" So, too, when Shelley addresses an apostrophe to his love and lets slip the exclamation: "Thy lips, oh slippery blisses!"

Such lapses do not prove that Wordsworth and Shelley were bad poets, but only that they could strain so hard for high-seriousness that their voices cracked. If, however, some poets let themselves fall into unconsciously ridiculous positions, there are always others ready to pick up the slip and to have fun with it. One of the most pompous and flat-footedly moral of the English poets was Robert Southey. The performance of his poems tends always to center around a spike of moral Gradgrindism which the performer proceeds to drive in with such graceless energy that the hammer splits and leaves him holding a shattered stump of the handle. We in the audience see his laborious earnestness, but the act is so clumsy that we cannot resist laughing it off the stage.

Lewis Carroll, the ever-graceful author of *Alice in Wonderland*, had a great gift for such laughter. His "Father William," a direct take-off of Southey's "The Old Man's Comforts and How He Gained Them," is as devastating a spoof as one may find in English poetry:

THE OLD MAN'S COMFORTS
AND HOW HE GAINED THEM

Robert Southey

"You are old, father William," the young man cried;
  "The few locks which are left you are grey;
You are hale, father William, a hearty old man;
  Now tell me the reason, I pray."

"In the days of my youth," father William replied,
  "I remember'd that youth would fly fast,
And abus'd not my health and my vigour at first,
  That I never might need them at last."

"You are old, father William," the young man cried,
  "And pleasures with youth pass away.
And yet you lament not the days that are gone;
  Now tell me the reason, I pray."

"In the days of my youth," father William replied,
  "I remember'd that youth could not last;
I thought of the future, whatever I did,
  That I never might grieve for the past."

"You are old, father William," the young man cried,
  "And life must be hast'ning away;
You are cheerful, and love to converse upon death;
  Now tell me the reason, I pray."

"I am cheerful, young man," father William replied;
  "Let the cause thy attention engage;
In the days of my youth, I remember'd my God,
  And He hath not forgotten my age."

FATHER WILLIAM

Lewis Carroll

"You are old, father William," the young man said,
  "And your hair has become very white;
And yet you incessantly stand on your head—
  Do you think, at your age, it is right?"

"In my youth," father William replied to his son,
  "I feared it might injure the brain;
But, now that I'm perfectly sure I have none,
  Why, I do it again and again."

"*You are old,*" *said the youth,* "*as I mentioned before,*
   And have grown most uncommonly fat;
Yet you turned a back-somersault in at the door—
   Pray what is the reason of that?"

"*In my youth,*" *said the sage, as he shook his grey locks,*
   "*I kept all my limbs very supple*
By the use of this ointment—one shilling the box—
   Allow me to sell you a couple?"

"*You are old,*" *said the youth,* "*and your jaws are too weak*
   For anything tougher than suet;
Yet you finished the goose, with the bones and the beak—
   Pray, how did you manage to do it?"

"*In my youth,*" *said his father,* "*I took to the law,*
   And argued each case with my wife;
And the muscular strength, which it gave to my jaw,
   Has lasted the rest of my life."

"*You are old,*" *said the youth,* "*one would hardly suppose*
   That your eye was as steady as ever;
Yet you balanced an eel on the end of your nose—
   What made you so awfully clever?"

"*I have answered three questions, and that is enough,*"
   Said his father; "*don't give yourself airs!*
Do you think I can listen all day to such stuff?
   Be off, or I'll kick you down stairs!"

The fun that Carroll had with his spoof is obvious, but it should not obscure an awareness of his skill in building his poem—his "act," as a juggler might say. The first question put to Father William, for example, accuses Southey of being turned upside down, and Father William's first reply openly accuses Southey of being brainless. There is really not much more one can say against a poet, yet Carroll, having already assassinated Southey, manages to keep his poem lively for three more question-and-answer turns. If each question-and-answer turn is thought of as a scene, what is the principle on which the scenes follow one another? Are they increasingly serious? Increasingly ludicrous? Increasingly trivial? Increasingly revealing of Father William's character? What is the order of progression in Southey's poem? What are the three virtues Southey's old man extols to the youth, and why did Southey develop them in the order given? Carroll found himself having such fun with his parody that he went on for one more question-and-answer than the original. What are the four points Carroll makes about Father William's character, and how does each parody comment on the points Southey makes?

Very often, when one is uncertain about a given poem, he may find useful clues to better understanding in other poems by the same poet. Carroll wrote a number of happy parodies, all of them aimed at deflating overserious morality. Another of Carroll's most memorable parodies is "The Crocodile," a spoof of Isaac Watts's "How Doth the Little Busy Bee":

AGAINST IDLENESS AND MISCHIEF

Isaac Watts

How doth the little busy bee
   Improve each shining hour,
And gather honey all the day
   From every opening flower!

How skillfully she builds her cell!
   How neat she spreads the wax!
And labours hard to store it well
   With the sweet food she makes.

In works of labour or of skill,
   I would be busy too;
For Satan finds some mischief still
   For idle hands to do.

In books, or work, or healthful play,
   Let my first years be passed,
That I may give for every day
   Some good account at last.

THE CROCODILE

Lewis Carroll

How doth the little crocodile
   Improve his shining tail,
And pour the waters of the Nile
   On every shining scale!

> *How cheerfully he seems to grin,*
> *How neatly spreads his claws,*
> *And welcomes little fishes in,*
> *With gently smiling jaws!*

Southey's Father William and Carroll's speak in what seem to be the same terms, yet to very different ends. Watts's little busy bee and Carroll's crocodile are also presented in similar terms. Both are described with a kind of pious unctuousness, yet the two are engaged in activities of quite a different moral color. Is it too much to argue that the crocodile is a happy hypocrite piously gobbling up the trusting fishes (including the poor fishes among the readers who are willing to take Watts's prettily shallow morality as a true rule of life)? Is it too much again to claim that the crocodile and Father William have a good deal in common—that both of them, in fact, accuse their originals of hypocrisy?

If Carroll's aim in these two poems is to show the ludicrousness and hypocrisy of the poems he lampoons, how do the lampoons achieve that aim? (How does a poem mean?) Clearly the two old men, the little busy bee, and the crocodile are symbols. Of what? One must never be in a hurry to "define" symbols for, as already noted, symbols are not pat equivalents but areas of meaning. What must not be missed, however, is that the real performance of Carroll's parodies arises from the way the symbol "crocodile" plays against the symbol "little busy bee." How many such interplays of meaning suggest themselves?

Whether or not one can identify Carroll's great skills as a poetic performer, no reader can fail to respond to Carroll's sense of fun. He has such a good time within his own mind that inevitably the reader is made happy in *his* mind. One of the most unusual and certainly one of the most delightful of Carroll's performances is "Jabberwocky":

JABBERWOCKY

Lewis Carroll

> *'Twas brillig, and the slithy toves*
> *Did gyre and gimble in the wabe:*
> *All mimsy were the borogoves,*
> *And the mome raths outgrabe.*
>
> *"Beware the Jabberwock, my son!*
> *The jaws that bite, the claws that catch!*

Beware the Jubjub bird, and shun
The frumious Bandersnatch!"

He took his vorpal sword in hand:
Long time the manxome foe he sought—
So rested he by the Tumtum tree,
And stood awhile in thought.

And, as in uffish thought he stood,
The Jabberwock, with eyes of flame,
Came whiffling through the tulgey wood,
And burbled as it came!

One, two! One, two! And through and through
The vorpal blade went snicker-snack!
He left it dead, and with its head
He went galumphing back.

"And hast thou slain the Jabberwock?
Come to my arms, my beamish boy!
O frabjous day! Callooh! Callay!"
He chortled in his joy.

'Twas brillig, and the slithy toves
Did gyre and gimble in the wabe:
All mimsy were the borogoves,
And the mome raths outgrabe.

Everyone knows that "Jabberwocky" is a "nonsense" poem: it may be found so listed in any number of anthologies. The word "jabber" in the title, followed by "wocky" (whatever that may mean), is itself descriptive: if there were such a thing as a "wocky" this is the way it might "jabber."

In case there were any doubt about the fun, Carroll "explains" this poem in *Through the Looking-Glass*. There, Alice and Humpty Dumpty discuss it, and Humpty Dumpty, after an unenlightening explanation of "brillig," goes on to explain "slithy":

Well, "slithy" means "lithe and slimy." "Lithe" is the same as "active."
You see it's like a portmanteau—there are two meanings packed up into
one word.

Later he identifies "mimsy" as another portmanteau word made up of "flimsy and miserable."

And with Humpty Dumpty's encouragement a number of people have hunted through "Jabberwocky" for other portmanteau words and for what has been packed into them. Such word-hunting is pleasant enough as a game, and it is clearly founded in the author's own directive. Where, moreover, there is such good reason for believing the poem to be "nonsense," little will be served by denying its character as such. But what is "nonsense"? Is it the same as "non-sense"? Suppose that Carroll had written not a poem but an orchestral *scherzo*, a simple but brilliant piece of fun-music: would one be so readily tempted to call such music "nonsense"? Let the Wocky jabber as it will—and beautiful jabber it is—there is still a second sort of performance to which the appearance of "non-sense" gives an especially apt flavor. And that second performance involves a great deal of "sense," if by "sense" one means "meaningful comment upon an identifiable subject."

One must go a long way round to identify the subject and the comment upon it. Even then his identifications cannot be more than good guesses. The long way round, however, has the advantage of rambling through some of the most attractive and most native of English poetry, and it will further serve to raise some basic questions about the nature of the poetic performance.

Assume for the sake of exploration that the performance of "Jabberwocky" does involve "sensible" comment on a subject. What sort of performance is it, and what clues are there to the nature of its subject? The beamish (whatever that is) boy is warned about a monster called the Jabberwock. The boy is warned to shun it, and also the Jubjub bird and the frumious (furious, ruminous, gloomious?) Bandersnatch (who "snatches at banter"?). Instead of shunning it, however, the boy hunts it, slays it, and is welcomed back as a conquering hero. Clearly, the tone of all this is mock-heroic.

"Father William" and "The Crocodile" provide any reader with reason enough to look for mockery in Carroll's poems. But what could he be mocking here? A first clue lies in the devices Carroll uses in his poetic performance. The poem is deeply indebted to the techniques of English ballads. Stanzas one and two of "Jabberwocky," for example, utter some sort of dark prophecy. In disregard of that prophecy, the hero goes forth to mortal combat. He succeeds in overcoming his dark fate and returns victorious to a hero's welcome. Variants of this basic action may be found in countless ballads. Sometimes the hero returns victorious, to be greeted with joy; sometimes he returns dying, to be saluted with a lament; sometimes the action takes a different turn. The pattern itself, however, is unmistakable, and in order to sense meaningfully what Carroll is doing with this pattern, the reader will have to take an excursion through English balladry, both "folk" and "literary."

A Note on

Humpty Dumpty

by J. B. Priestley

(1921)

ALICE *in Wonderland* and *Through the Looking-Glass* are, I understand, to be published for the first time in German. When I first learned this important fact, it surprised me for a moment, for I had thought that both these classics had by this time passed into all civilized tongues; but after some little reflection, I soon realized that if they had been popular in Germany, we should have known about it. It is not difficult to imagine what will happen when the *Alice* books are well known there, for we know what happened to Shakespeare. A cloud of commentators will gather, and a thousand solemn Teutons will sit down to write huge volumes of comment and criticism; they will contrast and compare the characters (there will even be a short chapter on Bill the Lizard), and will offer numerous conflicting interpretations of the jokes. After that, Freud and Jung and their followers will inevitably arrive upon the scene, and they will give us appalling volumes on *Sexualtheorie* of *Alice in Wonderland*, on the *Assoziationsfähigkeit und Assoziationsstudien* of Jabberwocky, on the inner meaning of the conflict between Tweedledum and Tweedledee from the *psychoanalytische und psychopathologische* points of view. We shall understand, for the first time, the peculiarly revolting symbolism of the Mad Hatter's Tea-Party, and my old friend, the Mad Hatter himself, will be shown to be a mere bundle of neuroses. And as for Alice—but no, Alice shall be spared; I, for one, am not going to be the first to disillusion the wistful shade of Lewis Carroll; may he remain in ignorance a little longer as to what there really was in Alice's mind, the Wonderland (save the mark!) in Alice.

How will Humpty Dumpty fare among the German critics and commentators? I shall be interested to learn, for there has always seemed to me about Humpty Dumpty the air of a solemn literary man, and I was driven to thinking about him only a few days ago, when I had been reading the work of a rather pontifical and humorless young critic whose name I would not divulge for the world. There is quite a little school of youngish critics in this country and America whose work, at once pretentious and barren, has always seemed to me to have a certain "note" in it that was vaguely familiar; but it was not until the other day that I realized where it was I had caught that manner, heard those accents, before. It was in *Through the Looking-Glass*. Humpty Dumpty has not had justice done to him; he is a prophetic figure, and Lewis Carroll, in drawing him, was satirizing a race of critics that did not then exist. Now that they do exist and put their insufferable writings before us at every turn, it is high time we learned to appreciate Carroll's character sketch for what it is—a master stroke of satire in anticipation. I do not say for one moment that such an explanation will exhaust the significance of Humpty Dumpty, for I should not be surprised if there are not other, deeper and more esoteric, interpretations of this character waiting to be discovered by members of the Theosophical Society and others; but it is Humpty Dumpty as a literary character that interests me, and so I shall confine myself to this one aspect. Let us approach the text while it is still unencumbered with German professors.

Alice, you will remember, discovers Humpty Dumpty (who has just been an egg in a shop) sitting on the top of a high and extremely narrow wall, and she takes him for a stuffed figure. This is, you will observe, our introduction to him: notice the *high* wall, so narrow that Alice "wondered how he could keep his *balance*" (the italics are mine) and the *stuffed figure*. Remember these things, and think of that darling of the tiny coteries, Mr. Blank, that owlish young critic: I say no more. It is characteristic of all such critics that they very quickly show a contempt for their audience; they are all for the select few, who can appreciate Flaubert and Stendhal and Chekhov and no one else. Humpty Dumpty strikes this note very early: "Some people," he remarks, at the very beginning of the talk, "have no more sense than a baby!" Immediately afterwards, he asks Alice what her name *means* and is annoyed because she does not know, a significant procedure that needs no comment from me. Then Alice, who represents the normal person, asks a question of the utmost importance—

"Don't you think you'd be safer down on the ground?" Alice went on, not with any idea of making another riddle, but simply in her good-natured anxiety for the queer creature. "That wall is so very narrow!"

Indeed, the whole passage is significant. Notice that Humpty Dumpty thinks that every simple question is a riddle, something for him to solve triumphantly, and he cannot understand that Alice, standing firmly on the ground, may be wiser than he and may be really giving advice and not seeking the answers to trifling conundrums. He, of course, prefers to be in the air, and the very *narrowness* of his wall appeals to him. Again, on the very same page, we discover him breaking into a sudden passion because Alice interrupts with "To send all his horses and all his men." What he thought a grand secret is in reality a mere commonplace, known to Alice and everybody else, and only his blind conceit has prevented him from discovering this fact before: there is no necessity to labor the point or to indicate the analogy. Very typical too is the pedantry he displays, shortly afterwards, in the discussion about Alice's age—

"I thought you meant 'How old are you?'" Alice exclaimed.
"If I'd meant that, I'd have said it," said Humpty Dumpty.

And the next moment, he shows his hand again by remarking: "Now if you'd asked *my* advice, I'd have said, 'Leave off at seven'—but it's too late now." Here is that characteristic reluctance to come to terms with reality, that love of fixed standards, rigidity, arrested development, that hatred of change and evolution, which always mark this type of mind.

It would not be difficult to follow the conversation step by step and find something typical of the fourth-rate critic in every remark that Humpty Dumpty makes; but we must pass on to the latter part of the chapter, in which the conversation turns upon literary themes. Here the clues to Carroll's real intention in writing the chapter are plain for everyone to see. After the talk about un-birthday presents, Humpty Dumpty, it will be remembered, exclaims: "There's glory for you!" Alice, of course, does not understand what he means by "glory," and says so, upon which he smiles contemptuously and cries: "Of course you don't—till I tell you." At every step now the satire becomes more and more direct, until we reach the very climax in Humpty Dumpty's cry of "Impenetrability! That's what I say!" Who does not know those superior beings who, when they write what they allege to be literary criticism, talk of "planes" and "dimensions," of "static" and "dynamic," of "objective correlative," and Jargon only knows what else! And here is Humpty Dumpty, swaying on his high and narrow wall and crying, in a kind of ecstasy, "Impenetrability!"—Humpty Dumpty, the very type and symbol of all such jargoneers. Alice, as usual, speaks for the sane mass of mankind when she remarks so thoughtfully, "That's a great deal to make one word mean." Of course it is a great deal, but then Humpty Dumpty and his kind pester us with their uncouth and inappropriate terms so that they may be spared the labor of thought and yet may convey the impression of great profundity. There is a certain periodical written for the benefit of superior persons in America, a periodical in which every article bristles with terrifying names and pretentious technical terms that really mean little or nothing, and if I had my way there would be scored across every page of that periodical, in the largest and blackest of letters, the blessed word "Impenetrability." But hardly less significant is Humpty Dumpty's reply to Alice's request that he should explain to her the meaning of the poem "Jabberwocky." For once he is eager, alert, on his mettle: "Let's hear it," he cries. "I can explain all the poems that ever were invented—and a good many that haven't been invented just yet." Of course he can, and so can all his tribe; they are forever explaining poems, forever mauling and manhandling their betters, the poets. But what, it may be asked, is meant by that reference to a good many poems "that haven't been invented yet"? For my part, I hold that it refers to the sketchy verses written by his friends, members of his little coterie, for such verses can hardly be said to have been invented, and it is only when they are explained by the friendly critic that they really come into existence as inventions at all. Finally, it is inevitable that we should discover that Humpty Dumpty, too, writes verse. This fact alone proves conclusively that Lewis Carroll, having had a sudden and disturbing vision of what was to come, meant this Humpty Dumpty episode to be a satire. True, the verses themselves are better, at least technically, than those we are treated to by the young critics who are aimed at, but it is extremely likely that our author, even in parody, felt that he ought not to fall below a certain standard. But the poem, if it can be called a poem, that Humpty Dumpty recites has certain characteristics that are by this time only too familiar to readers of verse: it has that abrupt manner, that sense of incompleteness, that suggestion of vague symbolism, which we know only too well. Such verses as—

> *The little fishes' answer was*
> *"We cannot do it, Sir, because—"*

and

> *And when I found the door was shut,*
> *I tried to turn the handle, but—*

leave us in doubt as to who are the posthumous victims of this satirical genius. And we have only to think of what we have suffered from such persons, and in particular (not to mince matters) Mr. Blank and Mr. Dash, to agree that once again Alice is made to speak for all of us when she exclaims, as she walks away from the absurd figure perched on the high and narrow wall, "Of all the unsatisfactory people I *ever* met. . . ." There is clearly no more to be said; the episode is at an end; Humpty Dumpty and all his later followers are annihilated.

Logic and Language in THROUGH THE LOOKING-GLASS

Patricia Meyer Spacks

(1961)

EVEN THE MOST hardy opponents of whimsy, those who resolutely refuse
to succumb to the charm of Pogo or Winnie-the-Pooh, have frequently
yielded to the appeal of Lewis Carroll's *Through the Looking-Glass*. Of
all books intended for children, *Through the Looking-Glass* and *Alice
in Wonderland* are probably the ones most read by adults with enjoyment.
And though the charm of the Looking-Glass world, by its very profundity and complexity, remains undefinable, certainly one of its many
sources of appeal for adults, and perhaps the one with most far-reaching
significance, is the special attitude toward language which the book

presents, an attitude brilliantly used as a weapon of social commentary. Through what appears to be mere verbal play, Carroll succeeds in suggesting that the apparent chaos of the dream-world is less disorderly than the lack of discipline in the real world, that the problem of appearance and reality has to do with value as well as perception.

In a review of a collection of French folk tales, W. H. Auden once remarked that characters in fairy tales are subject always to certain laws, despite the fact that their world is an emphatically unreal one. One of the two areas he mentions in which such laws inevitably operate is that of language: even the fairy-tale universe does not escape the rigorous logic of language. Auden is speaking, of course, of the folk tale, and *Through the Looking-Glass* is an extremely sophisticated example of the "literary" as opposed to the "folk" fairy tale. Yet in it, too, in a world consciously upside down and backwards, the logic of language holds sway—if to very different purpose from that of the folk tale.

The example quoted by Auden may help to clarify the point. "We can lie in language," he observes, "and manipulate the world as we wish, but the lie must make sense as a grammatical proposition." Then he quotes from an unnamed fairy tale:

"What are you doing there, good woman?" he asked.
"I'd like to take some sunshine home, a whole wheelbarrowful, but it's difficult, for as soon as I get it in the shade it vanishes."
"What do you want a wheelbarrowful of sunshine for?"
"It's to warm my little boy who is at home half dead from cold."

The logic here is that of the real world; its appearance in the fairy tale serves to confirm our faith in the sanity of our own environment.

But quite the reverse is true in *Through the Looking-Glass*, where rigid conformity to the logical demands of language suggests rather a sense of insanity in the ordinary world. Most commentators on Carroll have assumed the opposite: that the insanity is in the Looking-Glass world, not in our own. D. H. Monro, for example, in *Argument of Laughter*, remarks that Carroll's technique is "to take some well-worn, trite form of words, and explore it for unexpected and impossible meanings. The method is precisely the method of serious intellectual endeavor —of logic or mathematics. But the object is different. We are no longer concerned to find truth and order and new meaning. We are looking for fantasy and disorder and nonsense."

Only in the shallowest sense, however, does the trip through the Looking-Glass reveal disorder and nonsense. Carroll's world of fantasy is most profoundly, in its semantic aspects at least, the sort of world for which such a logician as Charles Dodgson might yearn: a world of truth and order. That it *seems* disorderly is a condemnation of the ordinary sloppy thinking of the reader and the sloppy traditions of his language; the apparent disorder concealing deep logic is an effective satiric weapon. But let us look at some examples.

At the very beginning of Alice's adventures, she finds herself in a garden full of talking flowers. She asks if they are not frightened at being out there alone, and the Rose replies that there's the tree in the middle to protect them.

> *"But what could it do, if any danger came?" Alice asked.*
> *"It could bark," said the Rose.*
> *"It says 'Bough-wough,'" cried a Daisy: "that's why its branches are called boughs!"*

A little later, Alice comments that she has never before known flowers to talk. She is instructed to feel the ground, discovers that it is very hard, and is told that usually gardeners make the beds too soft, so that the flowers are always asleep.

Perfectly simple puns, these, but puns with a purpose, puns which immediately establish a context. In the actual world, no real relation exists between the bark of a dog and the bark of a tree, and flowers in hard ground are as speechless as flowers in soft. In the topsy-turvy world behind the Looking-Glass, on the other hand, there is far more regard for the import of words: their meaning cannot be evaded simply by making distinctions between "bow-wow" and "bough-wough." And the unavoidable suggestion is that our everyday use of language is largely arbitrary and unaccountable.

The same sort of pun continues throughout the book, with ever deepening effect. The Rocking-horse-fly is made of wood and gets about by swinging itself from branch to branch; the Bread-and-butter-fly consists of thin slices of bread and butter, a crust, and a lump of sugar, and lives on weak tea with cream in it. But how is the more common horsefly like a horse, the butterfly related to butter? In the Looking-Glass world, jam every other day means never jam today—for "to-day isn't any *other* day, you know." Alice, who sees nobody on the road, is vastly admired by the

White King: accustomed to a more severely logical world than hers, he can only see somebody. The Frog can't understand why anyone should answer the door unless it has been asking something; he admonishes Alice for knocking at it: "Wexes it, you know." Alice, become a queen, is rebuked for attempting to slice a leg of mutton after she has been presented to it: "It isn't etiquette to cut anyone you've been introduced to."

All of this is extremely confusing for Alice, as confusing as dreams usually are. Yet the confusion is really a product of her own initial commitment to the ordinary world: she, not her Looking-Glass interlocutors, is actually illogical. And to the extent that readers participate in the sense of dream-chaos, the joke is on them—for the apparent illogic of the dream-world comes actually from a profound absence of chaos.

The significance of language and its demands is emphasized also in other ways. Principal spokesman, of course, is Humpty Dumpty, who has before now been quoted in serious articles on semantics. "There's glory for you!" he observes, and Alice fails to understand—as well she might.

"I don't know what you mean by 'glory,'" Alice said.

Humpty Dumpty smiled contemptuously. "Of course you don't—till I tell you. I meant 'there's a nice knock-down argument for you!'"

"But 'glory' doesn't mean 'a nice knock-down argument,'" Alice objected.

"When I use a word," Humpty Dumpty said in rather a scornful tone, "it means just what I choose it to mean—neither more nor less."

"The question is," said Alice, "whether you can make words mean so many different things."

"The question is," said Humpty Dumpty, "which is to be master—that's all."

Alice was too much puzzled to say anything, so after a minute Humpty Dumpty began again. "They've a temper, some of them—particularly verbs, they're the proudest—adjectives you can do anything with, but not verbs—however, I can manage the whole lot of them! Impenetrability! That's what I say!"

Nonsense? In a modern classic of semantics, *The Meaning of Meaning*, C. K. Ogden and I. A. Richards examine the usage of several noted modern philosophers with regard to the word "meaning." This is their conclusion: "In spite of a tacit assumption that the term is sufficiently understood, no principle governs its usage, nor does any technique exist whereby confusion may be avoided." Yet the most elementary principle of semantics is that agreement about the use of signs rather than the signs themselves enables us to communicate. With Humpty Dumpty's method of dealing with words, chaos is come again. For the severe social discipline of language suggested by the puns previously noted, he substitutes an altogether solipsistic discipline—but Ogden and Richards stand as eloquent witnesses to the prevalence of Solipsism in the usage of the real world. Again, the Looking-Glass world has the logical advantage: if Humpty Dumpty's technique would end by making communication impossible, at least he is clear-sighted enough to know what he is doing. In our world, failures of communication from similar causes are frequently complicated by our unwillingness to recognize high-handed dealings with language.

In his interpretation of "Jabberwocky," on the other hand, Humpty Dumpty shows that the satirist can find a target also in the effort to insist upon exactness. The poem itself, of course, is presented for Alice's mystification in the opening pages of the book. "Somehow it seems to fill my head with ideas," she says, "—only I don't exactly know what they are!" Humpty Dumpty has no such problem. When Alice asks him for an interpretation of the first stanza, he finds no difficulty attaching precise meanings to each word: "Well, '*outgribing*' is something between bellowing and whistling, with a kind of sneeze in the middle." But his interpretation—reducing the splendid stanza to an account of animals resembling badgers, lizards, and corkscrews, going through various gyrations in the plot of land around a sundial during the part of the afternoon when one begins broiling things for dinner—destroys the poem. One can hardly think of these grotesque animals and their sundial while appreciating the masterful narrative poetry of "Jabberwocky": it is an interpretation forgotten as soon as it is read. Surely, the filling of the head with cloudy ideas is a higher poetic achievement than the reduction of these ideas to the ridiculous. Alice asks for no more interpretations from Humpty Dumpty, and when he recites to her his own poem, a creation devoid of difficult words or leaps of imagination, it seems to her greater nonsense than the other: she doesn't know what it means either, but it doesn't fill her head with ideas.

But the ultimate point of Humpty Dumpty's method with language is the same as the point of the Gnat's exposition of Looking-Glass insect life. In both cases, the central revelation is the same: that language, the symbolic representation of experience, has power of its own. Thus anthropologists find that primitive magic depends upon an equation between the *names* of things and their souls, and semanticists learn that a shift of words in a crucial context equals a shift of emotion. Alice's adventures are an educative process, but even after her encounter with Humpty Dumpty, she never becomes quite wary enough. She is unprepared for the vagaries of the White Knight, who reveals to her that what the name of a song is called, the name of the song itself, what the song is called, and what the song really *is*, can all be different. She is accustomed to a world in which language is used more loosely: it is never used loosely in Looking-Glass Land.

And indeed the Word has power: this truth is demonstrated repeatedly. A case in point is the wood where things have no names. The Red Queen's final injunction to Alice has been, "Remember who you are!" In the mysterious wood, Alice forgets. The result is that she becomes effectively different. She walks through the forest with her arm around the neck of a fawn, which also has forgotten its name and nature. When names return to the two, on the farther edge of the wood, their friendly relationship is destroyed: the fawn darts away in fear, once he has attached appropriate labels to himself and his companion. Toward the end of the book, the White Queen relates the story of a thunderstorm which frightened her so much she couldn't remember her own name. Alice reflects, "I never should *try* to remember my name in the middle of an accident; Where would be the use of it?" But the White Queen is wiser than she; Alice should have learned by this time the high potency of names. As Pythagoras said, "The wisest of all things is Number, and next to this the Name-Giver."

Even the use of nursery rhymes here, so different from anything in *Alice in Wonderland*, is a demonstration of the force of language. The existence of the rhymes itself seems to determine the course of the action related to them: again, a dictum of Ogden and Richards is supported—that "the power of words is the most conservative force in our life." It is the power of words that eliminates the possibility of change from the Looking-Glass world: actions are by words eternally fixed, and no deviation from them is conceivable. Tweedledum and Tweedledee fight over their rattle not because they want to—quite the contrary—but because, in effect, the rhyme says they do, and therefore they must. They are forced on by a special sort of fate, the sort most appropriate to a work so largely dominated by preoccupation with language. This sense of fatality caused by the existence of a certain set of words is even stronger in the case of Humpty Dumpty, whose pompousness has an undertone of pathos because of the inevitability of his fall. In his case, the relation between rhyme and actuality is more pointed, as he brags about the fact that if he should fall, the king will send all his horses and men to pick him up. The humorist is here exploiting his special equivalent of tragic irony. So, too, with the King's Messenger, Haigha, words determine, in a simple and direct sense, events. Alice plays the children's game, "I love my love with an H," with his name; she feeds him with Ham sandwiches and Hay. When Haigha arrives, the King feels faint; his messenger opens the bag hanging around his neck, hands the King a ham sandwich, and then reports there is nothing left but hay. Alice has exercised no pre-science; the words have created the event. And when we hear of the Lion and the Unicorn fighting for the crown, we know with complete sureness that the action will continue through white bread and brown plum cakes, and drumming out of town: nothing else can possibly happen because the Word on the subject already exists.

So it seems apparent that language is a theme underlying virtually all the episodes of *Through the Looking-Glass*. Through four main devices Lewis Carroll makes his points about language: through the punning which demonstrates the looseness with which words are ordinarily used; through the personal discipline imposed on language by Humpty Dumpty and, less extensively, by the White Knight; through the emphasis on the importance of names; and through the convention that existent sets of words can determine patterns of events. The attitudes thus communicated add a special emphasis to the more obvious motif of the difficulty of distinguishing between appearance and reality.

This problem of appearance and reality is, of course, implicit or explicit in all dream narratives: if the action of the dream seems true, it implies the question of whether it is not essentially as true as the more solid waking world. In *Through the Looking-Glass*, the problem is certainly explicit. Tweedledum and Tweedledee show Alice the Red King asleep under a tree, and tell her that he is dreaming of her:

"And if he left off dreaming about you, where do you suppose you'd be?"

"Where I am now, of course," said Alice.

"Not you!" Tweedledee retorted contemptuously. "You'd be nowhere. Why, you're only a sort of thing in his dream!"

"If that there King was to wake," added Tweedledum, "you'd go out—bang!—just like a candle!"

The discussion continues, until Alice is reduced to tears by the repeated insistence that she is not real, only to be told, "You won't make yourself a bit realler by crying," and, a bit later, that she is not weeping real tears. The final question of the book is "who it was that dreamed it all," Alice or the Red King. "He was part of my dream, of course—but then I was part of his dream, too!" And the narrative proper is followed by a sentimental poem, which ends, "Life, what is it but a dream?"

The question of who is real, Alice or the Red King; which is real, the everyday world or the dream-world, is given added intensity by the special attitude toward language so closely involved in the narrative. For the dream-world is, as I have tried to show, a world which has as a dominant characteristic a high regard for the demands of language, a world in which language is taken seriously. It seems, to this extent, closer to the realm of absolute truth than the existence from which Alice escapes. If, in other words, it is not actually truer than the other world, it, in a sense, should be; by being more logical, it *seems* more true. Alice, loyal in essence to her ordinary life, although unfailingly courteous to representatives of the world behind the Looking-Glass, still has her doubts about the reality of the realm of her values; and these doubts are communicated to the reader. The questions raised by what most critics call Carroll's "word-play" are the questions of modern philosophers. A. J. Ayer, for example, speaks of "the naive assumption that definite descriptive phrases are demonstrative symbols"—that words have *essential* meanings rather than arbitrary ones. And Ogden and Richards carry the matter further: "No important question of verbal usage can be considered without raising questions as to the rank or level and the truth or falsity of the actual references which may employ them." But Carroll has antedated all three: the question of meaning and the question of value are the very crux of the dealings with language in *Through the Looking-Glass.*

For the satirist's foundation, inasmuch as he concerns himself with language here, is not—like Pope's, for example—in the socially accepted values of his time, or, like Byron's, in personal standards. The play with words, playful though it is, depends for its satiric effect on the assumed existence of some realm of absolutes, in which there is a real equation between a truth and its symbolic expression. The Looking-Glass world is far from this realm of absolutes, but not so far as the "real" world, where play with language is not so free, and where we too often fail to recognize the possibility that there may indeed be a significant difference between what a song is called and what it really is. As Swift, in his discussion of Houyhnhnms and Yahoos, sheds doubts on man's claim to be a rational animal, so Carroll, with none of Swift's venom but with equally high standards, suggests in *Through the Looking-Glass* the dubiety of the assumption that human communication is logical and accurate. Both men are concerned with modes of human action; Carroll's special genius, perhaps, lies in his ability to disguise charmingly the seriousness of his concern, to make the most playful quality of his work at the same time its didactic crux.

VII
Freudian
Interpretations

ALICE IN WONDERLAND

Psychoanalyzed

by A. M. E. Goldschmidt

(1933)

IN TREATING certain passages of *Alice in Wonderland* as products of the author's subconscious mind, it is not suggested that such an approach is defensible for all, or even for most, literature. The strangest fantasies may defy the judgment of the psychoanalyst of whatever school, when they are the work of a refined and eager sensibility, consciously operating in the wide field of human experience. On the other hand no critic upon whom the Freudian theory has made even the slightest impression can refrain from recognizing sexual symbolism in any medium, when it is very clearly manifested. The Freudian interpretation, for instance, of some of the curiosities of popular tales or rhymes must seem, to such a critic, irrefutable. There may be subsidiary interpretations, he feels, but the element of sexual symbolism, when once apparent, cannot be neglected.

But why should the fantasy of Lewis Carroll be placed in the category of naïve and spontaneous creations, as a fit subject for analysis, rather than be accorded the immunity which is due to a conscious work of art?[1] The answer is to be found in the nature of the author, considered as a conscious artist, and in the mental conditions under which the fantasy was composed. The story of *Alice* was begun in the course of a river party, the author telling it, quite impromptu, to three of his child-friends. We have his own word for it, that he simply said the first thing that came into his head. The story is in the form of a dream, and it has the strange spontaneity of a dream, at least in those earlier passages which will form the subject of our analysis; for there are some parts which are witty, coherent, intellectual, and deliberate—they are the work of the conscious mind, which occupied itself, as we know, with logic, mathematics, chess, acrostics, and parody. To the conscious mind was eventually committed the task of bringing to an artistic conclusion the original dreamlike fantasy. Long before reaching the end, the author tells us, he had "drained the wells of fancy dry," and the rest "had to be hammered out." In this latter part, even the nonsense is systematic—as, owing to the prearranged scheme of the chess problem, it remains in *Through the Looking-Glass*. But in the first part there is no system, the incidents and images are suggested by the subconscious, and their nature is erotic.

The symbolism begins almost at once. Alice runs down the rabbit-hole after the White Rabbit and suddenly finds herself falling down "what seemed to be a very deep well." Here we have what is perhaps the best-known symbol of coitus. Next, the dreamer (who identifies himself with Alice throughout) is seen pursuing the White Rabbit down a series of passages, and it is worth noting that Ştekel interprets the pursuit in dreams of something we are unable to catch as representing an attempt to make up a disparity in age. Now the dreamer enters a "long, low hall," round which are a number of doors, all locked. Alice despairs of getting out; but "suddenly she came upon a little three-legged table"; she finds upon it

a tiny golden key, and Alice's first idea was that this might belong to one of the doors of the hall; but alas! either the locks were too large,

*or the key was too small, but at any rate it would not open any of them.
However . . . she came upon a low curtain . . . and behind it was a little
door about fifteen inches high: she tried the little golden key in the lock,
and to her great delight it fitted! Alice opened the door and found that
it led into a small passage not much larger than a rat-hole: she knelt
down and looked along the passage into the loveliest garden you ever
saw. How she longed to get out of that dark hall, and wander about
among those beds of bright flowers and those cool fountains. . . .*

Here we find the common symbolism of lock and key representing
coitus; the doors of normal size represent adult women. These are disre-
garded by the dreamer and the interest is centered on the little door,
which symbolizes a female child; the curtain before it represents the
child's clothes.

The colorful language suggests the presence, in the subconscious, of
an abnormal emotion of considerable strength. There can be no doubt,
historically speaking, that this emotion was completely repressed, and
that Lewis Carroll's relations with his child-friends were of the most
harmless and delightful kind. Equally there can be little doubt of its
subconscious existence. Lewis Carroll was an unmarried clergyman of
the strictest "virtue," and his abnormal instinct is therefore more clearly
recognized, because scarcely complicated by other issues. It is difficult
to hold that his interest in children was inspired by a love of childhood
in general, and in any case based on a mental rather than a physical
attraction, in view of two facts: that he detested little boys, for whom,
writes a biographer "he had an aversion amounting to terror," and that
his friendships almost invariably ended with the close of childhood.

"About nine out of ten of my child friendships," he writes himself,
*"get shipwrecked at the critical point where the stream and river meet,
and the child friends once so affectionate become uninteresting acquaintances whom I have no wish to set eyes on again."*

Such a sudden revulsion of feeling would be inexplicable, if it had
been the character and personality of the child which absorbed his
interest. We must remember too that he was no gray-haired old gentleman
at the time *Alice* was first invented, but a young man of thirty. His friendships with children began when he was only twenty-three, but the development of his instinct, in later years, is convincingly illustrated by a dream
which he records in a letter. He was a great friend of the Terrys, and at
the time of the dream Marion, sister of Ellen, was acting the lead in a play
in London. Lewis Carroll dreamed that he went to see Mrs. Terry and

found Marion there, as a little girl. He then asked Mrs. Terry if he could take the child Marion to see the grown-up Marion act. The nature of the repressed wish is clear—he would like the admired actress to turn into a child, since children were more attractive to him.

The symbol of the door is replaced later in the story by that of a little house about four feet high, but meanwhile have occurred a series of incidents whose meaning we may briefly indicate here, although in the book they are as elaborate as they are striking. Alice alternately grows and shrinks—first on drinking the bottle marked "Drink Me," then on eating a cake, then on nibbling the mushroom. The phallic significance of these incidents is clear, and is borne out by the illustrations, particularly that of Alice's "immense length of neck, which seemed to rise like a stalk out of a sea of green leaves which lay far below her." Tenniel's illustrations, with which most nurseries are familiar, were not original, but copied directly from those of the author, which may be seen in the Everyman edition. They are of the most striking immediacy, in comparison with Tenniel's humorous, but fussy work, and indeed have something of the disturbing strangeness of surrealism.

The whole course of the story is perhaps to be explained by the desire for complete virility, conflicting with the desire for abnormal satisfaction. If sexual emotions may be divided into the lumbar and the thoracic, we can form a clearer idea of what is involved. The whole aim of the dreamer is to fulfill the thoracic emotion; the one, however, always involves the other; and on this occasion conflicts with it. The importance of the latter, however, in the dreamer's subconscious, when disconnected from the extraverted emotion, is seen by two further incidents, of an autoerotic significance, those of the sneezing baby and of the flamingo. Later, as we have said, the story comes under the control of the conscious mind, and there are no irrelevant incidents. But the reader, if he accepts our thesis in its main lines, may proceed to find for himself, in the earlier part, symbols of minor importance.

We might expect to find that these repressions, and the unconscious mental conflict they involved, caused Lewis Carroll trouble in later life. Indeed, he is described, in middle and old age, as morose, irritable, intractable, and subject to fits of depression. Had he lived today he might have undergone analysis, discovered the cause of his neurosis, and lived a more contented life. But in that case he might not have written *Alice in Wonderland*.

Psychoanalytic
Remarks on
ALICE
IN WONDERLAND
and Lewis Carroll

by Paul Schilder

(1938)

LEWIS CARROLL's *Alice in Wonderland* and *Through the Looking-Glass and What Alice Found There* are classics of stories for children. As far as I know nobody has tried so far to find out what is offered to children by these stories.

One would expect that the men writing for children should have or should have had a rich life and that this richness of experience might transmit something valuable to the child. Charles Lutwidge Dodgson (this is the real name of the author) lived a rather narrow and distorted life.[1] He came from a religious family. His father was interested in mathematics. His mother is described as gentle and kind. None of the biographies which I have at my disposal contains anything about the deeper relations between Charles and his parents. In none of the books can anything be found about his relations to his brothers and sisters. He was the oldest of eleven children, eight[2] of them being girls. We merely hear that he gave theatrical performances for them and that he died in 1898 at the age of sixty-five, at his sister's house, where for some twenty years it had been his custom to spend Christmas and other holidays. In his childhood he amused himself with snails and toads as pets. . . . He matriculated at Christ's Church in Oxford, his father's college, when he was eighteen. He was always a brilliant pupil. He spent the greater part of his life in Oxford, where he lectured in mathematics. He was ordained deacon in 1861 but never proceeded to priest's orders and preached also very rarely. This may have been partially due to his stammering, which he shared with others of his siblings. One of his biographers sees in this a hereditary taint due to the consanguinity between his father and his mother.

Alice in Wonderland appeared in 1865. In 1867 Dodgson made a trip to Russia with Dr. Liddon. The diary of this trip is meager and dull. He showed a great interest in churches. In 1871 *Through the Looking-Glass* appeared. He had no adult friends. He liked little girls and only girls. He had very little interest in boys but he occasionally showed interest in juvenile male actors. However, Mr. Bert Coote, one of the child-actors in whom he was interested, had a little sister who may have been the real cause of Carroll's interest. When a friend once offered to bring his boy to him, he declined, and said, "He thought I doted on all children but I am not omnivorous like a pig. I pick and choose."

Alice in Wonderland originated from stories told to Lorina, Alice, and Edith Liddell, the three daughters of the college Dean. Dodgson was particularly attracted to Alice, who was then about seven years old. He has photographed her in a pose which in its sensual innocence reminds one of pictures of Greuze. His interest in his child-friends usually ceased when they were about fourteen and he exchanged correspondence with them when they grew older. In his numerous diaries there is not the slightest suggestion of erotic interests. His friends, interviewed by Reed, testify in the same direction. He was prolific in writing letters to little girls in which he tried to amuse them. Some of his poems addressed to little girls are not very different from love poems. The dedication of *Through the Looking-Glass* reads:

> *Child of the pure unclouded brow*
> *And dreaming eyes of wonder! . . .*
> *Thy loving smile will surely hail*
> *The love-gift of a fairy-tale.*

The dedication of the *Hunting of the Snark* reads:

> *Inscribed to a dear Child: . . . .*
> *Girt with a boyish garb for boyish task. . . .*

Shy with adults, he easily got in contact with little girls whom he amused by storytelling and mechanical toys.

He seemingly was generally kind in his contacts with adults but extremely pedantic concerning the illustrations of his books and did not get along very well with his illustrators. He was interested in photography. He had considerable gifts for mathematics and wrote several books on the subject under his real name which, although not outstanding, won considerable acclaim. He was dry and uninspiring as a teacher. He was religious. He intended to write down some of his sermons, of which one on eternal punishment was dearest to him.

This material is scanty. We have therefore to turn to his work if we want to get deeper information.

One is astonished to find in his pleasant fairy stories the expression of an enormous anxiety. Alice, in *Through the Looking-Glass,* is "standing bewildered." "She does not know what to do." "She does not even know her name." "She cannot find the word 'tree'." When she wants to repeat a poem "another poem comes out, to her distress." "She moves and comes back to the same place."

Most of her anxieties are connected with a change of her body (body image). It is either too small or too big. When it is too big she gets squeezed, or she fills the room (for instance, the end scene in *Alice in Wonderland*). She feels separated from her feet. She does not find the gloves of the Rabbit. She is frightened when she hears continually about cutting heads off. She is threatened by the Duchess and by the Queen of Hearts. Time either stops or goes in the opposite direction. She has not the right ticket in the train. Animals pass remarks about her. The mutton she wants to eat starts talking. The food is taken away from her and the banquet scene ends in an uproar in which she is threatened by the candles, by the ladle, and by the bottles which have become birds. These are indeed nightmares full of anxiety. We are accustomed to find such dreams in persons with strong repressions which prevent final satisfactions. Alice, although bewildered, remains passive. Things happen to her. Only towards the end she revolts against the King and Queen of Hearts and she even shakes the Red Queen, which turns out to be the black kitten.

It is perhaps remarkable that she is never successful when she wants to eat. When she eats or drinks, she becomes merely bigger or smaller. Although she would like to cut the cake for the Lion and the Unicorn, she encounters great difficulties and finally she has no cake for herself. There are severe deprivations in the sphere of food and of eating. Alice does not get anything at the mad tea-party. Oral aggressiveness is found everywhere. The poem of the Walrus and the Carpenter is of an astonishing cruelty. The "lobster is crooked." Alice herself "frightens the Mouse and the birds by tales of devouring." There is also "an owl to be devoured by a panther." The "crocodile devours the little fish." Father William, as an old man, "eats the goose with the bones and the beak since his jaw got so strong by arguing with his wife." (It is remarkable that the little girls invited by Carroll got very little food.)

We find, also, preponderant oral sadistic trends of cannibalistic character.

There is no dearth of other cruelties. "The Queen of Hearts wants to chop off almost everybody's head." There is a serious discussion whether "one can cut off the head of the Cheshire Cat" when it appears alone. It is the fear of "being cut to pieces" which comes again and again into the foreground. The "head of the Jabberwocky is cut off too." The prisoner (the Messenger) "is threatened with death," as is the Knave of Hearts.

Thus there is a continuous threat to the integrity of the body in general.

I have shown that an extreme aggressiveness finally distorts space.[3] The loss of the third dimension plays an important part in Carroll's work. In *Sylvie and Bruno*, the warden's brother calls a boy a nail which stands out from the floor and has to be "hammered flat." In a letter written to a little girl about three cats which visited him, he tells that he knocked the cats down as flat as a pancake and that afterwards they were quite happy "between the sheets of blotting paper." It is perhaps in this respect remarkable that many of the figures are taken from cards and are reduced to cards again in the final scene. I have mentioned the distortions of

Alice's body. The egg-shaped Humpty Dumpty "falls" finally from the wall with a crash.

The stability of space is guaranteed by the vestibular apparatus and by postural reflexes. The stability of space is continually threatened. Alice is "going through the rabbit-hole" which functions like a chute. The White King and the White Queen make "rapid flights through the air." A "wind blows" which carries the Red Queen. "Bottles start to fly." "Candlesticks elongate." "A train is jumping over a river." It is an uncertain world. In addition, right and left are changed by the mirror. The King's whole "army tumbles and falls." So do the Red and White Knight. Father William "balances on his head." There is not much certainty in such a world. One does not wonder that Alice is rather afraid she might be a dream of the Red King.

Time does not escape distortion. It "either stands still or goes even in the opposite direction," although it is difficult even for Carroll to persist with such a distortion for a very long time. One of the letters he wrote to one of his little friends starts with the last word of the letter and finishes with the first: a complete reversal. After all, Carroll was a mathematician. It may be that ruthlessness towards space and time belong to the characteristics of the mathematical talent.

One may raise the question whether there is not a somatic basis for Carroll's pleasure in mirror writing (the first part of the Jabberwocky ballad is printed in mirror writing) and reversals, since he was a stammerer. Orton (especially in his Salmon lectures, 1936) has pointed to the organic basis of such combinations. However, left and right disorientation and reversals are very often symbolizations for the inability to find a definite direction in one's sexuality and for a wavering between the hetero- and homosexual component impulses.

There is an inexhaustible play with words in both *Alice* tales. "Pig" is misunderstood as "fig." As counterpart to "beautification" the word "uglification" is introduced. The shoes in the sea are made of "soles" and "eels." The whiting makes the "shoes and boots white." No wise fish would go anywhere without "porpoise." The tale about the Fury and the Mouse is arranged in a form of a "tail."[4]

We know this phenomenon very well. It occurs when the word is not taken merely as a sign but as a substance of its own. What the word signifies (the referent) diffuses into the sign. The sign becomes the object itself, quite in the same way as Pavlov's dogs react to the signal alone with salivation, which should be the reaction to the actual food. The word is handled as a substance, as any other substance. A "Rocking-horse-fly" is invented; it is made of wood. Humpty Dumpty can therefore say very well that he "lets the words work for him." Humpty Dumpty is furthermore right when he says that the words have the meanings he gives to them. Whenever one starts playing with words, the problem of negation and the problem of opposites will soon emerge. Alice "sees nobody" and the king admires her that "she can see nobody at such a distance." Humpty Dumpty prefers "un-birthday" presents, since there are 364 days in a year where one can get un-birthday presents more often. The Red Queen says that "she could show hills in comparison with which the hill seen could be called a valley." The sign function of language is substituted here by the most primitive attitude towards the sign function, on the basis of which no real orientation is possible and Alice remains bewildered.

The Jabberwocky poem uses new words which remind one of the language of dreams and of schizophrenics. Slithy—lithe and shiny; mimsy, flimsy and miserable; wabe—way before and way behind; gyre—to go around like a gyroscope; gimble—to make holes like a gimlet.

The Jabberwocky ballad's first few lines were published about ten years before the appearance of *Looking-Glass*, with a slightly different interpretation. Five years later, in *The Hunting of the Snark*, Carroll explains the principle of portmanteau words.[5] These are words which combine two words by what today we call condensation. We find these condensations when the forces of the system of the unconscious come into play. This is a rather ruthless treatment of words. They are handled without consideration. It depends "who is the master," says Humpty Dumpty. Words are "cut to pieces" and the pieces are arbitrarily united. Such an attitude towards words is found in early stages of mental development. In childhood there is an experimental stage in which the child tries to become clear about the sign function of words. In schizophrenia, such a treatment of words signifies the wish of the individual to give up definite relations to the world, which is, after all, a world of regular sequences and of meaning.

Lewis Carroll is considered as the master of "nonsense literature." One of his biographers even calls him the founder of nonsense literature. The Red Queen says, after having made nonsensical remarks, "but I have heard nonsense compared with which that would be as sensible as a dictionary." The Walrus and the Carpenter "go out in sunshine when it is night." The White Knight delights in nonsensical inventions. He carries a little box upside down so that "rain cannot come in," but the "clothes and the sandwiches have fallen out" (play against gravitation). He has a "mousetrap on horseback" (the play with spatial relations). Anklets around the feet of the horse protect against the bite of sharks (contraction of space). Freud says justly that nonsense in dreams and so-called unconscious thinking signifies contempt and sneering. We may expect that nonsense literature is the expression of particularly strong destructive tendencies, of very primitive character. No wonder that persons faced with so much destructive nonsense finally "do not know whether they exist" or whether "they are part of a dream and will vanish." Many things vanish: the fawn, the beard of a passenger, and, in *The Hunting of the Snark*, the baker disappears, faced by a snark which is a bojum. The scene in the store of the sheep changes suddenly. The figures in *Wonderland* taken from cards become a pack of cards again. The figures of *Looking-Glass* are in reality unanimated chess figures.

This is a world of cruelty, destruction, and annihilation. Alice, constantly threatened, still emerges bland and smiling. The kings and queens, the duchesses and knights are "reduced to nothingness." Perhaps it is this final outcome which is gratifying to the child and the adult reader and listener.

It is perhaps worth while to take a glimpse into the world of the child. It experiments continually with the qualities of space, with the shape of its own body, with mass and configuration. This is particularly obvious with children who are between three and four years old, as studies by L. Bender and me have shown.[6] But it can also be observed in younger and older people. It is interesting to compare the Mother Goose rhymes with *Alice* and *Through the Looking-Glass*. There we find a "crooked man who went a crooked mile, a crooked cat and a crooked mouse." "The cats of Kilkenny disappear." "A woman loses her identity after a part of her skirt is cut off." "The sheep leave their tails behind them." The King of France merely "goes up and down a hill with twenty-thousand men." "Elizabeth, Elspeth, Betsy, Bess are four persons and still one person." The similarity is obvious. George Saintsbury, in the *Cambridge History of English Literature*, has stressed this similarity too, and remarks about Carroll "there is something of the manipulations of mathematical symbols in the systematic absurdity and the nonsensical preciseness of his humor." It seems to me that the destructiveness of Carroll's nonsense goes further than the experimentation of the nursery rhymes.

What does all this mean? How did Carroll come to this queer world? It is a world without real love. The queens and kings are either absurd or cruel or both. We would suspect that Carroll never got the full love of his parents. In large families children very often feel neglected. We may suspect that Carroll, who so often shows feelings of guilt in his diary and who wrote the sermon on eternal punishment, had been educated rather strictly. He must have looked with suspicion at the many children who came after him. Are the kings and queens "symbols" for his parents? Alice also complains very bitterly that the "animals order her around so much." Are some of the animals also representatives of the parents?

All kinds of disagreeable animals appear in the two fairy tales. Carroll liked to play with toads and snails and earthworms. Alice is in continuous fear of being attacked or blamed by the animals. Do the insects represent the many brothers and sisters who must have provoked jealousy in Carroll?

We have at any rate the hypothesis that the demands of Carroll concerning the love of his parents were not fully satisfied. He may have found consolation in the one or the other of his siblings, especially in his sisters. It is remarkable that Alice does not report her adventures to her mother, but to her sister. It is also remarkable that Carroll, talking about her future, refrains from picturing her as a mother who tells stories to her own children. He lets her merely gather about her little children who are strangers. It is, by the way, also reported that Carroll showed jealousy when one of his former little friends married. We may suppose that Carroll expected from one of his sisters the love which he could not get from his mother. The biographical material at hand is not sufficient to decide the question.

We may furthermore suspect that he did not feel sure that he could get this love as the oldest brother and that he felt he might get this love if he would take the place of the parents, and especially the place of the mother. It may be also that he identified himself with one of the older sisters. He was, by the way, particularly sensitive towards the impersonation of females by males on the stage and resented it. Is this a defense against the unconscious wish to play the part of a woman, especially the part of the mother and a sister?

What was his relation to his sex organ anyhow? Fenichel has lately pointed to the possibility that little girls might become symbols for the phallus.[7] Alice changes her form continually; she is continually threatened and continually in danger. There may have been in Carroll the wish for feminine passivity and a protest against it. He plays the part of the mother to little girls but the little girl is for him also the completion of his own body. The little girl is his love object, substituting for the mother and substituting for the sister. These are complicated discussions and are not fully justified, since we do not know enough about the fantasy life of Carroll and probably shall never know about it. But on the basis of other experiences we are reasonably sure that the little girls substitute for incestuous love objects. Besides this object relation, there must have existed a strong tendency to identification, especially with female members of the family. As in all forms of primitive sexuality, the promiscuity in Carroll's relation to children is interesting. He seemingly tried to get in contact with a very great number of children and to "seduce" them in this way.

It is obvious that such object relations, loaded with insecurity and feelings of guilt, cannot remain satisfactory and must be accompanied by hostile and negative tendencies. These hostile tendencies did not find any open expression in Carroll's life. A strong superego and a strong moral consciousness protected him. The strength of the repression may be partially responsible for the depth to which the regression took place. All the hostile tendencies had therefore to come out in the particularly severe distortions in his work. It is possible that the mathematical ability and the constitutional difficulties to which I have pointed before may have something to do with the type and the depth of the regression. Since we do not know enough about the early history of Carroll, we cannot appreciate fully the relation between constitutional and individual factors in the type of regression, which is obvious in his work and in the structure of his love life. Most of the biographers stress the difference between the official personality of Carroll and the personality expressed in his literary work. Carroll himself has pointed this way by choosing a pseudonym and holding Charles Lutwidge Dodgson strictly separated from Lewis Carroll. We can understand his motives to do so. However, his stern morality, his dryness, his mathematical interests, are not separate parts of his personality but are the reaction and the basis of the tendencies which he expressed in his work.

I suspect that nonsense literature will originate whenever there are incomplete object relations and a regression to deep layers involving the relation of space and time on the basis of primitive aggressiveness.

Carroll appears to the writer of this essay as a particularly destructive writer. I do not mean this in the sense of a literary criticism, which does not concern us here. We may merely ask whether such a literature might not increase destructive attitudes in children beyond the measure which is desirable. There is very little in *Alice in Wonderland*, as in *Through the Looking-Glass*, which leads from destruction to construction. There is very little love and tenderness and little regard for the existence of others. Maybe we can have confidence that children will find a way to construction for themselves. At any rate, the child may be led to a mental experimentation which, although cruel, may sooner or later lead to a better appreciation of space, time, and words and so, also, to a better appreciation of other human beings. Problems of this type have to be decided by experience and by experimental approach.

What do children do with Carroll's work? We know very little about it. Preliminary impressions in adults who have read Carroll's books in childhood make it probable that the child uses Carroll's nonsense verses and anxiety situations in a way similar to the manner in which the child uses *Mother Goose Rhymes*. They take them as an understood reality which one can hope to handle better after one has played and worked with it. In comparison with other fairy stories, the dissociation resulting from extreme cruelty is more obvious in Carroll's work. One may be afraid that without the help of the adult, the child may remain bewildered and, alone, may not find his way back to a world in which it can appreciate love relations, space and time and words.

From

"Lewis Carroll's Adventures in Wonderland"

by *John Skinner*

(1947)

. . . It is impossible to gain conscious understanding of the life of Lewis Carroll or of the meaning of his written fantasy unless a psychoanalytic approach is used in the study. One of the outstanding characteristics of the stories of *Alice* is the dreamlike quality of the writing and of the situations which Alice and the others encounter. Lewis Carroll admitted this when he first wrote the manuscript but discarded all references to dreams when he rewrote the book for publication. However, the verse which opens the book makes the intention clear:

The dream-child moving through a land
Of wonders wild and new,
In friendly chat with bird or beast—
And half believe it true.

Lewis Carroll seems to have escaped from harsh world realities into his stories as others escape from painful situations in dreams. The story of *Alice's Adventures in Wonderland* was consciously designed for the entertainment of the children of Dean Liddell, a friend of the author at Oxford, and Lewis Carroll characterized his stories as love-gifts. However, he was not conscious of the motivation of the stories or of the source of their inspiration. The explanation of the fantasy came much later than the original creation, and Professor Dodgson was often hard put to explain what he had meant when he wrote as Mr. Carroll. *The Hunting of the Snark* was always a mystery, for audience and author, and in one of the letters which he wrote some years after the verse was published, Lewis Carroll says:

In answer to your question, "What did you mean the Snark was?" will you tell your friend that I meant that the Snark was a Boojum. I trust that she and you will now feel quite satisfied and happy. To the best of my recollection, I had no other meaning in mind, when I wrote it; but people have since tried to find the meaning in it. The one I like best (which I think is partly my own) is that it may be taken as an Allegory for the Pursuit of Happiness.

Although he made this explanation as "partly my own," it had been suggested in a letter written to him by three American children and represented the value which they had seen in the allegory rather than the meaning which Mr. Carroll had given it. He seems glad of an explanation, though made by another, and there is other evidence that he was never able to explain the meaning of the poem sufficiently, either to himself or others, for he also says:

Of course you know what a Snark is? If you do, please tell me: for I haven't an idea what it is like.

Lewis Carroll was as ignorant of the source of his material as we are often ignorant of the well-spring of the bizarre dreams of sleep:

. . . I added my fresh ideas, which seemed to grow of themselves upon the original stock; and many more added themselves when, years afterward, I wrote it all over again for publication . . . but whenever or how-

ever . . . it comes of itself. I cannot set invention going like a clock, by any voluntary winding up . . . Alice and The Looking Glass are made up almost wholly of bits and scraps, single ideas which come of themselves.

Lewis Carroll liked to invent portmanteau words which carried a double meaning and which telescoped several ideas into one word, just as a number of incidents may be symbolized in one event in a dream, but his explanations of these words were also made sometime after the word had been unconsciously written and given meaning. He writes the following explanation of the words in "Jabberwocky"; but it does not indicate a controlled, rational invention of words so much as a later analysis of meaning, which Mr. Carroll may mistrust even as he explains:

I'm afraid I can't explain "vorpal blade" for you—nor yet "tulgey wood"; but I did make an explanation once for "uffish thought"—It seems to suggest a state of mind when the voice is gruffish, the manner roughish, and the temper huffish. Then again, as to "burble": if you take the three verbs "bleat", "murmur" and "warble", and select the bits I have underlined, it certainly makes "burble": though I am afraid I can't distinctly remember having made it in that way.

He has said that the Snark was a mythological creature which was half snake and half shark, and this verse was written in reverse, in a sense, for the first line which occurred to him was the last line of the written poem:

For the Snark was a Boojum, you see.

There is a relationship between the two poems, *The Hunting of the Snark* and "Jabberwocky," for some of the nonsense words are common to both poems. The following explanation of the words in "Jabberwocky" was made in *Mischmasch* in 1855, one of the newspapers which Lewis Carroll wrote while at Oxford:

BRYLLYG *(derived from the verb to* BRYL *or* BROIL*). "The time of broiling dinner, i.e., the close of the afternoon."*
SLYTHY *(compounded of* SLIMY *and* LITHE*). "Smooth and active."*
TOVE. *A species of Badger. They had smooth white hair, long hind legs, and short horns like a stag; lived chiefly on cheese.*
GYRE, *verb (derived from* GYAOUR *or* GIAOUR, *"a dog"). To scratch like a dog.*
GYMBLE *(whence* GIMBLET*). "To screw out holes in anything."*
WABE *(derived from the verb to* SWAB *or* SOAK*). "The side of a hill" (from it's being* soaked *by the rain).*

MIMSY *(whence* MIMSERABLE *and* MISERABLE*).* *"Unhappy."*

BOROGROVE. *An extinct kind of Parrot. They had no wings, beaks turned up, and made their nests under sundials; lived on veal.*

MOME *(hence* SOLEMOME, SOLEMONE, *and* SOLEMN*).* *"Grave."*

RATH. *A species of land turtle. Head erect: mouth like a shark: forelegs curved out so that the animal walked on its knees: smooth green body: lived on swallows and oysters.*

OUTGRABE, *past tense of the verb to* OUTGRIBE. *(It is connected with old verb to* GRIKE, *or* SHRIKE, *from which are derived "shriek" and "creak").* *"Squeaked."*

Hence the literal English of the passage is: "It was evening, and the smooth active badgers were scratching and boring holes in the hillside; all unhappy were the parrots; and the grave turtles squeaked out."

There were probably sundials on the tops of the hill, and the "borogroves" were afraid that their nests would be undermined. The hill was probably full of the nests of "raths," which ran out squeaking with fear on hearing the "toves" scratching outside. This is an obscure, but yet deeply affecting relic of Ancient Poetry.

Lewis Carroll described this as Anglo-Saxon poetry and in *Carroll's Alice,* Professor Harry Morgan Ayres, Columbia University, traces characters and illustrations to an Anglo-Saxon source. He feels that "Haigha" and "Hatta" in *Through the Looking-Glass* are prototypes for the Hatter and the March Hare in *Alice's Adventures in Wonderland.* He believes that Haigha is a name coined from the name of an English authority on Anglo-Saxon, Daniel Henry Haigh. He also found the word "hatte" used in the Anglo-Saxon manuscripts, which may have been mistaken by Lewis Carroll as a family name although it is a translation of a verb, "is called."

Professor Ayres shows further that some of the costume detail in the Tenniel drawings is similar to the drawings in the early Anglo-Saxon manuscripts, particularly in the cross-gartering and the design of the shoes of Haigha and Hatta. His thesis is further supported by Lewis Carroll's references to "Anglo-Saxon attitudes" of "skipping and wriggling with great hands spread out on each side," which is an exact description of the flat, awkwardly articulated drawings in the early Anglo-Saxon manuscripts. Lewis Carroll called it an "attitude," with perhaps an intentional pun on the word "hatte," thus making it "(h)attitudes." There are other evidences that his imaginative characters were based on friends and acquaintances or other people who are familiar to all of us—teachers, nurses, butlers, gardeners, and other adults.

The practice of reversal permeates the life of Lewis Carroll, his stories, and his hobbies. Alice found herself in a world which reversed the accepted patterns of the world, and the story of the Looking-Glass is a story of complete reversal of the real world. In his own life, Lewis Carroll was obliged to write with the right hand rather than the left, and to reverse the character of Charles Dodgson in order to become Lewis Carroll. Everything worked backward for Alice, too, when she fell down the rabbit-hole into another world or when she stepped into the land behind the looking-glass. Lewis Carroll liked to write in reverse and sent letters which could be read only when they were held up to a mirror. He wrote the verse about the Jabberwock in reverse and the last line first.

One of the letters to a child-friend was written with the signature of Charles Dodgson as salutation and opens:

C. L. D. Uncle loving your

The letter is somewhat acid in tone, for Lewis Carroll was writing about a birthday gift which had not pleased him:

It was so nice of you to give me that pretty Antimacassar you had made for my grandfather. And how well it has lasted.

His life seems to indicate that he did not like his adult, masculine character and that he wished to change himself into a small, adventurous girl because he could not reverse the inexorable force which propelled him toward adult life. If he could have reversed his order in the family constellation, he could have displaced the progression of ten brothers and sisters who forced him to become the oldest child. He is clear in stating his feeling toward boy babies, and an important boy character, Bruno, appears in only one story, *Sylvie and Bruno*, although he is more like a little girl than like a little boy and Lewis Carroll did not complete the story until after twenty years of work. There are clear expressions of hostility toward boys, and the letters of Lewis Carroll include only one letter to a boy. It is full of rejection, with little friendliness in the tone:

I would have been very glad to write to you as you wish, only there are several objections. I think when you have heard them, you will see that I am right in saying "no". The first objection is, "I've got no ink . . ." The next objection is, "I've no time." You don't believe that, you say? Well, who cares? . . . The third and greatest objection is, my great dislike for children. I don't know why, I'm sure: but I hate them—just as one hates armchairs and plum pudding . . . So you see, it would never do to write to you. Have you any sisters? I forget. If you have, give them my love . . . I hope you won't be much disappointed at not getting a letter from

Your affectionate friend

Much of the humor of Lewis Carroll is based on reversal of the intention of an original thought and he parries the aggression of others by thrusting it back upon his opponent. The logical, childlike arguments of Alice are a perversion of adult logic and Lewis Carroll used this same device in some of his correspondence:

In some ways, you know, people that don't exist are much nicer than people that do. For instance, people that don't exist are never cross; and they never contradict you; and they never tread on your toes! Oh, they're ever so much nicer than people that do exist. However, never mind; you can't help existing; and I daresay you're just as nice as if you didn't.

Such logic is the peculiar delight of children who trap and overcome the restrictive adult by extending the original promise to an infinite, illogical, never-to-be-expected conclusion. It is also a sadistic, verbal revenge and we are all familiar with the person that cannot be convinced because of the illogical logic that protects him.

This tendency seems closely related to the teasing which we find in many of Lewis Carroll's letters and which is often openly hostile. He wrote the little boy a letter because he felt a compulsion to answer all letters and he pretended to meet the request, yet he denies he has written the letter, asks that the boy not feel too disappointed, while at the same time he inquires about the boy's sisters, to whom he sends his love. It is significant that he signed some letters "Sylvie" but he never used the name of Bruno, which further suggests his identification with his small girl characters rather than with the boys. He could never overcome this aversion to boys and writes in another letter:

My best love to yourself—to your Mother kindest regards—to your small, fat, impertinent, ignorant brother my hatred.

He does not seem to have enjoyed being a boy, although he remembers

Once I was a real boy

just as the Mock Turtle laments

Once I was a real turtle.

He was once asked to teach in a boys' school and wrote the following reply:

> To me they [boys] are not an attractive race of beings (as a little boy
> I was simply detestable) and if you wanted to induce me, by money, to
> come and teach them, I can only say you would have to offer more than
> £1000 per year.

A recent biographer, Florence Becker Lennon, feels that the verse of Lewis Carroll sometimes indicates an unresolved Oedipus conflict with a strong attachment to the mother. "Solitude," written when Dodgson was twenty-one, seems to support Mrs. Lennon's analysis:

> I'd give all wealth that years have piled,
>   The slow result of Life's decay,
> To be once more a little child
>   For one bright summer-day.

Although Mrs. Lennon does not frankly admit a Freudian analysis of this verse, there is sufficient symbolism in this poem and in another, "Stolen Waters," to support the thesis that Lewis Carroll remained at a childish level in his emotional life:

> I kissed her on the false, false lips—
> That burning kiss, I feel it now!

> "True love gives true love of the best:
>   Then take," I cried, "my heart to thee!"
> The very heart from out my breast
>   I plucked, I gave it willingly:
>   Her very heart she gave to me—
> Then died the glory from the west.

> In the gray light I saw her face,
>   And it was withered, old, and gray;
> The flowers were fading in their place,
>   Were fading with the fading day.

Lewis Carroll offers a solution to the insoluble dilemma of adulthood by substituting a state of childish existence, aimed not at the realization of a mature adult life, but fixed at a level of innocence in life until the adult-child passes into the larger innocence of death:

> "Be as a child—
> So shalt thou sing for very joy of breath—
> So shalt thou wait thy dying,

> *In holy transport lying—*
> *So pass rejoicing through the gate of death,*
> *In garment undefiled."*

There is a further indication of an unsolved emotional problem in Lewis Carroll's choice of young girls as love objects; young girls who were sisters; sisters who were young girls and thus one step removed from the mother who may not be loved because of the taboo of the father and of society. He stated his ideal of love as that of a young girl but stipulated that they must be young girls from outside the family. We have also seen that when Lewis Carroll reversed the family name, he omitted adoption of the paternal name but maintained the perversion of the mother's family name, just as his identifications remained with girl children instead of with boys. He seems to have solved his adolescent conflict by putting adult sexuality aside and remaining a passive compliant son who did not protest the loss of his masculine adulthood openly, but who apparently never loved an adult woman.

If this is true, his repression of feeling must have been deep and unrealized, which may explain in part the elaborate defenses which he created to protect himself from anxiety. We have seen that he created two personalities for himself and that he lived as Charles L. Dodgson or Lewis Carroll with equal facility and enjoyment. In the final analysis, we can expect that it was through such a defense that life became tolerable for him, and that he escaped eventual illness by splitting his personality into two forms. Dr. Paul Schilder felt that the anal-sadistic content of the stories of Lewis Carroll were significant, and most of the compulsions which he displayed are related to the retentive, hoarding, inflexible character of the anal personality, which seems to be supported in his dress, the cataloguing of letters and papers, the neatness of his room, his choice of note paper in graduated sizes, his scanty diet, his clean gloves, and the general neatness and precise exactness of his life. The exaggerated control of his environment seems to mirror a fear of the volatile and explosive unconscious wishes which he felt. Neither could he be certain what to expect from uncontrolled, free, and less restricted people in the world, so he shunned them and sought security in the presence of children, who are also immature adults. In later years, his fears bordered on the pathological, for he refused to drink from a sherry bottle other his own and he cut the pages of his manuscripts into strips when he mailed them to the illustrator, who was instructed to use a guide, mailed by separate post, in reassembling the manuscript.

There is a persistence of sexual feeling which cannot be denied, however, and Lewis Carroll was aware of some guilt in his relationships with his young friends, for he always felt that Mrs. Grundy was looking over his shoulder:

(being now an old man who can venture on things that "Mrs. Grundy" would never permit to a younger man) have some little friend to stay with me as a guest. My last friend was the little girl who lately played Alice.

Mrs. Grundy is a further censor of his activities in the following letter, which was written with so much nervousness that the original is hardly legible. It is a letter full of apology and fear but also full of persistence and anxious expectation when he invites a child to visit him:

You were so gracious the other day that I have nearly got over my fear of you. The slight tremulousness which you may observe in my writing, produced by the thought that it is you I am writing to, will soon pass off. Next time I borrow you, I shall venture on having you alone: I like my child friends best one by one: and I'll have Maggie alone another day, if she'll come (that is the great difficulty!). But first I want to borrow (I can scarcely muster courage to say it) your eldest sister. Oh, how the very thought of it frightens me! Do you think she would come? I don't mean alone: I think Maggie might come, too, to make it all proper. . . .

This letter is almost hysterical, pleading and suppliant, with mixed fear that he may be misunderstood and a further fear that he may lose the love of one child when he asks her to act as his intermediary with her sister. There is some biographical material which indicates that some parents were unwilling to permit their children to visit Lewis Carroll and he objected if the parents did not wish children to visit him unchaperoned. There was an open, unspecified disagreement between Mrs. Liddell and Mr. Dodgson which must remain mysterious until his diaries are published or until there is further biographical information concerning him. In addition to preferring his visitors alone, and resenting the interruption of parents, it was difficult for Lewis Carroll to share his friends with others. He sent the following gentle reprimand to one of the children whom he knew:

Oh, child, child! I kept my promise yesterday afternoon, and came

*down to the sea, to go with you along the rocks: but I saw you going
with another gentleman, so I thought I wasn't wanted just yet; so I
walked about a bit, and when I got back I couldn't see you anywhere,
though I went a good way on the rocks to look.*

His interest in figure-drawing seems a further sublimation of his
sexual interest in children. This never became a conscious sexual interest
and yet his preoccupation with girl children can scarcely be understood
in other terms. A woman friend who was also an artist worked with him
to secure suitable models and states that he considered twelve the ideal
age for his drawing, for he considered children too thin who were
younger. In later years, Lewis Carroll developed a close friendship with
Harry Furniss, the artist who illustrated several editions of his stories,
and in one of his letters, Lewis Carroll confesses his wish and the accompanying fear of social taboos:

*I wish I dared dispose with all costume: naked children are so per-
fectly pure and lovely, but Mrs. Grundy would be furious—it would never
do. Then the question is, how little dress would content her.*

Although he wrote about "children" in the letter, he did not mean all
children, but only little girls, for he states in another letter:

*I confess I do not admire naked boys, in pictures. They always seem
to need clothes—whereas one hardly sees why the lovely forms of girls
should ever be covered up.*

His interest in the figures of little girls and his love of little girls was the
eventual expression of his denial of adult sexual life. There is a cohesion
in the pattern if we recall his interest in photography, the costumes in
which he dressed his young friends, his summer vacations at the beach,
and the actual celibacy which he chose for himself, further enforced by
his association with the Church.

Love may assume many aspects when denied, and Dr. Schilder has
identified the sadism, unconsciously expressed in the fairy tales of Lewis
Carroll. This can be further illustrated in many of his letters, which
contain moralistic advice, corrections of speech and grammar, or playful
complaints when his young friends do not give him the love and attention
which he demands.

In one letter, he writes to apologize for having failed to congratulate
a child on her birthday and, although he called when no one was at

home, he imagined the following scene as preparation for the child's party:

I had just time to look into the kitchen, and saw your birthday feast getting ready, a nice dish of crusts, bones, pills, cotton-bobbins, and rhubarb and magnesia. "Now," I thought, "she will be happy!" And with a smiling face I went away.

He was very conscious of birthdays and some of his letters are complaints about the gifts he received. They are usually complaints in coy terms but the harshness is there, though disguised and softened:

Thank you very much for the napkin ring, but do you know I never use anything of the sort, so I hope you won't mind giving it to somebody else instead, and if you really want to make something for me, make me a little bag (say a square bag about the size of this note sheet); that would be really useful, and I should be really glad to have it.

At another time he had been promised a gift which had not been sent him, so he wrote the following letter to complain, although he reversed his feeling and wrote the letter as though he were writing to thank his young friend for the birthday present:

I have waited since January 27 to thank you for your letter and present, that I might be able to say the "scales" had come—But as they still don't come, I will wait no longer. Thank you for all your birthday wishes and for the "scales," whatever they are.

Although he was timid in his behavior, he dreaded the rejection that the timid person always fears and the following letters show his anger when he is neglected, although he also pretends that the loss of a friend more or less could mean little to him. There is also interesting incidental information about his voluminous letter-writing:

Please don't suggest to her to write, poor child. If she had got, as I have, more than 800 entries in her letter-register for this year, she wouldn't be particularly keen about adding one to the list.

Despite his friendships, there is a complaint of ultimate poverty of love in the wistful confession which Lewis Carroll made in another letter:

Of course there isn't much companionship possible, after all, between an old man's mind and a little child's—what there is, is sweet—and wholesome, I think.

He once wrote a child that he forgot what the story of *Alice* was about but he said:

I think it was about malice.

Some may feel that too great an emphasis has been placed on slight, incidental information about Lewis Carroll, as given in letters and articles, and yet it is precisely the slight and incidental which gives the deepest understanding of the forces which prompted him to fashion his life as he did. It is the chink in the armor which is dangerous, the vulnerable break in the defense, but it may also be the avenue to the heart and a true understanding of the individual.

There is a good deal of evidence which traces the characters in the stories of *Alice* to people known to Lewis Carroll. The following description of the White Rabbit might almost be a description of the personality of Lewis Carroll and seems to indicate the manner in which he introjected himself into his stories:

And the White Rabbit, what of him? Was he framed on the Alice lines or meant as a contrast? As a contrast, distinctly. For her "youth", "audacity", "vigour", and "swift directness" of "purpose", read "elderly", "timid", "feeble", and "nervously shilly-shallying" and you will get some-thing of what I meant him to be. I think the White Rabbit should wear spectacles. I am sure his voice should quaver, and his whole air to suggest a total inability to say "Boo" to a goose!

There is a persistence in Lewis Carroll's feeling that his writing should have meaning, even though he could not always give it, and it is the Red Queen who reminds Alice that:

Even a joke should have meaning.

It is important for our understanding, then, to relate the other clues concerning characters to the origins which Lewis Carroll has defined. Canon Duckworth accompanied Lewis Carroll on the boat trip the day he first told the story to the Liddell children and later Carroll sent a copy of the book to the Canon, with the inscription:

The Duck from the Dodo.

The Duck and the Dodo in Wonderland seem to have been created from the first syllables of the two names, Duckworth and Dodgson. It is also interesting to recall the symbol of the Dodo bird, which is stupid, ineffective, and aimless, which may be related to the stammering inef-fectual life which Lewis Carroll lived and which in turn may also be related to his speech, for a stammered pronunciation of Dodgson produces "Dodo" as the first syllable.

When the Dormouse tells the story of the three little girls who lived in the treacle well—Elsie, Lacey, and Tilly—he uses variations of the names of the children Lavinia, Alice, and Edith. Elsie is a pronunciation of the initials of Lavinia Charlotte; Lacie is an anagram for Alice; and Tillie was the pet name used for Edith. Later, Lory, the parrot, may be traced to Lorina, and Eaglet is a childish pronunciation of the name Edith.

It is possible to recognize the prototype of many familiar people in the stories of Lewis Carroll and to populate them with acquaintances whom we also wish to caricature. The reader may do this unconsciously and yet Lewis Carroll seems to have written many of his stories as an overt expression of malice, clothed in the socially acceptable form of whimsy. The inconsistency of the adult world is always apparent, but also apparent in the inconsistencies of the life of Lewis Carroll and of his acquaintances. The stories are filled with an endless procession of people in masquerade and somewhat ridiculous as a result: queens, kings, footmen, servants, teachers, gardeners, and other everyday people of everyday life.

Lewis Carroll suffered from insomnia, although he sometimes denied it, and one of his young friends said that his most absurd ideas came to him when he was almost asleep. He walked long distances during the day and invented a system of cryptograph writing which enabled him to write his thoughts in the dark. Although he worked hard during the day and exhausted himself physically, he was often unable to fall asleep, and he wrote *Pillow Problems* to provide ways of occupying his mind when he was sleepless.

It was perhaps on the threshold of sleep that Lewis Carroll felt most keenly his discovery that if "live" is spelled backward it becomes "evil," for it is in this period of mental dusk that the darker thoughts of the mind threaten to penetrate into consciousness. Lewis Carroll expressed this same sentiment in speaking of the Snark:

> *I engage with the Snark—every night after dark—*
> *In a dreamy delirious fight. . . .*

He could never explain this creature of his imagination, searched for but never found, although he realized that it was not quite nonsense:

> *.. Still, you know, words mean more than we mean to express when we use them: so a whole book ought to mean more than the writer meant.*

He never found a role for himself in the world, either, and remained with a portmanteau personality, now open as Lewis Carroll, now closed behind the armor of Charles L. Dodgson. He could not grasp the essential role of an adult, masculine person and he fumbled for his identity only to find it was usually expressed in a soft, feminine, plastic identification with young girl children. He was a pedantic, forbidding adult as Charles L. Dodgson and in this role openly presented himself to the world, but as Lewis Carroll he became an adult, unmarried, secluded male spinster. In later years, he became more openly the character of Lewis Carroll, and the querulous and complaining characteristics of his behavior were said to be more pronounced.

Lewis Carroll was not a quiet, shy, passive person in all respects, but revolt was expressed in a bland, limited, and inhibited way. Stories are made from words and words are intended to be spoken, so Lewis Carroll lived and protested through his stories while Professor Dodgson lived and protested in pamphlets or letters to the newspapers. Overt displacement of the shadowy authority of the father was never realized, but Lewis Carroll was created from the spiritual rib of Charles Lutwidge Dodgson and authority became divided and dilute, so seemed less threatening.

There was a similar dilution in his own personality and his basic sexual conflict remained unexpressed, his sexual wishes disguised by his interest in young girls, while he guarded against overt sexuality by discarding his friends when they became adolescents. If women were necessary, they were necessary as mothers or sisters, not as wives or friends, which may bring us close to the basic source of the creative impulse of Lewis Carroll.

He could never slay the dragon and become the hero, the traditional role of the young hero in classic myths, for there is no hero in *The Hunting of the Snark*. At the crucial moment the hero disappears, vanishes, and admits that he cannot even identify his enemy or find him:

> *But if ever I meet with a Boojum, that day,*
> *In a moment (of this I am sure),*
> *I shall softly and suddenly vanish away—*
> *And the notion I cannot endure!*

This is perhaps the only solution of the dilemma of Charles Lutwidge Dodgson, who did not dare to become adult. Dr. Martin Grotjahn, in a psychological analysis of *Ferdinand the Bull*, had shown a similar inclination in this modern, mythical character who refused to become an adult bull, fighting in the bull ring, so remained the eternal child sitting quietly under the paternal cork-tree, smelling the beautiful flowers. Dr. Grotjahn explains the appeal of the book to the adult when he says:

Adults like to read this book to children, telling them in this way that Ferdinand enjoys everlasting love, peace, and happiness so long as he behaves like a nice little calf who does not grow up. In this case the book is used as a clear-cut castration threat, like most famous books for children.

Lewis Carroll also remained a child and in this role solved the problem which we all have faced when growing up. It is perhaps this unconscious identification with him which makes us understand him when he speaks to us through his stories and which will also make Alice live forever as a child of the collective world unconscious.

About the

Symbolization of

ALICE'S ADVENTURES IN WONDERLAND

by Martin Grotjahn

(1947)

"That's the most important piece of evidence we've heard yet," said the King, rubbing his hands; "so now let the jury ———"

"If any one of them can explain it," said Alice, (she had grown so large in the last few minutes that she wasn't a bit afraid of interrupting him), "I'll give him sixpence. I don't believe there's an atom of meaning in it."

The jury all wrote down, on their slates, "She doesn't believe there's an atom of meaning in it," but none of them attempted to explain the paper.

Previous analytic remarks
concerning Lewis Carroll and
Alice in Wonderland[1]

THE STRANGE CASE of Alice's adventures in Wonderland has attracted the attention of psychoanalysts several times before. Most recently, John Skinner[2] pointed out how some character traits and possibly neurotic features of the author, Lewis Carroll, may have found expression in the strange symbolizations of his early, and to even higher degree, his later writings.

In her book, *Victoria Through the Looking-Glass,* Florence Becker Lennon[3] takes issue with Freud's[4] theories on wit and humor. With the superiority of the professional historian and art critic towards the outsider and intruder, she misrepresents Freud, disregards completely later analytic contributions[5] to the problems of aesthetics and the comic; she then proceeds to ridicule psychoanalysis and to demonstrate its alleged limitations.

Ten years ago, Paul Schilder[6] expressed his views on *Alice in Wonderland.* His interpretation is another example of analytic interest in literature on folklore as documented from early writings of Freud to most recent publications by Hanns Sachs.

Paul Schilder points out how much anxiety in Alice is connected with a change in her body image, how often she was orally frustrated and never succeeded in eating anything, and how much oral aggressivity was found everywhere in the story. Besides the body image, time and space are distorted, which Schilder links with "extreme aggressivity." The preference for mirror writing is taken as a possible indication for a right-left disturbance and, as such, as a sign of an organic disorder. The inexhaustible play with words is considered as an almost schizophrenic symptom and analyzed according to Freud's interpretation of speech in the Schreber case. The word's significance diffuses into the sign, the word comes to its own life; Humpty Dumpty "lets the word work for him." At other places, words are "cut to pieces" and live forth as such, unite with other parts and take on new meaning—or no meaning at all. Paul Schilder concludes "that nonsense literature will originate whenever there are incomplete object relations and a regression to deep layers involving the relation of space and time on the basis of primitive aggressiveness." It may be added that this inner relationship between regressive expression of aggression and the distortion of body, time, and space is found not only in literature, but also in modern painting. The fluid, or almost fluid, watches and timepieces in the pictures by Salvador Dali, his stereotyped, almost spaceless dimensions, give a clear illustration of such disintegration.

Lewis Carroll appeared to Paul Schilder as a "particularly destructive writer" and it was feared that this literature, so lacking of construction, with so little love and tenderness and regard for other people, may be bewildering and confusing for children.

The Symbolic Equation:
Girl = Phallus

Two years before Paul Schilder wrote down his remarks about *Alice,* Otto Fenichel[7] wrote a very important contribution for the understanding of symbols under the title: "The Symbolic Equation: Girl=Phallus." Schilder applies Fenichel's opinion that little girls may symbolically express the phallus. What we know about Lewis Carroll, his personality development and behavior, as summarized and related to his writings recently by John Skinner, suggests a central position of this symbolic equation Girl=Phallus in the interpretation of Alice, who, after all, is the brainchild of Lewis Carroll and serves for the outlet of his unconscious fantasies and needs.

Such a symboli-equation is most strikingly, and almost undisguisedly, presented in reality in the form, figure, and function of the tambour majorette, a young girl, marching in front of a large body of men, united with them but still demonstratively put in front of them, exhibiting herself as a part of the group without interfering with the exhibition of this group. She does not compete for more attention or applause by the crowd than the men are to get who follow her, but she takes over a certain, always sexual component of this exhibitionistic, parading behavior of men in the marching group. Supposedly, she is loved by the men of the unit—actually, she is not genitally loved but narcissistically admired, and after her parade she is not treated like a woman, but like a tired little child, badly in need of a rest. She then behaves like a penis post coitum. She emphasizes her symbolic meaning by her high hat, preferably adorned by a feather or pompon; she is usually stripped down to the essentials of her clothing but it is important that the essentials of her body remain well hidden. She invariably sports enormously oversized boots which look as if they were designed for a giant, approximately the size of all men of the unit combined in one. As if all of this would not be enough, she is given a stick in her hand which she twirls around untiringly. Moving like a four-gaited horse and demonstrating her surplus energy and potency by every move, she bends like a phallus so erected that almost the bursting point is reached. At times, the performance is so obvious that it loses the character of a symbolization and assumes the feature of a pantomime, the lowest form of theatrical performance.

The great dynamic and economic function of the majorette is her (or his?) unifying influence upon the group: she drains—and on a non-genital level even satisfies—certain sexual feelings with their possibly disturbing qualities and leaves undisturbed the feelings which are non-genital and therefore especially fit for mass and group formation. Her second important function is her acting as a "connecting link" between the masculine marching unit and the admiring crowd. She is the focus or hot point of tension between crowd on the sidewalk and group on the march.

The symbolism of the Girl = Phallus can be shown in a vast multitude of variations, ranging from the awe-inspiring heroine to the Vargas girl used as a pinup, or the lucky charm of female figures on the cockpit of an airplane. The paintings of the Girl = Phallus have one special phallic feature: they picture the girl in a state of erective strength, her form almost bursting from the second into the third dimension.

It is very important to recognize for the understanding of the symbolization of *Alice in Wonderland* that the phallus must be represented only by a girl, not by a boy. It also must be a sexually undifferentiated girl, not yet a fully developed woman. The sexually undifferentiated boy is better suited for a highly sublimated symbolization: the angel. There are no female angels.

The reality of the penis makes the male better fixed for a quite different symbolization: namely, that of the devil, the principal of evil and sin. Lucifer, too, like the majorette, shows a multitude of phallic symbols: his horns, his spear, his tail, his hoofs. They, however, represent symbolically more the purpose of the genitals than their narcissistically so highly evaluated beauty. And it seems that according to infantile beliefs and, in later stages, according to our unconscious, there remains the pessimistic opinion that all purpose is bad. Purpose spoiled the play and turned it into work; purpose changed narcissistic admiration into conquest and competition.

Between the symbolic equation Girl = Phallus and the devil stands a third symbolization which is needed for the interpretation of *Alice's Adventures in Wonderland*. The Girl = Phallus symbolizes the narcissistically admired phallus—admired but not used—as the majorette is exhibited but not used in any other sexual way. The devil symbolizes in contrast the sinful function of the penis. In between stands the *Däumling* of Andersen's fairy tales or the dwarfs of Snow White or the little imaginary men of our children who live an adventurous life in the body of the giant. The unconscious may use the phallus, stripped of all sexual potentialities, but still omnipotent and all-knowing, penetrating, and victorious. In a symbolic way, the final answer is given to the question: "What price castration?" The symbolic aspects of the "castrated phallus" have been shown by Helene Deutsch[8] in her analytic interpretation of Don Quixote and by Fritz Moellenhoff[9] in his paper about the popularity of Mickey Mouse.

The Symbolization in *Wonderland*

John Skinner has given the possible unconscious motives in Lewis Carroll's personality as known to us today which may have prompted him to indulge in the Wonderland fantasies. Regardless of the unconscious motives and intentions of the author, he succeeded in creating a fantasy of enduring value with great fascination for all of us. It should be possible, therefore, aside from personal motivation and meaning, to point out and to interpret some of the relations between the *Adventures* and the unconscious of the reader. Without this appeal to the unconscious of the reader, the *Adventures* would have remained what they originally were: a highly regressive daydream of the Reverend Charles Dodgson. His schizoid personality, his compulsive character traits, his often paranoid behavior, his regressive attitude and loving fascination by sexually undifferentiated child-actresses, his childhood experiences as the son of a minister and the oldest of eleven siblings—all this gave him the qualifications to create the *Adventures* and to be joined there by his friends, with whom he had so little contact on this side of Wonderland.

Lewis Carroll created in literature what Melanie Klein tried to call science in the framework of her theories. Evidence that Alice represents the symbolic equation Girl = Phallus and her adventures represent a trip back into the mother's womb is easily gathered in the book: a rabbit leads Alice "down the tunnel" and the descent is "very slow." She comes to a room with "doors all around" but they are "all locked." Alice wants to "shut up like a telescope" and, sure enough, with the help of some magic fluid, she finds herself being "only ten inches high."

At the opening of Chapter II is a picture of Alice which is almost too obvious for words, and which could be easily misinterpreted as obscene: Alice is elongated to the extreme, has a small head, a long neck, a trunk without shoulders or hips, which is continued without curves into the pillar-like legs. The arms are small and practically non-existent, the dress emphasizes the phallic appearance of the girl, asking almost teasingly: "Who in the world am I?" The illustrating artist, John Tenniel, betrays here his secret, intuitive understanding of Carroll's symbolism and gives it perfectly fitting visual expression.

In the pool of tears, representing the water from where all life and babies come, Alice seems to find all of the ten brothers and sisters of Lewis Carroll in the form of Duck and Dodo, Lory and Eaglet "and several other curious creatures." How to get dry again after the swim in the pool of tears is easily said: by learning "the driest thing I know," about William the Conqueror.

There is also a hostile way of growing: Alice grows so fast that she almost threatens to burst the whole house she is in; "as a last resource, she put one arm out of the window, and one foot up the chimney." In its destructiveness for mother and child, hostile fantasies could hardly be better expressed.

The Pigeon seems to know that little girls are snakes and intend to destroy all eggs, stating most clearly: "They are a kind of serpent, that is all I can say." What Alice herself thinks of children in Wonderland, especially boys, is also clearly expressed: the baby turns into a pig. Down there time stands still, and it is "always six o'clock now."

Finally Alice meets the Queen, who is as dreadful as and yet quite like the Duchess. The King is only vaguely outlined and not very impressive. There are again "ten children," as in Charles Dodgson's family (not counting Charles himself). The Queen mother seems to give life freely and she takes it away with even greater ease, nullifying the whole effort of creation and destruction, ending it all in a catastrophic tumbling down of a pack of cards. As it might have been predicted, nobody can go down into the mothers unpunished, so Alice has to face the trial of the Queen and King. She solves the situation by retreating into reality and awakening.

The Lobster Quadrille:
High Point or Disintegration
of Symbolization?

Like dreams dreamed in the same night, some of Alice's adventures show the same motive in different degrees and variations of disguise. The process of symbolization becomes more and more regressive, and this seems to be true not only for the story of *Alice in Wonderland*, but quite generally for all later works of Lewis Carroll. Words assume more and more their own meaning and finally have lost their object cathexis, as in a schizophrenic psychosis. Fantastic animals take over the progress of the story to ever higher extent. What in the beginning of the story seemed to have been a rediscovery of an old childhood enjoyment, to ridicule intelligence, logic, time, and space, becomes later a world of its own, again resembling a psychotic break with reality or at least presenting the scars of such a break. At first, the reactivation of the primary process could be accomplished in the service of the author's ego; later it looks as if the poet's ego had to compromise in order to hold things together. The danger point occurs approximately in Chapter VIII, "The Queen's Croquet-Ground." The "Mock Turtle's Story" and the "Lobster Quadrille" are full of such disintegrated symbolisms, interwoven with something called "morals," as, for example:

"Tut, tut, child!" said the Duchess. "Everything's got a moral, if only you can find it." And she squeezed herself up closer to Alice's side as she spoke. . . .

" 'Tis so," said the Duchess: "and the moral of that is—'Oh, 'tis love, 'tis love, that makes the world go round!' " . . .

" 'Take care of the sense, and the sounds will take care of themselves.' "

This integration or individualization or overcathexis of the symbolization does not necessarily influence the poetic or artistic value of the poem's work. As in *Faust*, Part II, or in Dante's *Inferno*, the highest point in Alice's voyage to the end of the night can probably be described only in words and symbols as used in the "Lobster Quadrille." Almost as in a catatonic rigor, words are of no meaning any more and even the feelings probably are far "beyond the pleasure principle." Alice can describe the state of her existence—should she, would she care to describe it—on the rocky shores of the ocean, only in the allegoric picture of the lobsters dancing a quadrille. The highest artistic experience is not necessarily identical with the highest artistic expression.

The Awakening of Alice

In accordance with the fact of increasing disintegration of symbolization is the fact that Alice's rebirth or awakening is the book's weakest part. As in Charles Dodgson's real life, the conflict seems to have remained unsolved. He was much better in putting Alice to sleep than in waking her up. The reader follows willingly down the road to the mothers, but the way back to reality and life he has to make by himself.

So to speak, the awakening from *Alice's Adventures* demands more from the ego's integrative powers than the awakening from a fairy tale. Here again the regressive character of the symbolization becomes obvious. In the fairy tales of Grimm and Andersen the regression leads only to the reactivation of magic-mystic ways of the infantile levels of thinking and fantasies. In the last part of the *Adventures* the regression goes much further and the solution does not seem to be an ego integration but a compromise formation.

From the point of analytic interpretation as developed here, the question of the value of Carroll's book for the mental health or education of children becomes meaningless. As in all good books for children, it is not only for children, but for the child in all men. The lack of love, of regard for other people, the intense cruelty, the rebellion against rhyme and reason, the final distortion of everything seen through the looking-glass does not matter.

If I should formulate the analytic meaning of the reading experience of Carroll's *Adventures*, I would formulate it in a way similar to that in which Hanns Sachs[10] once formulated the aim of analysis. Such books as Lewis Carroll's *Alice's Adventures in Wonderland* lead to an artistic and testing regression; they open a temporary guilt-free and relatively anxiety-free communication to the unconscious. Necessary repression and sublimation are achieved more easily and with healthier results when the communication with the creative unconscious is kept alive, free, and open.

From "The Character of Dodgson as revealed in the Writings of Carroll"

by Phyllis Greenacre

(1955)

DODGSON WAS REGARDED as an eccentric by his students and his contemporaries, and although some saw him as dull and boring, the picture in retrospect is interesting and at times colorful. In his boyhood he had been so adept manually that he not only made his own marionettes and theater, but on one occasion he made for a sister a very tiny set of tools, complete in a case, only one inch long. He, like the White Knight, was an inventor—of gadgets, of puzzles, riddles, games, and conundrums, as well as many mnemonic devices.[1] During a great deal of his adult life he apparently suffered from an intractable insomnia; and he constructed many of his inventions, seemingly, as a way of keeping his mind busy during the long hours of the night. He invented an instrument which he called a nyctograph for making records in the dark. He worked out most of his inventions entirely in his mind, only making a record on completion.

To those who did not know him well he seemed "stiff and donnish" (Collingwood's words), and Mark Twain found him "the stillest and shyest full-grown man" except for Uncle Remus that he had ever met. During several hours of conversation in a group, Carroll contributed nothing but an occasional question.[2] On the other hand, Twain found him interesting to look at. The shyness may have been increased by his stammering and by his deafness (left ear), but it was almost all-pervasive, except with his little girls. Only occasionally in some meeting would he flash out with an incisive witticism—and he was generally more amusing when enticed into a monologue than in a conversation. He was slight ... and rather drab in appearance. It is said that the two sides of his face did not match. He habitually put his right hand in front of his mouth while lecturing and was sufficiently self-critical that he drew a caricature of himself in this position. As he grew older, his face became more feminine in cast, an effect possibly enhanced by his wearing his hair rather long. His effeminacy was sufficiently obvious that some of his less sympathetic students once wrote a parody of his parodies and signed it "Louisa Caroline."

He disliked garish colors, preferred pinks and grays, and is said to have requested one of the little girls not to visit him in a red dress.[3] He himself wore unobtrusive clothing, except that he habitually went without an overcoat, wore a tall hat, and black cotton gloves. He stood so straight that he seemed to be leaning backward, and is also said to have staggered a little, i.e., veering more to one side than the other. In spite of this he was a tremendous walker—and in 1897, six months before his death, he noted walking seventeen to twenty miles on each of two days with only one day in between.

There was a tinge of the crank inventor in his attitudes. For the most part he carried out his mental researches without much reference to the activities in the outer world, although he was a habitual publisher of his ideas, either in articles in magazines or by letters to the newspapers. Thus he invented a new method of reckoning postage which he sent to the post-office department; a new method of scoring and eliminating in tennis matches, sent to the Lawn Tennis Association; a new method of voting when more than two choices are present. In 1876, he "invented" proportional representation, although it had been invented by Thomas Hare and debated in Parliament in 1867.

From an early age he was interested in time, and wrote and lectured many times on the subject "Where does the day begin?" He spent much time writing people all over the world to discover how they dated letters at a specific time, but he paid no attention to the Prime Meridian Conference held in Washington, D.C., to settle the question of the International Date Line. He seemed always to be in some kind of battle with time, attempting to avoid being caught by time or trying to entrap time himself. He often refused invitations for a specific time but would announce his intention to come at a later, unspecified time.

For twenty-one years (approximately 1870-1891), he consistently wrote in purple ink; and then suddenly stopped. The significance of this is unclear. But ink itself had great meaning. Throughout his stories it is used as the agent for reviving creatures who faint out of terror or excitement.

Not only was he a compulsive publisher of his ideas, but he was a compulsive indexer. He kept a record of all the letters he wrote or received, cross-indexed for topical content. At the time of his death, this registry contained more than 98,000 items. He was something of a collector, too, having a number of music boxes and more than two hundred fountain pens.

He frequently carried a little black bag, much like a doctor's bag, filled with safety pins, puzzles and games of his own making, pencils and paper, handkerchiefs and other articles to aid little girls on railroad trains and at the seashore, and to entice them into a fuller acquaintance. One is reminded here of the original railroad whose victims must be thrice flattened by the engine of Love before first aid is granted. Now, Mr. Dodgson being older, gave prophylactic help.

With adults he was sometimes pompous. For over forty years he kept a record of all his dinner parties, including a statement of the seating arrangements and the menu for the occasion. He often invited little girls to lunch, with instructions to them to leave their brothers at home. In his middle life he frankly loathed little boys, and refused to stand in church until after the boy choir had passed, as he wished to prevent the boys from becoming conceited. He was known to invite a lady to dinner but stipulate that she should leave her husband at home.

His sensitivity to fits and convulsions has already been described. He also had a recurrent preoccupation with cords and knots—not only was the baby tied into a knot by Alice, but the Mouse's tail was also knotted, as was the Tangled Tale. Carroll also sent Macmillan a diagram of just how all packages to him should be wrapped, how the cords should be tied, and where the knots should be placed. In packing for vacation trips, he had a great many portmanteaus (luggage as well as words) with contents wrapped in paper in individual packets, sometimes tied as well. Consequently paper very much increased the size and weight of his luggage.

The illustrators of Carroll's books found him a difficult man to work with: exacting in the extreme, wishing to dictate many details to the illustrator who should somehow reproduce exactly Carroll's own mental picture of the scene, almost as though the artist might photograph Carroll's own imagery. Sir John Tenniel, Henry Holiday, and Harry Furniss all found their tasks arduous, and Furniss, a conscious caricaturist and much younger than Carroll, tried to outdo him in eccentricity and threatened to strike when Carroll became too strongly demanding. While Furniss' account has been discredited by some as burlesquing the situation—and he almost surely embellished his description of it somewhat—yet it is too much in accord with other traits of Dodgson-Carroll to be completely discarded. Furniss, who was the illustrator for *Sylvie and Bruno*, worked with Carroll from 1885 to 1892, when Carroll had more and more retired into Dodgson and his peculiarities had somewhat deepened. He had become solitary, had given up much of his always moderate social life, abandoned his photography and his teaching, but continued to live at Oxford and work on his manuscripts. He is generally reported to have become increasingly vain, secretive, and even a little suspicious. He rarely accepted invitations to dine, but would "drop in" at a less exactly appointed time; if he did go out to dinner, he sometimes took his own bottle of wine with him. He became more and more burdened by his own prominence and had refused to accept mail addressed to Carroll at Oxford; at the same time he published frequently and that, often trivia. According to Furniss' account, Carroll sent him an elaborate document committing him to secrecy about the manuscript. He seemed to wish to make sure that Furniss' wife did not see a picture or look at the manuscript before publication—a stipulation to which Furniss did not agree and so refused to sign the document. But still cautious that others might see prematurely the precious *Sylvie and Bruno* manuscript, which he considered his best work, he prepared the manuscript by cutting it into horizontal strips of four or five lines each, then placed the whole lot in a sack and shook it up. Taking out piece by piece, he pasted the strips down as they happened to come. All strips had already been marked with code hieroglyphics according to which they might be properly reassembled. Furniss reports that he sent the whole batch back with another threat to strike. This jumbled manuscript had been delivered at night.[4] Furniss found that Carroll wanted him to assemble his illustrations from almost as many fragments as were represented in the manuscript. The author would send the illustrator quantities of photographs showing this or that feature which he found inspiring, or would request him to visit friends or even strangers to collect "fragments of faces" which Carroll had thought suitable for the illustrations.

Roger L. Green (editor of the *Diaries* recently published), in a *Story of Lewis Carroll*, neutralizes the Furniss account of the mischmasch manuscript, explaining it rather on the basis that the manuscript, which was frankly made up of a number of short stories and sketches, had not yet been properly assembled. That Carroll had a feeling for mischmasch as well as for order and was constantly taking things apart, jumbling them, and reassembling them, cannot be denied.[5] How much Furniss caricatured is an additional question.

Two other preoccupations were so conspicuous both in his life and in his writing as to be clinically noteworthy, viz. 1) special attitudes toward eating and breathing, and 2) his relationship to animals, especially to cats.

Attitudes toward Eating and Breathing

Eating (or drinking) and breathing are of course psychologically very close together. In certain respects the latter appears as a kind of ghost or spirit of the former. Both were exceedingly important in Carroll's life. He was himself rather slight in stature. This, combined with his somewhat stiff erectness made him appear taller than he was. He was abstemious, eating and drinking little. A biscuit and sherry constituted his lunch very often. He was somewhat appalled by the healthy appetite of some of his little girl friends. Nonetheless, he was greatly preoccupied with eating. His early sketches tended to make people either abnormally fat or abnormally thin. The interest in food and its "nothingness" represented in air is interestingly apparent in one of his early drawings: a sketch of a family taking food in homeopathic doses, in which a butler announces that only a billionth of an ounce of bread is left in the house and that this must be saved for next week, and the mother orders that a trillionth more should be ordered from the baker. One child asks whether another should have "another molecule" and an older sister deplores that her present glasses have not permitted her to see a nonillionth which has come her way. The whole family party has the grim appearance of those suffering from anorexia nervosa, and the humor has an "Emperor's New Clothes" type of satire, expressed of course in another medium. This cartoon appeared in the *Rectory Umbrella*, which dates from Dodgson's period between Rugby and Oxford. A complementary cartoon, appearing in the same magazine, was a sketch purporting to be a caricature of Joshua Reynolds' painting, "The Age of Innocence." The Dodgson version shows a young hippopotamus, obviously well fed, who, "seated under a shady tree, presents to the contemplative mind a charming union of youth and innocence" (written by Charles L. Dodgson, the Editor of the *Rectory Umbrella*).

The question of eating or being eaten is introduced into the Wonderland adventures before Alice gets fairly down the rabbit-hole, with her ponderings as to whether cats eat bats or bats eat cats. Subsequently, eating and drinking magically change her body size; the contents of the "Drink Me" bottle, which she finds on the glass table, suddenly shrinks her; whereas the "Eat Me" cake reverses this. Similarly, nipping from another bottle near the looking-glass in White Rabbit's house enlarges her and the pebbles that turn into cakes reduce her. And so it goes. She frightens the Mouse by talking about Dinah the cat, who is such a good mouser, and she finds herself singing about the Crocodile who "welcomes little fishes in with gently smiling jaws." Time is suddenly involved when the turning of the earth on its axis gets mixed with the preparation of the soup by the Duchess's cook; and again, this problem crops up in the eternally revolving and mad tea-party in which the old subject "When does the day begin?" is revived. Food is the source of trouble and guilt with the Seven of Hearts threatened with decapitation for bringing the cook tulip bulbs instead of onions, and again in the grand trial scene when the Knave of Hearts is being tried for having stolen the tarts.

This same gastrointestinal axis to the world's turning appears in some of the early poetry written during Charles's adolescence, especially the moralistic poems dealing with hostility between siblings: "Brother and Sister" (1845), a rollicking rhyme ending with the moral "Don't stew your sister"; and "The Two Brothers," (1853) which relates the tale of a boy who baited his fishhook with a younger brother and so broke their sister's heart "into three" and provoked the lament, "One of the two will be wet through and through and t'other will be late to tea." Similarly, in parody "The Lady of the Lake" becomes "The Lady of the Ladle."

One can well imagine that sibling rivalry may have been expressed early and drastically among the children of the Daresbury clergyman, in terms of food preference and privileges. Edwin, who was probably the target of the "Age of Innocence" cartoon, was born after the family had moved to Croft and somewhat more affluent circumstances. He was an innocent infant of three to four at the time of the drawing of the cartoon (1849-1850). The Caucus-Race in *Alice's Adventures in Wonderland,* in which all the animals, large and small, must have prizes, appears as the solution for, or warding off of, such jealousy and rivalry, with Alice rather than the youthful Charles playing the role of arbiter.

In *Through the Looking-Glass,* changes in body size and proportions are lacking, but the time-space relationship is still puzzling and appears in changes in space appreciation outside the body as indicated by the varying rates of speed necessary to cover apparently similar distances, or sometimes any distance at all. Volcanic explosions seem to have occurred when Alice picked up the White King and Queen and moved them so rapidly that they became breathless. Alice herself floated rather than walked downstairs simply by touching the handrail with her fingertips. Again, there was the eventful race in which the Queen seized Alice by the hand and ran breathlessly and with toes barely touching the ground, but without actually changing their location on the chessboard. A little later the Queen said good-bye and vanished seemingly into thin air. Then there was the railroad journey in which the entire train rose straight up in the air, in crossing a brook, and Alice presently found herself talking to a giant Gnat which fanned her with its wings. At this point flying seems to pervade the picture. The Rocking-horse-fly swung itself from branch to branch while a Bread-and-butter-fly crawled at her feet. People were threatened with the extinction of going out like the flame of a candle; and in the final scene, which is a banquet rather than a trial (in contrast to Wonderland), Alice finds herself pressed between the two Queens in a way that lifts her into the air, while the candles suddenly shoot upward to the ceiling and all the dishes develop wings. Food was certainly not unimportant in the Looking-Glass World, only it was not as ubiquitous as in Wonderland. In the former, movement through the air appears rather as the reverse of passage of food into the body.

Charles Dodgson considered whether air was healthy or morbid with nearly the same intensity of concern which he gave to food and drink, which he catalogued so constantly. His apprehension of infection was great and he had such concern about contaminated or unhealthy air in general that at times he stuffed all the cracks under doors and windows, and had an elaborate system of keeping the temperature equalized throughout his rooms, causing him to make repeated daily rounds of his series of thermometers.

Gertrude Chataway, one of Carroll's little girl friends to whom he dedicated *The Snark*—and it will be recalled that the Boojum Snark caused any onlooker to vanish into thin air—described Mr. Dodgson as follows:

Next door there was an old gentleman [actually aged 43!] who interested me immensely. He would come onto his balcony which joined ours, sniffing the air with his head thrown back and would walk right down the steps on to the beach with his chin in the air, drinking in the fresh breezes as if he could never have enough ... Whenever I heard his footsteps, I flew out to see him coming and one day when he spoke to me my joy was complete ... In a very little while I was as familiar with the interior of his lodgings as with my own ... He often took his cue [in telling stories] from [the child's] remarks ... so that the story seemed a personal possession ... It was astonishing that he never seemed tired or to want other society ... He [later] told me it was the greatest pleasure he could have to converse freely with a child and feel the depths of her mind ... I don't think he ever really understood that we whom he had known as children, could not always remain such.

A letter from Carroll to little Miss Chataway, written October 3, 1875, explains that he will *drink her health* instead of sending her a present. Then, finding a pun in this phrase, he continued,

But perhaps you will object ... If I were to sit by you and to drink your tea, you wouldn't like that. You would say "Boo-hoo! Here's Mr. Dodgson's drunk all my tea and I haven't got any left!" I am very much afraid Sybil will find you sitting by the sad sea-wave and crying

"Boo! Hoo! Mr. Dodgson's drunk my health and I haven't got any left!"
Your mother will say [to the doctor] "You see she would go and make
friends with a strange gentleman, and yesterday he drank her health! . . .
The only way to cure her is to wait until next birthday and then for her
to drink his health." And then we shall have changed healths. I wonder
how you'll like mine! Oh Gertrude, I wish you would not talk such
nonsense! . . . Your loving friend. Lewis Carroll.

Miss Chataway's first description of the man breathing in health with
his exuberant sniffing of the sea air is a reverse side of the same picture
as that given elsewhere of his elaborate precautions against breathing in
contaminated air, especially that emanating from a letter received from
one of the Bowman children who suffered from scarlet fever. In this
Chataway letter, the idea of the gift of drinking the health and the
turning by a pun of this intensely positive attitude to the extreme opposite
—a destructive vampirish sucking or swallowing up—is implicitly suggested, with a merry ghoulishness. It also contains an elaboration of
childhood's idea—with its modicum of truth—that our bodies and hence
our identities are determined by what we eat.

The Relation to Animals

The animals in the *Alice* books far outnumber the human beings, even
as they probably did in the gardens at Daresbury and Croft, and Charles
continued always to be in communion with them. He has his favorites and
his dis-favorites (to coin a Carrollian word). Among the less loved were
dogs. Although an oversized puppy appears amiably enough in the
Wonderland garden, there is evidence that in actual life Dodgson did not
enjoy dogs, and when one rushed violently at him on a visit to the
Arnolds, he refused ever to return there unless the dog were destroyed.
(One may venture the conjecture that the dog was a male.) He sent the
Arnolds an exact diagram of the canine tooth marks on his trouser leg,
and when the dog was not abolished, he continued on friendly terms with
the family but arranged to see them outside of their own home. In
general, however, he seems to have been charming with and charmed by
small animals and to have treated them in whimsy as somewhat superior
to human beings, whom they either replaced or in part represented.

Among all the animals, the cat has a special place. Not only were there

Dinah, the white kitten, and the black kitten (who became royalty), but there was the Cheshire Cat as well.[6] In Carroll's letters (about 1863) to another little girl friend, Agnes Hughes, he developed fantasies about cats in quite a significant way. He had sent Agnes many kisses, apparently with some instructions for dividing them up, at which the child apparently demurred. He replied:

You lazy thing! What? I'm to divide the kisses myself, am I? Indeed and I won't take the trouble to do anything of the sort. But I'll tell you how to do it. First you take four of the kisses, and that reminds me of a very curious thing that happened to me at half-past four yesterday. Three visitors came knocking at my door, begging me to let them in. When I opened the door, who do you think they were? You will never guess. Why they were three cats! . . . They all looked so cross and disagreeable that I took up the first thing I could lay my hands on which happened to be the rolling pin and knocked them all down as flat as pancakes: "If you come knocking at my door," I said, "I shall come knocking at your heads." That was fair, wasn't it? Yours affectionately . . .

Again, one ventures the thought that the troublesome cats were little males (or at least made him aware of maleness); and it is worth noting that the preceding letter to Agnes carried a postscript in which Carroll had sent his love to the little Agnes and his kindest regards to her mother, but "to your fat impertinent ignorant brother my hatred—and I think that is all." It was in turn followed by more cat letters:

About the cats, you know. Of course I didn't leave them lying flat on the ground like dried flowers. I picked them up, and I was as kind as I could be to them. I lent them a portfolio for a bed—they would not have been comfortable in a real bed, you know; they were too thin; but they were quite happy between the sheets of blotting paper, and each of them had a pen wiper for a pillow. Well then I went to bed; but first I lent them three dinner bells to ring in the night in case they wanted anything in the night. You know I have three dinner bells,—the first (which is the largest) is rung when dinner is nearly ready; the second (which is rather larger) is rung when it is quite ready; and the third (which is as large as the other two put together) is rung all the time I am at dinner. Well, I told them they might ring if they happened to want anything—and as they rang all the bells all night, I suppose they did want something or other, only I was too sleepy to attend to them. In the morning I gave them some rat-tail jelly and buttered mice for breakfast, and they were as discontented as they could be. They wanted some boiled pelican but of course I knew that would not be good for them. So all I said was "Go to

Number two Finborough Road and ask for Agnes Hughes and if it's really good for you, she'll give you some." Then I shook hands with them all and wished them good-bye, and drove them up the chimney. They seemed very sorry to go and they took the bells and the portfolio with them. I didn't find this out until after they had gone, and then I was sorry too, and wished them back again. How are Arthur, and Amy, and Emily? Do they still go up and down Finborough Road and teach the cats to be nice to the mice? I'm very fond of all cats in Finborough Road. Give them my love—Who do I mean by "them"? Never mind. Your affectionate friend—

And another letter to Amy, the sister of Agnes, contained the following:

You have asked after those three cats. Ah, the dear creatures. Do you know, ever since that night they first came, they have never left me? Isn't it kind of them? Tell Agnes this, she will be interested to hear it. And they are so kind and thoughtful: Do you know, when I had gone out for a walk the other day, they got all my books out of the book-case and opened them all to page 50 because they thought that would be a nice useful page to begin at. It was rather unfortunate, though: because they took my bottle of gum, and tried to gum pictures upon the ceiling (which they thought would please me), and by accident they spilt a quantity of it all over the books. So when they were shut up and put by, the leaves all stuck together and I can never read page 50 again in any of them! However they meant it very kindly, so I wasn't angry. I gave them a spoonful of ink as a treat, but they were ungrateful for that and made dreadful faces. But of course, as it was given them as a treat, they had to drink it. One of them has turned black since: it was a white cat to begin with. Give my love to any children you happen to meet. Also I send two kisses and a half for you to divide with Agnes, Emily, and Godfrey. Mind you divide them fairly. Yours affectionately—

These letters are perhaps as self-revealing as anything, except *Sylvie and Bruno*, that Carroll ever wrote. They show readily enough the fluctuating aggressiveness with an urge to cruelty and then to affectionate playfulness; but there are expressed, further, more disguised but equally powerful complex trends which will be delineated in the discussion of the dynamics of the Carroll-Dodgson character formation.

The Main Themes in Carroll's Writing

The two *Alice* books, *Alice's Adventures in Wonderland* and *Through the Looking-Glass*, furnish naturally a starting place for the study of the thematic content of Carroll's fantasies; then *The Hunting of the Snark* and *Sylvie and Bruno*—with of course secondary consideration of his poetry and miscellaneous writings.

Wonderland

Alice in a state of sleepy boredom saw a rabbit run past her, nervously looking at his watch and talking to himself about being late. Her curiosity aroused, she followed him down a rabbit-hole which seemed very long indeed, but after a time turned into another long passage, which in turn became a long low hall with locked doors all around it. She found a tiny golden key which opened a small door hidden behind curtains, and gave her a view into a beautiful garden which she longed to enter. The story deals with her vicissitudes in getting into the garden and finally with the unexpected events within.

In brief, Alice goes through a series of bodily changes, always induced by eating or drinking something, except in the last instance, where her change in form is due to the fan (nosegay of flowers in the first version) which she picks up and holds after it has been dropped by the Rabbit.[7] Sometimes she is enlarged and again she becomes too small to reach even the door handle. In two of her enlarged states it is her neck which grows especially long, and she is once mistaken for a serpent as she coils her neck down through the tree branches in order to see underneath them. In her small states, she once suffers from her chin hitting her feet and apparently has no neck at all, and again is threatened with going out like a candle.

She has feelings of alienation both from her body and from her mind, believes that she may have become somebody else, and tests her identity with problems in arithmetic, trials of her memory, and school lessons to see if she still knows the things she has learned, as she has repeatedly found herself saying nonsense. The great charm of the tale lies in the panorama of grotesque caricature expressed in the general mixture and fusion of identities of the animals, insects, and strange human beings whom Alice meets. Through all this is a cacophony of cruelty so extreme as to be ridiculous: animals eat each other up, a baby turns into a pig and is abandoned to wander away into the forest, decapitation is a general threat, and a Cheshire Cat does appear smiling, though separated from its own body. Even words are always changing *their* identities through punning. All this appears against a backdrop of illogical time and spatial relations, and an attitude of gentle puzzlement on Alice's part. In general, the irrational changes in size are confined to sudden changes in Alice's own body.

Finally, however, entrance into the beautiful garden, the home of the royal family, is achieved. But the bedlam is, if anything, worse. The main characters are an animated pack of cards: the Spades are the gardeners, the Clubs are the police force, the Diamonds are the courtiers, and the whole garden is ruled by the Hearts. It is interesting to consider here that the suit of cards, the Royal Family, has exactly the same number of members as the Dodgson family. There are admonitions of love, but a threat of execution permeates the place, and the Queen of Hearts seems madly lustful for everyone's head. Irritability and rage prevail, only, as the Mock Turtle explains, the executions, like everything else, are not real. "It's all her [the Queen's] fancy, that: they never executes nobody, you know." Finally it develops that the Knave of Hearts is being tried for having stolen tarts made by the Queen, and he in turn is in danger of execution. Alice is surprised to find herself called as a witness, and upsets the courtroom both literally (for she has again become gigantic) and figuratively by her rebellion against the nonsensical course of the trial. A final bit of evidence is produced in the form of an unsigned letter, written in rhyme, indicating that the tarts have been returned. It is a masterpiece of confused identities, expressed in pronouns, and concludes—

> *They all returned from him to you,*
> *Though they were mine before. . . .*
>
> *My notion was that you had been*
> *(Before she had this fit)*
> *An obstacle that came between*
> *Him, and ourselves, and it.*

The Queen goes into another fit of rage while denying that she is subject to fits and demands an indefinite sentence. Alice declares a verdict must be given first and finds herself threatened with decapitation by the Queen, and defiantly replies: "Who cares for a pack of cards?" Whereupon the whole pack rises up in the air to hurl itself against her, and she awakes to find that she had been having a nightmare.

In a curious epilogue to the main tale, Alice recounts the dream to her sister, who in turn dreams the dream over, and in a half-awake state

. . . pictured to herself how this same little sister of hers would, in the aftertime, be herself a grown woman; and how she would keep, through all her riper years, the simple and loving heart of her childhood; and how she would gather about her other little children, and make their *eyes bright and eager with many a strange tale, perhaps even with the dream of Wonderland of long ago*

—truly an immortality of innocence as unreal and fantasied as were the executionary threats of the Queen of Hearts.

Looking-Glass

This was written seven years after Carroll had told the tale of *Wonderland* to the three little girls on the river and Alice is a little older than she was in *Wonderland*. Its plot follows, with similarities and reversals, that of *Wonderland*. The story opens with the theme of punishment: Alice reproaching her kitten for its faults and threatening punishment, only to think of her own fate if her punishments were accumulated and given to her at once. In a final threat to put the kitten through the mantel looking-glass, Alice discovers she can go through herself into that land of reversal, only a small bit of which can be seen ordinarily. It is the space behind the clock. Thus *Looking-Glass* begins with guilt and possible punishment rather than ending so; and time is involved (in the White Rabbit's watch and the mantel clock) in both adventures. In *Looking-Glass,* inanimate objects have come alive; the pictures on the wall move and the face of the clock grins, while the chess pieces on the hearth become the active inhabitants of the land. The motif of the game, expressed in the card game of *Wonderland,* is now experienced more fully as the game of chess, and concern about external space, not merely our own body change, plays a primary role, with the time theme secondary. In fact, in all *Looking-Glass* Land, Alice never once changes size herself, although objects external to her change frequently and distance has a troublesome way of contracting, expanding, and reversing itself. There is the same wish to get into the garden, but this is achieved early in the tale and without trouble. Alice floats downstairs so rapidly that she steadies herself by clutching the doorknob at the garden entrance.

The garden is full of pert flowers whom Alice finally threatens to decapitate (pick) in order to subdue them. While attempting to reach a hill from which to have a better view of the garden, Alice encounters the Red Queen of chess, now grown life-size, whom she has previously seen on the hearth and frightened by lifting her rapidly through the air. There is now a reversal, in that the Red Queen forces Alice to run breathlessly through the air with her, but without reaching anyplace. The rest of *Looking-Glass* is involved with Alice's progress through the chess game of life until she can be crowned a queen herself, on attaining the Eighth Square. Each square has its own adventures, which in general are not so frightfully exciting as those of *Wonderland*. Alice is repeatedly confronted with the facts that space, time, and even memory and cause-and-effect may be reversed and run in either direction, this unreliability causing much confusion. The Red King and Queen are the main characters, much less fierce than the King and Queen of Hearts, and they have counterparts in the untidy but well-meaning White King and Queen. Several fights or threats of fights occur—notably between Tweedledum and Tweedledee, and the Lion and the Unicorn. Finally, Alice encounters the White Knight, who plays a role partly like and partly opposite to that of the Knave of Hearts in *Wonderland*. The White Knight cannot possibly be accused of any crime—he is just too muddled, awkward, and generally impotent. He continually falls from his horse in every direction except over its head, and he carries dangling from his saddle any number of futile contrivances, each of which he owns to be his own invention. Alice has repeatedly to pick him up and get him seated again, and in one final rescue has to pull him out of a ditch, where he has plunged head foremost. The Knight amiably explains: "What does it matter where my body happens to be? My mind goes on working all the same. In fact the more head downward I am, the more I keep inventing new things." (Thus the White Knight seems to be in a state of chronic partial alienation between head and body, resembling in this the Cheshire Cat.) Finally the White Knight sings Alice a song about an old man a-sitting on a gate, which is sung to the tune of "I give thee all, I can no more"[8] and parodies Wordsworth's "The Leech-Gatherer."[9] He is disappointed that Alice does not weep. The White Knight then says farewell, foolishly smiling and begging her to wave her handkerchief in good-bye to him by way of encouragement, after which she will go on into the Eighth Square and queenship, as indeed happens.

As preparation for queenship, Alice is sent through a course of training by the Red and White Queens—a training and an examination which have a shadowy resemblance to a trial; and she is finally obligated to give a dinner party to celebrate her royal debut—all this under the malicious and officious direction of the Red Queen. The party ends, however, in chaos and confusion, not unlike the end of the trial scene—only again, instead of Alice changing size, the objects on the dinner table become large and animated: the candles shoot up to the ceiling, the plates develop wings, the soup ladle is threatening, and complete pandemonium is about to prevail until Alice, in reaction to the emergency, literally turns the table by pulling the cloth off and dumping the whole mess on the floor. She then turns to attack the Red Queen who had provoked the perversity of the dinner party, but finds the Queen again shrunken to chess-piece size. She awakes shaking the Red Queen, only to find she is really shaking her kitten.[10]

While the manifest plots of the *Alice* books are thus similar and simple in structure, it is not their plots which are generally remembered, but their various absurdly irrational incidents with the apparent triumph of sheer but rhythmical nonsense. Perhaps no book except the Bible is quoted as often in unlikely places and by improbable people as *Alice*. For in the account of Alice's experiences there is always some vividly mad vignette which can be used for comparison and relief in most of life's troubling dilemmas. The plot, however, the penetration into the hidden or secret garden and the difficulties encountered there, is in essence the most universal plot of mankind, whether stimulated by the sublibrarian's vision of the little girls playing in the Dean's garden, or from the gardens at Croft and Daresbury traversed by the engine of Love and inhabited by the civilized but combatant worms and caterpillars, or more remotely derived from that garden where Adam and Eve ate of the apple and the serpent of sophistication lurked nearby.

From

"Further Insights"

by Géza Róheim

(1955)

. . . WE TURN NOW to the writings of Lewis Carroll, where a literary parallel may be found to our patient's schizophrenic manipulation of time, food, words, and reality. Interestingly enough, the patient himself once told me that his experiences in life were similar to those of *Alice in Wonderland*. The comparison is not a forced one, and I am not the first one to explain Lewis Carroll's work along psychoanalytic lines. Schilder (1938) has already discussed the oral and destructive nature of *Alice in Wonderland*.

In Lewis Carroll's writings the oral trauma (or the oral situation, to express the same thing more cautiously) is always breaking through the polite superficialities. For example, we attend a "Mad Tea-Party" with Alice, the March Hare, the Mad Hatter, and the Dormouse. It is a *mad* tea-party. The March Hare *is* as mad as a March Hare, and so is the Mad Hatter; while Dormouse (*dormeuse*), with his continual tendency to fall asleep, represents withdrawal. In view of all this we expect to find a duplication of schizophrenic mechanisms in this part of the narrative, and we are not disappointed.

The March Hare reproves Alice for not saying what she means.

"I do," Alice hastily replied; "at least—at least I mean what I say— that's the same thing, you know."

The Mad Hatter objects that this is not the same thing. What, we may ask, are they quarreling about? The real meaning of the dispute seems to point to the ancient problem of words and meanings.

"Not the same thing a bit!" said the Hatter. "Why, you might just as well say that 'I see what I eat' is the same as 'I eat what I see'!"

The main thing about this tea-party is that time has stopped. It is always six o'clock, and they are always having tea. Alice is told that if she were on good terms with time, rather than beating or killing "him," she could (instead of doing her lessons in the morning) set the clock for half-past one and it would be dinnertime. The Hatter, it may be noted, originally went mad when the Queen said: "He's murdering time! Off with his head!" If "time" here means the ends of tension, or oral satisfaction, we can see that the Hatter's aggression touches off anxiety and counteraggression in the Queen.

The Mad Hatter appears again at the trial scene. The trial is about some stolen tarts:

> *The Queen of Hearts, she made some tarts,*
> *   All on a summer day:*
> *The Knave of Hearts, he stole those tarts*
> *   And took them quite away!*

The Mad Hatter is asked to testify:

"I'm a poor man, your Majesty," the Hatter began, in a trembling voice, "and I hadn't begun my tea—not above a week or so—and what with the bread-and-butter getting so thin—and the twinkling of the tea—"

This is followed by the schizophrenic play on words that runs right through the entire book.

Aggressions plays an important role in our theory of the oral trauma. The infant's aggressive tendencies are mobilized by frustration; but, in view of the expected retaliation and the identification with the mother's body, this aggression results in anxiety. In Chapter VI of *Alice in Wonderland* we encounter the Duchess, who is a counterpart of the Queen, both with her motto "Chop off her head" and with the baby who is really a pig. The Duchess sings a lullaby, shaking the baby violently at the end of every line:

> *Speak roughly to your little boy,*
> *   And beat him when he sneezes:*
> *He only does it to annoy,*
> *   Because he knows it teases.*

Since they are busy putting pepper into the soup to make the child sneeze, the cycle of aggression and counteraggression is complete.

Lewis Carroll, though strongly attracted to little girls, disliked little boys. On one occasion he declined to see a friend's boy and said:

He thought I doted on all children but I am not omnivorous like a pig. I pick and choose.

(It may be noted parenthetically that the infant at the breast is a pig—or he is an omnivorous pig in relation to the other children in the family. This is very similar to our patient's complaint that people thought he ate like a hog.)

The whole story of *Alice in Wonderland* begins with the problems of time and orality. The Rabbit takes his watch from his pocket and finds it is late. When Alice falls down the hole, the first thing she notices is a jar labeled "Orange Marmalade." To her very great disappointment, the jar is empty (the oral trauma). She is afraid that she will drop the empty jar and kill somebody underneath her (aggression). Then she hopes that the people at home will not forget to feed Dinah, her cat (that is, give it some milk at teatime), and she continues in a dreamy sort of way:

Do cats eat bats? Do bats eat cats?

The same theme of oral tension may be found in a famous poem by Lewis Carroll, *The Hunting of the Snark.* It begins with a play on the words "fuming" and "furious," which are condensed into a new word, "frumious," very much in the way our patient played with words and coined neologisms. The poem then introduces a person who enters a ship and has completely forgotten his name. He answers to any loud cry such as "Fry me!" or "Fritter my wig!" His intimate friends call him Candle Ends, while his enemies refer to him as Toasted Cheese. The journey is full of oral difficulties. The Baker can only bake a bridal cake; the Butcher can only kill beavers. What is the mysterious Snark they are pursuing? It seems to symbolize food, because the first mark of a Snark is its taste, which is meager but hollow and crisp.

The Snark is also connected with the anxiety about disappearing. Some Snarks are Boojums; and if you happen to see a Snark who is a Boojum, you simply disappear. When the Baker finally finds the Snark and it turns out to be a Boojum, he vanishes in the middle of a word. (This is exactly similar to our patient's anxiety that the words will disappear in him, or that he will disappear in the word. It is our interpretation that the patient deals with the oral trauma by identifying himself with the *vanishing breast* or nipple, which is the source of life. When the breast vanishes, he himself vanishes. The awful thing, he says, is that his parents did not know it when he left home.) During the Barrister's Dream in *The Hunting of the Snark*, the Snark defends a pig in court—the pig is charged with *deserting his sty*. This is also of great interest because the pig is a symbol of the baby in *Alice in Wonderland*.

But the significant person in *The Hunting of the Snark* is the captain of the expedition, the Bellman. In addition to his remarkable lamp, in which the Snark-disappearing motive is indicated—because there is no shore, no goal, only the sea—his ideas about reaching his destination are somewhat peculiar: his navigational charts are blank.

> *This was charming, no doubt: but they shortly found out*
> *That the Captain they trusted so well*
> *Had only one notion for crossing the ocean,*
> *And that was to tingle his bell.*

The interpretation I suggest is that the Bellman is hungry, he is a child crying for food.

This is clarified by a passage in one of Lewis Carroll's letters:

You know I have three dinner-bells—the first (which is the largest) is rung when dinner is nearly ready; the second (which is rather larger) is rung when it is quite ready; and the third (which is as large as the other two put together) is rung all the time I am at dinner.

The importance of the oral trauma and the similarity of Lewis Carroll's literary fantasy to schizophrenic fantasy are further illuminated by a reading of *Through the Looking-Glass,* a sequel to *Alice in Wonderland.* At the beginning and end of this book, Alice is playing with her cat, Dinah, and with Dinah's kittens. Alice is half asleep. In the dream that follows, the black kitten turns into the Red Queen; the white kitten, into the White Queen. At the end of the dream Alice herself becomes a Queen; with the result that there are three queens, the Red Queen, the White Queen, and Queen Alice. The obvious conclusion is that the two kittens are Alice's siblings—the situation is one of sibling rivalry.

Early in *Through the Looking-Glass,* Alice is scolding Kitty, alias the Red Queen, for her faults:

Number two: you pulled Snowdrop away by the tail just as I had put down the saucer of milk before her! What, you were thirsty, were you? How do you know she wasn't thirsty too!

The kitten's punishment is that she will have to go without her dinner; and then Alice meditates on what would happen if she herself had to go without her dinner. We conclude, therefore, that the Red Queen is Alice and that she is trying in the fantasy to keep all the milk for herself, so that her sister should have none. We recall also that Alice had once frightened her old nurse by suddenly shouting in her ear that they play a game in which Alice would pretend to be a hungry hyena and the nurse would be a bone!

It is significant that Lewis Carroll (Charles Lutwidge Dodgson) had ten siblings. He was the oldest child in the family, and he therefore had plenty of opportunity to feel jealous of his younger siblings and (we conjecture) to develop cannibalistic fantasies about the rivals who took his place with the mother. In *Through the Looking-Glass* there is the well-known story of the Walrus and the Carpenter. They take all the little Oysters for a walk and then, although they "deeply sympathize," they eat the whole lot. There is also the very significant passage at the end of *Through the Looking-Glass,* where Alice is Queen and a feast is given in her honor. The first course is a leg of mutton. The Red Queen introduces them to each other: "Alice—Mutton, Mutton—Alice." Having been introduced to the mutton, Alice cannot eat it. In this way she is in danger of missing her entire dinner; so when, notwithstanding the introduction, she cuts a slice of pudding, the Pudding says:

"What impertinence!" said the Pudding. "I wonder how you'd like it if I were to cut a slice out of you, you creature!"

If the successive courses at the dinner represent the siblings whom Alice wanted to eat, we can understand why she cannot eat them after being personally acquainted with them, or after being introduced to them. This would mean that the siblings, instead of being mere fantasy objects, have become personal and real; they are friends and cannot be eaten.

It is worth recalling in this connection that, among the Pitjentara of Australia, every second child is eaten by the siblings and parents in order to give them a kind of double strength; but if the baby survives until it acquires a name, the period of danger is over and it will not be eaten.

But what happens at Alice's banquet? The Red Queen and the White Queen, her rivals in this situation, are transformed into soup and a leg of mutton, thus confirming our interpretation of the nature of the courses at the dinner.

In Chapter V of *Through the Looking-Glass* the White Queen goes rushing through the woods and keeps whispering something to herself that sounds like "Bread-and-butter, bread-and-butter." This is followed by the theme of disappearing food (or breast). The White Queen offers to engage Alice as her maid. The salary is twopence a week and "jam every other day." The Queen explains that there is jam tomorrow and jam yesterday, but never jam today. The Queen eventually turns into an old Sheep, in whose shop Alice experiences some interesting difficulties; everything that Alice tries to take hold of disappears, and the egg she finally buys becomes Humpty Dumpty.

The disappearing food also explains Alice's anxieties at the beginning of *Alice in Wonderland*. She dwindles when she eats one kind of food, and she becomes so tiny that she is afraid of disappearing. Another kind of food makes her so big that there is scarcely any room for her in the house. Diminution in size is the opposite of growth and refers to the oral situation in which one is subject to attack. When Alice is so big that she fills the whole house, the Rabbit throws a cartload of pebbles at her. These are transformed into cakes; but as soon as she eats a cake, she begins to shrink. The food that makes Alice small is the disappearing nipple (subject-object identification), while her colossal size represents oral aggression and body-destruction fantasies.

In Chapter V of *Alice in Wonderland*, Alice is so tall that she reaches above the trees. The Pigeon says that she is a serpent and must be after her eggs (that is, the young ones). The whole narrative deals with creatures whom one ordinarily eats, or who are eaten by the cat and dog, and with whom Alice is required to meet on terms of friendship and equality. This touches off guilt feelings of the oral type. In Chapter X of the same book the Mock Turtle tells Alice that "perhaps you have never been introduced to the Lobster." Alice is just going to say, "I once tasted—" and then checks herself in time. The same thing occurs with the Whiting. Similarly, Alice's idea of starting a pleasant conversation with the Mouse (who may be French) is to ask, "*Où est ma chatte?*"

We see that oral destructiveness and sibling rivalry must have played a part in the formation of these fantasies. Their similarity to schizophrenia is equally striking. First of all there is the continual play on words. What does the Whiting do under the sea? It does the boots and shoes. Boots on land being done with blacking, they are done under the sea with whiting. Likewise, the shoes are made of soles and eels, and it is impossible to do anything without a porpoise (purpose), and so on *ad infinitum*.

After the episode with the "Looking-Glass Insects," Alice comes to the country where things lose their names and she loses her name. We have adequately described our patient's fears of losing his name.[1] As indicated above, the loss of one's name reflects the separation of words and objects. In schizophrenia, the connection between the preconscious cathexis and the world of objects is lost at first and then there is an attempt to restore this connection; but this attempt is only half successful and the words are dealt with as if they were objects.

The restoration of these destroyed connections, *the way back*, is represented by Humpty Dumpty. He overemphasizes the connection between word and object.

"Must *a name mean something?*" *Alice asked doubtfully.*
"*Of course it must,*" *Humpty Dumpty said with a short laugh:* "my *name means the shape I am—and a good handsome shape it is, too.*"

Humpty Dumpty represents an attempt to return to the world of object relations, but it is an unsuccessful attempt. The reinvested cathexis is now in the words, and these become persons and depend on their master, the subject.

"*When* I *use a word . . . it means just what I choose it to mean— neither more nor less. . . . When I make a word do a lot of work like that . . . I always pay it extra.*"

It is appropriate that Humpty Dumpty should be made the representative of an unsuccessful attempt at restoration. This is undoubtedly determined by the rhyme from which he originates. We all know that Humpty Dumpty sat on a wall, had a great fall, and that all the King's horses and men could not put poor Humpty Dumpty together again.

In the parallel we are drawing between Alice and our patient there is an additional and very striking feature. In *Through the Looking-Glass,* Alice too has her "bugs." A hoarse voice speaks and Alice thinks, "It sounds like a horse." And an extremely small voice close to her ear says, "You might make a joke on that—something about 'horse' and 'hoarse,' you know." The owner of the small voice must be inside Alice, because he repeats her thoughts. When it does this once again, Alice says, "Don't tease so. . . . If you're so anxious to have a joke made, why don't you make one yourself?" The little voice sighed deeply; it sounded *very* unhappy. It was such a wonderfully small sigh that Alice would not have heard it at all had it not come quite close to her ear. "I know you are a friend," the little voice went on. "A dear friend, and an old friend. And you won't hurt me, though I *am* an insect." Then Alice sees the insect: it is a gnat, the size of a chicken.

A discussion follows about insects and their names. In this country, we learn, there is a Rocking-horse-fly instead of a Horse-fly; a Snap-dragon-fly (its body is made of plum pudding) instead of a Dragon-fly; and a Bread-and-butter-fly instead of a Butterfly.

Its wings are thin slices of bread-and-butter, its body is a crust, and its head is a lump of sugar.

The Bread-and-butter-fly, it may be noted, lives on weak tea with cream in it.

The bugs, as in the case of our patient, are internalized objects. The similarity goes even further. Our patient's bugs have to do with the disappearance of food. Alice's bugs are made of food. The patient's bugs are closely connected with his dread about the loss of his name. The Gnat, while humming around Alice's head, says to her: "I suppose you don't want to lose your name?"

Additional examples could easily be adduced. They would only be supernumerary at this point. There is no doubt that there are numerous and striking similarities between the fantasy world of *Alice in Wonderland* and the fantasies of our patient.

From "The Thinking of the Body":

COMMENTS ON THE IMAGERY OF CATHARSIS IN LITERATURE

by Kenneth Burke

(1966)

CATHARSIS[1] is usually considered in the grand style (in terms of such sacrifices and victimage as attain their fulfillment in the ritualistic use of the "scapegoat" for poetic purposes). But there are humbler modes of "mortification" available to imaginative writing. And I have here illustrated the point by close inspection of certain texts: *Alice in Wonderland,* Wagner's *Ring,* Flaubert's *The Temptation of St. Anthony,* the *Prometheus Bound* of Aeschylus, the poetry of Mallarmé—also some poems and stories of my own. Persons who insist on keeping the subject of the poetic imagination *salonfähig* (or, as the dictionary might put it, "suitable for discussion in the drawing room") will resent such analysis. So let us offer these pages simply as a contribution to what I elsewhere call the "Beauty Clinic."

Since the idea of purgation readily includes connotations of physical excretion, and since good writers are thorough in the range of their imaginings, it is almost inevitable that (through the subterfuges of poetic invention) good literature would readily and naturally encompass this area of expression, though often by ingenious subterfuge, as particularly in the case of our first example.

Alice in Wonderland

In this ingenious fantasy, we submit, the chapter "Pig and Pepper" is to be viewed as a circuitous description of "child training." Here, by the subterfuges (the "miraculism"?) of nonsense and fantasy, the disciplinary punishment for *crepitus ventris* can be humorously transformed into the advice given in the Duchess's song:

> *Speak roughly to your little boy,*
> *And beat him when he sneezes. . . .*

In brief, when we read this perverse reference to "sneezing," I am suggesting that here is a time to remember the euphemisms in Gilbert Murray's translation of *The Frogs* (where the translator systematically substitutes "sneeze" for Aristophanes' references to a farcical nether noise). As for the grunting which began when the child "had left off sneezing," and which led Alice to say, "that's not at all a proper way of expressing yourself": the double meaning (the "self-expressive" grunt as "purgative") is simultaneously concealed and revealed by the developments of the plot: the grunting child becomes a grunting pig. Or, more literally, what at first was taken for a grunting child turns out to be a pig. This is a roundabout way of saying that such a grunt is piggish, an animal noise. And as we shall see in a few moments, there are good reasons for locating this "grunt" with relation to the reverse end of the animal.

What about the conceit of the Cheshire Cat, which, "beginning with the end of its tail" disappeared all but its grin, until that too was gone? By what labyrinthine route did the author hit upon this ingenious invention? If our interpretation about the sneeze and the grunt is correct, then it might well follow that the vaporous grin is the deceptive translation of odor into terms of sight. To introduce a grammatical element here: the grin would be the *essence* of the "cat." And what kind of essence? The associational bridge might be contrived through "Cheshire," which would belong in the olfactory bit by reason of its connection with the almost proverbial Cheshire cheese.

The whole kitchen scene would be a reversal of motives, a "dizzy" transcendence by concealment through nonsense, so that food could perversely stand for its opposite, offal. (See Freud's *Basic Writings:* "The ugliest as well as the most intimate details of sexual life may be thought of or dreamed of in apparently innocent allusions to culinary operations.") Hence the ambiguities of the kitchen "pot" which "seemed to be full of soup," and into which the cook put too much sternutatory "pepper."

The only two creatures in the kitchen that did *not* sneeze were the "cook" and the cat. Presumably it did not disturb the "cook" because she stood for mother or nurse. And it did not disturb the cat because the cat was the very "soul" of the creation (its transcendent actuality). Other pertinent details: the fishlike and froglike footmen, with their impaired *dignity*; the Fish-footman's remark, " I shall sit here . . . on and off, for days and days"; his irrelevant *whistling* that leads to nothing;[2] the Duchess on a "stool" (she is the unpresentable counterpart of Alice's primness). The theme was introduced by the episode of the insolent Caterpillar, "smoking," and seen by Alice "beyond" the mushroom (that is, beyond the phallic?). Alice here was worried about a "poem" that *wouldn't come out right* ("It all came different," she complained). It was a poem about a busy bee (a creature proverbial for its attention to "duty," which we here interpret in the French sense of *devoirs*).

The anal-oral reversibility is continued in the scene of the Mad Tea-Party, with its rudeness so embarrassing to Alice, the prim, well-trained potty-girl. The reversal centers about the theme of the eating from dirty plates. It is paralleled intellectually in the inventions that get things inside out, upside down, and backwards—and is repeated in the principle of reversal that is clearly indicated in the title of the sequel, *Through the Looking-Glass*. The set of the footmen's heads in the previous chapter, (being held so far back that they are turned upwards rather than forwards) is thus seen to represent not just the comic exaggeration of a servant's pride in his master's dignity, but also the principle of a burlesqued human face such as is suggested by a *cul nu*. The three at the dirty table (Mad Hatter, March Hare, and Dormouse) presumably include connotations of the Demonic Trinity (the one asleep, to deflect the dormant sexuality of the child?). And a glance at Tenniel's drawing of Mad Hatter and March Hare, attempting to stuff the Dormouse into the teapot, now makes the cloacal "ambiguities" here startlingly clear.

This principle of reversibility is incipiently present as early as the initial "fall" down the rabbit-hole. The internality of this fall is represented in Alice's speculations during her descent, "I must be getting somewhere near the centre of the earth." The principle of *reversibility* with regard to food is ambiguously introduced when she sleepily decides that there is no difference between the two questions, "Do cats eat bats?" and "Do bats eat cats?" The jingle of the final episode (with its interpretation, "'If she should push the matter on'—that must be the Queen") leads into the "stuff and nonsense" of the Queen's intellectualistic putting of the hind end foremost: "Sentence first—verdict afterwards."

The circling about the table, and the reference (in the epilogue) to this "never-ending meal," suggest that we might eventually trail the fantasy back to the digestive tract as primal worm, Ouroboros, ever circling back upon itself, the "mystic" dreaming stage of vegetal metabolism in which the taking-in and the giving-off merge into one another (a kind of possibility which, at this stage, we shall mention without further argument).

But, for one final set of observations designed to indicate the puns underlying this "nonsense," we might note the author himself ambiguously attests to such enigmas, in saying that the story follows the pattern of a chess game (a "Cheshire" game? a "cheese" game?) where Alice is to "win in eleven moves." Here our point about the "Duchess" is borne out by Alice's "coronation," in line with popular witticisms about the "throne." And the outline of the game tells us exactly when Alice "leaves egg on shelf," a double meaning in keeping with popular witticisms involving the outlaw meanings of "egg."

ALICE IN WONDERLAND:

The Child as

Swain

by William Empson

(1935)

IT MUST SEEM a curious thing that there has been so little serious criticism of the *Alices,* and that so many critics, with so militant and eager an air of good taste, have explained that they would not think of attempting it. Even Mr. de la Mare's book, which made many good points, is queerly evasive in tone. There seems to be a feeling that real criticism would involve psychoanalysis, and that the results would be so improper as to destroy the atmosphere of the books altogether. Dodgson was too conscious a writer to be caught out so easily. For instance, it is an obvious bit of interpretation to say that the Queen of Hearts is a symbol of "uncontrolled animal passion" seen through the clear but blank eyes of sexlessness; obvious, and the sort of thing critics are now so sure would be in bad taste; Dodgson said it himself, to the actress who took the part when the thing was acted. The books are so frankly about growing up that there is no great discovery in translating them into Freudian terms; it seems only the proper exegesis of a classic even where it would be a shock to the author. On the whole, the results of the analysis, when put into drawing-room language, are his conscious opinions; and if there was no other satisfactory outlet for his feelings but the special one fixed in his books, the same is true in a degree of any original artist. I shall use psychoanalysis where it seems relevant, and feel I had better begin by saying what use it is supposed to be. Its business here is not to discover a neurosis peculiar to Dodgson. The essential idea behind the books is a shift onto the child, which Dodgson did not invent, of the obscure tradition of pastoral. The formula is now "*child*-become-judge," and if Dodgson identifies himself with the child, so does the writer of the primary sort of pastoral with his magnified version of the swain. (Dodgson took an excellent photograph, much admired by Tennyson, of Alice Liddell as a ragged beggar girl, which seems a sort of example of the connection.) I should say indeed that this version was more open to neurosis than the older ones; it is less hopeful and more a return into oneself. The analysis should show how this works in general. But there are other things to be said about such a version of pastoral; its use of the device prior to irony lets it make covert judgments about any matter the author was interested in.

There is a tantalizing one about Darwinism. The first Neanderthal skull was found in 1856. *The Origin of Species* (1859) came out six years before *Wonderland*, three before its conception, and was very much in the air, a pervading bad smell. It is hard to say how far Dodgson, under cover of nonsense, was using ideas of which his set disapproved; he wrote some hysterical passages against vivisection and has a curious remark to the effect that chemistry professors had better not have laboratories, but was open to new ideas and doubted the eternity of hell. The 1860 meeting of the British Association, at which Huxley started his career as publicist and gave that resounding snub to Bishop Wilberforce, was held at Oxford, where Dodgson was already in residence. He had met Tennyson in '56, and we hear of Tennyson lecturing him later on the likeness of monkeys' and men's skulls.

The only passage that I feel sure involves evolution comes at the beginning of *Wonderland* (the most spontaneous and "subconscious" part of the books), when Alice gets out of the bath of tears that has magically released her from the underground chamber; it is made clear (for instance about watering-places) that the salt water is the sea from which life arose; as a bodily product it is also the amniotic fluid (there are other forces at work here); ontogeny then repeats phylogeny, and a whole Noah's Ark gets out of the sea with her. In Dodgson's own illustration as well as Tenniel's there is the disturbing head of a monkey and in the text there is an extinct bird. Our minds having thus been forced back onto the history of species, there is a reading of history from the period when the Mouse "came over" with the Conqueror; questions of race turn into the questions of breeding in which Dodgson was more frankly interested, and there are obscure snubs for people who boast about their ancestors. We then have the Caucus-Race (the word had associations for Dodgson with local politics; he says somewhere, "I never go to a Caucus without reluctance"), in which you begin running when you like and leave off when you like, and all win. The subtlety of this is that it supports Natural Selection (in the offensive way the nineteenth century did) to show the absurdity of democracy, and supports democracy (or at any rate liberty) to show the absurdity of Natural Selection. The race is not to the swift, because idealism will not let it be to the swift, and because life, as we are told in the final poem, is at random and a dream. But there is no weakening of human values in this generosity; all the animals win, and Alice, because she is Man, has therefore to give them comfits, but though they demand this they do not fail to recognize that she is superior. They give her her own elegant thimble, the symbol of her labor, because she too has won, and because the highest among you shall be the servant of all. This is a solid piece of symbolism; the politically minded scientists preaching progress through "selection" and *laissez-faire* are confronted with the full anarchy of Christ. And the pretense of infantilism allows it a certain grim honesty; Alice is a little ridiculous and discomfited, under cover of charm, and would prefer a more aristocratic system.

In the *Looking-Glass* too there are ideas about progress at an early stage of the journey of growing up. Alice goes quickly through the First Square by railway, in a carriage full of animals in a state of excitement about the progress of business and machinery; the only man is Disraeli, dressed in newspapers—the new man who gets on by self-advertisement, the newspaper-fed man who believes in progress, possibly even the rational dress of the future.

> . . . *to her great surprise they all* thought *in chorus (I hope you understand what* thinking *in chorus means—for I must confess that I don't), "Better say nothing at all. Language is worth a thousand pounds a word!"*
>
> *"I shall dream about a thousand pounds tonight, I know I shall," thought Alice.*
>
> *All this time the Guard was looking at her, first through a telescope, then through a microscope, and then through an opera-glass. At last he said, "You're traveling the wrong way," and shut up the window and went away.*

This seems to be a prophecy; Huxley in the Romanes lecture of 1893, and less clearly beforehand, said that the human sense of right must judge and often be opposed to the progress imposed by Nature, but at this time he was still looking through the glasses.

> *But the gentleman dressed in white paper leaned forwards and whispered in her ear, "Never mind what they all say, my dear, but take a return-ticket every time the train stops."*

In 1861 "many Tory members considered that the prime minister was a better representative of conservative opinions than the leader of the opposition." This seems to be the double outlook of Disraeli's conservatism, too subtle to inspire action. I think he turns up again as the Unicorn when the Lion and the Unicorn are fighting for the Crown; they make a great dust and nuisance, treat the commonsense Alice as entirely mythical, and are very frightening to the poor King to whom the Crown really belongs.

> *"Indeed I shan't," Alice said rather impatiently. "I don't belong to this railway journey at all—I was in a wood just now—and I wish I could get back there!"*

When she gets back to the wood it is different; it is Nature in the raw, with no names, and she is afraid of it. She still thinks the animals are right to stay there; even when they know their names "they wouldn't answer at all, if they were wise." (They might do well to write nonsense books under an assumed name, and refuse to answer even to that.) All this is a very Kafka piece of symbolism, less at ease than the preceding one; *Wonderland* is a dream, but the *Looking-Glass* is self-consciousness.

But both are topical; whether you call the result allegory or "pure non-sense" depends on ideas about progress and industrialization, and there is room for exegesis on the matter.

The beginning of modern child-sentiment may be placed at the obscure edition of *Mother Goose's Melodies* (John Newbury, 1760), with "maxims" very probably by Goldsmith. The important thing is not the rhymes (Boston boasts an edition of 1719. My impression is that they improved as time went on) but the appended maxims, which take a sophisticated pleasure in them. Most are sensible proverbs which the child had better know anyway; their charm (mainly for the adult) comes from the unexpected view of the story you must take if they are not to be irrelevant.

AMPHION'S SONG OF EURYDICE.

I won't be my Father's Jack,
I won't be my Father's Jill,
I won't be the Fiddler's Wife,
And I will have music when I will.

T'other little Tune,
T'other little Tune,
Prithee Love play me
T'other little Tune.

MAXIM.—Those Arts are the most valuable which are of the greatest Use.

It seems to be the fiddler whose art has been useful in controlling her, but then again she may have discovered the art of wheedling the fiddler. The pomp of the maxim and the childishness of the rhyme make a mock-pastoral compound. The pleasure in children here is obviously a derivative of the pleasure in Macheath; the children are "little rogues."

Bow wow wow
Whose dog art Thou?
Little Tom Tinker's Dog.
Bow wow wow.

Tom Tinker's Dog is a very good Dog; and an honester Dog than his Master.

Honest ("free from hypocrisy" or the patronizing tone to a social inferior) and *dog* ("you young dog") have their *Beggar's Opera* feelings here; it is not even clear whether Tom is a young vagabond or a child.

This is a pleasant example because one can trace the question back. Pope engraved a couplet "on the collar of a dog which I gave to His Royal Highness"—a friendly act as from one gentleman to another resident in the neighborhood.

> I am his Highness' dog at Kew.
> Pray tell me, sir, whose dog are you?

Presumably Frederick himself would be the first to read it. The joke carries a certain praise for the underdog; the point is not that men are slaves but that they find it suits them and remain good-humored. The dog is proud of being the prince's dog and expects no one to take offense at the question. There is also a hearty independence in its lack of respect for the inquirer. Pope took this from Sir William Temple, where it is said by a fool: "I am the Lord Chamberlain's fool. And whose are you?" was his answer to the nobleman. It is a neat case of the slow shift of this sentiment from fool to rogue to child.

Alice, I think, is more of a "little rogue" than it is usual to say, or than Dodgson himself thought in later years:

loving as a dog . . . and gentle as a fawn; then courteous,—courteous to all, *high or low, grand or grotesque, King or Caterpillar . . . trustful, with an absolute trust. . . .*

and so on. It depends what you expect of a child of seven.

. . . she had quite a long argument with the Lory, who at last turned sulky, and would only say, "I'm older than you, and must know better." And this Alice would not allow, without knowing how old it was, and as the Lory positively refused to tell its age, there was no more to be said.

Alice had to be made to speak up to bring out the point—here the point is a sense of the fundamental oddity of life given by the fact that different animals become grown-up at different ages; but still, if you accept the Lory as a grownup, this is rather a pert child. She is often the underdog speaking up for itself.

A quite separate feeling about children, which is yet at the back of the pertness here and in the Goldsmith, since it is needed if the pertness is to be charming, may be seen in its clearest form in Wordsworth and Coleridge; it is the whole point of the "Ode to Intimations" and even of

"We are Seven." The child has not yet been put wrong by civilization, and all grownups have been. It may well be true that Dodgson envied the child because it was sexless, and Wordsworth because he knew that he was destroying his native poetry by the smugness of his life, but neither theory explains why this feeling about children arose when it did and became so general. There is much of it in Vaughan after the Civil War, but as a general tendency it appeared when the eighteenth-century settlement had come to seem narrow and inescapable; one might connect it with the end of dueling; also when the scientific sort of truth had been generally accepted as the main and real one. It strengthened as the aristocracy became more puritan. It depends on a feeling, whatever may have caused that in its turn, that no way of building up character, no intellectual system, can bring out all that is inherent in the human spirit, and therefore that there is more in the child than any man has been able to keep. (The child is a microcosm, like Donne's world, and Alice too is a stoic.) This runs through all Victorian and Romantic literature; the world of the adult made it hard to be an artist, and they kept a sort of taproot going down to their experience as children. Artists like Wordsworth and Coleridge, who accepted this fact and used it, naturally come to seem the most interesting and in a way the most sincere writers of the period. Their idea of the child, that it is in the right relation to Nature, not dividing what should be unified, that its intuitive judgment contains what poetry and philosophy must spend their time laboring to recover, was accepted by Dodgson and a main part of his feeling. He quotes Wordsworth on this point in the "Easter Greeting"—the child feels its life in every limb; Dodgson advises it, with an infelicitous memory of the original poem, to give its attention to death from time to time. That the dream books are

> *Like Pilgrim's withered wreaths of flowers*
> *Plucked in a far-off land*

is a fine expression of Wordsworth's sense both of the poetry of childhood and of his advancing sterility. And the moment when Alice finds herself dancing with Tweedledum and Tweedledee, so that it is difficult to introduce herself afterwards, is a successful interruption of Wordsworthian sentiment into his normal style.

. . . she took hold of both hands at once: the next moment they were dancing round in a ring. This seemed quite natural (she remembered

afterwards), and she was not even surprised to hear music playing: it
seemed to come from the tree under which they were dancing, and it
was done (as well as she could make it out) by the branches rubbing one
across another, like fiddles and fiddle-sticks. . . . "I don't know when I
began it, but somehow I felt as if I'd been singing it a long long time!"

This is presented as like the odd behavior of comic objects such as soup
tureens, but it is a directer version of the idea of the child's unity with
nature. She has been singing a long long time because she sang with no
temporal limits in that imperial palace whence she came. Yet it is the
frank selfishness of the brothers, who, being little boys, the horrid, are
made into a satire on war, and will only give her the hands free from
hugging each other, that forces her into the ring with them that produces eternity. Even here this puts a subtle doubt into the eternities open
to the child.

For Dodgson will only go halfway with the sentiment of the child's
unity with nature, and has another purpose for his heroine; she is the
free and independent mind. Not that this is contradictory; because she is
right about life, she is independent from all the other characters who
are wrong. But it is important to him because it enables him to clash the
Wordsworth sentiments with the other main tradition about children
derived from rogue-sentiment. (For both, no doubt, he had to go some
way back; the intervening sentiment about children is that the great
thing is to repress their Original Sin, and I suppose, though he would
not have liked it, he was among the obscure influences that led to the
cult of games in the public schools.)

One might say that the *Alices* differ from other versions of pastoral
in lacking the sense of glory. Normally the idea of including all sorts of
men in yourself brings in an idea of reconciling yourself with nature and
therefore gaining power over it. The *Alices* are more self-protective; the
dream cuts out the real world and the delicacy of the mood is felt to cut
out the lower classes. This is true enough, but when Humpty Dumpty says
that glory means a nice knock-down argument, he is not far from the
central feeling of the book. There is a real feeling of isolation and yet just
that is taken as the source of power.

The obvious parody of Wordsworth is the poem of the White Knight,
an important figure for whom Dodgson is willing to break the language
of humor into the language of sentiment. It takes off "Resolution and
Independence," a genuine pastoral poem if ever there was one; the endur-

ance of the leech-gatherer gives Wordsworth strength to face the pain of the world. Dodgson was fond of saying that one parodied the best poems, or anyway that parody showed no lack of imagination, but a certain bitterness is inherent in parody; if the meaning is not "This poem is absurd" it must be "In my present mood of emotional sterility the poem will not work, or I am afraid to let it work, on *me*." The parody here will have no truck with the dignity of the leech-gatherer, but the point of that is to make the unworldly dreaminess of the Knight more absurd; there may even be a reproach for Wordsworth in the lack of consideration that makes him go on asking the same question. One feels that the Knight has probably imagined most of the old man's answers, or anyway that the old man was playing up to the fool who questioned him. At any rate, there is a complete shift of interest from the virtues of the leech-gatherer onto the childish but profound virtues of his questioner.

The main basis of the joke is the idea of absurd inventions of new foods. Dodgson was well-informed about food, kept his old menus, and was wine-taster to the College; but ate very little, suspected the High Table of overeating, and would see no reason to deny that he connected overeating with other forms of sensuality. One reason for the importance of rich food here is that it is the child's symbol for all luxuries reserved for grownups. I take it that the fascination of soup and of the Mock Turtle who sings about it was that soup is mainly eaten at dinner, the excitingly grown-up meal eaten after the child has gone to bed. When Alice talks about her dinner she presumably means lunch, and it is rather a boast when she says she has already met whiting. In the White Knight's song and conversation these little jokes based on fear of sensuality are put to a further use; he becomes the scientist, the inventor, whose mind is nobly but absurdly detached from interest in the pleasures of the senses and even from "good sense."

"*How* can *you* go on talking so quietly, head downwards?" Alice asked, as she dragged him out by the feet, and laid him in a heap on the bank.

The Knight looked surprised at the question. "What does it matter where my body happens to be?" he said. "My mind goes on working all the same. In fact, the more head downwards I am, the more I keep inventing new things.

"Now the cleverest thing that I ever did," he went on after a pause, "was inventing a new pudding during the meat-course."

This required extreme detachment; the word "clever" has become a signal that the mind is being admired for such a reason. The more absurd the assumptions of the thinking, for instance those of scientific materialism, the more vigorous the thought based upon it. "Life is so strange that his results have the more chance of being valuable because his assumptions are absurd, but we must not forget that they are so." This indeed is as near the truth as one need get about scientific determinism.

One reason for the moral grandeur of the Knight, then, is that he stands for the Victorian scientist, who was felt to have invented a new kind of Roman virtue; earnestly, patiently, carefully (it annoyed Samuel Butler to have these words used so continually about scientists), without sensuality, without self-seeking, without claiming any but a fragment of knowledge, he goes on laboring at his absurd but fruitful conceptions. But the parody makes him stand also for the poet, and Wordsworth would have been pleased by this; he considered that the poet was essentially one who revived our sense of the original facts of nature, and should use scientific ideas where he could; poetry was the impassioned expression of the face of all science; Wordsworth was as successful in putting life into the abstract words of science as into "the plain language of men," and many of the *Lyrical Ballads* are best understood as psychological notes written in a form that saves one from forgetting their actuality. The Knight has the same readiness to accept new ideas and ways of life, such as the sciences were imposing, without ceasing to be good and, in his way, sensible, as Alice herself shows for instance when, in falling down the rabbit-hole, she plans a polite entry into the Antipodes and is careful not to drop the marmalade onto the inhabitants. It is the childishness of the Knight that lets him combine the virtues of the poet and the scientist, and one must expect a creature so finely suited to life to be absurd because life itself is absurd.

The talking-animal convention and the changes of relative size appear in so different a children's book as *Gulliver*; they evidently make some direct appeal to the child, whatever more sophisticated ideas are piled onto them. Children feel at home with animals conceived as human; the animal can be made affectionate without its making serious emotional demands on them, does not want to educate them, is at least unconventional in the sense that it does not impose its conventions, and does not make a secret of the processes of nature. So the talking animals here are a child-world; the rule about them is that they are always friendly though childishly frank to Alice while she is small, and when she is big (suggesting grown up) always opposed to her, or by her, or both. But talking animals in children's books had been turned to didactic purposes ever since Aesop; the schoolmastering tone in which the animals talk nonsense to Alice is partly a parody of this—they are really childish but try not to look it. On the other hand, this tone is so supported by the way they can order her about, the firm and surprising way their minds work, the abstract topics they work on, the useless rules they accept with so much conviction, that we take them as real grownups contrasted with unsophisticated childhood. "The grown-up world is as odd as the child-world, and both are a dream." This ambivalence seems to correspond to Dodgson's own attitude to children; he, like Alice, wanted to get the advantages of being childish and grown up at once. In real life this seems to have at least occasional disadvantages both ways; one remembers the little girl who screamed and demanded to be taken from the lunch table because she knew she couldn't solve his puzzles (not, apparently, a usual, but one would think a natural reaction to his mode of approach)—she clearly thought him too grown-up; whereas in the scenes of jealousy with his little girls' parents, the grownups must have thought him quite enough of a child. He made a success of the process, and it seems clear that it did none of the little girls any harm, but one cannot help cocking one's eye at it as a way of life.

The changes of size are more complex. In *Gulliver* they are the impersonal eye; to change size and nothing else makes you feel "this makes one see things as they are in themselves." It excites wonder, but of a scientific sort. Swift used it for satire on science or from a horrified interest in it, and to give a sort of scientific authority to his deductions, that men, seen as small, are spiritually petty and, seen as large, physically loathsome. And it is the small observer, like the child, who does least to alter what he sees and therefore sees most truly. (The definition of potential, in all but the most rigid textbooks of electricity, contents itself with talking about the force on a *small* charge which doesn't alter the field *much*. The objection that the small alteration in the field might be proportional to the small force does not occur easily to the reader.) To mix this with a pious child's type of wonder made science seem less irreligious and gave you a feeling that you were being good because educating a child; Faraday's talks for children on the chemical history of a candle came out in 1861, so the method was in the air. But these are special uses of a material rich in itself. Children like to think of being so small that they could hide from grownups and so big that they could control them, and to do this dramatizes the great topic of growing up, which both *Alices* keep to consistently. In the same way the charm of "Jabberwocky" is that it is a code language, the language with which grownups hide things from children or children from grownups. Also, the words are such good tongue-gestures, in Sir Richard Paget's phrase, that they seem to carry their own meaning; this carries a hint of the paradox that the conventions are natural.

Both books also keep to the topic of death—the first two jokes about death in *Wonderland* come on pages 3 and 4—and for the child this may be a natural connection; I remember believing I should have to die in order to grow up, and thinking the prospect very disagreeable. There seems to be a connection in Dodgson's mind between the death of childhood and the development of sex, which might be pursued into many of the details of the books. Alice will die if the Red King wakes up, partly because she is a dream-product of the author and partly because the Pawn is put back in its box at the end of the game. He is the absent husband of the Red Queen who is a governess, and the end of the book comes when Alice defeats the Red Queen and "mates" the King. Everything seems to break up because she arrives at a piece of *knowledge*, that all the poems are about fish. I should say the idea was somehow at work at the end of *Wonderland* too. The trial is meant to be a mystery; Alice is told to leave the court, as if a child ought not to hear the evidence, and yet they expect her to give evidence herself.

> "What do you know about this business?" the King said to Alice.
> "Nothing," said Alice.
> "Nothing whatever?" persisted the King.
> "Nothing whatever," said Alice.
> "That's very important," the King said, turning to the jury. They were just beginning to write this down on their slates, when the White Rabbit interrupted: "Unimportant, your Majesty means of course," he said, in a very respectful tone, but frowning and making faces as he spoke.
> "Unimportant, of course, I meant," the King hastily said, and went on to himself in an undertone, "important—unimportant—unimportant—important—" as if he were trying which word sounded best.

There is no such stress in the passage as would make one feel there must be something behind it, and certainly it is funny enough as it stands. But

I think Dodgson felt it was important that Alice should be innocent of all knowledge of what the Knave of Hearts (a flashy-looking lady's man in the picture) is likely to have been doing, and also important that she should not be told she is innocent. That is why the King, always a well-intentioned man, is embarrassed. At the same time Dodgson feels that Alice is right in thinking "it doesn't matter a bit" which word the jury write down; she is too stable in her detachment to be embarrassed, these things will not interest her, and in a way she includes them all in herself. And it is the refusal to let her stay that makes her revolt and break the dream. It is tempting to read an example of this idea into the poem that introduces the *Looking-Glass*.

> *Come, harken then, ere voice of dread,*
> *With bitter summons laden,*
> *Shall summon to unwelcome bed*
> *A melancholy maiden!*[1]

After all, the marriage bed was more likely to be the end of the maiden than the grave, and the metaphor firmly implied treats them as identical.

The last example is obviously more a joke against Dodgson than anything else, and though the connection between death and the development of sex is, I think, at work, it is not the main point of the conflict about growing up. Alice is given a magical control over her growth by the traditionally symbolic Caterpillar, a creature which has to go through a sort of death to become grown up, and then seems a more spiritual creature. It refuses to agree with Alice that this process is at all peculiar, and clearly her own life will be somehow like it, but the main idea is not its development of sex. The butterfly implied may be the girl when she is "out" or her soul when in heaven, to which she is now nearer than she will be when she is "out"; she must walk to it by walking away from it. Alice knows several reasons why she should object to growing up, and does not at all like being an obvious angel, a head out of contact with its body that has to come down from the sky and gets mistaken for the Paradisal serpent of the knowledge of good and evil, and by the pigeon of the Annunciation, too. But she only makes herself smaller for reasons of tact or proportion; the triumphant close of *Wonderland* is that she has outgrown her fancies and can afford to wake and despise them. The *Looking-Glass* is less of a dream-product, less concentrated on the child's situation, and (once started) less full of changes of size; but it has the same end; the governess shrinks to a kitten when Alice has grown from a Pawn to a Queen and can shake her. Both these clearly stand for becoming grown up and yet in part are a revolt against grown-up behavior; there is the same ambivalence as about the talking animals. Whether children often find this symbolism as interesting as Carroll did is another thing; there are recorded cases of tears at such a betrayal of the reality of the story. I remember feeling that the ends of the books were a sort of necessary assertion that the grown-up world was after all the proper one; one did not object to that in principle, but would no more turn to those parts from preference than to the "Easter Greeting to Every Child that Loves Alice" (Gothic type).

To make the dream-story from which *Wonderland* was elaborated seem Freudian one has only to tell it. A fall through a deep hole into the secrets of Mother Earth produces a new enclosed soul wondering who it is, what will be its position in the world, and how it can get out. It is a long low hall, part of the palace of the Queen of Hearts (a neat touch), from which it can only get out to the fresh air and the fountains through a hole frighteningly too small. Strange changes, caused by the way it is nourished there, happen to it in this place, but always when it is big it cannot get out and when it is small it is not allowed to; for one thing, being a little girl, it has no key. The nightmare theme of the birth-trauma, that she grows too big for the room and is almost crushed by it, is not only used here but repeated more painfully after she seems to have got out; the Rabbit sends her sternly into its house and some food there makes her grow again. In Dodgson's own drawing of Alice when cramped into the room with one foot up the chimney, kicking out the hateful thing that tries to come down (she takes away its pencil when it is a juror), she is much more obviously in the fetus position than in Tenniel's. The White Rabbit is Mr. Spooner, to whom the spoonerisms happened, an undergraduate in 1862, but its business here is as a pet for children which they may be allowed to breed. Not that the clearness of the framework makes the interpretation simple; Alice peering through the hole into the garden may be wanting a return to the womb as well as an escape from it; she is fond, we are told, of taking both sides of an argument when talking to herself, and the whole book balances between the luscious nonsense-world of fantasy and the ironic nonsense-world of fact.

I said that the sea of tears she swims in was the amniotic fluid, which is much too simple. You may take it as Lethe in which the souls were bathed before rebirth (and it is their own tears; they forget, as we forget our childhood, through the repression of pain) or as the "solution" of an

intellectual contradiction through Intuition and a return to the Unconscious. Anyway, it is a sordid image made pretty; one need not read
Dodgson's satirical verses against babies to see how much he would dislike a child wallowing in its tears in real life. The fondness of small girls
for doing this has to be faced early in attempting to prefer them, possibly
to small boys, certainly to grownups; to a man idealizing children as free
from the falsity of a rich emotional life, their displays of emotion must
be particularly disconcerting. The celibate may be forced to observe
them, on the floor of a railway carriage for example, after a storm of
fury, dabbling in their ooze; covertly snuggling against mamma while
each still pretends to ignore the other. The symbolic pleasure of dabbling
seems based on an idea that the liquid itself is the bad temper which
they have got rid of by the storm and yet are still hugging, or that they
are not quite impotent, since they have at least "done" this much about
the situation. The acid quality of the style shows that Dodgson does not
entirely like having to love creatures whose narcissism takes this form,
but he does not want simply to forget it as he too would like a relief from
"ill-temper"; he sterilizes it from the start by giving it a charming myth.
The love for narcissists itself seems mainly based on a desire to keep
oneself safely detached, which is the essential notion here.

The symbolic completeness of Alice's experience is, I think, important. She runs the whole gamut; she is a father in getting down the hole,
a fetus at the bottom, and can only be born by becoming a mother and
producing her own amniotic fluid. Whether Carroll's mind played the trick
of putting this into the story or not, he has the feelings that would correspond to it. A desire to include all sexuality in the girl-child, the least
obviously sexed of human creatures, the one that keeps its sex in the
safest place, was an important part of their fascination for him. He is
partly imagining himself as the girl-child (with these comforting characteristics), partly as its father (these together make *it* a father), partly
as its lover—so it might be a mother—but then, of course, it is clever and
detached enough to do everything for itself. He told one of his little girls
a story about cats wearing gloves over their claws: "For you see, 'gloves'
have got 'love' inside them— there's none outside, you know." So far from
its dependence, the child's independence is the important thing, and the
theme behind that is the self-centered emotional life imposed by the
detached intelligence.

The famous Cat is a very direct symbol of this ideal of intellectual detachment; all cats are detached, and since this one grins, it is the amused observer. It can disappear because it can abstract itself from its surroundings into a more interesting inner world; it appears only as a head because it is almost a disembodied intelligence, and only as a grin because it can impose an atmosphere without being present. In frightening the King by the allowable act of looking at him, it displays the soul-force of Mr. Gandhi; it is unbeheadable because its soul cannot be killed; and its influence brings about a short amnesty in the divided nature of the Queen and Duchess. Its cleverness makes it formidable—it has very long claws and a great many teeth—but Alice is particularly at home with it; she is the same sort of thing.

The Gnat gives a more touching picture of Dodgson; he treats nowhere more directly of his actual relations with the child. He feels he is liable to nag at it, as a gnat would, and the Gnat turns out, as it is, to be alarmingly big as a friend for the child, but at first it sounds tiny because it means so little to her. It tries to amuse her by rather frightening accounts of other dangerous insects, other grownups. It is reduced to tears by the melancholy of its own jokes, which it usually can't bear to finish; only if Alice had made them, as it keeps egging her on to do, would they be at all interesting. That at least would show the child had paid some sort of attention, and it could go away and repeat them to other people. The desire to have jokes made all the time, it feels, is a painful and obvious confession of spiritual discomfort, and the freedom of Alice from such a feeling makes her unapproachable.

"Don't tease so," said Alice, looking about in vain to see where the voice came from. "If you're so anxious to have a joke made, why don't you make one yourself?"

The little voice sighed deeply: it was very *unhappy, evidently, and Alice would have said something pitying to comfort it, "if it would only sigh like other people!" she thought. But this was such a wonderfully small sigh, that she wouldn't have heard it at all, if it hadn't come* quite *close to her ear. The consequence of this was that it tickled her ear very much, and quite took off her thoughts from the unhappiness of the poor little creature.*

"I know you are a friend," *the little voice went on;* "a dear friend, and an old friend. And you won't hurt me, though I *am* an insect."

"What kind of insect?" Alice inquired, a little anxiously. What she really wanted to know was, whether it could sting or not, but she thought this wouldn't be quite a civil question to ask.

"What, then you don't—" *the little voice began....*

"Don't know who I am! Does anybody not know who I am?" He is afraid that even so innocent a love as his, like all love, may be cruel, and yet it is she who is able to hurt him, if only through his vanity. The implications of these few pages are so painful that the ironical calm of the close, when she kills it, seems delightfully gay and strong. The Gnat is suggesting to her that she would like to remain purely a creature of nature and stay in the wood where there are no names.

> "... *That's a joke. I wish you had made it.*"
> "*Why do you wish I had made it?*" *Alice asked.* "*It's a very bad one.*"
> *But the Gnat only sighed deeply, while two large tears came rolling down its cheeks.*
> "*You shouldn't make jokes,*" *Alice said,* "*if it makes you so unhappy.*"
> *Then came another of those melancholy little sighs, and this time the poor Gnat really seemed to have sighed itself away, for, when Alice looked up, there was nothing whatever to be seen on the twig, and, as she was getting quite chilly with sitting so long, she got up and walked on.*

The overpunctuation and the flat assonance of "long—on" add to the effect. There is something charmingly prim and well-meaning about the way she sweeps aside the feelings that she can't deal with. One need not suppose that Dodgson ever performed this scene, which he can imagine so clearly, but there is too much self-knowledge here to make the game of psychoanalysis seem merely good fun.

The scene in which the Duchess has become friendly to Alice at the garden-party shows Alice no longer separate from her creator; it is clear that Dodgson would be as irritated as she is by the incident, and is putting himself in her place. The obvious way to read it is as the middle-aged woman trying to flirt with the chaste young man.

> "*The game's going on rather better now,*" *she said. . . .*
> "*'Tis so,*" *said the Duchess:* "*and the moral of that is—'Oh, 'tis love, 'tis love, that makes the world go round!'*"
> "*Somebody said,*" *Alice whispered,* "*that it's done by everybody minding their own business!*"
> "*Ah, well! It means much the same thing,*" *said the Duchess, digging her sharp little chin into Alice's shoulder as she added,* "*and the moral of that is—'Take care of the sense, and the sounds will take care of themselves.'*"
> "*How fond she is of finding morals in things!*" *Alice thought to herself.*

Both are true because the generous and the selfish kinds of love have the same name; the Duchess seems to take the view of the political economists, that the greatest public good is produced by the greatest private selfishness. All this talk about "morals" makes Alice suspicious; also, she is carrying a flamingo, a pink bird with a long neck. "The chief difficulty Alice found at first was in managing her flamingo . . . it *would* twist itself round and look up in her face."

"I dare say you're wondering why I don't put my arm round your waist," the Duchess said, after a pause: "the reason is, that I'm doubtful about the temper of your flamingo. Shall I try the experiment?"

"He might bite," Alice cautiously replied, not feeling at all anxious to have the experiment tried.

"Very true," said the Duchess: "flamingoes and mustard both bite. And the moral of that is—'Birds of a feather flock together.'"

Mustard may be classed with the pepper that made her "ill-tempered" when she had so much of it in the soup, so that flamingos and mustard become the desires of the two sexes. No doubt Dodgson would be indignant at having this meaning read into his symbols, but the meaning itself, if he had been intending to talk about the matter, is just what he would have wished to say.

The Duchess then jumps away to another aspect of the selfishness of our nature.

"It's a mineral, I think," said Alice.

"Of course it is," said the Duchess, who seemed ready to agree to everything that Alice said: "there's a large mustard-mine near here. And the moral of that is—'The more there is of mine, the less there is of yours.'"

One could put the same meanings in again, but a new one has come forward: "Industrialism is merely as greedy as sex; all we get from it is a sharper distinction between rich and poor." They go off into riddles about sincerity and how one can grow into what one would seem to be.

This sort of "analysis" is a peep at machinery; the question for criticism is what is done with the machine. The purpose of a dream on the Freudian theory is simply to keep you in an undisturbed state so that you can go on sleeping; in the course of this practical work you may produce something of more general value, but not only of one sort. Alice has, I understand, become a patron saint of the Surrealists, but they do not go in for Comic Primness, a sort of reserve of force, which is her chief charm. Wyndham Lewis avoided putting her beside Proust and Lorelei, to be danced on as a debilitating child-cult (though she is a bit of pragmatist too); the present-day reader is more likely to complain of her complacence. In this sort of child-cult the child, though a means of imaginative escape, becomes the critic; Alice is the most reasonable and responsible person in the book. This is meant as charmingly pathetic about her as well as satire about her elders, and there is some implication that the sane man can take no other view of the world, even for controlling it, than the child does; but this is kept a good distance from sentimental infantilism. There is always some doubt about the meaning of a man who says he wants to be like a child, because he may want to be like it in having fresh and vivid feelings and senses; in not knowing, expecting, or desiring evil; in not having an analytical mind; in having no sexual desires recognizable as such, or out of a desire to be mothered and evade responsibility. He is usually mixing them up—Christ's praise of children, given perhaps for reasons I have failed to list, has made it a respected thing to say, and it has been said often and loosely—but a man can make his own mixture; Carroll's invective hardly shows which he is attacking. The praise of the child in the *Alices* mainly depends on a distaste not only for sexuality but for all the distortions of vision that go with a rich emotional life; the opposite idea needs to be set against this: that you can only understand people or even things by having such a life in yourself to be their mirror; but the idea itself is very respectable. So far as it is typical of the scientist, the books are an expression of the scientific attitude (e.g. the Bread-and-butter-fly) or a sort of satire on it that treats it as inevitable.

The most obvious aspect of the complacence is the snobbery. It is clear that Alice is not only a very well-brought-up but a very well-to-do little girl; if she has grown into Mabel, so that she will have to go and live in that poky little house and have next to no toys to play with, she will refuse to come out of her rabbit-hole at all. One is only surprised that she is allowed to meet Mabel. All through the books odd objects of luxury are viewed rather as Wordsworth viewed mountains: meaningless, but grand and irremovable; objects of myth. The whiting, the talking leg of mutton, the soup-tureen, the tea-tray in the sky, are obvious examples. The shift from the idea of the child's unity with nature is amusingly complete; a mere change in the objects viewed makes it at one with the conventions. But this is still not far from Wordsworth, who made his mountains into symbols of the stable and moral society living among them. In part, the joke of this stands for the sincerity of the child that criticizes the folly of convention, but Alice is very respectful to conventions and interested to learn new ones; indeed, the discussions about the rules of the game of conversation, those stern comments on the isolation of humanity, put the tone so strongly in favor of the conventions that one feels there is nothing else in the world. There is a strange clash on this topic about the three little sisters who lived on treacle, discussed at the Mad Tea-Party. "They couldn't have done that, you know," Alice gently remarked, "they'd have been ill." "So they were," said Dormouse, "*very* ill." The creatures are always self-centered and argumentative, to stand for the detachment of the intellect from emotion, which is necessary to it and yet makes it childish. Then the remark stands both for the danger of taking as one's guide the natural desires ("this is the sort of thing little girls would do if they were left alone") and for a pathetic example of a martyrdom to the conventions; the little girls did not mind *how* ill they were made by living on treacle, because it was their rule, and they knew it was expected of them. (That they are refined girls is clear from the fact that they do allegorical sketches.) There is an obscure connection here with the belief of the period that a really nice girl is "delicate" (the profound sentences implied by the combination of meanings in this word are [a] "you cannot get a woman to be refined unless you make her ill" and, more darkly, [b] "she is desirable because corpse-like"); Dodgson was always shocked to find that his little girls had appetites, because it made them seem less pure. The passage about the Bread-and-butter-fly brings this out more frankly, with something of the willful grimness of Webster. It was a creature of such high refinement that it could only live on weak tea with cream in it (tea being the caller's meal, sacred to the fair, with nothing gross about it).

A new difficulty came into Alice's head.

> "*Supposing it couldn't find any?*" *she suggested.*
> "*Then it would die, of course.*"
> "*But that must happen very often,*" *Alice remarked thoughtfully.*
> "*It always happens,*" *said the Gnat.*
> *After this, Alice was silent for a minute or two, pondering.*

There need be no gloating over the child's innocence here, as in Barrie; anybody might ponder. Alice has just suggested that flies burn themselves to death in candles out of a martyr's ambition to become Snapdragon-flies. The talk goes on to losing one's name, which is the next stage on her journey, and brings freedom but is like death; the girl may lose her personality by growing up into the life of convention, and her virginity (like her surname) by marriage; or she may lose her "good name" when she loses the conventions "in the woods"—the animals, etc., there have no names because they are out of reach of the controlling reason; or, when she develops sex, she must neither understand nor name her feelings. The Gnat is weeping and Alice is afraid of the wood but determined to go on. "It always dies of thirst" or "it always dies in the end, as do we all"; "the life of highest refinement is the most deathly, yet what else is one to aim at when life is so brief, and when there is so little in it of any value." A certain ghoulishness in the atmosphere of this, of which the tight-lacing may have been a product or partial cause,[2] comes out very strongly in Henry James; the decadents pounced on it for their own purposes but could not put more death wishes into it than these respectables had done already.

The blend of child-cult and snobbery that Alice shares with Oscar Wilde is indeed much more bouncing and cheerful; the theme here is that it is proper for the well-meaning and innocent girl to be worldly, because she, like the world, should know the value of her condition. "When we were girls we were brought up to know nothing, and very interesting it was"; "Mamma, whose ideas on education are remarkably strict, has brought me up to be extremely short-sighted; so do you mind my looking at you through my glasses?" This joke seems to have come in after the Restoration dramatists as innocence recovered its social value; there are touches in Farquhar and it is strong in the *Beggar's Opera*. Sheridan has full control of it for Mrs. Malaprop.

I don't think so much learning becomes a young woman. . . . But, Sir Anthony, I would send her, at nine years old, to a boarding school, in order to learn a little ingenuity and artifice. Then, sir, she should have a supercilious knowledge in accounts; and as she grew up, I would have her instructed in geometry, that she might learn something of the contagious countries; but, above all, Sir Anthony, she should be mistress of orthodoxy, that she might not mis-spell, and mispronounce words so shamefully as girls usually do; and likewise that she might reprehend the true meaning of what she is saying.

Dodgson has an imitation of this which may show, what many of his appreciators seem anxious to deny, that even *Wonderland* contains straight satire. The Mock Turtle was taught at school

Reeling and Writhing, of course, to begin with . . . and then the differ-

ent branches of Arithmetic—Ambition, Distraction, Uglification and Deri-
sion ... Mystery, ancient and modern, with Seaography; then Drawling
—the Drawling-master ... used to come once a week; he taught us
Drawling, Stretching, and Fainting in Coils.

Children are to enjoy the jokes as against education, grownups as
against a smart and too expensive education. Alice was not one of the
climbers taught like this, and firmly remarks elsewhere that manners
are not learned from lessons. But she willingly receives social advice like
"curtsey while you're thinking what to say, it saves time," and the doctrine that you must walk away from a queen if you really want to meet
her has more point when said of the greed of the climber than of the
unself-seeking curiosity of the small girl. Or it applies to both, and
allows the climber a sense of purity and simplicity; I think this was a
source of charm, whether Dodgson meant it or not. Alice's own social
assumptions are more subtle and all-pervading; she always seems to
raise the tone of the company she enters, and to find this all the easier
because the creatures are so rude to her. A central idea here is that the
perfect lady can gain all the advantages of contempt without soiling
herself by expressing or even feeling it.

> *This time there could be no mistake about it: it was neither more nor*
> *less than a pig, and she felt that it would be quite absurd for her to*
> *carry it any further.*
> *So she set the little creature down, and felt quite relieved to see it*
> *trot away quietly into the wood. "If it had grown up," she said to her-*
> *self, "it would have made a dreadfully ugly child; but it makes rather a*
> *handsome pig, I think." And she began thinking over other children she*
> *knew, who might do very well as pigs, and was just saying to herself,*
> *"if only one knew the right way to change them—" when she was a*
> *little startled by seeing the Cheshire Cat sitting on the bough of a tree*
> *a few yards off.*
> *The Cat only grinned when it saw Alice. It looked good-natured, she*
> *thought: still it had very long claws and a great many teeth, so she felt*
> *that it ought to be treated with respect.*

The effect of cuddling these mellow evasive phrases—"a good deal"
—"do very well as"—whose vagueness can convey so rich an irony and
so complete a detachment while making so firm a claim to show charming good will, is very close to that of Wilde's comedy. So is the hint of
a delicious slavishness behind the primness, and contrasting with the
irony, of the last phrase. (But then, Dodgson feels the Cat deserves

respect as the detached intelligence—he is enjoying the idea that Alice and other social figures have got to respect Dodgson.) I think there is a feeling that the aristocrat is essentially like the child because it is his business to make claims in advance of his immediate personal merits; the child is not strong yet, and the aristocrat only as part of a system; the best he can do, if actually asked for his credentials, since it would be indecent to produce his pedigree, is to display charm and hope it will appear unconscious, like the good young girl. Wilde's version of this leaves rather a bad taste in the mouth because it is slavish; it has something of the naïve snobbery of the high-class servant. Whistler meant this by the most crashing of his insults—"Oscar now stands forth unveiled as his own 'gentleman'"—when Wilde took shelter from a charge of plagiarism behind the claim that a gentleman does not attend to coarse abuse.

Slavish, for one thing, because they were always juggling between what they themselves thought wicked and what the society they addressed thought wicked, talking about sin when they meant scandal. The thrill of *Pen, Pencil and Poison* is in the covert comparison between Wilde himself and the poisoner, and Wilde certainly did not think his sexual habits as wicked as killing a friend to annoy an insurance company. By their very hints that they deserved notice as sinners they pretended to accept all the moral ideas of society, because they wanted to succeed in it, and yet society only took them seriously because they were connected with an intellectual movement which refused to accept some of those ideas. The Byronic theme of the man unable to accept the moral ideas of his society and yet torn by his feelings about them is real and permanent, but to base it on intellectual dishonesty is to short-circuit it, and leads to a claim that the life of highest refinement must be allowed a certain avid infantile petulance.

Alice is not a slave like this; she is almost too sure that she is good and right. The grownup is egged on to imitate her not as a privileged decadent but as a privileged eccentric, a Victorian figure that we must be sorry to lose. The eccentric, though kind and noble, would be alarming from the strength of his virtues if he were less funny; Dodgson saw to it that this underlying feeling about his monsters was brought out firmly by Tenniel, who had been trained on drawing very serious things like the British Lion weeping over Gordon, for *Punch*. Their massive and romantic nobility is, I think, an important element in the effect; Dodgson did not get it in his own drawings (nor, by the way, did he give all the young men eunuchoid legs) but no doubt he would have done so if he had been able. I should connect this weighty background with the tone of worldly goodness, of universal but not stupid charity, in Alice's remarks about the pig: "I shall do my best even for you; of course one will suffer, because you are not worth the efforts spent on you; but I have no temptation to be uncharitable to you because I am too far above you to need to put you in your place"—this is what her tone would develop into; a genuine readiness for self-sacrifice and a more genuine sense of power.

The qualities held in so subtle a suspension in Alice are shown in full blast in the two Queens. It is clear that this sort of moral superiority involves a painful isolation, similar to those involved in the intellectual way of life and the life of chastity, which are here associated with it. The reference to *Maud* (1855) brings this out. It was a shocking book; mockery was deserved; and its improper freedom was parodied by the flowers at the beginning of the *Looking-Glass*. A taint of fussiness hangs over this sort of essay, but the parodies were assumed to be obvious (children who aren't forced to learn Dr. Watts can't get the same thrill from parodies of him as the original children did) and even this parody is not as obvious as it was. There is no doubt that the flowers are much funnier if you compare them with their indestructible originals.

> . . . whenever a March-wind sighs
> He sets the jewel-print of your feet
> In violets blue as your eyes . . .

> . . . the pimpernel dozed on the lea;
> But the rose was awake all night for your sake,
> Knowing your promise to me;
> The lilies and roses were all awake . . .

> Queen rose of the rosebud garden of girls. . . .

> There has fallen a splendid tear
> From the passion-flower at the gate.
> She is coming, my dove, my dear;
> She is coming, my life, my fate;
> The red rose cries, "She is near, she is near;"
> And the white rose weeps, "She is late;"
> The larkspur listens, "I hear, I hear;"
> And the lily whispers, "I wait."

"It isn't manners for us to begin, you know," said the Rose, "and I really was wondering when you'd speak." . . .

"How is it you all talk so nicely?" Alice said, hoping to get it into a better temper by a compliment. . . .

"In most gardens," the Tiger-lily said, "they make the beds too soft, so that the flowers are always asleep."

This sounded a very good reason, and Alice was quite pleased to know it. "I never thought of that before!" she said.

"It's my opinion that you never think at all," the Rose said, in a rather severe tone.

"I never saw anybody that looked stupider," a Violet said, so suddenly, that Alice quite jumped; for it hadn't spoken before. . . .

"She's coming!" cried the Larkspur. "I hear her footstep, thump, thump, along the gravel-walk!"

Alice looked round eagerly and found that it was the Red Queen—

the concentrated essence, Dodgson was to explain, of all governesses. The Tiger-lily was originally a passionflower, but it was explained to Dodgson in time that the passion meant was not that of sexual desire (which he relates to ill-temper) but of Christ; a brilliant recovery was made after the shock of this, for Tiger-lily includes both the alarming fierceness of ideal passion (chaste till now) and the ill-temper of the life of virtue and self-sacrifice typified by the governess (chaste always). So that in effect he includes all the flowers Tennyson named. The willow-tree that said Bough-wough doesn't come in the poem, but it is a symbol of hopeless love anyway. The pink daisies turn white out of fear, as the white ones turn pink in the poem out of admiration. I don't know how far we ought to notice the remark about beds, which implies that they should be hard because even passion demands the virtues of asceticism (they are also the earthy beds of the grave); it fits in very well with the ideas at work, but does not seem a thing Dodgson would have said in clearer language.

But though he shied from the Christian association in the complex idea wanted from "Passion-Flower," the flowers make another one very firmly.

"But that's not your fault," the Rose added kindly. "You're beginning to fade, you know—and then one can't help one's petals getting a little untidy."

Alice didn't like this idea at all: so, to change the subject, she asked "Does she ever come out here?"

"I daresay you'll see her soon," said the Rose. "She's one of the thorny

kind."[3]

"*Where does she wear the thorns?*" *Alice asked with some curiosity.*
"*Why, all round her head, of course,*" *the Rose replied.* "*I was won-dering you hadn't got some too. I thought it was the regular rule.*"

Death is never far out of sight in the books. The Rose cannot help standing for desire, but its thorns here stand for the ill-temper not so much of passion as of chastity, that of the governess or that involved in ideal love. Then the thorns round the Queen's head, the "regular rule" for suffering humanity, not yet assumed by the child, stand for the Passion, the self-sacrifice of the most ideal and most generous love, which produces ugliness and ill-temper.

The joke of making romantic love ridiculous by applying it to undesired middle-aged women is less to be respected than the joke of the hopelessness of idealism. W. S. Gilbert uses it for the same timid facetiousness but more offensively. This perhaps specially nineteenth-century trick is played about all the women in the *Alices*—the Ugly Duchess who had the aphrodisiac in the soup (pepper, as Alice pointed out, produces "ill-temper") was the same person as the Queen in the first draft ("Queen of Hearts and Marchioness of Mock Turtles") so that the Queen's sentence of her is the suicide of disruptive passion. The Mock Turtle, who is half beef in the picture, with a cloven hoof, suffers from the calf-love of a turtledove; he went to a bad school and is excited about dancing. (He is also weeping for his lost childhood, which Dodgson sympathized with while blaming its exaggeration, and Alice thought very queer; this keeps it from being direct satire.) So love is also ridiculous in young men; it is felt that these two cover the whole field (Dodgson was about thirty at the time) so that, granted these points, the world is safe for chastity. The danger was from middle-aged women because young women could be treated as pure, like Alice. Nor indeed is this mere convention; Gilbert was relying on one of the more permanent jokes played by nature on civilization, that unless somewhat primitive methods are employed, the specific desires of refined women may appear too late. So far as the chaste man uses this fact, and the fact that men are hurt by permanent chastity less than women in order to insult women, no fuss that he may make about baby women will make him dignified. Dodgson keeps the theme fairly agreeable by con-necting it with the more general one of self-sacrifice—which may be useless or harmful, even when spontaneous or part of a reasonable convention, which then makes the sacrificer ridiculous and crippled, but which even then makes him deserve respect and may give him unexpected sources of power. The man playing at child-cult arrives at Sex War here (as usual since, but the comic Lear didn't), but not to the death or with all weapons.

The same ideas are behind the White Queen, the emotional as against the practical idealist. It seems clear that the *Apologia* (1864) is in sight when she believes the impossible for half an hour before breakfast, to keep in practice; I should interpret the two examples she gives as immortality and putting back the clock of history; also, Mass occurs before breakfast. All through the Wool and Water chapter (milk and water but not nourishing, and gritty to the teeth) she is Oxford, the life of learning rather than of dogmatic religion. Everyone recognizes the local shop, the sham fights, the rowing, the academic old Sheep, and the way it laughs scornfully when Alice doesn't know the technical slang of rowing; and there are some general reflections on education. The teacher willfully puts the egg a long way off, so that you have to walk after it yourself, and meanwhile it turns into something else; and when you have "paid for" the education, its effects, then first known, must be accepted as part of you whether they are good or bad. Oxford as dreamy may be half satire, half acceptance of Arnold's "adorable dreamer" purple patch (1865).

Once at least in each book a cry of loneliness goes up from Alice at the oddity beyond sympathy or communication of the world she has entered—whether that in which the child is shut by weakness, or the adult by the renunciations necessary both for the ideal and the worldly way of life (the strength of the snobbery is to imply that these are the same). It seems strangely terrible that the answers of the White Queen, on the second of these occasions, should be so unanswerable.

> *By this time it was getting light. "The crow must have flown away, I think," said Alice: "I'm so glad it's gone. I thought it was the night coming on."*

Even in the rhyme the crow may be fear of death. The rhymes, like those other main structural materials, chess and cards, are useful because, being fixed, trivial, odd, and stirring to the imagination, they affect one as conventions of the dream-world, and this sets the tone about conventions.

"I wish I could manage to be glad!" the Queen said. "Only I never can remember the rule. You must be very happy, living in this wood, and being glad whenever you like."

So another wood has turned out to be nature. This use of "that's a rule" is Sheridan's in *The Critic;* the pathos of its futility is that it is an attempt of reason to do the work of emotion and escape the dangers of the emotional approach to life. There may be a glance at the Oxford Movement and dogma. Perhaps chiefly a satire on the complacence of the fashion of slumming, the remark seems to spread out into the whole beauty and pathos of the ideas of pastoral; by its very universality her vague sympathy becomes an obscure self-indulgence.

"Only it is so very lonely here!" Alice said in a melancholy voice; and, at the thought of her loneliness, two large tears came rolling down her cheeks.

"Oh, don't go on like that," cried the poor Queen, wringing her hands in despair. "Consider what a great girl you are. Consider what a long way you've come to-day. Consider what o'clock it is. Consider anything, only don't cry!"

Alice could not help laughing at this, even in the midst of her tears. "Can you keep from crying by considering things?" she asked.

"That's the way it's done," the Queen said with great decision: "nobody can do two things at once, you know. Let's consider your age to begin with—how old are you?"

We are back at once to the crucial topic of age and the fear of death, and pass to the effectiveness of practice in helping one to believe the impossible; for example, that the aging Queen is so old that she would be dead. The helplessness of the intellect, which claims to rule so much, is granted under cover of the counterclaim that since it makes you impersonal, you can forget pain with it; we do not believe this about the Queen chiefly because she has not enough understanding of other people. The jerk of the return to age, and the assumption that this is a field for polite lying, make the work of the intellect only the game of conversation. Humpty Dumpty has the same embarrassing trick for arguing away a suggestion of loneliness. Indeed, about all the rationalism of Alice and her acquaintances there hangs a suggestion that there are, after all questions of pure thought, academic thought, whose altruism is recognized and paid for, though meant only for the upper classes to whom the conventions are in any case natural habit; like that suggestion that the scientist is sure to be a gentleman and has plenty of space, which is the fascination of Kew Gardens.

The Queen is a very inclusive figure. "Looking before and after" with the plaintive tone of universal altruism, she lives chiefly backwards, in history; the necessary darkness of growth, the mysteries of self-knowledge, the self-contradictions of the will, the antinomies of philosophy, the very Looking-Glass itself, impose this; nor is it mere weakness to attempt to resolve them only in the direct impulse of the child. Gathering the more dream-rushes, her love for man becomes the more universal, herself the more like a porcupine. Knitting with more and more needles, she tries to control life by a more and more complex intellectual apparatus—the "progress" of Herbert Spencer; any one shelf of the shop is empty, but there is always something very interesting—the "atmosphere" of the place is so interesting—which moves up as you look at it from shelf to shelf; there is jam only in the future and our traditional past, and the test made by Alice, who sent value through the ceiling as if it were quite used to it, shows that progress can never reach value, because its habitation and name is heaven. The Queen's scheme of social reform, which is to punish those who are not respectable before their crimes are committed, seems to be another of these jokes about progress:

"But if you hadn't *done them," the Queen said, "that would have been better still; better, and better, and better!" Her voice went higher with each "better," till it got quite to a squeak at last.*

There is a similar attack in the Walrus and the Carpenter, who are depressed by the spectacle of unimproved nature and engage in charitable work among oysters. The Carpenter is a Castle and the Walrus, who could eat so many more because he was crying behind his handkerchief, was a Bishop, in the scheme at the beginning of the book. But in saying so one must be struck by the depth at which the satire is hidden; the queerness of the incident and the characters takes on a Wordsworthian grandeur and aridity, and the landscape defined by the tricks of facetiousness takes on the remote and staring beauty of the ideas of the insane. It is odd to find that Tenniel went on to illustrate Poe in the same manner; Dodgson is often doing what Poe wanted to do, and can do it the more easily because he can safely introduce the absurd. The Idiot Boy of Wordsworth is too milky a moonlit creature to be at home with Nature as she was deplored by the Carpenter, and much of the technique of the rudeness of the Mad Hatter has been learned from Hamlet. It is the ground-bass of this kinship with insanity, I think, that makes it so clear that the books are not trifling, and the cool courage with which Alice accepts madmen that gives them their strength.

This talk about the snobbery of the *Alices* may seem a mere attack, but a little acid may help to remove the slime with which they have been encrusted. The two main ideas behind the snobbery, that virtue and intelligence are alike lonely, and that good manners are therefore important though an absurd confession of human limitations, do not depend on a local class system; they would be recognized in a degree by any tolerable society. And if in a degree their opposites must also be recognized, so they are here; there are solid enough statements of the shams of altruism and convention and their horrors when genuine; it is the forces of this conflict that make a clash violent enough to end both the dreams. In *Wonderland* this is mysteriously mixed up with the trial of the Knave of Hearts, the thief of love, but at the end of the second book the symbolism is franker and more simple. She is a grown Queen and has acquired the conventional dignities of her insane world; suddenly she admits their insanity, refuses to be a grown Queen, and destroys them.

"I can't stand this any longer!" she cried, as she seized the tablecloth in both hands: one good pull, and plates, dishes, guests, and candles came crashing down together in a heap on the floor.

The guests are inanimate and the crawling self-stultifying machinery of luxury has taken on a hideous life of its own. It is the High Table of Christ Church that we must think of here. The gentleman is not the slave of his conventions because at need he could destroy them; and yet, even if he did this, and all the more because he does not, he must adopt while despising it the attitude to them of the child.

VIII
Jungian
and
Mythic

From

a Letter to

Lewis Carroll on

"Jabberwocky"

by Dr. Robert Scott,
DEAN OF ROCHESTER
(1871)

ARE WE TO SUPPOSE, after all, that the Saga of Jabberwocky is one of the universal heirlooms which the Aryan race at its dispersion carried with it from the great cradle of the family? You really must consult Max Müller about this. It begins to be probable that the *origo originalissima* may be discovered in Sanskrit, and that we shall by and by have a *Iabrivokaveda*. The hero will turn out to be the Sun-God in one of his *Avatars*; and the Tumtum tree the great Ash *Yggdrasil* of the Scandinavian mythology.

ALICE

as Anima:

THE IMAGE OF WOMAN
IN CARROLL'S CLASSICS

by *Judith Bloomingdale*

(1971)

ALICE's *Adventures in Wonderland* and *Through the Looking-Glass* can best be described as the harrowing of the Victorian Hell. Alice herself is Carroll's Beatrice—the Muse of his Comedy. Her fall down the rabbit-hole is that of Eve—Adam's soul mate, or *anima*—and her ultimate coronation as Queen of the Looking-Glass World is an unconscious anticipation of the Assumption of Mary as Queen of Heaven, which became Catholic dogma in 1950.[1] As Mary completes with Her maternal nature the incompleteness of the Trinity and fulfills in this divine destiny the task given Her on earth, Alice in her own time is Victoria Regina, heiress of all the ages. (Indeed, Carroll liked to pretend that he had received letters from the Queen.)

Jung has defined the *anima* as the archetypal image of woman that compensates the masculine consciousness of every man. As he noted in *The Development of Personality,* "Every man carries within him the eternal image of woman, not the image of this or that particular woman, but a definite feminine image. This image is fundamentally unconscious, an hereditary factor of primordial origin engraved in the living organic system of the man, an imprint or 'archetype' of all the ancestral experiences of the female, a deposit, as it were, of all the impressions ever made by woman. . . . Since this image is unconscious, it is always unconsciously projected upon the person of the beloved, and is one of the chief reasons for passionate attraction or aversion."[2] The power of the *anima* is that of *eros,* or feeling.

Circumstances led Carroll to personify his inner image of woman in Alice, the heroine of his most famous books. She figures in the drama of Wonderland-Looking-Glass as a positive *anima* who moves from innocence to experience, unconsciousness to consciousness. As Jung has demonstrated, there are four stages in the normal development of the *anima:* "The first stage is best symbolized by the figure of Eve, which represents purely instinctual and biological relations. The second can be seen in Faust's Helen: She personifies a romantic and aesthetic level that is, however, still characterized by sexual elements. The third is represented, for instance, by the Virgin Mary—a figure who raises love (*eros*) to the heights of spiritual devotion. The fourth type is symbolized by Sapientia, wisdom transcending even the most holy and the most pure. Of this another symbol is the Shulamite in the Song of Solomon. (In the psychic development of modern man this stage is rarely reached. The Mona Lisa comes nearest to such a wisdom *anima.*)"[3] The place of Alice in this hierarchy is that of Beatrice, the child-woman who inspired Dante to begin his triumphant journey from Hell to Heaven.

To complicate matters, Alice is in turn possessed by the *animus,* the image of man that compensates the feminine consciousness. The *animus* corresponds to the *Logos,* or Word, and influences a woman's thinking.[4] Both powers are notably disturbed in their functioning in the worlds of Wonderland and the Looking-Glass. Alice, who is significantly at the age of reason, suffers memory losses and tries vainly to make "sense" of nonsense—*logic* is the key theme of the book. All the characters except

Alice are "touchy, irritable, moody, jealous, vain and unadjusted"⁵—characteristics of the man possessed by the *anima*, who "intensifies, exaggerates, falsifies and mythologizes all emotional relations with his work and with other people of both sexes."⁶ This is certainly the case with the characters in *Wonderland* and *Looking-Glass*.

By way of contrast, and as Jung states in "The Relations Between the Ego and the Unconscious," a woman's *animus* does not appear as one person, but as a plurality of persons, ". . . a supreme moral authority that tells her with remorseless precision and dry matter-of-factness what she is doing and for what motives. . . . [It is] a 'Court of Conscience' . . . [a] collection of condemnatory judges, a sort of College of Preceptors . . . rather like an assembly of fathers or dignitaries of some kind who lay down incontestable, 'rational,' *ex cathedra* judgments . . . [that] take the form of so-called sound common sense, [or] appear as principles that are like a travesty of education: 'People have always done it like this,' or, 'Everybody says it is like that.'"⁷ What better description of the trial scene in *Wonderland* is there than this!

And what better description of the Victorian system of education? The endless moralizing endemic to that exclusively patriarchal order typifies Alice's every encounter with the figures in Wonderland and the Looking-Glass World. This is surely the way Victorian society must have appeared to a little (Liddell) girl intent on making sense of a pre-eminently "sensible" world whose denial of social equality to women typically sentimentalized its feminine unconscious either as angel or whore. It is precisely this sentimentality that Carroll attacks by way of his art. The little sisters who live at the bottom of the treacle well are obviously in danger of drowning in sugar, spice, and everything nice before Carroll comes to their rescue.

It is the heroine Alice who enables Carroll to perform his own heroic artistic task. By serving as the Beatrice of his journey, she becomes the *mediatrix* to his psychic universe. As Jung has stated: "The natural function of the *animus* (as well as of the *anima*) is to . . . function as a bridge, or a door, leading to the images of the collective unconscious."⁸

The genesis of *Alice* is to be found in the facts of Charles Dodgson's personal history.⁹ Born the eldest of eleven children to an "angel" mother and a rector father, Carroll's unique place in his mother's graces was usurped after only one and one-half years by another baby, a girl

(Caroline), then another, then finally another boy, to whom years later Carroll wrote from away, "Roar not, lest thou be abolished." His own roar, which had been so long suppressed, came out in volcanic force in the *Alice* books.

The figure of the mother with nursing baby, the Madonna, can be seen in grotesque form in the "Pig and Pepper" chapter of *Wonderland*, when the hideous Duchess shouts a violent lullaby—"Speak roughly to your little boy"—which Carroll's mother never did; she merely "kissed away" all his justifiable anger at being so soon deprived of her attentions. Carroll's lifelong preoccupation with cats and kittens (or "kitts," identified with kisses)[10] reveals a fixation on the feminine, an equation of maternal love with the kind of care bestowed upon her kittens by Dinah, Alice's totem animal. In a telltale phrase, Carroll once spoke of "nursing the cat." But the soft, furry, sweet cat has claws. As Tennyson said, nature is "red in tooth and claw." It is this aspect of "Mother Nature" that predominates in *Wonderland*. The undisputed Queen (of Hearts!) of this kingdom is a Shiva, a tyrant whose fiat is "Off with his head!" In a matriarchal household ruled by velvet paws, the male mouse is in continual danger of emasculation—the *Wonderland* Mouse's attenuated tale ends in "death." Carroll's fight for identity in the nursery and later in the rectory garden was a Darwinian struggle for survival. The typical flower in the Looking-Glass-World garden is no wallflower, but a veritable virago—true Tiger-lily. Carroll's ego, a Humpty Dumpty (egg), was in perpetual peril of falling, never to be put together again. Indeed, Humpty Dumpty is the archetypal image of Platonic man—seen as the union of white and yolk, *yang* and *yin,* enclosed within a thin shell of brittle skin. His defensive hypersensitivity to a little girl's curiosity is a reflection of the touchiness of a boy too long exposed to feminine eyes. It is the anguished cry of a little boy forced to spend the first years of his life in the almost exclusive company of sisters (of which Carroll ultimately had seven).

Paralleling the precarious development of masculine identity was Carroll's apparent image of woman as victim, a kind of Christian martyr whose duty was in Pauline terms to present her body as a living sacrifice to God. His lifelong obsession with victims of epileptic fits, his eagerness to learn all he could so as to be of help to the sufferer, point to intense curiosity concerning the "fit" of a woman in labor. In the trial scene of *Wonderland,* the King inquires of the Queen, "—you never had fits, my dear, I think?" The regular repetition of the birth drama (trauma) in the isolated rural rectory led to an irreconcilable split in Dodgson. The disparity between the relentlessly inculcated Christianity of self-sacrificing love and the real screams of his mother in labor set up in the young boy a rebellion against the flesh that left his psychic development arrested at the prepubertal level.

Ultimately, then, Charles Dodgson refused to assume the one-sided, aggressive sexual role nature had prescribed, and identified instead with the feminine to the extent of repudiating his given (Christian) name for that of Lewis Carroll (Louisa Caroline), after two of his sisters. This refusal was precipitated by the trauma of transition from a matriarchal household to the rough milieu of Rugby—which accounts also for his lifelong distrust of little boys. A study of Carroll's handwriting at twelve, the age at which he left the sheltered rectory garden (later to figure in the *Alice* books as the goal of Alice's quest, the paradise of childhood), and that at twenty, shows a change from a precociously mature extroverted adjustment to a decidedly introverted one.[11] This reversal was largely brought about by his mother's death at the time of his entrance into Oxford.

So died the "very rebellious nature"[12] one expert had noticed in Dodgson's adolescent hand. It is as though he had made an heroic adjustment to the given home situation, where he achieved identity only at the cost of his own real needs as a growing, curious, intelligent boy. The boy whose constant refrain was "Please explain" yielded to the gentle but insistent demands of his mother that he be brave, courteous, obedient, with all the other Boy Scout virtues, only to be thrust rudely from this rural Eden into the Hell of Rugby. And we all know that Hell is not too strong a word for the realities of the English public school. Dodgson, labeled a "muff" by one of his peers, survived in this crude games-oriented environment only by retreating to the safe, respected role of scholar, behind which *persona* he hid for the rest of his life. Charles Dodgson at twenty, the time of his mother's death, was a victim of psychic exhaustion. And with her died his last hope of achieving a love so long denied him. At the beginning of his academic, worldly career his life as a man was effectively ended. Ten years later he wrote a poem that spoke of a woman with "false, false lips,"[13] evidently his mother.

In Jungian terms, the man who is a victim of a mother complex sees her as the "enveloping, embracing and devouring element. . . . His *eros* is passive, like a child's; he hopes to be caught, sucked in, enveloped and devoured. He seeks, as it were, the protecting, nourishing, charmed circle of the mother, the condition of the infant released from every care, in which the outside world bends over him and even forces happiness upon him."[14]

As Jung has also stated, the man possessed by the *anima* sees all of life as a game or puzzle.[15] This perception seems to be the missing link between the two personalities of Charles Dodgson and Lewis Carroll. The pedantic mathematician, poor lecturer to boys at Oxford, is at the same time the fascinating teller of enchanted tales to little girls. And of course the chief activities in Wonderland and the Looking-Glass world are the games of croquet and chess, with riddles and word-play abounding.

It is a mystery how Alice Liddell came to be Carroll's Muse, whose "pure, unclouded brow and dreaming eyes of wonder" inspired him to write his only happy "love poems," the prefatory ones to both books. In her he somehow recovered an image, long lost, of the ideal girl-woman— first incarnated in his mother, a very young woman at the time of his birth. As Phyllis Greenacre has noted, it is a common situation for the subject of an unresolved Oedipal fixation to be attracted to a woman as many years his junior as his mother was his senior. When Dodgson met Alice, she was not quite four years old. But he marked the day in his diary with "a white stone." For him this symbol seems to have had a numinous significance. Whiteness is the color of purity and innocence; it is the perfect color, containing all others. The stone seems to have for Carroll a mystic connotation similar to that of the Rock in Judeo-Christian tradition—the Rock of Moses that became Christ, the stone that the builders rejected but that became the cornerstone of the Church. In short, it is the philosopher's stone of the alchemists, symbol of the Self.[16] In choosing the dreamchild Alice as his heroine, Carroll made of her journey through Wonderland—the psychic underground—and the Looking-Glass World—or Purgatory—a Pilgrim's Progress from this world to a hoped-for better.

Carroll's choice of a girl child, a heroine rather than a hero, is also significant in that it affirms the androgynous nature of the presexual self. As Jung states in *The Psychology of the Child Archetype*, "The child paves the way for a future change of personality. In the individuation process, it anticipates the figure that comes from the synthesis of conscious and unconscious elements in the personality. It is therefore a symbol which unites the opposites; a mediator, bringer of healing, . . . one who makes whole . . . it can be expressed by roundness, the circle or sphere, or else by the quaternity as another form of wholeness. I have called this wholeness that transcends consciousness the 'Self.' The goal of the individuation process is the self."[17]

Alice as child-heroine undergoes the experiences ascribed by Jung to the mythical child—i.e. abandonment, invincibility, and hermaphroditism.[18] The child is all that is abandoned and exposed and at the same time divinely powerful; the insignificant, dubious beginning, and the triumphal end.[19]

The King and Queen of Hearts serve as the divine syzygy of the mythological drama—the parents of the "royal" child. The King has been rendered effectively impotent by the wrath of the Queen—the wrath that Carroll's real queen-mother never expressed, but that he obviously felt she should have. The crime in Wonderland that must be paid for is that of the Knave of Hearts, who stole the tarts, suffered the punishment of beating "full sore," and "vowed he'd steal no more." In Freudian terms the crime of incest is punished by impotence or abdication of all ambition to become king. The Knave remains content to be merely a bumbling White Knight, a Don Quixote forever tilting futilely at windmills. The world of Wonderland is a great courtroom where the guilty individual, the child, is arraigned before a mad audience on whose ears the word of reason falls without effect. But the sentence declared by the diabolical Queen—"Off with her head!"—fails of execution because Alice at last rebels. "'Who cares for *you*?' said Alice (she had grown to her full size by this time). 'You're nothing but a pack of cards!'" Like the child who dared perceive that the Emperor wore no clothes, Alice in her innocent indignation speaks not only for herself and for the "Knave," but for all children who are threatened by adults with unjust punishments. And to a child, injustice is the one unpardonable sin. One thinks of Dickens' orphan heroes, punished not for their own crimes but for the crimes of the society that made them its victims and even scapegoats.

As a real girl-child, Alice has only the stereotyped future prescribed for her by Victorian mores: if fortunate, a good marriage and motherhood; if unfortunate, spinsterhood. But as dreamchild, she can even in maturity move "through a land/Of wonders wild and new," the Wonderland of Carroll's imagination.

Most of all, Carroll bids Alice,

> *Come, harken then, ere voice of dread,*
>   *With bitter tidings laden,*
> *Shall summon to unwelcome bed*
>   *A melancholy maiden!*

The voice is that of the Bridegroom, Death, with the emphasis not, I submit, on the latter, but on the former. For Carroll the "unwelcome bed" was the marriage bed, which had become for his mother the grave —she had died in middle age, the perfect wife and mother. Since it was the Bridegroom Death that ultimately robbed Charles Dodgson of all hope for full maternal love, he vowed in his celibacy never to commit against "a melancholy maiden" the "crime" of all bridegrooms save Christ. Viewed in this light, the *Alice* books are a "love gift of a fairy-tale" to his mother as she might have been—the Eternal Virgin, Child-Woman, Alice the Queen:

> *Still she haunts me, phantomwise,*
>   *Alice moving under skies*
> *Never seen by waking eyes. . . ."*

For Carroll the golden key of innocent love opened the door that led to "the beautiful garden, [with] the bright flower-beds and the cool fountains." He could enter only with Alice, his "Lady Soul,"[20] the earthly paradise of imagination where childhood's "golden afternoons" are eternal.

II

The central riddle of *Wonderland* that must be solved is that which Alice asks the Duchess concerning the Cheshire Cat: "Please would you tell me . . . why your cat grins like that?" As the cat is traditionally feminine (as the dog is masculine), the Cheshire Cat's presence in the central, far-from-silent tableau of *Wonderland*, the emotionally (pepper) charged kitchen of the Duchess's house, is that of the Eternal Feminine. The mad grin of the appearing and disappearing gargoyle, which literally "hangs over" the heads of the participants in the game of life, is an insane version of the enigmatic smile of the "Mona Lisa," the mask of the Sphinx—supreme embodiment of the riddle of the universe.

The Duchess here plays the role of the Great Mother, the "loving and terrible mother" . . . the paradoxical Kali of Indian religion,[21] a role she shares with the Queen of Hearts of the Trial scene. That the Duchess flings her abused baby to Alice: "Here! You may nurse it a bit, if you like!" is a foreshadowing of the role Alice is later to assume in the Looking-Glass world.

The heroic task that Alice as child-heroine must perform in *Wonderland* is to assert in the face of a primitive, threatening universe the reasonableness of her own (and the Knave of Hearts') right to exist, and actively to rebel against the social order that sentences to death ("Off with her head!") all those who demur from its mad decrees. Both of these are summed up in the climax of the drama, the Trial scene in which the vicious Queen overrules her mild consort's reasonable order:

> *"Let the jury consider their verdict," the King said. . . .*
> *"No! No!" said the Queen. "Sentence first—verdict afterwards."*
> *"Stuff and nonsense!" said Alice loudly. "The idea of having the sentence first!"*
> *"Hold your tongue!" said the Queen, turning purple.*
> *"I won't!" said Alice.*
> *"Off with her head!" the Queen shouted at the top of her voice. Nobody moved.*
> *"Who cares for you?" said Alice (she had grown to her full size by this time). "You're nothing but a pack of cards!"*

And Alice wakes up from her dream-turned-nightmare—but the riddle of the Cheshire Cat remains unanswered.

In the Looking-Glass world that Alice next enters, she finds herself on a higher plane of existence than the Hell of Wonderland. As the heroine who dared challenge the tyranny of the Queen of that kingdom, she finds that she is to be made a queen herself if she can successfully complete her moves as White Pawn in the "great huge game of chess that's being played—all over the world—if this *is* the world at all, you know." She also admits to a secret desire—"I wouldn't mind being a Pawn, if only I might join—though of course I should *like* to be a Queen, best." The Red and White Queens of this kingdom are notably more agreeable than the Queen of Hearts and aid Alice in her journey. What has made this transformation possible?

The missing link between *Wonderland* and *Looking-Glass* and the real climax of their drama is the mythological event revealed in the "nonsense" of the famous "Jabberwocky" poem. The child-hero of this drama is, significantly, a boy—a miniature St. George: and like the traditional Christian hero, the deed he performs is that of rescuing a damsel in distress—i.e., the princess, or *anima*, about to be devoured by the dragon, which here symbolizes the evil attributes of the mother archetype.[22] Here the threat of the terrible Queen of Wonderland is turned against herself in the apotheosized form of the Jabberwock:

> *One, two! One, two! And through and through*
> *The vorpal blade went snicker-snack.*
> *He left it dead, and with its head*
> *He went galumphing back.*

The awe-ful deed is done. The son-hero is received with joy by his father and the goal of atonement (at-one-ment) with the masculine principle is achieved.

At once Alice finds herself in the garden she has long sought to enter. The garden is here a positive mother symbol,[23] no longer wild nature, but cultivated, tended, fostered—in short, the Garden of Live Flowers. (In the garden-croquet-ground of the Queen of Hearts, the white roses were being painted red, the color of blood.) The asperity of the beautiful flowers, however, reveals that the negative aspects of the feminine have by no means been dispelled.

The Red Queen, the governess-like mentor of Alice's *Looking-Glass* journey, is an extension of the positive character of the Duchess of *Wonderland*, the most promising of whose "morals" was, "Oh, 'tis love, 'tis love, that makes the world go round!" When Alice tenders her secret wish to be Queen, the Red Queen only smiles pleasantly and says, "That's easily managed. You can be the White Queen's Pawn. . . . When you get to the Eighth Square you'll be a Queen . . . we shall be Queens together, and it's all feasting and fun!"

The White Queen is as helpless and vague as the Red Queen is helpful and precise; Alice must assume the role of "lady's maid" in an attempt to bring order to the former's disheveled person. The two queens together form the polarity of experience and naïveté that is finally symbolically resolved when the two queens lie down to sleep like children with their heads in Queen Alice's lap.

In the last important move before her coronation, Alice is rescued from a Red Knight "brandishing a great club," by a White Knight—the apotheosis of the positive *animus*, the Jabberwock-slayer grown up, the "knight in shining armor" of chivalry and romance. Like Chaucer's "verray, parfit, gentil knight," he is the type of Christian hero whose function is to serve his Lady. Though it is his avowed function to conduct Alice safely to the end of the wood, it is in fact she who helps him by waving her handkerchief in encouragement as he rides out of sight. It is not so much the actual help tendered her by her rescuer that Alice remembers, but the vividness of his presence, "the mild blue eyes and kindly smile of the Knight—the setting sun gleaming through his hair, and shining on his armour in a blaze of light that quite dazzled her—" This is the mystical moment for Alice. Not her own coronation, but that of the true King of the Looking-Glass World. Not a mighty world conquerer, but the gentle man, the pure and innocent hero, the risen Christ radiant with scars—Christ as Clown. With his armor on, and as drawn by Tenniel, the White Knight is the crucified human figure with the head of an ass that Harvey Cox in his *The Feast of Fools*[24] cites as one of the earliest representations of Christ: "Because the foolishness of God is wiser than men; and the weakness of God is stronger than men" (Paul, I Corinthians). The White Knight is the advent of Christ the harlequin into the consciousness of an age that has forgotten how to laugh. Most of all, the very awkwardness of his comic falls constitute a clown—like choreography that is a mock parallel to the dance of David before the ark of the Lord—the joyful dance of the *Logos*,[25] Christ "the incarnation of festivity and fantasy."[26] As has been noted by a contemporary theologian, Hugo Rahner, the Hebrew word in the Book of Proverbs that describes the activity of the *Logos* can better be described as "dance."[27] Or as song. " 'You are sad,' " the Knight said in an anxious tone: 'Let me sing you a song to comfort you.' " The song he sings is sung to the tune, "I give thee all, I can no more." Christ the suffering servant.

As absurd hero of his age, the White Knight sums up the history of Western civilization: he is at once Christ, St. George, the Knight of the Grail, Lancelot, Don Quixote, and finally modern man, none of whose ingenious "inventions" have really "worked"—in the sense that they have not brought him happiness. It is the paradox of her protector's power and powerlessness that evokes in Alice the "little scream of laughter" that marks the joyous epiphany of the book. She *sees* in her Knight's "gentle foolish face," in his "mild blue eyes and kindly smile," the face of the Lord of Life.

The coronation of Queen Alice that follows is the true Feast of Fools. Far from being a dignified affair, it is a boisterous banquet where the "feasting and fun" promised by the Red Queen turn into an hilarious apocalypse in which Alice is literally elevated (the bodily Assumption of Mary):

the two Queens pushed her so, one on each side, that they nearly lifted her up into the air. "I rise to return thanks—" Alice began: and she really did *rise as she spoke, several inches; but she got hold of the edge of the table, and managed to pull herself down again—*

It is the mock crowning and elevation of Alice to the position of Queen of the Looking-Glass World that also parallels the passion of Christ the clown. As He was deserted, denied, taunted in His royal robes, crowned with thorns and humiliated, made to drink the bitter vinegar of man's scorn and lifted up on the cross as "King of the Jews," so is she deserted by her sleeping companions, mocked by the powerful, crowned with a very heavy, tight golden crown, made to drink "sand [mixed] with cider," "wool [mixed] with the wine"; starved at her own triumphal banquet—the mock queen of a mad world.

So at the end of her journey, Alice/Beatrice hears with Carroll/Dante "the laughter of the universe" (*"un riso dell universo"*). The Human Comedy is potentially Divine. The Hell of Wonderland, "where there is no hope and no laughter," the purgatory of Looking-Glass World, "where there is no laughter, but there is hope," has given way to the Paradise ushered in by the White Knight, "when hope is no longer necessary and laughter reigns."[28]

And what has really made Alice Queen of the Looking-Glass World? Throughout her journey she has exhibited (to enumerate the qualities Carroll attributes to her) curiosity, courage, kindness, intelligence, courtesy, dignity, a sense of humor, humility, sympathy, propriety, respect, imagination, wonder, initiative, gratitude, patience, affection, thoughtfulness, integrity, and a sense of justice in the face of an outrageous universe. It is notable that Alice assumes increasingly maternal characteristics in her journey. She is entrusted with the care of the baby the Duchess has rejected in Wonderland, listens with sympathy to the tales of all the characters, intercedes on behalf of the Knave of Hearts, clasps "her arms . . . lovingly round the soft neck of the Fawn," serves as peacemaker in the sibling rivalry between Tweedledum and Tweedledee, "a-dresses" the White Queen (i.e., serves as lady's maid), passes round the cake at the fight of the lion and unicorn, encourages the White Knight, and is finally requested to sing a "soothing" lullaby to the Red and White Queens, who fall asleep in her lap like children (babies?).

Finally, then, it is her capacity for compassion that distinguishes Alice the Queen. The true ending of the dreams of Wonderland and Looking-Glass is the wish of Alice's older sister for her little sister that serves as the coda for *Wonderland*:

Lastly, she pictured to herself how this same little sister of hers would, in the after-time, be herself a grown woman; and how she would keep, through all her riper years, the simple and loving heart of her childhood; and how she would gather about her other little children, and make their eyes bright and eager with many a strange tale, perhaps even with the dream of Wonderland of long ago; and how she would feel with all their simple sorrows, and find a pleasure in all their simple joys, remembering her own child-life, and the happy summer days.

Love is the golden crown that makes Alice the true Queen of Hearts.

ALICE'S
Journey to the End
of Night
by Donald Rackin
(1966)

IN THE CENTURY now passed since the publication of *Alice's Adventures in Wonderland,* scores of critical studies have attempted to account for the fascination the book holds for adult readers. Although some of these investigations offer provocative insights, most of them treat Carroll in specialized modes inaccessible to the majority of readers, and they fail to view *Alice* as a complete and organic work of art. Hardly a single important critique has been written of *Alice* as a self-contained fiction, distinct from *Through the Looking-Glass* and all other imaginative pieces by Carroll. Critics also tend to confuse Charles Dodgson the man with Lewis Carroll the author; this leads to distorted readings of *Alice* that depend too heavily on the fact, say, that Dodgson was an Oxford don, or a mathematician, or a highly eccentric Victorian gentleman with curious pathological tendencies. The results are often analyses which fail to explain the total work's undeniable impact on the modern lay reader unschooled in Victorian political and social history, theoretical mathematics, symbolic logic, or Freudian psychology. It seems time, then, that *Alice* be treated for what it most certainly is—a book of major and permanent importance in the tradition of English fiction, a work that still pertains directly to the experience of the unspecialized reader, and one that exemplifies the profound questioning of reality which characterizes the mainstream of nineteenth-century English literature.

The fact that Carroll's first version of *Alice's Adventures in Wonderland* was called *Alice's Adventures under Ground* is surprisingly prophetic. Perhaps even the final version would be more appropriately entitled *Alice's Adventures under Ground,* since, above all else, it embodies a comic horror-vision of the chaotic land beneath the manmade groundwork of Western thought and convention.

Alice's dogged quest for Wonderland's meaning in terms of her aboveground world of secure conventions and self-assured regulations is doomed to failure. Her only escape is in flight from Wonderland's complete anarchy—a desperate leap back to the aboveground certainties of social formalities and ordinary logic. Her literal quest serves, vicariously, as the reader's metaphorical search for meaning in the lawless, haphazard universe of his deepest consciousness. Thus, the almost unanimous agreement among modern critics that *Alice* is a dream-vision turns out to be far more than a matter of technical classification. If it were merely that, one might dismiss the work (and some critics have) as simply a whimsical excursion into an amusing, childlike world that has little relevance to the central concerns of adult life and little importance in comparison to the obviously "serious" works that explore these concerns. But if "dream-vision" is understood as serious thinkers (ranging from medieval poets to modern psychologists) have so often understood it, as an avenue to knowledge that is perhaps more meaningful—and frequently more horrifying—than any that the unaided conscious intellect can discover, then it provides an almost perfect description of the very substance of Carroll's masterpiece.

Merely to list the reverses Alice encounters in Wonderland is to survey at a glance an almost total destruction of the fabric of our so-called logical, orderly, and coherent approach to the world. Practically all pattern, save the consistency of chaos, is annihilated. First, there are the usual modes of thought—ordinary mathematics and logic: in Wonderland they possess absolutely no meaning. Next are the even more basic social and linguistic conventions: these too lose all validity. Finally, the fundamental framework of conscious predication—orderly time and space—appears nowhere except in the confused memory of the befuddled but obstinate visitor from aboveground. Alice, therefore, becomes the reader's surrogate on a frightful journey into meaningless night. The only difference between Alice and the reader—and this is significant—is that she soberly, tenaciously, childishly refuses to accept chaos completely for what it is, while the adult reader almost invariably responds with the only defense left open to him in the face of unquestionable chaos—he laughs. Naturally he laughs for other reasons, too. But the essence of Alice's adventures beneath commonly accepted ground is the grimmest comedy conceivable, the comedy of man's absurd condition in an apparently meaningless world.

If *Alice's Adventures in Wonderland*, then, is best viewed as a grimly comic trip through the lawless underground that lies just beneath the surface of our constructed universe, what gives the work its indisputable relevance to that universe, what keeps *Alice* itself from becoming formless, inconsistent, and confusing? The answer to this question is at once an explanation of *Alice's* literary nature and a tentative glimpse at a fundamental problem of modern man.

Let us begin at the beginning. Alice enters upon her journey underground simply because she is *curious*: she follows the White Rabbit down the rabbit-hole, "never once considering how in the world she was to get out again"[1] With the fearlessness of the innocent child, the intellectual and spiritual recklessness of a heedless scientist or saint, Alice takes her gigantic and seemingly irreversible leap into the world beneath and beyond ordinary human experience.

Significantly, Alice brings along with her a number of things from that old world aboveground, the most important being her belief in the simple orderliness of the universe. For example, in the midst of her long fall she retains her old belief in regular causal relations and puts the empty marmalade jar back into a cupboard in order to avoid "killing somebody underneath," whatever "killing" may mean to her. She wonders, as she falls and falls, about many things—all in terms of the world she has left behind, as if she had not really left it at all. She wonders what latitude or longitude she has arrived at, even though "latitude" and "longitude" are meaningless words to her and meaningless measurements under the ground. She wonders whether she will come out on the other side of the earth, where people called "The Antipathies" walk with their heads downwards (a prophetic pun, for the majority of the "people" she will meet will be truly "Antipathies" to Alice).

Already a pattern is discernible: Alice's assumptions are typically no more than her elders' operating premises, which she maintains with a doctrinaire passion that is almost a caricature of immature credulity. For her, these premises are empty words, yet her faith in their validity is almost boundless. Carroll thus economically establishes one important facet of his protagonist before her adventures and her quest for meaning begin in earnest: she has reached that stage of development where the world appears completely explainable and unambiguous, that most narrow-minded, prejudiced period of life where, paradoxically, daring curiosity is wedded to uncompromising literalness and priggish, ignorant faith in the fundamental sanity of all things. With a few deft strokes, Carroll has prepared us for Alice's first major confrontation with chaos. She is ready to cope with the "impossible" in terms of the "possible," and we are ready to understand and laugh at her literal-minded reactions.

To all of us the concept of constant or predictable size is fairly important; to a child of seven or eight it is often a matter of physical and mental survival. However, since Alice wants to pass through the tiny door into the "loveliest garden you ever saw," she herself wishes the destruction of the principle of constant size: she wishes she could find the way to shut up like a telescope. Fortunately, "so many out-of-the-way things had happened lately" that she has "begun to think that very few things indeed [are] really impossible." Here Alice's mind is operating along logical lines established before her arrival in the confusing underground. She deals with the impossible as if it had to conform to the regular causal operations of her old world aboveground. But the adult reader knows better: in addition to recognizing the fallacies of Alice's reasoning in terms of traditional aboveground logic, the reader also realizes that in an underground world where "impossibility" is, as it were, the rule, Alice has no right to assume that the old logic itself still applies. The fact that Alice's illogical reasoning holds true in this case merely indicates that if Wonderland operates on any firm principle, that principle most certainly runs counter to the normal logic of the everyday world.

In any event, Alice is comparatively successful this time—her apparent logic seems to hold true. No doubt her first limited successes and her ability more or less to control events at the beginning serve to make her later setbacks all the more perplexing. Besides, although her ability to change her size at will is at first pleasurable (as it well might be to children, who often equate size with power), it soon becomes a mixed blessing. Although she "had got so much into the way of expecting nothing but out-of-the-way things to happen, that it seemed quite dull and stupid for life to go on in the common way," rapid, almost haphazard changes from ten inches to nine feet are usually accompanied by downright dangerous circumstances like deep pools of tears and frightfully cramped quarters. Nevertheless, even here Wonderland still bears some relationship to aboveground causality: growing big or small still seems to have predictable effects. Amidst all the comedy, however, the ominous destructive process has begun: two reasonably constant aspects of ordinary existence—natural growth and predictable size— have already lost their validity. Whether or not Alice recognizes it, a wedge has been driven into her old structure of meaning.

It is only natural that in such circumstances of confusion, a child would try to relate himself to the secure stability of the past. Alice soon says,

> *Dear, dear! How queer everything is today! And yesterday things went on just as usual . . . if I'm not the same, the next question is, "Who in the world am I?" Ah, that's the great puzzle!*

This fallacious and ironically comic "in-the-world" approach bears watching. Earlier Alice followed the Rabbit, "never once considering how in the world she was to get out again." Alice typically persists in fruitless attempts to relate her truly "out-of-the-world" adventures to her previous "in-the-world" assumptions. Perhaps sensing that her aboveground identity rested on arbitrary, constructed systems like arithmetic, she attempts to re-establish it by reciting her rote-learned lessons:

> *Let me see: four times five is twelve, and four times six is thirteen, and four times seven is—oh dear! I shall never get to twenty at that rate!*

But Alice is in Wonderland, where old assumptions—that rabbits cannot talk, that longitude and latitude can always plot position, that size and growth must be fairly regular—have already proven ridiculously invalid. Of course, her arithmetic (as some specialists have pointed out) still makes sense,[2] but only to a relatively sophisticated mind; and even then the sense it makes only serves to strengthen a vision of the arbitrary nature of common aboveground approaches to meaning. Alice herself has an intuition of this truth when she asserts, "However, the Multiplication Table doesn't signify: let's try Geography." But even before she begins her confused geography recitation ("London is the capital of Paris," and so on), the reader suspects that she is again headed for failure, since the ordinary concept of space, too, is already on its way to oblivion.

Directly after these amusing arithmetical and geographical set-backs, Alice attempts to establish her previous identity by reciting Watts's moral verses about the busy bee and Satan's mischief for idle hands. Once again it is all wrong. Even her voice sounds "hoarse and strange," as if taking some uncontrollable, demonic delight in the parody ("How doth the little crocodile"). In this one short comic poem, another aboveground principle is subverted. For regardless of the patent sentimentality of verses like "How doth the little busy bee / Improve each shining hour," they are for many a child the only morality he yet knows (indeed, the very triteness of such verses reflects a truth about the seemingly more sincere moral aphorisms of adults). Alice's comic recitation also subverts the sentimental convention that animals are innately moral,[3] and this subversion ties in neatly with Alice's later encounters with the animals of Wonderland: for the most part they will not be like Watts's busy little bee; they will be more like Alice's nasty crocodile. Hence, moral precepts, like orderly growth, are meaningless or cruelly twisted in Wonderland. And with so many familiar, comforting concepts already lost, Alice naturally begins to sense her isolation. She wishes that those she left aboveground would call her back because she is "so *very* tired of being all alone here!"

A number of psychoanalytic interpretations of *Alice* stress the importance of this motif of self-identity.[4] Psychoanalytic techniques, however, seem rather superfluous in this case: most adult readers easily recognize that this most crucial aboveground convention—the nearly universal belief in permanent self-identity—is put to the test and eventually demolished in Wonderland. Alice is constantly perplexed with the same question: "Who am I?" When, in the fourth chapter, the White Rabbit orders her about like his servant Mary Ann, Alice (attempting, as usual, to relate her adventures to some orderly pattern applicable to aboveground experience) accepts the new role and imagines how the new identity will follow her back to her old world, where her cat Dinah will order her about in the same fashion. In addition, her continuing changes in size represent a variation of the self-identity theme, since to a child differences in size represent definite changes in actual identity. Alice's tortured "What *will* become of me?" in reaction to her apparently uncontrolled growth and her fearful acceptance of the role as servant to a rabbit are, then, more than the amusing responses of a little girl to general confusion. They are her reactions to the destruction of three basic aboveground assumptions —orderly growth, the hierarchy of animals and men, and consistent identity.

Not only is Alice's previous identity meaningless in Wonderland; the very concept of permanent identity is invalid. A pack of cards can be a group of people, a child can turn into a pig, a cat's grin can exist without a cat. Even inanimate objects like stones lack simple consistency; in the fourth chapter, when the White Rabbit and his group throw pebbles at Alice, who is trapped by her enormous size in the house which is now far too small for her, she notices "with some surprise, that the pebbles [are] all turning into little cakes." Well schooled in the aboveground principles of regular causality and by now quite determined to assume that the same principles are operative in this Wonderland of impossibilities, Alice proceeds in her doggedly logical manner:

> If I eat one of these cakes . . . it's sure to make some change in my size; and, as it can't possibly make me larger, it must make me smaller, I suppose.

It is the "I suppose" that humorously hints at what may be happening somewhere deep within Alice. Pedestrian as her mind is, she is beginning to get a glimmer of the "principle" of Wonderland—that it operates on *no* principle whatsoever. Yet her subsequent eating of the pebbles that are now little cakes represents her stubborn determination to act as if her aboveground order still obtains.

From the very beginning of the underground adventures, another worldly convention—that verbal communication is potentially logical and unambiguous—has been surreptitiously assailed. Finally, when Alice and the strange animals emerge soaking from her pool of tears, linguistic order dissolves completely, appropriately in a dramatized pun. The Mouse announces in all seriousness that he will dry them: his method is to recite a passage from a history textbook, the "driest thing" he knows. Here Wonderland, through the comic agency of the Mouse and his "dry" history lesson, subverts a fundamental principle of everyday language. His confusion of symbol and object has far-reaching metaphysical signif-icance, but all we need note here is that this confusion is one more contribution to the clear pattern of destruction running through all of Alice's adventures.

Much of the humor in this chapter, which begins with the semantic mix-up over the word *dry*, is based on similar linguistic mayhem. The assembled creatures cannot accept language on its own grounds. They want it to do what it cannot do. For one thing, they want it to be logical. When the Mouse states in his "dry" tale that "the patriotic Archbishop of Canterbury Stigand found it advisable," he is interrupted by the Duck, who wants to know the antecedent noun for "it" before the Mouse has a chance to continue. Here is a twist in Wonderland's destructive strategy: instead of contradicting the validity of man-made constructs and conven-tions by merely carrying on without them, Wonderland manages in the very act of using them to be far more subversive. Actually, the Duck's demand is a dramatic *reductio ad absurdum* of traditional grammar. He implicitly puts aboveground linguistic assumptions to the test by asking language to do what is finally impossible—to be consistently unambiguous. Such a new turn in strategy enriches the complexity of the humorous attack on aboveground convention and our illusion of cosmic order. By demanding that language be consistently sequential, Wonderland, so to speak, destroys the false logic of language with logic itself. This new strategy demonstrates one more weapon in Wonderland's comic arsenal: whenever the world aboveground claims to be strictly consistent—as in space, size, or mathematics—Wonderland is, by its very operations, mad-deningly inconsistent. But whenever the world aboveground is admittedly inconsistent—as in grammar—then Wonderland strenuously demands com-plete consistency. Such an oblique attack forces the reader to remember what he always knew—one cannot expect ordinary language to be unam-biguous like mathematics. However, the urgent, rude insistence of Won-derland creatures (like the Eaglet's cry "Speak English!" or, later, the March Hare's "say what you mean" with its implication that language is not reversible like mathematical equations), neatly satirizes the common world's illogicality; and so, in the midst of all the fun, one more conventional prop of order begins to crumble.

As Chapter III progresses, this conventional prop finally disintegrates. When Alice asks the Dodo what a Caucus-Race is (that is, when she asks him to define a word with other words) and thereby unwittingly tests a fundamental aspect of language, his only answer is "the best way to explain it is to do it." When the Mouse asserts that his "is a long and a sad tale," Alice replies, "It *is* a long tail . . . but why do you call it sad?" When the Mouse says "not," Alice thinks he refers to a *knot*.[5] Here, then, another aboveground assumption (one that perplexed Charles Dodgson all his life)—that ordinary language, whether written or spoken, has at least the potential to be univocal—dissolves as swiftly and easily as the smiling Cheshire Cat. And as Alice's adventures continue, this comic subversion of linguistic convention increases in both scope and intensity.[6]

In Chapter V, "Advice from a Caterpillar," the destruction of the aboveground hierarchy of animals and men obviously steps up in intensity. This chapter also continues the attack on Alice's belief in orderly language and relates that belief to another set of worldly conventions, the customs of social etiquette. The Caterpillar plays a role similar to Humpty Dumpty's in *Through the Looking-Glass*. Although he is by no means the incisive, dictatorial critic of language that Humpty Dumpty is, he is just as rude in his disparagement of Alice's linguistic habits. The Caterpillar also demonstrates by his actions that the conventions of etiquette in social intercourse are meaningless in Wonderland. Alice has already suffered the rudeness of the White Rabbit, but the brusque orders of that timid authoritarian are almost polite in comparison to the barbarisms of the Caterpillar. Alice's own politeness to the Caterpillar increases at first in practically inverse proportion to his mounting rudeness. As his demands upon her patience reach fantastic heights, she makes it a point to address him as "Sir" and to reply "very politely" to his ridiculously unfair criticisms of her speech, "swallowing down her anger as well as she [can]." This amusing reaction by Alice, occurring as it does in many places in Wonderland, is another example of her attempt to find an order underground that somehow corresponds to the order of her previous life. Certainly, in that life it is sometimes the most impolite, imperious people who command the most respect and obedience; and to a child under the domination of inscrutable adults such a paradox may appear to be orderly and right.

The most impolite remark of the Caterpillar is his very first laconic question. Its crudeness is magnified when he repeats it contemptuously— "Who are *You?*" With characteristic comic understatement, the narrator observes that "this was not an encouraging opening for a conversation." Indeed, in the light of Alice's many previous troubles about self-identity, the direct question becomes far more than a matter of ordinary impoliteness.

Alice responds with another attempt to recall a rote-learned, moralistic poem from her past. This time she recites in response to the gruff commands of the Caterpillar, but the result is the same—it comes out all wrong. "You are old, father William," the lively parody of Southey's didactic verses, is, like "How doth the little crocodile," more than a humorous poem. It is, in this context of outlandish impoliteness, a kind of versified paraphrase of the almost immoral rudeness of the Caterpillar. Alice's Father William seems the antithesis of Southey's pious, temperate old man who has come gently to the end of his days. Her Father William has the air of an impolite old rake, and a conniving one at that:

> *"In my youth," said the sage, as he shook his grey locks,*
> *"I kept all my limbs very supple*
> *By the use of this ointment—one shilling the box—*
> *Allow me to sell you a couple?"*

The Caterpillar is thus closer to the truth than Alice is when he tells her that her recitation is not, as she says, merely wrong because "some of the words have got altered"; it is, as he asserts, "wrong from beginning to end," because it runs counter to the whole moral spirit of the original poem. Again in a recitation, Alice has yielded to that uncontrollable imp within her and joined willingly in the comic destruction of aboveground convention.

The rudeness of the Caterpillar contributes to the continuing antipathy between Alice and the creatures of Wonderland. Generally, she is met with condescension or mistrust, and most of the creatures she encounters are quick to contradict her. No doubt there is an element of fear in their authoritarian rudeness: they probably suspect that Alice, somewhat like an adult with children, holds the power of life and death over them. She can reject them, seemingly destroy them with a few words like "nonsense" or "You're nothing but a pack of cards!" But whatever their motives, these creatures of Wonderland are, according to all of Alice's acquired standards of social decorum, extremely discourteous (in fact, since they are strangers and Alice is something like a guest, they should be more polite, not less). Alice, clinging to her aboveground code of behavior, is either assiduously polite or ignorantly determined to educate them in her old etiquette. Significantly, most of her rules consist of "don'ts," obviously laid down by adults and now taken on complete faith by this literal-minded and priggish child. At the Mad Tea-Party, for example, Alice says to the Mad Hatter, "You should learn not to make personal remarks. . . . It's very rude." But here again, as in Wonderland's attacks on her illogical language, Alice's conventions are wittily turned upon themselves: when she violates her own dogmatic principle of decorum and rudely says to the Hatter, "Nobody asked *your* opinion," he "triumphantly" retorts, "Who's making personal remarks now?" And poor Alice finds herself at a new impasse: she does "not quite know what to say to this." She has been tested by her own principle and has been discredited, and she is, significantly, at a loss for *words*.

In the same chapter with the Caterpillar, Carroll touches so lightly upon another absurd "impossibility" that it almost escapes our attention the way it completely escapes Alice's. The Caterpillar leaves Alice with a rudeness so blatant that it is funny.

> *It yawned once or twice . . . got down off the mushroom, and crawled away into the grass, merely remarking, as [it] went, "One side will make you grow taller, and the other side will make you grow shorter."*

Alice, in a quandary, thinks to herself: "One side of *what*?" And the Caterpillar says, " 'Of the mushroom,' . . . just as if she had asked it aloud." No more is said of this unusual occurrence, but readers may well be impressed by such clairvoyance. For it is still one of our cherished aboveground beliefs that communication between separate minds necessitates some exchange of tangible symbols, and, even if we admit the validity of extrasensory phenomena, we do so with some wonder. But the Caterpillar, naturally, accepts his clairvoyance as a matter of course— there is not the slightest trace of wonder in his nonchalant attitude. The fact that Alice fails to relate this extraordinary occurrence to her pre-Wonderland experience is, in part, explained by the nonchalance of the Caterpillar: she obviously misses the significance of his mental feat. However, this unwitting acceptance by Alice may also mark an incipient change in her motivation. Perhaps at this point she has begun unconsciously to sense that Wonderland is *not* in any way like her old world aboveground, even though she will vainly attempt in later adventures to find or construct a meaningful connection.

In Chapter VI an important aspect of the chaos is that the creatures here, like the clairvoyant Caterpillar, rarely consider their environment or their actions as anything but normal. To them there is certainly nothing wonderful about Wonderland. This is made explicit when a large plate comes skimming out the door, barely missing the Frog-Footman's head, and we are told that the Footman continues what he is doing, "exactly as if nothing had happened." This acceptance of chaos by the inhabitants of Wonderland has at least two significant relations to the book's whole meaning. First, it serves to pique further Alice's curiosity about the "rules" of Wonderland. Since the creatures do not think their lives and world are in any way strange or disorderly, Alice takes this attitude—albeit incorrectly—as a sign that there has to be an order. In general, she fails to consider consciously the possibility that the very anarchy of their realm may be directly related to their own heedless and irrational behavior—that they live in chaos and thus act accordingly. Indeed, her reason, ordering mechanism that it is, is totally incapable of functioning outside the bounds of some kind of order. Second, the creatures' acceptance of chaos can be viewed as a fantastic parody of what happens every day in the world aboveground. Here, in fact, may be the correlation between the two worlds that Alice seeks but never fully discovers. The creatures aboveground, with their constructs and arbitrary conventions, act in the same way. If the Frog-Footman, say, were to visit the London of the 1860's, would not the average Englishman's nonchalant acceptance of such preposterous notions as orderly time and space strike him as insane? This gently comic exposure of the relativity of order that we find in Lewis Carroll's fiction has been discussed by a number of critics, but none has pointed out its organic function in *Alice*. It is an important component of the book's vision of universal anarchy; for what mankind (or Alice in her Wonderland) typically desires is not an adjustable frame of meaning, but an unambiguous and permanent order. Alice's reaction to the Frog-Footman's argumentativeness is representative of her total reaction to this universal anarchy: "It's really dreadful . . . the way all the creatures argue. It's enough to drive one crazy!" Like her previous "I suppose," the key words "dreadful" and "crazy" subtly reveal what is happening to Alice without her knowing it; she is slowly coming to an

unconscious perception of Wonderland's maddening—and dangerous—
nature.

Soon Alice meets the Duchess, whose hilarious rudeness surpasses even
the Caterpillar's. Alice again responds with her best manners. The
Duchess, like the Frog-Footman, takes no notice of the bedlam around
her: surrounded by the howling of the baby, the kitchen utensils thrown
by the cook, and the general disorder, the Duchess single-mindedly persists in her barbarous treatment of the baby and her guest Alice. Her
"lullaby" is another of Wonderland's subversive parodies. For example, a
verse of the original poem by David Bates reads:

> Speak gently to the little child!
>   Its love be sure to gain;
> Teach it in accents soft and mild;
>   It may not long remain.[7]

The Duchess sings:

> *Speak roughly to your little boy,*
>   *And beat him when he sneezes:*
> *He only does it to annoy,*
>   *Because he knows it teases.*

This parody, like the earlier ones uttered by Alice, actively denies Alice's
previous moral code. The Duchess, so fond of aphorisms, here recom-
mends what Alice's world would call sheer cruelty. Moreover, the Duchess practices what she preaches, constantly shaking and tossing the baby
as she sings her "lullaby." The baby soon turns into an ugly, grunting
pig—right in Alice's hands. Such a dramatized reversal of the conventional sentimental attitude towards children (the Duchess even shouts
"Pig!" at the baby) is something besides a hit at aboveground morality—
it is more like a denial of a customary emotional response. We may note
here that Carroll himself, usually so fearful of committing any social
impropriety, could not in his letters and conversation always restrain his
deep-seated disgust with all babies. But such information merely corrob-
orates what any adult reader easily perceives: the baby-pig episode
humorously portrays the arbitrary nature of conventional attitudes
towards infants. We need go no further than the text; Alice herself muses
about "other children she knew, who might do very well as pigs."

In this same chapter, Alice has her famous conversation with the
Cheshire Cat. In the light of Wonderland's increasing destruction of the

common world's principal foundations for sanity and order, the Cat's remarks become especially important. He is the one creature who explicitly presents Alice with an explanation of the chaos that surrounds her. When Alice asserts, "I don't want to go among mad people," the Cat replies, "Oh, you can't help that . . . we're all mad here. I'm mad. You're mad." Alice answers, "How do you know I'm mad?" And the Cat says, "You must be . . . or you wouldn't have come here." Through this brief exchange, the amused reader—not Alice—gets a tentative, fleeting glimpse at the "meaning" of Wonderland that Alice instinctively seeks. In addition, the enigmatic Cat, who vanishes and appears as easily as he smiles, here intimates that Alice's curiosity is madness or at least the motive-power behind her mad act—her leap into this insane land. That Alice is, as the Cat states, just as mad as the natives of Wonderland is still difficult for the reader to admit, indeed even to perceive. For Alice comes from and alone represents the ordinary reader's world, which, for the sake of his existence as well as hers, must appear sane. The narrator says, "Alice didn't think that [his syllogism] proved it [her madness] at all," and the reader laughs and tacitly agrees, forgetting that the Cat's reasoning can be just as valid as Alice's. For Alice, the Cheshire Cat, and the reader are all now in Wonderland. Alice apparently learns nothing from the Cat's important revelation. While she is "not much surprised" at his vanishing—for she is "getting so well used to queer things happening"—she still fails to perceive Wonderland's meaning for those who live by the illusory principles of aboveground order. Furthermore, after being told specifically by the Cheshire Cat that the Hatter and the March Hare are both mad, Alice, when she meets them in her next adventure, remains uninstructed and stubbornly persists in her attempts to relate their disordered actions to her old notions of sanity.

Is it because Alice is a child that she fails after all this to see Wonderland for what it is? Is it her youthful ignorance that makes her miss the dangerous significance of a grin without a cat—an attribute without a subject? All she can think at this point is:

Well! I've often seen a cat without a grin, . . . but a grin without a cat! It's the most curious thing I ever saw in all my life!

But this represents the response of most adults, too. In a sense, we are all childishly ignorant in the face of supreme danger; for woven into the whole complex fabric of implications in this laughable colloquy with the

Cat is one implication that easily escapes our attention: another above-ground operating principle—the seemingly indestructible bond between subject and attribute—has been graphically subverted by the appearance of a cat's grin without a cat.

In Chapter VII Alice's old concept of time dissolves, in one of the funniest and yet most grimly destructive scenes in the book. While many other common bases of order continue to be subverted in this adventure, "A Mad Tea-Party" focuses on time, one major aboveground system that still appears to have some validity. Up to this point, the attack on time has been only incidental and certainly not overwhelming, and time still has had some meaning because the narrative itself has progressed through a vague chronological framework.

In the beginning of "A Mad Tea-Party," Alice comes upon a situation that apparently has had no temporal beginning and probably will never have an end. The March Hare, Mad Hatter, and Dormouse sit at a tea-table, engaged in a truly endless succession of tea and pointless conversation (perhaps a representation of a child's view of polite mealtimes). In the midst of all the disconnected talk, the Hatter suddenly asks Alice, as if it were a test, "What day of the month is it?" and, like the White Rabbit, looks at his watch "uneasily." This question opens a whole series of ridiculous comments on watches and time. These comments themselves seem pointless; and their complete lack of coherence or sequence intensi-fies the chapter's pervasive atmosphere of timelessness (especially since Alice, like the ordinary nineteenth-century reader, still clings to her old conception of time as linear and progressive).

When the Hatter admits that his riddle about the raven and the writ-ing desk has no answer, Alice sighs, "I think you might do something better with the time . . . than wasting it in asking riddles that have no answers." The Hatter replies, "If you knew Time as well as I do . . . you wouldn't talk about wasting *it*. It's *him*." This nonsensical personification of time continues in the conversation that follows. Amidst the by now familiar puns that tend to destroy linguistic order, like those on beating or killing time, time itself, like a person, is revealed as malleable, recalci-trant, or disorderly. Such a view of time as finite and personal, of course, comically subverts the aboveground convention of time's infinite, orderly, autonomous nature. This finally puts time in its proper place—another arbitrary, changeable artifact that has no claim to absolute validity, no binding claim, in fact, to existence. Since time is now like a person, a kind

of ill-behaved child created by man, there is the unavoidable danger that
he will rebel and refuse to be consistent. That is exactly what has happened in this Wonderland tea-party: the Hatter says time "won't do a
thing I ask! It's always six o'clock now"; that is, it is always tea-time.
Time is thus frozen, and one of the most important concepts of common
human experience is laughed out of existence.

Wonderland seems to compensate for this frozen time by substituting
space—the creatures move around the tea-table in a kind of never-ending
game of musical chairs. We might take this substitution of space as
Carroll's hint at a more accurate conception of time; but, like the underlying accuracy of Alice's confused multiplication in Chapter II, this
subtle hint at the reality of "reality" is a bit too sophisticated for most
readers, as it certainly is for poor Alice. Besides, the concept of space, as
we have seen, has already been demolished. At this midway point in the
narrative, then, the destruction of the foundations of Alice's old order is
practically complete.

Alice, in Chapter VII, has almost reached rock bottom in her descent
into chaos—betokened by the word "mad," which is part of the title of the
chapter, part of the name of one principal character, and part of the
common epithet applied to another ("mad as a March Hare"). Her
dramatic experience of the subversion of the aboveground system of
meaning seems complete, but there is at least one foundation of that old
system that remains intact. Despite the fact that inanimate objects like
stones have lost stable identity, they have up to Chapter VIII remained
within the class of *inanimate* objects—with the possible exception hinted
at in Chapter VII that tea-trays can fly like bats.

"Twinkle, twinkle, little bat"—Carroll's charming parody of Jane
Taylor's nursery rhyme "The Star"—occupies a rather pivotal position in
the pattern of destruction I have been tracing. First, the poem uses, as
parodies do in general, the original verses as part of the total context.
Carroll's substitutions (*bat* for *star, at* for *are, you fly* for *so high,* and *tea-
tray* for *diamond*) must be considered in the light of Jane Taylor's poem.
Viewed this way, Carroll's poem becomes a compressed statement of
much of the destruction that has already taken place in Wonderland, as
well as a gentle hint at what is to come in the next chapter. A bat represents to most readers ugly nature—active and predatory; a star, on the
other hand, usually connotes beautiful, remote, static nature. Moreover,
"what you're at" and "fly" intensify the Darwinian, predatory, gross

struggle image and increase the humorous incongruity between Carroll's lines and Miss Taylor's. All this harks back to the earlier comic subversion of the sentimental view of animal morality seen in such verses as "How doth the little crocodile," another hit at false piety and false natural history in popular nursery rhymes. This, in turn, leads the reader's mind back to the original star, whose moral connotations have now been subverted: it no longer seems to deserve the purity implied by "diamond." In addition, "Twinkle, twinkle, little bat," with its delightful mix-up of animate bat with inanimate star and flying tea-tray with flying bat, serves as an appropriate transition to Chapter VIII, where the fabricated separation between animate and inanimate objects is finally destroyed.

Immediately after the highly subversive Mad Tea-Party, Alice meets in Chapter VIII a whole new set of creatures—playing cards that are alive —so alive, in fact, that one has become one of the most well-known "persons" in English literature, the furious Queen of Hearts. Carroll's method of making these cards appear human is an example of his technical ability throughout *Alice*. For one thing, he skillfully employs devices which make their conversations with Alice seem natural. Almost immediately, one of the gardeners, the two of spades, speaks in a slight dialect (dialects have been attributed previously to a number of animals). Carroll also carefully indicates the volume and emotional quality of the dialogue—a kind of humorous reversal of the aboveground notion that speech is a primary distinction between animals and men. Some card-characters merely "say" their lines, others "shout" or "roar"; some are "silent," or speak in "a low, hurried tone"; Alice herself gives "a little scream of laughter," and the Queen sometimes speaks "in a voice of thunder." Another device for making these inanimate objects appear human and their scenes realistic is the inclusion of already well-established characters like the White Rabbit and the Duchess, whose "humanness" is now taken for granted and who here respond to the playing-card Queen as if she were supremely vital.

In this way another aboveground principle—that there is a distinct cleavage between the animate and inanimate worlds—is humorously overthrown. One thing, however, remains constant: these card-creatures are just as irrational and chaotic as all the previous animal inhabitants of the insane underground. Indeed, the chaos is compounded when these inanimate-objects-turned-human treat the normally live creatures of Alice's former existence as inanimate artifacts. Wonderland has again turned the tables, hereby using live animals like hedgehogs and flamingos for croquet balls and mallets. Alice, still clinging to her "in-the-world" approach, says to the Cheshire Cat, "you've no idea how confusing it is all the things being alive." The Cat, of course, has no idea how confusing it is, since he neither possesses nor is possessed by Alice's old, aboveground standards of regularity. Moreover, this appeal to the Cat marks another step in Alice's slowly disintegrating sense of order: although she still clings to her old constructed concepts of reality, she forgets completely what the Cat is and where he dwells.

Since Alice rarely relinquishes her notions of order without some struggle, it is fitting that in "The Queen's Croquet-Ground" she should try to remind herself of the aboveground distinction between live and inanimate entities. When the Queen of Hearts rudely demands, as so many other creatures have demanded, that Alice identify herself, Alice "very politely" says: "My name is Alice, so please your Majesty," but adds to herself, "Why, they're only a pack of cards, after all. I needn't be afraid of them!" At this point, Alice is not yet prepared to say such a thing aloud. Nevertheless, this silent comment may indicate that Alice is beginning to sense the final danger inherent in Wonderland—her own destruction—and is beginning to fall back on her only defense against this ultimate devastation which has lurked ominously beneath all the rest of her problems. She is falling back on those now inoperative aboveground principles which, illusory or not, can preserve her sanity and her very existence.

Alice has many reasons for such subversive thoughts. She has certainly been cheated: the Queen's Croquet-Ground—with its painted flowers, its exasperating and insane game, its wild and dangerous creatures—is that same "beautiful garden" she has been seeking from the outset. Perhaps it is the realization that her arduous journey beneath the grounds of her old, dull, constricted world of rote-lessons and unexplainable, arbitrary adult rules has brought her, not to "those beds of bright flowers and those cool fountains," but to a chaotic place of madness ruled by a furious Queen who orders executions with almost every breath—perhaps it is the realization of all this that encourages Alice to begin her rebellion.

A more important reason for Alice's drift toward rebellion is that she has begun to sense that her quest for unambiguous meaning and immortal order is fruitless. Haphazard as her trip may at first seem, Alice has nevertheless been moving towards the grounds of Wonderland which correspond to the grounds of her old world. The rulers of Wonderland (the King and Queen of Hearts) and their "beautiful garden" have been Alice's spiritual goal almost from the beginning, and it is appropriate that the rulers and court of Wonderland should hold the secret of their realm's meaning and be the ultimate source of its order. The fact that they are court cards and hearts emphasizes their central, vital position, as does the fact that they are introduced with names written all in capital letters, a device stressed by Carroll in his revisions. Ironically, Alice is for once correct in judging Wonderland on the basis of her previous "in-the-world" experience. But what do these repositories of meaning and order turn out to be? Mere abstract, manufactured, and arbitrary symbols—just a pack of cards, pictures of kings and queens, men and women. Their grounds of meaning turn out to be croquet grounds and their principles the rules of an insane, topsy-turvy *game*.

Alice's first realization that she need not be afraid because, "after all," she is dealing with a mere pack of cards has an effect, although an impermanent one, on her subsequent behavior. Immediately after her brief insight, she is extremely rude to the Queen, so rude that Alice herself is "surprised at her own courage." She interrupts the Queen's repeated "Off with her head!" by saying " 'Nonsense!' . . . very loudly and decidedly." The King's and Queen's immediate reaction to this single word is significant: the "Queen was silent" and "the King laid his hand upon her arm and timidly said, 'Consider, my dear: she is only a child!' " Among other things, this reaction of the rulers of Wonderland is a humorous, metaphorical equivalent of the aboveground world's reaction to the ridiculous challenge of a Wonderland. When either is named for what it is, it is left, as it were, speechless. Paradoxically, by the power of one of the most artificial constructs of all—the world—these rulers are rendered powerless, that is, without words. That the child Alice has had this supreme power all along goes without saying. Alice, however, does not realize the potency of her weapon or, for that matter, that she even has a weapon. Hence, even though she can say to herself that "they're only a pack of cards, after all. I needn't be afraid of them!" she soon reverts to her seemingly unwarranted fear: "Alice began to feel very uneasy: to be sure, she had not as yet had any dispute with the Queen, but she knew that it might happen any minute, 'and then,' thought she, 'what would become of me? They're dreadfully fond of beheading people here: the great wonder is, that there's any one left alive!' "

From this point to the end of the adventures, it is the main business of the narrative that underlies all the fun and gay nonsense to trace Alice's preparation for her final, overt denial of Wonderland, the destruction of her fearful vision for the sake of her identity and sanity. To gain strength and courage for that act of denial, Alice seeks the aid of allies (meanwhile, of course, she continues to play what she has already viewed as a crazy game). In Chapter VIII she makes the mistake of assuming that the Cheshire Cat is such an ally. She spies his grin in the air and says, "It's the Cheshire Cat: now I shall have somebody to talk to." But when Alice, "feeling very glad she had some one to listen to her," complains to the Cat about the game she is playing—saying "they don't seem to have any rules in particular"—his only reply is the apparent non sequitur, "How do you like the Queen?" He, of course, sees no fault in a game without any rules but a mad queen's; if he were to play the insane games aboveground with their many arbitrary "rules," he would probably find them as disturbing as Alice finds the mad, seemingly ruleless croquet game of Wonderland.

In much the same way that she mistakes the Cheshire Cat for an ally, Alice mistakenly assumes that "logical" rules still have validity. At the very beginning of the next chapter ("The Mock Turtle's Story"), she meets the Duchess again, and, finding that previously irascible creature in good humor, assumes that her anger was merely the result of the pepper in her soup. "Maybe it's always pepper that makes people hot-tempered," Alice muses. And she begins to extrapolate from her new-found hypothesis, "very much pleased at having found out a new kind of rule." Here, although there is the prominent "Maybe," Alice reveals that she still stubbornly believes there is a cause-effect order in Wonderland and one that can be applied to her own world too: this, in spite of all the mounting evidence to the contrary. The Duchess herself is the personified *reductio ad absurdum* of Alice's attitude toward rules: the Duchess finds a "moral" in everything. Alice is faced with a new curious problem: once again Wonderland forces her aboveground assumptions to the final test, and once again it laughs them out of existence. Poor, dogged Alice, however, is unable to see the "moral" in the Duchess's preoccupation with finding morals; that is, Alice fails to perceive that such remarks as "Everything's got a moral, if only you can find it" are essentially satirical counterthrusts at her own determination to find the rules in Wonderland.

Finally, Alice meets two creatures who seem capable of serving as allies—the Gryphon and the Mock Turtle, two of the most fantastic characters in Wonderland's whole laughable gallery. For both of these animals, nonsensical as they are, seem to see Wonderland for what it is, at least for what it is to Alice. When Alice recounts to them her adventures, the Gryphon says, "It's all about as curious as it can be." When Alice attempts to recite another moralistic Watts poem ("'Tis the voice of the sluggard") and again twists it into a cruel, amoral, survival-of-the-fittest commentary on nature, the Mock Turtle asserts that "it sounds uncommon nonsense" and says, "It's by far the most confusing thing *I* ever heard!" Their words "curious," "nonsense," and "confusing" are drawn, of course, from Alice's vocabulary.

This sympathy for Alice, it should be observed, is not as simple as it first appears. For one thing, the solicitude of the Gryphon and Mock Turtle is—as their names suggest—undoubtedly false. Both creatures are palpable sentimentalists: the Mock Turtle's mawkish song about beautiful soup, sung in "a voice choked with sobs," is the measure of their sentimentality. Once again Wonderland tests an aboveground convention by carrying it to its extreme: here, instead of attacking one particular kind of aboveground sentiment such as the common emotional response to babies or to stars and bees, Wonderland comically overthrows sentiment itself. Alice cannot hope to find genuine sympathy and real allies in the Gryphon and Mock Turtle. In any event, she has no time to react, for the great trial (of the last chapters) is about to begin.

Before turning to that trial, we should try to assess the full function of the Mock Turtle and Gryphon in the Wonderland motif of subversion. After the Queen's croquet game, no remnant of ordinary aboveground order remains intact. The only order poor Alice can possibly perceive in Wonderland is the consistent antipathy of all the creatures towards her and all her previous assumptions. Now, Chapters IX and X serve to subvert and finally destroy the "order" of Wonderland itself, because here the two sentimental friends, the Gryphon and the Mock Turtle, argue neither with each other (as most of the other creatures do) nor with Alice's aboveground assumptions. In a sense they *are* the allies she seeks: they take her side, seeing her adventures and reverses as she sees them.[8] This sympathy—whether genuine or false—breaks Wonderland's pattern of antipathy and is perhaps the ultimate destruction: order, as Alice once knew it, is now so hopelessly snarled that she must, in literal self-defense, take that inevitable leap back to her own insane, illusory, but livable world of arbitrary logic and convention.

If "The Queen's Croquet-Ground" has convinced Alice that her quest for Wonderland's principle of order in the personalities or games of Wonderland's playing-card rulers is pointless, the last two chapters of the book reveal that even beyond these rulers and their mad croquet-ground there is no fundamental law, save perhaps the furious Queen's "Off with his head!"—and even that persistent demand, Alice has been told by the Gryphon, is never obeyed: "It's all her fancy, that: they never executes nobody, you know." At the end, Alice is finally brought to what should be the last refuge of order—the court of law.

Chapter XI begins with a crowd scene. As the chapter progresses, we realize that many of the creatures Alice has encountered from the beginning are assembled here. This strengthens the impression that the trial is the final test of Wonderland's meaning, the appropriate conclusion of Alice's quest for law and order. What is on trial here is not really the Knave of Hearts. What is on trial is the "law" itself, whether it be the law of Wonderland or, by extension, the law wherever it is encountered. Alice has already lost faith in her own search for the law of Wonderland, but then she forgets even that loss. In the final trial, where her forgotten suspicions return to become a frightful apperception of the total intransigent chaos underlying her artificial world, Alice is moved to her only salvation—a complete and active denial of the horrible, unacceptable truth.

In these last two chapters, after all the destruction of the old bases of order, all that is left is the hollow form of things. The trial now appears in its true light: since the world in which the trial takes place is without order or meaning, the trial is a pointless formality, another game without rules and without a winner. And when Alice is herself forced to participate and is again drawn into the mad proceedings, her rebellion is inevitable.

That Alice at the beginning of the trial has not yet abandoned her old cherished faith in order is revealed in a number of ways. The narrator tells us that

Alice had never been in a court of justice before, but she had read about them in books, and she was quite pleased to find that she knew the name of nearly everything there.

Once more, Alice persists in viewing the underground bedlam from an "in-the-world" perspective. Part of the witty comedy here, naturally, derives from the fact that many adult readers *have* been in a court: they know that this Wonderland court is an outlandish travesty (especially when it is called a "court of *justice*"). Yet they also sense that at the core there is a great deal of similarity between "real" trials aboveground and this insanely unjust trial of the Knave of Hearts. They also sense the significance of Alice's comfort in finding that she can name the items in the court—another illustration of Wonderland's incessant attack on man's groundless linguistic habits, intensified when the narrator ironically remarks that Alice was rather proud of her ability to name everything in the court, "for she thought, and rightly too, that very few little girls of her age knew the meaning of it all." An even more important result of Alice's "in-the-world" approach to the trial is that she will again be frustrated, this time by the fact that while the Wonderland trial is similar in outward form to "real" trials, it characteristically ignores or subverts all the significant principles.

The last chapter is called "Alice's Evidence." The title itself has a multiple meaning. Literally, Alice is forced to participate actively in the insanity of Wonderland by giving "evidence," even though she has now grown so large that she can at any second rebel if she so desires. More important, Alice in this last scene acquires the "evidence" she needs in order to make her decision about Wonderland. At first, Alice reacts with fear; when she is called to the stand, she cries out, " 'Here!' . . . quite forgetting in the flurry of the moment how large she had grown in the last few minutes." Along with this fear, however, is a growing sense of the meaninglessness of the trial (and thus, she thinks, of all Wonderland). When she looks over the jurymen's shoulders and sees the nonsense they are writing, Alice says to herself, "it doesn't matter a bit." Here she is becoming just as subversive towards Wonderland as Wonderland has been towards her and her aboveground principles. Soon Alice is courageously contradicting the King and Queen openly.

> *"That* proves *his guilt, of course,"* said the Queen: *"so, off with—."*
> *"It doesn't prove anything of the sort!"* said Alice.

And after the White Rabbit reads his major piece of evidence against the Knave of Hearts, the mad poem full of unclear pronoun references, Alice daringly states aloud:

> *"If any one of them* [the jury] *can explain it,"* . . . (she had grown so large in the last few minutes that she wasn't a bit afraid of interrupting him [the King]), *"I'll give him sixpence. I don't believe there's an atom of meaning in it."*

Finally, when the Queen asserts, "Sentence first—verdict afterwards," Alice says loudly, "Stuff and nonsense!" The Queen turns purple with rage, Alice actively denies the Queen's demand to be silent with a forceful "I won't!" and the whole underground adventure explodes and disintegrates.

We see here, with the progression from Alice's thinking "to herself" to her final words said "loudly" and her absolute refusal to keep silent, that part of her rebellion rests on her growing ability to speak the necessary words—to give the necessary "evidence." In Chapter VIII Alice was outwardly polite while she inwardly said, "they're only a pack of cards, after all." At the end, she is completely open, and she terminates her nightmarish adventure with her own weapon of destruction, her loudly proclaimed, "You're nothing but a pack of cards!"

Alice's final, overt rejection of Wonderland, her flight from the frightful anarchy of the world underneath the grounds of common consciousness, is a symbolic rejection of mad sanity in favor of the sane madness of ordinary existence. Perhaps it is best to view the normal conscious mind as an automatic filtering and ordering mechanism which protects us from seeing the world in all its chaotic wonder and glory—at least it seems best to view the mind this way when we attempt an explanation of the serious theme that emerges from the delicious, sprightly wit and humor of *Alice's Adventures in Wonderland*. When Alice at last names her tormentors a pack of cards and thereby ends her underground journey, her mind, by that very assertion, imposes an artificial but effective order upon that which can never be organically ordered. By the time Alice and the reader reach this last scene in Wonderland it should be quite obvious to all that language itself is an inadequate construct. Yet it is by this construct that Alice preserves her sanity and identity. She uses words to put all Wonderland into a category of manufactured, nonhuman, arbitrary entities—"a pack of cards." Insane as her act may be in terms of what Wonderland has demonstrated, it provides her with the means to dispel her vision and thus protect herself from the dangers of complete perception. Alice has thus come full circle: her mad curiosity led her to the vision of absurdity; her failure led her to dismay; and her instinct for survival, assured identity, and sanity led her to escape from her final horrifying perception.

It must be remembered that *Alice's Adventures in Wonderland* is not a piece of formal philosophy; it is, instead, a comic myth of man's insoluble problem of meaning in a meaningless world. Thus, the fact that Alice herself is unaware of the significance of her journey to the end of night and unaware of her reasons for finally denying the validity of her vision is by no means a flaw in the book. Alice, as the mythical representative of all her fellows aboveground, acts appropriately and appropriately is unaware of the meaning of her actions. Although Alice's quest for meaning is unfulfilled and she consciously learns nothing, she does survive because an instinctual "lesson" takes over at the moment of supreme danger. Unlike the artificial, illusory lessons of her nursery reading, schoolroom, or elders, the innate and unconscious drive for identity and self-preservation cannot be perverted by either Wonderland or the world above. The question is not whether this drive is a valid principle, but whether it is pragmatically sound. In *Alice* it is. And upon its pragmatic soundness rests the validity of all the other illusory principles and conventions. Alice's quest for reasonable experience whisks her back to her only possible, albeit artificial, world, where the ultimately irrational makes life sane.

Thus, the book is paradoxically both a denial and an affirmation of order—a kind of catharsis of what can never be truly purged but what must, for sanity's sake, be periodically purged in jest, fantasy, or dream. The Wonderland creatures and their world are not a pack of cards, after all. They are, so to speak, more "real" than so-called reality. But waking life, as most of us know it, must function as if they are unreal, as if chaos is amusing "nonsense."

On the surface, then, *Alice* is clearly not true to ordinary experience. Indeed, it is destructive of the very groundwork of that experience. Yet the book is certainly true to an extraordinary experience familiar to us all, the dream. For the apparently nonsensical elements of *Alice*, like timelessness, spacelessness, and fusion of discrete entities, are, as modern psychology has demonstrated, what lie just below the surface of rational consciousness and what we experience every night in the dream state.

I began this essay by pointing out the similarity between *Alice* and the traditional literary dream-vision. Some may argue that *Alice* would be better classified as a "nightmare-vision" because a nightmare is an unsuccessful dream, while a dream is a method whereby the dreamer successfully works out and solves in dramatic form a deep-seated problem, often a problem whose existence the conscious faculties will not allow themselves even to admit. Certainly Alice does deal with and dramatize what

is by nature and definition outside the awareness of the everyday conscious intellect; and some readers assume that Alice's dream does not
come to any satisfying conclusion, that the problem of the disorder beneath man-made order is left unsolved; but I have argued here that this
is not so, that *Alice's Adventures in Wonderland* solves the problem by
a kind of alogical dreamwork affirmation of man's artificially constructed
universe. Whether or not every reader's unconscious can be satisfied
with this extrarational solution is, it seems to me, an unanswerable and
finally irrelevant question. Alice's unconscious is what matters and it
is here that we can be sure the conclusion is satisfactory. After waking,
she runs off for tea because "it's getting late" (and this after the timeless
Mad Tea-Party), "thinking while she ran, as well she might, what a
wonderful dream it had been," completely at ease in her mad but possible world above the chaos of Wonderland.

IX
Psychedelic

White

Rabbit

by Grace Slick

(1966)

ONE PILL makes you larger
   And one pill makes you small.
And the ones that mother gives you
   don't do anything at all.
Go ask Alice
   when she's ten feet tall.

And if you go chasing rabbits
   And you know you're going to fall.

Tell 'em all who got a smokin' caterpillar
   has given you the call.
Call Alice
   when she was just small.

When men on the chessboard
   get up and tell you where to go.
And you've just had some kind of mushroom,
   and your mind is moving low,
Go ask Alice
   I think she'll know.

When logic and proportion
   have fallen sloppy dead,
And the White Knight is talking backwards,
   and the Red Queen's lost her head,
Remember what the Dormouse said:
Feed your head,
   feed your head.

Lewis Carroll—

The First Acidhead

by *Thomas Fensch*

(1968)

ALICE BEGAN the whole thing by falling—down and down and down until she thought she would fall through the middle of the earth.

She was after the White Rabbit—that curious rabbit with a waistcoat and a pocket watch. And she had fallen down a rabbit-hole.

And when she hit bottom she was in a long, low hall, in which there was a three-legged table with a bottle on it marked DRINK ME and a box under it marked EAT ME. And with some logic—for the bottle was *not* marked POISON—Alice drank it. It tasted like cherry tarts, custard, pineapple, roast turkey, toffee, and hot buttered toast, all at the same time.

And it put her uptight.

"What a curious feeling," Alice said. "I must be shutting up like a telescope."

She shrank until she was ten inches tall.

"It might end, you know, in my going out altogether, like a candle. I wonder what I should be like then?"

And she tried to imagine what the flame of a candle is like after it is blown out, but she had never seen one like that.

She stopped shrinking at ten inches and ate the cake that was marked EAT ME.

"Curiouser and curiouser," cried Alice. . . . "Now I'm opening out like the largest telescope that ever was! Good-bye feet!"

And that's only the beginning.

When you take something that tastes like cherry tarts, custard, pine-apple, roast turkey, toffee, and toast at the same time and makes you grow and shrink—baby, that's tripping out.

Lewis Carroll told it like it is—and he told it in 1865. And if you don't believe him, you can listen to the same thing today by the Jefferson Airplane. The Airplane's lead singer, Grace Slick, pays her tribute to Carroll in their single, "White Rabbit."[1]

> One pill makes you larger,
>   and one pill makes you small.
> And the ones that Mother gives you
>   don't do anything at all—
> Go ask Alice,
>   when she's ten feet tall. . . .
>
> And if you go chasing rabbits,
>   and you know you're going to fall,
> Tell them a hookah-smoking character
>   has given you the call;
>
> Call Alice—when she was just small. . . .

That "hookah-smoking character" is the Caterpillar that sits on the mushroom, smoking. Alice meets him later.

"Who are You?" said the Caterpillar.

"I—I hardly know, Sir, just at present—at least I know who I was when I got up this morning, but I think I must have changed several times since then."

The changing is the thing—what *is* normal?

> When logic and proportion
>   have fallen far be dead,
> And the White Knight is talking backwards
>   And the Red Queen's off her head. . . .

That's psychedelics—baby—now.

And there is no mention of *what* the Caterpillar smokes in his hookah. Then Alice meets the Cheshire Cat. He gives her directions to the Mad Hatter and the March Hare, but cautions, ". . . they're both mad.

"But I don't want to go among mad people," says Alice.

"Oh, you can't help that," says the Cat. "We're all mad. I'm mad. You're mad." And he disappears—leaving only his smile, which fades from sight long after the rest of him.

Alice meets the Mad Hatter and the March Hare—and the Dormouse. And here's the only place where the Jefferson Airplane's song differs from Lewis Carroll:

> And the White Knight is talking backwards
>   and the Red Queen's off her head . . .
> Remember what the Dormouse said:
>   Feed your head,
>   Feed your head. . . .

In other words, take some acid and trip out. Only the Dormouse never said that in Carroll's book anyway. He was tripping out already and didn't make much sense.

The Dormouse fell asleep and woke up, fell asleep again—tried to join the conversation and failed and fell asleep so much that the Mad Hatter had to pour hot tea on his nose to keep him awake. Then the Dormouse kept mumbling "Twinkle, twinkle, twinkle, twinkle," and the rest had to force him to stop.

Alice left the Mad Hatter and the March Hare and the rest, and the last she saw of them, they were focing the Dormouse into the teapot. It was, as Alice says, "the stupidest tea-party I ever saw in my life," and shows you how far things can go on a trip.

In case you think this was all a nineteenth-century mistake, consider the author Lewis Carroll.

His name wasn't Lewis Carroll. It was Charles Lutwidge Dodgson and he was a mathematician at Oxford University. But even for his time, he was freaky.

He was a fantastic mathematician—really brilliant at it[2]—but he didn't remember right from left, confused people and places, and generally was a living contradiction. It is doubtful that he ever knew of the nineteenth-century equivalent of LSD, but *Alice in Wonderland* echoes the confused, surrealistic world—the world of the LSD trip.

Down the rabbit-hole truth is meaningless, illusions are everything, and words mean what the speakers want them to mean at the moment and no longer. In the end, all the world of fantasy, of the Dormouse and the White Rabbit and the Kings and Queens and Cats, all of it turns into a pack of cards—and a dream.

And you can get the same thing for five dollars—a pill of acid that will fit easily into the palm of your hand.

And as Grace Slick and the Jefferson Airplane tell it:

> Remember what the Dormouse said:
> Feed your head,
> feed your head.

Notes

Auden: "Today's 'Wonder-World' Needs Alice"

1 Lorina was nicknamed Ina, and under that name appears in some essays that follow. [Ed.]

Strong: "Lewis Carroll"

1 If there ever was a definition II, it was omitted by the typesetter of the *Cornhill Magazine* at time of the essay's original appearance in print. [Ed.]

Woolf: "Lewis Carroll"

1 By capitalizing the word "Life," Mrs. Woolf may have been referring to Collingwood's *The Life and Letters of Lewis Carroll* (1898), or more likely—writing as she was in 1939—to Langford Reed's *The Life of Lewis Carroll* (1932). The third probability is that Mrs. Woolf was merely citing the life Carroll led as his Life, with characteristic Carrollian capitalization. [Ed.]

Lennon: "Escape through the Looking-Glass"

1 Falconer Madan, co-author of *Handbook of the Literature of C. L. Dodgson.*
2 *Carroll's Alice* (New York, 1936), by Harry Morgan Ayres.
3 Letter from Miss Dodgson.
4 *The Life and Letters of Lewis Carroll* (London, 1898), by Stuart Dodgson Collingwood.
5 *Swift and Carroll* (New York, 1955), by Dr. Phyllis Greenacre.
6 *The White Knight—A Study of C. L. Dodgson* (Edinburgh, 1952), by Alexander L. Taylor.
7 *Nothing Dies,* by J. W. Dunne.
8 *The Annotated Alice* (New York, 1960), ed. Martin Gardner.

Salmon: From " Literature for the Little Ones "

1 The reviewer meant, of course, the Reverend Charles Lutwidge Dodgson.

Leach: "*Alice in Wonderland* in Perspective"

1 Roger W. Holmes. "The Philosopher's *Alice in Wonderland,*" *Antioch Review,* XIX (1959), pp. 133–49 (see also C. J. Woollen: "Lewis Carroll: Philosopher," *Hibbert Journal,* XLVI (1947), pp. 63–8); Alexander L. Taylor: *The White Knight: A Study of C. L. Dodgson* Edinburgh, London, 1952), p. vi; Phyllis Greenacre: *Swift and Carroll: A Psychoanalytic Study of Two Lives* (New York, 1955); William Empson: *Some Versions of Pastoral* (London, 1955), pp. 253–94. Empson says, for example, that "the rule" about talking animals in *Alice* "is that they are always friendly though childishly frank to Alice when she is small, and when she is big (suggesting grown-up) always opposed to her, or by her, or both" (p. 266). But he is sound in saying that they remind one of adults.
2 "A Day of Misfortune," in *Anthology of Children's Literature,* ed. by Edna Johnson, Evelyn R. Sickles, and Frances C. Sayers; 3rd ed. (Boston, 1959), pp. 1123–26.
3 *Ibid.,* p. 1120.

Gordon: "The *Alice* Books
and the Metaphors of Victorian Childhood"

I wish to express thanks for the useful advice offered me during the writing of this essay by John Vogelsang, Chris Snodgrass, and Irving Massey, three enthusiastic colleagues.—JAN B. GORDON

1 Florence Becker Lennon: *The Life of Lewis Carroll* (New York, 1962), Chapter 4.

2 For the fine points of this distinction between children's literature and abandoned adult literature, see the splendid essay by Isabelle Jan: "Children's Literature and Bourgeois Society Since 1860," *Yale French Studies*, pp. 43, 57–72. Miss Jan finds that the linguistic reversals and word games that abound in so much late-nineteenth-century children's literature are related to the *stade du miroir*, the "mirror phase" of identity location in child development.

3 Elie Halevy: *England in 1815* (London, 1924), p. 72.

4 Philippe Ariès, "At the Point of Origin," *Yale French Studies*, pp. 15–27, 43.

5 Michel Foucault: *The Order of Things* (New York, 1970), p. 174.

6 Gaston Bachelard: *The Poetics of Space* (New York, 1964), pp. 196 ff.

7 Michel Foucault: *Madness & Civilization* (New York, 1967), pp. 164 ff.

8 The investigation of the literature dealing with the Victorian child's education is an unmined source of information applicable to an understanding of the concept of childhood. One of the few essays that expounds the differences between conflicting theories of development is that by Terry H. Gra-

bar: "'Scientific' Education and Richard Feverel," *Victorian Studies*, XIV, 2 (Dec. 1970), pp. 130–41.

9 See Gillian Avery: *Nineteenth-Century Children* (London, 1965) for an elaboration of themes common to the literature of childhood in the period. Whatever other characteristics children's literature may share, it seldom exhibits the characteristics of the *Bildungsroman*, the typical apprentice-novel, primarily because children have little conception of a difference between artifice and play. That distinction, as Susanna Millar and other child psychologists have suggested, arises much later in the child's development.

10 Harry Levin: "Wonderland Revisited," *Kenyon Review*, XXVII, pp. 608–14.

11 In one important sense, Alice stops growing when she runs out of room and feels herself enclosed by impacted space. One thinks immediately of all those overcrowded and overdecorated Victorian interiors, which were phenomenologically filled. So many of Landseer's paintings show the child virtually suffocating, entrapped in a space that has been transformed into artifact. Obviously, those children who escaped such impingement of being did so by manufacturing their own spaces, and the metaphor for that activity may well be the artist.

Sewell: "Lewis Carroll
and T. S. Eliot as Nonsense Poets"

1 Ezra Pound in the Cantos refers to Mr. Eliot as either "the Rev. Eliot" or "Old

Possum," as if he, too, saw the dilemma
of the connection.

2 For the end of the poem particularly,
the Baker in *The Hunting of the Snark*

is also a helpful commentator: "I said
it in Hebrew, I said it in Dutch, I said
it in German and Greek," etc.

Holmes: "The Philosopher's Alice"

1 Martin Gardner says "White Pawn
(Alice) to play, and win in eleven

moves." See *The Annotated Alice*, p.
172. [Ed.]

Leslie: "Lewis Carroll and the Oxford Movement"

1 I owe the profound suggestion that
Humpty Dumpty may represent Verbal

Inspiration to the Reverend Ronald
Knox.

Taylor: "Through the Looking-Glass"

1 Stuart Dodgson Collingwood: *The
Life and Letters of Lewis Carroll* (London, 1898), p. 138; Williams and Falconer: *Lewis Carroll Handbook* (New
York, 1962), p. 236.

2 *A Selection from the Letters of Lewis
Carroll to his Child-Friends* (London,
1933) ed. by Evelyn M. Hatch, p. 79.

3 Collingwood, p. 173.

4 Williams and Falconer, pp. 48–9.

5 E. T. Bell: *History of Mathematics, p.*
555, Note 15.

6 *Ritual Worship*, p. 13.

7 Florence Becker Lennon: *The Life of
Lewis Carroll* (New York, 1962), pp.
174–5.

8 *Ibid.*, p. 131.

9 *Cornhill Magazine*, July, 1932.

10 Helmut Gernsheim: *Lewis Carroll:
Photographer* (New York, 1949).

Milner: "The Poems in *Alice in Wonderland*"

1 Note that in this version the order of
stanzas differs from that reprinted in
Gardner's *Annotated Alice*. Moreover,
Milner omits the penultimate stanza,

and attributes the original poem to G.
W. Lanford. Gardner's evidence favors
David Bates. [Ed.]

Goldschmidt: "*Alice in Wonderland* Psychoanalyzed"

1 J. S. Bayliss first discovered the possibilities of an analysis of *Alice*, and

some of his valuable interpretations are
included in this essay.

Schilder: "Psychoanalytic Remarks on
Alice in Wonderland and Lewis Carroll"

1 The following books were chiefly used for this article: Langford Reed: *The Life of Lewis Carroll* (London, 1932); Walter de la Mare: *Lewis Carroll* (London 1932); *The Lewis Carroll Book* (New York. The Dial Press; 1931), with an introduction by Richard Herrick; Lewis Carroll: *The Russian Journal and Other Selections*, ed. by John Francis McDermott (New York: Dutton; 1935); Belle Moses: *Lewis Carroll in Wonderland and at Home* (New York, 1910); Stuart Dodgson Collingwood: *The Life and Letters of Lewis Carroll* (London, 1898).

2 Schilder here makes the same error as John Skinner was later to make in his 1947 essay, "Lewis Carroll's Adventures in Wonderland," only a portion of which is reprinted in this volume. The fact is there were seven girls and four boys born to the Reverend and Mrs. Charles Dodgson [Ed.].

3 Cf. my paper "Psychoanalysis of Space," *International Journal for Psychoanalysis*, XVII (1936).

4 Not all the phrases within quotation marks are Carroll's actual words. They are used in this manner to indicate situations, etc. [Ed.].

5 The *original* explanation of Carroll's portmanteau words was given by Humpty Dumpty in Chapter VI of *Looking-Glass*. The author here refers to Carroll's further explanations in the Preface to *The Hunting of the Snark*.

6 "Form as a Principle in Play of Children," *The Journal of Genetic Psychology*, IL (1936), pp. 254–61. The same problems are to be found in obsession neurosis: "*Zur Psychoanalyses der Geometrie, Arithmetik und Physik*," *Imago*, XXII (1936), pp. 389–95.

7 "*Die symbolische Gleichung: Mädchen =Phallus*," *Internationale Zeitsch. für Psychoan.*, XXII (1936), pp. 299–315.

Grotjahn: "About the Symbolization of
Alice's Adventures in Wonderland"

1 Lewis Carroll: *Alice's Adventures in Wonderland*. (New York: Modern Library; 1937).

2 Reprinted in this volume. See pp. 293–307. [Ed.]

3 Florence Becker Lennon: *Victoria Through the Looking-Glass* (New York, 1945).

4 Sigmund Freud: *Wit and Its Relation to the Unconscious* (London, 1905), pp. 633–803.

5 As summarized, for instance, in Martin Grotjahn's "The Importance of Freud's Book *Wit and Its Relation to the Unconscious*, A Note on Teaching Psychoanalysis," *Samiksa, Journal of* the Indian Psychoanalytic Society, I, 1 (1947), pp. 39–49.

6 Reprinted in this volume. See pp. 283–92. [Ed.]

7 Otto Fenichel: "*Die Symbolische Gleichung: Mädchen=Phallus*," *Int. Zeitschrift f.P.A.* XXII (1936), pp. 299–315.

8 Helene Deutsch: "Don Quixote and Don Quixotism," *The Psychoanalytic Quarterly*, VI, 2 (April 1937), pp. 215–222.

9 Fritz Moellenhoff: "Remarks on the Popularity of Mickey Mouse," *American Imago*, I, 19 (June 1940), pp. 19–32.

10 Hanns Sachs: "Observation of a Train-
ing-Analyst," *Psychoanalytic Quarterly,*   XVI, 2 (1947), pp. 157–68.

Greenacre: "The Character of Dodgson
as Revealed in the Writings of Carroll"

1 Dodgson "turned out nearly 200 little
printed pamphlets, many of which
consist of only a single sheet. Nearly
60 were devoted to topics in mathematics and logic; over 30 were concerned with games he invented or
were schemes for ciphering. Nearly
50 were related to Christ Church—
its little quarrels, its proposals for
change, its regulations. . . . Over 50
were devoted to miscellaneous subjects—how not to catch cold, how to
score tennis tournaments, on second-
hand books, proposals for a new
dramatic institute and for a bowdler-
ized Shakespeare for young girls, how
to play billiards on a circular table
. . . how to write and register correspondence, common errors in spelling,
on the profits of authorship, an adver-
tisement for selling a house, a questionnaire based on the rules for
commissions chargeable on overdue
postal orders, how to memorize dates,
etc. etc. . . . In one series [of pamph-
lets] he describes an unbelievably
complicated variant on croquet, successive editions making it less and less
likely that anyone would ever learn
the rules." Quoted from Warren
Weaver.

2 See Editor's Note in the *Diaries* under
July 26, 1879.

3 Warren Weaver, who has examined
many of Lewis Carroll's manuscripts,
letters, and notations, writes in
"Alice's Adventures in Wonderland:
Its Origin and Its Author" (*Princeton
University Library Chronicle, XIII,*
1951):

"Every example I have ever seen is
written with black ink up to June

27, 1870; in purple from Dec. 16,
1870 to Dec. 7, 1890; and then
black thereafter, except
a) one item dated January 27, 1871,
written in purple ink but cor-
rected in black.
b) one item dated June 10, 1872, in
black.
c) one item dated June 12, 1872 in
black with purple corrections.
Every example I have seen is dated February 5, 1891, or later is in black."

4 Compare this with the account of
Swift's anonymous delivery of his manuscript at night.

5 Compare the alleged treatment of the
manuscript with the following stanza
from *Poeta Fit, Non Nascitur*:

*For first you write a sentence
And then you chop it small;
Then mix the bits and sort them out
Just as they chance to fall:
The order of the phrases makes
No difference at all.*
In *Phantasmagoria,* 1869

6 The Cheshire cat did not originate
with Carroll, but is part of the folklore of the county in which he was
born. Its appearance in *Wonderland,*
however, has made it so famous that
its earlier existence is often overlooked.
The phrase "grinning like a Cheshire
cat" or "grinning like a chessy cat" appears in various writings before 1865.
Wolcott (Peter Pindar) wrote in 1792,
"Lo, like a Cheshire cat our court will
grin." There seem to be two main
theories regarding its origin: One is
based on the fact that a cheese was
formerly made in Cheshire molded like
a grinning cat. This has a peculiar Car-

rollian appeal, as it provokes the fantasy that the chessy cat may eat the rat that would eat the cheese. It reminds one further of the current phrase for a smugly smiling person, "He looks like the cat that has eaten the canary," and again we ask with Alice, "Do cats eat bats, or bats eat cats?" The explanation for the grin given by Brewer, however, is that the cats there knew that Cheshire is the County Palatine, and the idea is so funny that they are perpetually amused by it. (Certainly a cat may look at—and laugh at—a king.) Another explanation offered is that a lion rampant being the crest of an influential noble family of Cheshire, a cat's head became substituted for it due to the maladroit work of a painter who made signs for inns and other public places. Thus the cat became associated with Cheshire. The most coherent explanation, offered by Michael Perkins, relates the grinning Cheshire cat to the "witch cat" which began to grin on Hallowe'en in the Isle of Man and frightened observers all the way to Scotland. This cat was probably derived from the Palug Cat which the Welsh Triads record as having been kittened by the sow Henwen under the spell of the magician Coll, at Collfrew, at the Black Stone in Menai Straits. In North Wales, the cat bogey (which reappears in our grinning Jack-o'-Lantern) was a black hog with a "cutty" tail. It seems related then to the Manx cat of the Isle of Man. The Dodgsons made a family excursion to Beaumaris when Charles was a young boy, and the Menai Bridge reappears in his rhymes about the aged, aged man. The cat without a tail, or the Manx cat, becomes then converted into the cat without a head, or the head without a body, and is part of the decapitation and body-mutilation theme so apparent in Carroll's writing.

7 The close connection between the air (which is set in motion by the fan or given special significance when breathed in from the nosegay) and eating and drinking is again apparent.

8 Thomas Moore: "My Heart and Lute," in *Poetry and Pictures.*

9 "Resolution and Independence."

10 This whole picture reminds one inevitably of Carroll's attack on the cats of Finborough Road.

Róheim: "Further Insights"

1 Not included in the portion of Dr. Róheim's book excerpted here. [Ed.].

Burke: "The Thinking of the Body"

1 [These] pages are concerned with ways in which the functions of bodily excretion attain expression (sometimes direct, more often indirect) in works of the imagination. They were written in connection with a book I am writing on the subject of Poetics which, since the days of Aristotle's famous treatise, has variously concerned itself with processes of "catharsis" in art.

2 Recall in this connection the Aristophanic detail in Samuel Beckett's story "Yellow" (*New World Writing*, No. 10), explicitly concerned with a reference to bowel movements in a hospital: "He whistled a snatch outside the duty-room."

Empson: "Alice in Wonderland: The Child as Swain"

1 The second line of this poem is quoted by Martin Gardner as reading "with bitter *tidings*," not "summons." [Ed.]

2 It was getting worse when the *Alices* were written. In what Hugh Kingsmill calls "the fatal fifties" skirts were so big that the small waist was not much needed for contrast, so it can't be blamed for the literary works of that decade.

3 Empson here quotes from the early text of the second chapter of *Looking-Glass*, perhaps Dent's Everyman's Library. The later text, as reprinted in The Modern Library edition and elsewhere, has the Rose reply, "She's one of the kind that has nine spikes, you know." Just as Carroll changed his Passion-flower to a Tiger-lily when it was pointed out to him that the name was an allusion to Christ, so too must he have come to see the crown of thorns as a Christly reference and changed it in later versions [Ed.].

Bloomingdale: "Alice as *Anima*: The Image of Woman in Carroll's Classic"

1 "The solemn proclamation of the *Assumptio Mariae* which we have experienced in our own day is an example of the way symbols develop through the ages. The impelling motive behind it did not come from the ecclesiastical authorities, who had given clear proof of their hesitation by postponing the declaration for nearly a hundred years, but from the Catholic masses, who have insisted more and more vehemently on this development. Their insistence is, at bottom, the urge of the archetype to realize itself." C. J. Jung, in "The Sign of the Fishes," *AION: Researches into the Phenomenology of the Self*, Vol. 9, part II, *Collected Works of C. G. Jung*. New York: Pantheon; 1959. P. 87.

2 *The Development of Personality*, Vol. 17, *Collected Works of C. G. Jung*. New York: Pantheon; 1964. P. 198.

3 "The Process of Individuation," by M.-L. von Franz, in *Man and His Symbols*, conceived and edited by C. G. Jung. Garden City: Doubleday; 1964. P. 185.

4 *The Development of Personality, loc. cit.*

5 "Concerning the Archetypes with Special Reference to the Anima Concept," *The Archetypes and the Collective Unconscious*, Vol. 9, Part I, *Collected Works of C. G. Jung*. New York: Pantheon; 1968. Pp. 54–72.

6 *Ibid.*

7 "Anima and Animus," II, from "The Relations Between the Ego and the Unconscious," *The Basic Writings of C. G. Jung*. New York: The Modern Library; 1959. Pp. 177–78.

8 From unpublished seminar notes, "Visions" I, printed in the Glossary of *Memories, Dreams, Reflections*. New York: Random House; 1963. P. 380.

9 Biographical facts taken from Phyllis Greenacre's *Swift and Carroll: A Psychoanalytic Study of Two Lives*. New York: International Universities Press; 1955; and John Skinner's "Lewis Carroll's Adventures in Wonderland," in *Psychoanalysis and Literature: An Anthology*, edited by Hendrik M. Ruitenbeek. New York: E. P. Dutton; 1964.

10 Greenacre, *loc. cit.*, pp. 117–207.

11 Derek Hudson, *Lewis Carroll*. London: Constable and Co., Ltd.; 1955.

Pp. 58–76.

12 *Ibid.*, p. 66.

13 Greenacre, *loc. cit.*, p. 132.

14 C. G. Jung, III "The Syzygy: Anima and Animus" *Psyche & Symbol*, ed. by Violet S. de Laszlo. New York: Doubleday; 1958. Pp. 9–22.

15 *Ibid.*, p. 11.

16 von Franz, *loc. cit.*, p. 210.

17 "The Psychology of the Child Archetype," *The Archetypes and the Collective Unconscious*, pp. 151–81.

18 *Ibid.*

19 *Ibid.*

20 *Psyche & Symbol*, p. 11.

21 "Psychological Aspects of the Mother Archetype," *The Archetypes and the Collective Unconscious*, pp. 75–110.

22 *Ibid.*, p. 82.

23 *Ibid.*, pp. 75–110.

24 Chapter 10, "Christ the Harlequin," *The Feast of Fools*. New York: Harper & Row; 1969. Pp. 139–57.

25 *Ibid.*

26 *Ibid.*

27 *Ibid.*

28 *Ibid.*

Rackin: "Alice's Journey to the End of Night"

1 All references in my text to *Alice's Adventures in Wonderland* are to *The Annotated Alice*, ed. Martin Gardner (New York, 1960).

2 See, e.g., Alexander L. Taylor: *The White Knight: A Study of C. L. Dodgson* (London, 1952), pp. 46–47.

3 Alice's twisted nursery verses often make for more Darwinian sense than do their original models. See the essay by William Empson, pp. 344–73, for some comments on the Darwinian theory behind much of Carroll's subversive satire.

4 See, e.g., Phyllis Greenacre, *Swift and Carroll: A Psychoanalytic Study of Two Lives* (New York, 1955).

5 Harry Morgan Ayres, in *Carroll's Alice* (New York, 1936), pp. 63–5, points out that these misunderstandings derive from a peculiarity of English—"it is rich in homophones." This peculiarity, Ayres feels, accounts for the particular verbal nonsense which characterizes English humor. Ayres also states that effective communication depends to a great extent on the emotional attitude of the listener: since words are "mere sounds thrown out to a listener as clues to the mental state of the speaker with respect to things or actions," all the speaker can hope is that "the listener will piece these clues together intelligently and above all sympathetically." Is it possible, then, to assume that Alice's misunderstandings (*tale* vs. *tail, not* vs. *knot,* etc.) hint at the beginning of Alice's revolt against the maddening chaos of Wonderland? Is she here being covertly antagonistic and playing the same game that Wonderland plays all along—that is, asking her opponent to do what is finally impossible?

6 Chapter III foreshadows another feature of linguistic confusion that will reach its absurd apex in the hilarious final pages of the book. The Mouse's tale, printed emblematically in the shape of a mouse's long tail, is about the law; and certainly our ordinary conceptions of the law depend in great measure on the common assumption that language, at the bottom of most law, is potentially unambiguous. The word *trial* itself ideally connotes a suspension of judgment as well as a final decision. But in the Mouse's tail-tale, as in the final trial of *Alice* (and in many trials of expressionistic fiction since 1865), the prosecutor can also be the judge and jury, and the judgment can be passed before the trial has begun.

7 Quoted by Roger Lancelyn Green in

The Lewis Carroll Handbook (London, 1962), p. 281.

8 Note how the Mock Turtle's song that accompanies the Lobster Quadrille twists the sadistic original—" 'Will you walk into my parlour?' said the spider to the fly"—into an innocuous nursery rhyme. This parody demonstrates that Wonderland refuses to be consistent to itself: if the aboveground rhymes tend to hide or deny Darwinian theory, Wonderland's poems will be vengefully Darwiniana; but if above-ground rhymes admit the cruelty of nature, then Wonderland produces harmless nonsense verses where the creatures of the sea join in dance or owls and panthers share pies.

Fensch: "Lewis Carroll: The First Acidhead"

1 Note the discrepancies between Fensch's quotations from the lyrics, and the lyrics themselves. Variants include "hookah-smoking character" for "hookah-smoking caterpillar," "sloppy dead" for "be dead," "off her head" for "lost her head" and "heed your head" for "feed your head." [Ed.]

2 Fensch here differs from Harry Levin and others in this volume who maintain that Carroll was at best a mediocre mathematician. It would be of interest to learn what documentation Fensch has that Carroll was really "fantastic" at it. Perhaps he had read Strong's memoir. [Ed.]

About the Authors

ANONYMOUS continues to be one of the most widely read poets and critics in the English language. His work is marked by a great versatility of style.

W. H. AUDEN was born in York, England, in 1907, and educated at Oxford. He has been an American citizen since 1946. His poems—which range in subject matter from politics to psychology to Christianity—have earned the Pulitzer Prize, the National Book Award, the Bollingen Prize, the Guinness Poetry Award, and the National Medal for Literature. His recent books include two volumes of critical essays, *The Dyer's Hand* (1962) and *Secondary Worlds* (1969); as well as *Collected Shorter Poems* (1967) and *Collected Longer Poems* (1969).

JUDITH BLOOMINGDALE was born in Cohoes, New York, in 1939. She took her undergraduate and graduate degrees from Syracuse University, where she taught for a short time. More recently she has served as an editor with The Macmillan Company, publishers. Her poetry and criticism have appeared in a variety of journals, including *Modern Poetry Studies*, *The English Record*, *Prairie Schooner*, *Papers of the Bibliographical Society of America*, and the *New York Times*.

KENNETH BURKE, born in Pittsburgh in 1897, was educated at Ohio State and Columbia. For a number of years he taught at Bennington, and has lectured at many universities, including Chicago and Syracuse. Most recently he was Regents Professor at the University of California, Santa Barbara. Among his books are *The Philosophy of Literary Form*, *A Grammar of Motives*, and *Language as Symbolic Action*.

JOHN CIARDI, born in 1916, was educated at Bates and at Tufts. He has taught English at Harvard and Rutgers. Since 1956 he has been poetry editor of the *Saturday Review*. He is author of many collections of poetry, including *As If*, *Poems New and Selected* (1955), *In Fact* (1963), and *Lives of X* (1971). His translations of Dante are widely used in the classroom, as is his *How Does a Poem Mean?* from which the essay in this volume was extracted.

WALTER DE LA MARE (1873-1956) was an English poet of unusually sensitive and imaginative lyrics in traditional forms, as well as a much underrated writer of short stories. His books include *The Return* (1910), *Peacock Pie* (1913), *Motley and Other Poems* (1918), *Broomsticks* (1925), *On the Edge* (1930), and a novel, *Memoirs of a Midget* (1921). His complete poems were published here in 1970.

WILLIAM EMPSON was born in England in 1906 and graduated from Cambridge, where he studied with I. A. Richards. From 1941 to 1946 he was Chinese Editor for the BBC. He has taught at the Bunrika Daigaku in Tokyo, Peking National University, and since 1953 has been Professor of English Literature at Sheffield University. His influential volumes of criticism are *Seven Types of Ambiguity* (1930), *Some Versions of the Pastoral* (1935), and *The Structure of Complex Words* (1951). His *Collected Poems* appeared in 1955.

THOMAS FENSCH (born in 1943) is the author of *The Lion and the Lambs* and the highly satirical *Alice in Acidland.* He is a graduate of Ashland College and the University of Iowa's journalism school, from which he received his M.A. in 1967. He has written numerous magazine articles for a variety of publications, and, like Lewis Carroll, is a photographer.

ROBERT GRAVES (born in 1895) is the prolific English poet, novelist, and essayist, perhaps best known for his extraordinary love poems, his poems protesting the horrors of World War I, and his highly subjective study, *The White Goddess.* Among Mr. Graves's many books are *Goodbye to All That* (1929), an autobiography; and *Claudius the God* (1924) and *I Claudius* (1934), unusual historical novels with a psychological approach to their subject. He was elected Professor of Poetry at Oxford in 1961.

A[NTHONY] M[AURICE] E[LIM] GOLDSCHMIDT was a young British man of letters who was killed in action in North Africa in April, 1943, at the age of 31, while serving as a lieutenant in the Royal Artillery. His "Alice" essay, anticipating and perhaps even parodying the Freudian interpretations that were to follow, was penned while an undergraduate at Oxford, where he was a scholar at Harrow and an exhibitioner at Balliol College. At Oxford he also edited the undergraduate paper, *The Cherwell.* He later was a contributor to *Horizon.* Under the name Anthony Maurice he collaborated with Terence Rattigan on a play, *Follow the Leader* (1940); under the name Anthony Goldsmith he collaborated with Derek Hudson on a farce, *On the Slant* (written in 1933, but unpublished until 1945), and the admirable translation of Flaubert's *L'education sentimentale*, which appeared in the Everyman's Library (1941).

JAN B. GORDON is an assistant professor of English at State University of New York at Buffalo. A native Texan with advanced degrees from Princeton, he held a Leverhulme Visiting Lectureship to the University of Warwick, United Kingdom, in 1966-67. A frequent essayist on the relationship between *fin-de-siècle* visual and verbal art, he has contributed to *Kenyon Review, Criticism, Victorian Studies,*

Commonweal, Salmagundi, Southern Review, and *Journal of Art and Aesthetics Criticism.*

ROGER LANCELYN (GILBERT) GREEN was born in 1918. One of the leading experts on both Lewis Carroll and the Reverend C. L. Dodgson, he is editor of *The Lewis Carroll Diaries* and currently is co-editing with Morton H. Cohen more than three thousand of Carroll's letters.

PHYLLIS GREENACRE (born in 1894) is Professor of Clinical Psychiatry, Cornell University Medical School, and a practicing psychoanalyst in New York City. She has edited a volume, *Affective Disorders,* and is the author of both *Trauma, Growth and Personality* and *Swift and Carroll: A Psychoanalytic Study of Two Lives.*

HORACE GREGORY, born in Milwaukee in 1898, studied classical literature at the University of Wisconsin under the distinguished Latinist, William Ellery Leonard. From 1934 until his retirement in 1960, Mr. Gregory taught Classical Literature and Modern Poetry at Sarah Lawrence College. His books include critical studies of D. H. Lawrence, Amy Lowell, and Dorothy Richardson, in addition to seven collections of his own verse, for which he has received the Russell Loines Award, the Academy of American Poets Award, and the Bollingen Prize. His autobiography, *The House on Jefferson Street,* was published in 1971.

MARTIN GROTJAHN holds an M.D. degree and lives in Los Angeles. His psychoanalytical studies of children's literature have appeared in several journals, notably *The American Imago.*

JOHN P. HINZ (born in 1927) took his B.A. from the City College in New York and his advanced degrees from Columbia. He has taught at City College and, more recently, Richmond College in Staten Island. During 1961-62 he was a Fulbright Guest Professor at the University of Graz in Austria.

ROGER W. HOLMES, Chairman of the Department of Philosophy at Mount Holyoke College, is author of *The Rhyme of Reason, The Idealism of Giovanni Gentile, Exercises in Logic,* and *An Outline of Logic.* He is active in educational FM and TV work in Massachusetts. In addition, he is the inventor and builder of an electronic machine to test truth functions up to five variables in the field of symbolic logic.

GEORGE LANNING (born in 1925), former editor of the *Kenyon Review,* is the author of three novels (*This Happy Rural Seat, The Pedestal,* and *Green Corn Moon*) and co-author with Robie Macauley of *Technique in Fiction.* His stories have been included in both the *Best American Short Stories* and *O. Henry* annual collections. He received his education at The New School for Social Research and at Kenyon College.

ELSIE LEACH is a professor of English at San José State College in California. She received her B.A., M.A., and Ph.D. from UCLA. Her interests are widespread: besides specializing in seventeenth-century literature, she has written on such diverse characters as Saul Bellow, Dylan Thomas, and John Wesley, as well as Lewis Carroll.

SIR SHANE LESLIE, born in London in 1885, was a friend of Tolstoi and a man of letters who wrote appreciations of Aeschylus, Milton, Huysmans, Stendhal, and Thomas Aquinas, among others. He was a reviewer for the *Daily Telegraph* and the *Sunday Times*. He stood twice for Parliament as an Irish Nationalist and was twice defeated.

FLORENCE BECKER LENNON (born in 1895) is author of *Farewell to Walden* and *Forty Years in the Wilderness*, as well as *Victoria Through the Looking-Glass*. The latter was reprinted in an extensively revised edition in 1962, under the title *The Life of Lewis Carroll*, and again in 1971 in a Dover edition. For many years Mrs. Lennon conducted a program of poetry readings and discussions on radio station WEVD in New York. For the past thirty years she has lived in Boulder, Colorado.

HARRY LEVIN (born in 1912) is Irving Babbitt Professor of Comparative Literature at Harvard University. He has also been Visiting Professor at the Sorbonne, the Salzburg Seminar in American Studies, Tokyo University, and the University of California (Berkeley). Professor Levin has held a Guggenheim Fellowship, an award by the American Institute of Arts and Letters, and is a Fellow of the American Academy of Arts and Sciences and a chevalier of the Legion of Honor. His books include *James Joyce: a Critical Introduction* (1941), *The Overreacher: A Study of Christopher Marlowe* (1952), *Contexts of Criticism* (1957), *The Power of Blackness* (1958), and *The Question of Hamlet* (1959).

FLORENCE MILNER was a contributor to *The Bookman* in the first decade of this century. Her research into the forgotten originals for Car-

roll's poetic parodies resulted in the first such comparative study, making possible those that have followed.

ROBERT PHILLIPS (born 1938), the editor of this volume, has taught at Syracuse University and the New School, and currently is an editor of *Modern Poetry Studies*. He is the author of a book of poetry (*Inner Weather*, 1966), a book of short stories (*The Land of Lost Content*, 1970), and a forthcoming critical study of the English writer and painter, Denton Welch. He has published essays on Yeats, Joyce, Dylan Thomas, and others.

J. B. PRIESTLEY, born in 1894, is the English novelist, playwright, and journalist. He is best-known as the author of *The Good Companions* (1929) and *Angel Pavement* (1930), both popular novels compared by critics to Dickens' early work; and *Dangerous Corner*, a novel later dramatized as a play of the same name. His critical works include *The English Novel* (1927) and *Literature and Western Man* (1960).

DONALD RACKIN was born in Newark, New Jersey, in 1933. He took his B.A. from Rutgers in 1954, his M.A. from Columbia in 1955, and his Ph.D. in language and literature from the University of Illinois in 1964. Since 1962 he has been on the faculty of the Department of English at Temple University.

GÉZA RÓHEIM, the late psychoanalyst, was author of numerous studies, including *The Riddle of the Sphinx* (1934), *The Origin and Function of Culture* (1943), *The Gates of the Dream* (1953), and a posthumous volume, *Magic and Schizophrenia* (1955). His lively discussions demonstrated a wide knowledge of the beliefs and practices of black magic incantations.

EDWARD SALMON was a frequent book reviewer in the second half of the last century, publishing in *Nineteenth Century* and elsewhere.

ROBERT SCOTT (1811-1887) was born in Devonshire. Educated at Shrewsbury and Christ Church, Oxford, he received his B.A. in 1833. In 1835 he was made a fellow of Balliol, and in 1854, Master of Balliol. A lexicographer, he was made Professor of Exegesis at Oxford in 1861, a post he held until 1870 when he became Dean of Rochester. Although Dr. Scott published two books of his sermons, he is best remembered for his collaboration with H. C. Liddell on the great Greek-English Lexicon (1843). He is also the German translator of Carroll's "Jabberwocky," which he published in 1872 as "Der Jammerwoch"!

PAUL SCHILDER, M.D. and Ph.D., at the time of his essay was Research Professor, Department of Psychiatry, Medical College of New York University, and a member of the Psychiatric Division of Bellevue Hospital. His speech against exposing children to the dangerous corruption of Lewis Carroll's books, delivered before the American Psychoanalytical Society, caused considerable furor in the press in late 1936 and early 1937. He has contributed to *International Journal for Psychoanalysis; The Journal of Genetic Psychology*; and elsewhere.

ELIZABETH SEWELL, British philosopher, poet, and critic, is the author of *Paul Valéry, The Structure of*

Poetry, The Field of Nonsense, and *The Orphic Voice.* She has taught at Ohio State, Vassar, Fordham, Princeton, and Bennett College. Recently her poems were issued by University of North Carolina Press.

JOHN SKINNER (born 1925) is a psychoanalyst and the author of many professional articles. In 1964 he was a contributor to *Psychoanalysis and Literature,* an important symposium edited by Hendrik M. Ruitenbeek. Dr. Skinner lives in Los Angeles.

GRACE SLICK is a member of and lead singer for a Rock group with the highly imaginative name, The Jefferson Airplane. Her original lyrics have been anthologized in Richard Goldstein's *The Poetry of Rock* (1969).

PATRICIA MEYER SPACKS (born in 1929) is author of *The Varied God*: A Critical Study of Thomson's "The Seasons" (1959). She is Chairman of the English Department at Wellesley College.

THOMAS BANKS STRONG, nineteenth-century cleric, was Dean of Christ Church and later Bishop of Oxford. He was an associate of Lewis Carroll.

ALLEN TATE (born in 1891) is the noted Tennessee poet, novelist, critic, teacher, and editor. Tate's career began as an editor of the *Fugitive* (1922), and his interest in regionalism is displayed in contributions to the symposia *I'll Take My Stand* (1930), *The Critique of Humanism* (1930), and *Who Owns America?* (1936), as well as in interpretive biographies of Stonewall Jackson (1928) and Jefferson Davis (1929). He is, however, best known for his literary essays, collected in 1959, and for his metaphysical and highly satirical poems, most recently gathered as *The Swimmers and Other Selected Poems* (1971).

ALEXANDER L. TAYLOR (born 1909) lives in Ayr, Scotland, and is the author of *The White Knight*, a detailed and unique study of Lewis Carroll published in 1952; and co-author of *Bairnsangs* (MacMillan, London, 1955). Educated at Ayr Academy and Glasgow University, he currently is Principal Teacher of English at Cumnock Academy, Ayrshire, which he describes as "a large comprehensive with a staff shortage." During 1969-70 he was an exchange teacher at Willamette High School, Eugene, Oregon, which experience provided the material for his book-in-progress.

EDMUND WILSON (born in 1895) is recognized as the chronicler of the literary world in America and Europe from the early twenties to the present time. After education at Princeton he served as an editor of *Vanity Fair*, and later joined the staffs of the *New Republic* and the *New Yorker*. He is the author or editor of more than twenty-four books, including *A Prelude* (1967), described as the first installment of his autobiography. Of his earlier books perhaps the best known is *Axel's Castle* (1931), a study of symbolism and imaginative literatures.

VIRGINIA WOOLF (1882–1941) was the brilliant novelist and essayist and a member of the famous "Bloomsbury Group." Her books include *The Voyage Out* (1915), *Jacob's Room* (1923), *Mrs. Dalloway* (1925), *To the Lighthouse* (1927), *The Waves* (1931), and *Between the Acts* (1941). She was married to Leonard Woolf, a noted journalist, political thinker, and author of one of the important multi-volume autobiographies of recent years. Together, the Woolfs founded the Hogarth Press, which published books by Katherine Mansfield, T. S. Eliot, and E. M. Forster as well as by Mrs. Woolf.

ALEXANDER WOOLLCOTT (1887-1943) was born in the Fourierist colony called the North American Phalanx, in New Jersey. He became a well-known journalist, drama critic, and writer in New York, carrying on as well a radio program called "The Town Crier." Here and in his many articles for the *New Yorker*, he gained a great reputation for sentimentality and sharp wit. He is the author of several books, among them *Shouts and Murmurs* (1922), *While Rome Burns* (1934), and the anthologies *The Woollcott Reader* (1935) and *Woollcott's Second Reader* (1937).

An ALICE Checklist

Selected Criticism
and Comment
(1865-1971)

Aikman, C. M.: "Lewis Carroll," *New Century Review*, V (January 1899), pp. 17–33.

Alexander, Peter: "Logic and the Humor of Lewis Carroll," *Proceedings of the Leeds Philosophical and Literary Society*, VI (1951), pp. 551–66.

Anon.: "Children's Books," *The Athenaeum*, 1900 (December 16, 1865), p. 844.

_____: "Immortal Alice," *The Living Age*, CCCXLII (March 1932), pp. 53–7.

_____: "A Century of Alice," *Newsweek* (July 12, 1965), p. 86.

_____: "Alice, One Hundred. Being a Catalogue in Celebration of the 100th Birthday of *Alice's Adventures in Wonderland*" Victoria, B.C., 1966.

Arnold, Ethel M.: "Reminiscences of Lewis Carroll," *Atlantic*, CXLIII (June 1929), pp. 782–9.

Auden, W. H.: "The Man who Wrote 'Alice,'" *New York Times Book Review* (February 28, 1954), p. 4.

_____: "Today's 'Wonder-World' Needs Alice," *New York Times Magazine* (July 1, 1962), p. 5.

Ayres, Harry Morgan: *Carroll's Alice*. New York: Columbia University Press; 1936.

_____: "Carroll's Withdrawal of the 1865 Alice," *Huntington Library Bulletin*, VI (1934), pp. 153–63.

_____: "Lewis Carroll and the Alice Books," *Columbia University Quarterly*, XXIV, 2 (June 1932).

Bacon, Deborah: "The Meaning of Nonsense: A Psychoanalytical Approach to

Lewis Carroll." Columbia University. Unpublished doctoral dissertation; 1951.

Beerbohm, Max: "Alice Again Awakened," *Around Theatres*, New York: Knopf; 1930. Pp. 107–12.

Bernadete, Doris: "Alice Among the Professors," *Western Humanities Review*, V (1951), pp. 239–47.

Bloch, Robert: "All in a Golden Afternoon," *Fantasy & Science Fiction*, June 1956.

Bloomingdale, Judith: "Alice as *Anima*: The Image of Woman in Carroll's Classic," *Aspects of Alice*, edited by Robert Phillips. New York: Vanguard; 1971.

Boas, Guy: "Alice," *Blackwood's Magazine*, CCXLII (December 1937), pp. 740–6.

Bond, W. H.: "The Publication of Alice's Adventures in Wonderland," *Harvard Library Bulletin*, X, 3 (Autumn 1956).

Bowman, Isa: *The Story of Lewis Carroll*. London: J. M. Dent; 1899.

Boynton, Mary Fuertes: "An Oxford Don Quixote," *Hispania*, XLVIII (1964), pp. 738–50.

Braithwaite, R. B.: "Lewis Carroll as Logician," *The Mathematical Gazette*, XVI (May 1933).

Buckley, Jerome Hamilton: *The Victorian Temper*. New York: Vintage; 1964. Pp. 2–3.

Burke, Kenneth: "The Thinking of the Body," *Language as Symbolic Action*. Berkeley: University of California Press, 1966. Pp. 308–44.

Burpee, Lawrence J.: "Alice Joins the Immortals," *Dalhousie Review*, XXI (1941), pp. 194–204.

Burt, Maxwell Struthers: *Malice in Blunderland*. New York: Scribners; 1935.

Cammaerts, Emile: *The Poetry of Nonsense*. New York: E. P. Dutton; 1926.

Carroll, Lewis: *The Russian Journal and Other Selections*, ed. John Francis McDermott. New York: Dutton; 1935.

Cecil, David: "Lewis Carroll and Alice," *The Spectator*, CXLIX (July 16, 1932), pp. 74–5.

Chesterton, G. K.: "Both Sides of the Looking-Glass," *The Spice of Life and Other Essays*. Beaconsfield: Darwen Finlayson; 1964. Pp. 66–70.

————: "A Defense of Nonsense," *The Defendant*, 1901.

————: "Lewis Carroll" and "How Pleasant to Meet Mr. Lear," *A Handful of Authors*. New York: Sheed & Ward; 1953.

Ciardi, John: "A Burble Through the Tulgey Wood," *How Does a Poem Mean?* Boston: Houghton, Mifflin; 1959. Pp. 678–85.

Cohen, Morton N.: "Letters from Wonderland," *New York Times Book Review* (November 15, 1970), p. 2.

Collingwood, Stuart Dodgson: *The Life and Letters of Lewis Carroll*. London: Unwin; 1898.

————: *Diversions and Digressions of Lewis Carroll*. New York: Dover Publications; 1961.

Costa, P.: "Lewis Carroll parodie Walton: The Vision of the Three Ts," *Hommage à Paul Dottin,* XLIX, 1965. Pp. 175–84.

Coveney, Peter: *The Image of Childhood.* Baltimore: Penguin Books; 1967. Pp. 242–9.

Crofte-Cooke, Rupert. *Feasting with Panthers: A New Consideration of Some Late Victorian Writers.* New York: Holt, Rinehart & Winston; 1968, Pp. 140–59, 242–3, 291–2.

Darwin, Bernard: "The White Knight's Stamp-Case," *The Spectator,* CLXII (March 10, 1939), pp. 400–01.

De la Mare, Walter: *Lewis Carroll.* London: Faber & Faber; 1932.

————, ed.: *The Eighteen-eighties.* London: Royal Society of Literature of the United Kingdom; 1930. Pp. 218–55.

Deleuze, Gilles: *Logique du Sens.* Paris: Editions de Minuit; 1969.

Demijohn, Thom: *Black Alice. An Evil Fairy Tale.* New York: Avon Books; 1970. (Novel.)

Dobson, Austin: "Proem," *Alice's Adventures in Wonderland.* London: Heinemann; 1907.

Dodgson, Charles Lutwidge: *The Diaries of Lewis Carroll.* New York: Oxford University Press; 1954.

Duhamel, P. Albert: "Humpty Dumpty, Lil' Abner, and Ralph Waldo Emerson," *Delta Epsilon Sigma Bulletin,* VII (1962), pp. 39–44.

Dupont, V.: "Le monde et les personnages animaux dans Alice au pays de merveilles," *Hommage à Paul Dottin,* XLIX, 1965. Pp. 133–73.

Dyson, A. E.: "Trial by Enigma," *Twentieth Century,* CLX (1956), pp. 49–64.

Earnest, Ernest: "The Walrus and the Carpenter," *CEA Critic,* XXVI, iii (1963), p. 1.

Eastman, Max: *The Enjoyment of Laughter.* New York: Simon & Schuster; 1936.

Edgar, Randolph: "The Author of Alice," *The Bellman* (March 22, 1913).

Empson, William: "Alice in Wonderland: The Child as Swain," *Some Versions of Pastoral.* London: Chatto & Windus; 1935. New York: New Directions; 1938.

Eperson, D. B.: "Lewis Carroll, Mathematician," *The Mathematical Gazette,* XVII (May 1933), pp. 92–100.

Ettleson, Abraham: *Lewis Carroll's Through the Looking-Glass Decoded.* New York: Philosophical Library; 1966.

Evans, Luther H.: "The Alice Manuscript," *Alice's Adventures Under Ground,* Ann Arbor: University Microfilms; 1964.

Fadiman, Clifton: "Maze in the Snow," *Party of One.* Cleveland: World Publishers; 1955. Pp. 404–10.

Fensch, Thomas: *Alice in Acidland.* New York: A. S. Barnes; 1970.

————: "Lewis Carroll: The First Acidhead," *Story: The Yearbook of Discovery.* New York: Four Winds Press; 1969. Pp. 253–6.

Field, Richard Montgomery: *Alice's Adventures in Atomland in the Plastic Age.* South Duxbury, Mass., 1949.

Finkenstaedt, Thomas: "The Cheshire Cat of the Labour Ministry," *Lebende*

Sprachen, II (1957), pp. 9–10.

Firman, Catharine: "Lewis Carroll, Oxford Satirist," *Claremont Quarterly*, VIII, 1 (1960), pp. 69–72.

Frye, Northrop: *Anatomy of Criticism. Four Essays*. Princeton: Princeton University Press; 1957. Pp. 225, 310.

Furniss, Harry: *Confessions of a Caricaturist*. London: Bradbury, Agney & Co.; 1902.

―――――: *Some Victorian Men*. London: John Lane; 1924.

―――――: "Lewis Carroll," *Strand Magazine* (April 1908).

Gardner, Martin: "Introduction," *The Annotated Alice*. New York: Clarkson N. Potter, Inc., 1966. Pp. 7–16.

―――――, ed.: *The Annotated Snark*. New York: Simon & Schuster; 1962.

―――――: "Introduction," *Alice's Adventures Under Ground*. New York: Whittlesey-McGraw; 1965.

―――――: "Introduction," *The Nursery Alice*. New York: Dover Publications; 1966. Pp. v–xi.

―――――: "Introduction to the Dover Edition," *Alice's Adventures Under Ground*. New York: Dover Publications; 1965. Pp. v–xi. (A facsimile of the 1864 manuscript.)

Garnet, William: "Alice Through the (Convex) Looking Glass," *Mathematical Gazette*, IX (May 1918–January 1919), pp. 237–98.

Gernsheim, Helmut: *Lewis Carroll, Photographer*. New York: Chanticleer Press; 1949.

―――――: "Preface to the Dover Edition," *Lewis Carroll, Photographer*. New York: Dover Publications; 1969.

Gilbert, A.: "From Oxford to Wonderland," *Over Famous Thresholds*, pp. 151–72.

Godman, Stanley. "Lewis Carroll at the Sea Side," *London Times*, July 27, 1957.

―――――: "Lewis Carroll's Sister: Henrietta Dodgson," *Notes & Queries*, V. (1958), pp. 38–9.

―――――: "Lewis Carroll's Final Corrections to *Alice*," *London Times Literary Supplement* (May 2, 1958), p. 248.

―――――: "On All Fours," *Times Literary Supplement* (March 7, 1958).

Goldschmidt, A. M. E.: "*Alice in Wonderland* Psychoanalysed," *New Oxford Outlook* (May 1933), pp. 68–72.

Goldstein, Richard: *The Poetry of Rock*. New York: Bantam Books; 1969. Pp. 8, 107, 113.

Gordon, Jan B.: "The *Alice* Books and the Metaphors of Victorian Childhood," in *Aspects of Alice*, ed. Robert Phillips. New York: Vanguard, 1971.

Graves, Robert: "Alice," *Collected Poems*. Garden City: Doubleday; 1961. P. 59.

―――――: *The White Goddess*. New York: Vintage; 1960. Pp. 375, 496, 499.

Green, Roger Lancelyn: *The Story of Lewis Carroll*. London: Methuen; 1949.

―――――: "Introduction," *The Works of Lewis Carroll*. Feltham: Spring Books; 1965. Pp. 11–18.

―――――: "Introduction," *Alice in Wonderland and Through the Looking-Glass*.

London: Dent, Everyman's Library; 1965.

————: "The Gryphon and the Jabberwock," *Times Literary Supplement* (March 3, 1957), p. 136.

————: "The Real Lewis Carroll," *The Quarterly Review*, January 1954.

————: *Lewis Carroll.* London: Bodley Head; 1960.

————: *Lewis Carroll.* New York: Henry Z. Walck; 1962.

————, ed.: *The Diaries of Lewis Carroll*, 2 vols. New York: Oxford University Press; 1953.

Greenacre, Phyllis: *Swift and Carroll: A Psychoanalytic Study of Two Lives.* New York: International Universities Press; 1955.

Gregory, Horace: "Foreword," *Alice in Wonderland.* New York: New American Library, Signet Classics; 1960. Pp. v–x.

————: "On Lewis Carroll's *Alice* and Her White Knight and Wordsworth's 'Ode' on Immortality," *The Shield of Achilles.* New York: Harcourt, Brace; 1944. Pp. 90–105. (Reprinted in *Collected Essays.* New York: Grove Press; 1971.)

Grotjahn, Martin: "About the Symbolization of *Alice's Adventures in Wonderland*," *American Imago*, IV (1947), pp. 32–41.

Gussow, Mel: "Gregory's *Alice in Wonderland* Tunnels to Daylight," *New York Times* (September 7, 1970), p. 20.

Halpern, Sidney: "The Mother-Killer," *Psychoanalytic Review*, LII, 2 (1965), pp. 71–4.

Hargreaves, C.: "Alice's Recollections of Carrollian Days," *Cornhill Magazine* (July 1932).

Hatch, Beatrice: "Lewis Carroll (Charles Lutwidge Dodgson)," *Strand Magazine*, 15 (April, 1898), pp. 412–23.

Hatch, Evelyn M.: *A Selection from the Letters of Lewis Carroll to His Child-Friends.* London: Macmillan & Co.; 1933.

————: "Recollections of Lewis Carroll," *The Listener*, LIX (1958), p. 198.

Heron, Flodden W.: "The 1866 Appleton *Alice*," *The Colophon*, New Series I, 3 (1936), pp. 422–7.

Herrick, Richard: *The Lewis Carroll Book.* New York: Dial Press; 1931.

Hinz, John: "Alice Meets the Don," *South Atlantic Quarterly*, LII (1953), pp. 253–66.

Holmes, Roger W.: "The Philosopher's *Alice in Wonderland*," *Antioch Review*, XIX (1959), pp. 133–49.

Hubbell, George Shelton: "The Sanity of Wonderland," *Sewanee Review* (October 1927), pp. 587–98.

————: "Triple Alice," *Sewanee Review* (April 1940), pp. 174–96.

Hudson, Derek: *Lewis Carroll.* London: Constable; 1954.

————: *Lewis Carroll*, in *Writers and Their Work No. 96.* London: Longmans, Green; 1958.

————: "Lewis Carroll and G. M. Hopkins: Clergymen on a Victorian See-Saw," *The Dalhousie Review*, L, 1 (1970), pp. 83–7.

Hutton, Laurence: *Literary Landmarks of Oxford.* New York: Scribners; 1903.

Johnson, Edgar: "Divided Don in the Looking-Glass," *Saturday Review*, XXXVIII (February 26, 1955), p. 16.

Kalem, T. E.: "Into a Laughing Hell," *Time* (October 26, 1970), p. 93.

Kenner, Hugh: "Alice in Empsonland," *Gnomon*. New York: McDowell, Obolenksy; 1956. Pp. 249–62.

Kent, Muriel: "The Art of Nonsense," *Cornhill Magazine*, CXLIX (April 1934), pp. 478–87.

Kerr, Walter: "Carroll Knew the Dark Side First," *New York Times* (October 18, 1970), section D, p. 3.

Kirk, Daniel F.: "A Day in Dodgsonland," *Colby Library Quarterly*, VI (1962), pp. 158–68.

————: *Charles Dodgson, Semeiotician*. Gainesville: University of Florida Press; 1963.

Koestler, Arthur: *The Act of Creation*. New York: Macmillan; 1964. P. 67.

Krutch, Joseph Wood: "Psychoanalyzing Alice," *The Nation*, CXLIV (January 30, 1937), pp. 129–30.

————: "Lewis Carroll's Subconscious," *The Nation*. CLXXVIII (March 27, 1954), pp. 262–3.

Jung, Carl G.: "Approaching the Unconscious," in *Man and His Symbols*, Garden City: Doubleday; 1964. Pp. 53–4.

Lanning, George: "Did Mark Twain Write *Alice in Wonderland?*", in *Carrousel for Bibliophiles*, ed. W. Targ. New York: Duschnes; 1947. Pp. 358–61.

Leach, Elsie: "*Alice in Wonderland* in Perspective," *Victoria Newsletter*, XXV (1964), pp. 9–11.

Leathes, C. S.: "Lewis Carroll as Story-Teller," *Saturday Review*, LXXXV (January 25, 1898), pp. 102–10.

Lehmann, John: "*Alice in Wonderland* and Its Sequel," *Revue des Langues Vivantes* (Brussels), XXXII (1966), pp. 115–30.

Lennon, Florence Becker: *Victoria Through the Looking-Glass*. New York: Simon & Schuster, 1945.

————: *The Life of Lewis Carroll*. New York: Collier Books; 1962. (A new and extensively revised edition of the above.)

Leslie, Shane: "Lewis Carroll and the Oxford Movement," *London Mercury* (July 1933), pp. 233–9.

Lester, Elenore: "Taking a Trip with Andre and His *Alice*," *New York Times* (November 1, 1970), section D, p. 3.

Levin, Harry: "Wonderland Revisited," *Kenyon Review*, XXVII (1965), pp. 591–616.

Lincoln, E.: "Lewis Carroll, Dreamer," *Writing of Informal Essays*, ed. Mary Ellen Chase and M. E. MacGregor. Books for Libraries, 1928. Pp. 318–31.

Livingston, Flora V.: *The Harcourt Amory Collection of Lewis Carroll in the Harvard College Library*. Cambridge: Harvard College Library; 1932.

Losel, F.: "The First German Translation of *Alice in Wonderland*," *Hermathena*, XLIX (1964), pp. 66–79.

Lucas, Edward Verrall: "Charles Lutwidge Dodgson," *Dictionary of National Biography*, Supplement II (1901), pp. 142–4.

Lloyd, J. O. K.: "Annotated *Alice*," (London) *Times Literary Supplement*, (January 14, 1965), p. 27.

Macy, John: "Her Majesty's Jesters," *Bookman*, LXXIII (April 1931), pp. 146–57.

Madan, Falconer: *The Lewis Carroll Centenary in London, 1932*. London: J & E Bumpus; 1932.

Masslick, George B.: "A Book Within a Book," *English Journal*, X (March 1921), pp. 119–29.

Maynard, Theodore: "Lewis Carroll: Mathematician and Magician," *Catholic World*, CXXXV (1932), pp. 193–201.

McDermott, John Francis: "Introduction," *Collected Verse of Lewis Carroll*. New York: E. P. Dutton; 1929.

Mespoulet, Marguerite: *Creators of Wonderland*. New York: Arrow Editions; 1934.

Milner, Florence: "The Poems in *Alice in Wonderland*," *Bookman*, XVIII (September 1903), pp. 13–16.

Monro, D. H.: *Argument of Laughter*. Melbourne, 1951.

Montgomery, Lall F.: "The Eastern Alice," *Literature East & West*, VII (1963), pp. 3–9.

Morgan, C.: *The House of Macmillan, 1843–1943*. New York, 1943.

Morton, Richard: "*Alice's Adventures in Wonderland* and *Through the Looking-Glass*," *Elementary English*, XXXVIII (December 1960), pp. 509–13.

Moses, Belle: *Lewis Carroll in Wonderland and at Home*. New York: D. Appleton & Co.); 1910.

Nathan, George Jean: "Alice in Wonderland: Dramatization," *Theatre Book of the Year, 1946–47*. New York: Knopf; 1947. Pp. 362–4.

Newall, Peter: "Alice's Adventures in Wonderland from an Artist's Stand-Point," *Harper's*, CIII (October 1901), pp. 712–17.

Nicholson, Hubert: *A Voyage to Wonderland and Other Essays*. London: Heineman; 1947.

Oates, Joyce Carol: *Wonderland*. New York: Vanguard; 1971. (Novel.)

O'Brien, Hugh: "Alice in Wonderland: The 'French Lesson-Book,' " *Notes & Queries*, X (1963), p. 461.

O'Day, Edward F.: *The Father of Alice*. San Francisco: Lantern; 1917.

Orwell, George: "Nonsense Poetry," *Shooting an Elephant*. London: Faber & Faber; 1945.

Parisot, H.: *Lewis Carroll*. Paris, 1952.

Partridge, H. M. and D. C.: *The Most Remarkable Echo in the World*. Hastings-on-Hudson, N.Y.: H. M. Partridge; 1933.

Phillips, Robert: "Foreword," *Aspects of Alice*. New York: Vanguard; 1971.

Pitcher, George: "Wittgenstein, Nonsense and Lewis Carroll," *Massachusetts Review*, VI, 3 (Spring–Summer 1965), pp. 591–611.

Porter, Katherine Anne; Bertrand Russell; and Mark Van Doren: "Carroll: *Alice in Wonderland*," *New Invitation to Learning,* ed. Mark Van Doren. New York, 1942. Pp. 206–20.

Priestley, J. B.: "A Note on Humpty Dumpty," *I for One.* New York: Dodd, Mead; 1921. Pp. 191–9.

Rackin, Donald: "The Critical Interpretations of Alice in Wonderland: A Survey and Suggested Reading." University of Illinois: unpublished doctoral dissertation; 1968.

————. "Alice's Journey to the End of the Night," *PMLA,* LXXXI (1966), pp. 313–26.

Rae, John: *New Adventures of Alice.* Chicago: P. F. Volland; 1917.

Reed, Langford: *The Life of Lewis Carroll.* London: W. & G. Foyle; 1932.

————: "Foreword," and "The Beginning of Alice," *Further Nonsense Verse and Prose by Lewis Carroll.* New York: Appleton; 1921.

Reichert, Klaus: "Der Geheime Verführer," *Lewis Carroll: Briefe an kleine Mädchen.* Frankfurt: Insel Verlag; 1967. Pp. 103–10.

Richardson, Joanna: *The Young Lewis Carroll.* London: Parrish; 1964.

Róheim, Géza: "Further Insights," *Magic and Schizophrenia.* Bloomington: Indiana University Press; 1955. Pp. 201–20.

Ros, Amanda M'Kittrick: "Lewis Carroll: a Hasty Evaluation," *Bayonets of Hasty Sheen.* East Sheen: Alfred Ashley & Son; 194–.

Russell, A. S.: "Lewis Carroll: Tutor and Logician," *The Listener* (January 13, 1932).

Salmon, Edward: "Literature for the Little Ones," *Nineteenth Century,* XXII (October 1887), pp. 563–80.

Schickel, Richard: *The Disney Version.* New York: Simon & Schuster, 1968. Pp. 178, 284, 295–6.

Schilder, Paul: "Psychoanalytic Remarks on *Alice in Wonderland* and Lewis Carroll," *The Journal of Nervous and Mental Diseases,* LXXXVII (1938), pp. 159–68.

Serra, Cristobel. "Dos principles de absurdismo ingles: Edward Lear y Lewis Carroll," *Papeles de Son Armadans* (Majorca), XXXIV (1965), pp. lix–lxiv.

Sewell, Elizabeth: "Lewis Carroll and T. S. Eliot as Nonsense Poets," *T. S. Eliot,* ed. Neville Braybrooke. New York: Farrar, Straus; 1958. Pp. 49–56.

————: *The Field of Nonsense.* London: Chatto & Windus; 1952.

Shaw, John Mackay: *The Parodies of Lewis Carroll.* Talahassee: Florida State University Library; 1960.

Shepard, Richard F.: "Take Lewis Carroll, Add Soul . . .", *New York Times* (April 24, 1969), p. 40.

Skinner, John: "Lewis Carroll's Adventures in Wonderland," *American Imago,* IV (1947), pp. 3–31.

Spacks, Patricia Meyer: "Logic and Language in *Through the Looking-Glass,*" *ETC,* XVIII (1961), pp. 91–100.

Squire, J. C.: "By Lewis Carroll," *Essays at Large.* New York: G. H. Doran; 1923. Pp. 24–9.

Stafford, Jean: "The Jabberwock Anatomized," *The Griffen*, IX, 6 (June 1960), pp. 2–11.

Strong, T. B.: "Lewis Carroll," *Cornhill Magazine*, New Series IV (March 1898), pp. 303–10.

Sutherland, Robert Donald: "Language and Lewis Carroll," *Dissertation Abstracts*, XXV (1964), pp. 2522–3.

Tate, Allen: "Last Days of Alice," *Poems*. Chicago: Swallow Press; 1961. P. 115.

Taylor, Alexander L.: *The White Knight: A Study of C. L. Dodgson*. Edinburgh: Oliver & Boyd; 1952.

Tollemache, Lionel Arthur: "Reminiscences of Lewis Carroll," *Among My Books*. London: L. Arnold; 1898.

Tindall, William York: *Forces in Modern British Literature, 1885–1956*. New York: Vintage; 1956. Pp. 216, 230, 244, 287.

Tucker, Martin, ed. *The Critical Temper*, Vol. III. New York: Frederick Unger; 1969. Pp. 48–50.

Untermeyer, Louis: "Introduction," *Alice in Wonderland*. New York: Collier Books; 1962. Pp. 5–11.

Vail, Robert W. G.: *Alice in Wonderland: The Manuscript and the Story*. New York: N.Y. Public Library; 1928.

Van Doren, Dorothy: "Mr. Dodgson and Lewis Carroll," *The Nation*, CXXXIII (Dec. 2, 1931), pp. 607–9.

Walpole, Hugh: "Preface," *Alice's Adventures in Wonderland*, Centenary Edition. London: Macmillan; 1932.

Waugh, Evelyn: "Carroll and Dodgson," *The Spectator*, CLVI (October 3, 1939), p. 511.

Weaver, Warren: *Alice in Many Tongues: The Translations of Alice in Wonderland*. Madison: University of Wisconsin Press; 1964.

_____: *Lewis Carroll: Correspondence Numbers*. Scarsdale, 1940.

_____: "Lewis Carroll and a Geometrical Paradox," *American Mathematical Monthly*, XLV (April 1938), pp. 234–6.

_____: "Lewis Carroll: Mathematician," *Scientific American*, CXCIV (April 1956), pp. 116–20.

_____: "The Parrish Collection of Carrolliana," *Princeton University Library Chronicle*, XVII (1956), pp. 85–91.

Weinfield, Henry: "A Note Toward The Poetics of Lewis Carroll," *Promethean*, XVII, 1 (1969–70), pp. 36–8.

Westfeldt, Martha J.: *Alice in Hueyland*. New Orleans, 1935.

White, Elwyn Brooks: *Alice Through the Cellophane*. New York: John Day; 1933.

Whyte, Walter: "Lewis Carroll," *Poets and Poetry of the Nineteenth Century*, ed. Alfred H. Miles. London: Routledge; 1905. Pp. 443–54.

Williams, Sidney H., and Falconer Madan: *Lewis Carroll Handbook*, rev. by Roger Lancelyn Green. New York: Oxford University Press; 1962.

Wilson, Edmund: "C. L. Dodgson: The Poet Logician," *The Shores of Light*. New York: Farrar, Straus; 1952. Pp. 540–50.

Winterich, J. T.: "Lewis Carroll and Alice in Wonderland," *Books and the Man.* New York: Greenberg; 1929. Pp. 266–90.

Wood, James: *The Snark Was a Boojum: A Life of Lewis Carroll.* New York: Pantheon; 1966.

Woollcott, Alexander: "Introduction," *Complete Works of Lewis Carroll.* London: Nonesuch Press; 1939. (Reprinted in America in the Modern Library Giant edition; also in the Modern Library edition of *Alice in Wonderland.*)

Woolen, C. J.: "Lewis Carroll: Philosopher," *Hibbert Journal,* XLVI (1947), pp. 63–8.

Woolf, Virginia: "Lewis Carroll," *The Moment and Other Essays.* New York: Harcourt; 1948. Pp. 81–3. (Reprinted in *Collected Essays,* Vol. I, pp. 254–5.)

Wyatt, Horace Matthew: *Malice in Kultureland.* London: The Car Illustrated; 1914.

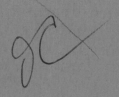